MONETARY STANDARDS AND EXCHANGE RATES

In this volume an international team of distinguished monetary economists examine the historical experience of exchange rate behavior under different monetary regimes. The main focus is on metallic standards and fixed exchange rates, such as the gold standard. With its combination of thematic overviews and case studies of the key countries and periods, the book greatly enhances our understanding of past monetary systems.

The volume is divided into three parts. Part I evaluates the various monetary systems. The performance of metallic regimes is compared with the other monetary systems of human history, using criteria such as growth, inflation and general economic stability. Part II is concerned with the detailed behavior of exchange rates under historical metallic regimes. Much attention is paid to the bimetallic standard of both gold and silver. Part III examines the different behavior of metallic standards in the center countries and at the periphery.

The book will be welcomed primarily by economic historians and general historians with an interest in monetary history, and also by scholars of macroeconomics and international economics.

Maria Cristina Marcuzzo is Associate Professor of Economics at the University of Rome, La Sapienza. A specialist in classical monetary theory and in the Cambridge School of economics, she is the co-author (with A. Rosselli) of *Ricardo and the Gold Standard* and co-editor of *The Economics of Joan Robinson.* She has published articles in *Economica, Revue d'Economie Politique, Cambridge Journal of Economics* and *Review of Political Economy.*

Lawrence H. Officer is Professor of Economics at the University of Illinois. He has been Visiting Professor at the University of Chicago, Research Consultant at the Bank of Canada, and Consultant at the International Monetary Fund. His academic specialities are monetary history and international economics, and his most recent book is *Between the Dollar–Sterling Gold Points: Exchange Rates, Parity and Market Behaviour.*

Annalisa Rosselli is Associate Professor of Economics at the University of Rome, Tor Vergata. She graduated in mathematics and studied at the London School of Economics. Her publications center on the history of economic thought and on economic history. She is the co-author (with M.C. Marcuzzo) of *Ricardo and the Gold Standard.*

Routledge Explorations in Economic History

1. Economic Ideas and Government Policy
Contributions to Contemporary Economic History – Sir Alec Cairncross

2. The Organization of Labour Markets
Modernity, Culture and Governance in Germany, Sweden, Britain and Japan – Bo Stråth

3. Currency Convertibility in the Twentieth Century
The Gold Standard and Beyond – Edited by Jorge Braga de Macedo, Barry Eichengreen and Jaime Reis

4. Britain's Place in the World
Import Controls 1945–1960 – Alan S. Milward and George Brennan

5. France and the International Economy
From Vichy to the Treaty of Rome – Frances M.B. Lynch

6. Monetary Standards and Exchange Rates – Edited by M.C. Marcuzzo, L.H. Officer and A. Rosselli

MONETARY STANDARDS AND EXCHANGE RATES

Edited by

Maria Cristina Marcuzzo, Lawrence H. Officer and Annalisa Rosselli

LONDON AND NEW YORK

First published 1997
by Routledge
2 Park Square, Milton Park, Abingdon, Oxfordshire OX14 4RN

Simultaneously published in the USA and Canada
by Routledge
711 Third Avenue, New York, NY 10017

First issued in paperback 2014

Routledge is an imprint of the Taylor and Francis Group, an informa business

Typeset in Garamond by
J&L Composition Ltd, Filey, North Yorkshire

British Library Cataloguing in Publication Data
A catalogue record for this book is available from the British Library

Library of Congress Cataloging in Publication Data
Monetary standards & exchange rates/edited by Maria Cristina Marcuzzo, Lawrence H. Officer & Annalisa Rosselli.
p. cm.
Includes bibliographical references and index.
1. Money–History. 2. Foreign exchange rates. 3. Gold standard–History. 4. Bimetallism. 5. Monetary policy. I. Marcuzzo, Maria Cristina, 1948– . II. Officer, Lawrence H. III. Rosselli, Annalisa.
HG231.M583 1997
332.4′5–dc21 96–50052
CIP

ISBN 13: 978-1-138-86584-6 (pbk)
ISBN 13: 978-0-415-14297-7 (hbk)

CONTENTS

FIGURES

TABLES

CONTRIBUTORS

Marie-Thérèse Boyer-Xambeu is Professor of Economics at the University of Paris 7. She co-authored (with G. Deleplace and L. Gillard) *Private Money and Public Currencies: The 16th Century Challenge* and *Bimétallisme, taux de change et prix de l'or et de l'argent (1717–1873)*. She has also published articles on the monetary theory of Thornton and Goschen.

Marcello de Cecco is Professor of Monetary Economics at the University of Rome, La Sapienza. He has taught at the European University Institute in Florence and at the University of Siena. An expert on the gold standard, he is the author of *Money and Empire* and of entries in *The New Palgrave Dictionary of Money and Finance.*

Richard N. Cooper was appointed Chairman of the National Intelligence Council on June 1, 1995. He is Maurits C. Boas Professor of International Economics at Harvard University (on leave). His previous positions include Chairman of the Federal Reserve Bank of Boston, Professor of Economics and Provost at Yale University, and several appointments in the US government. He is the author of various books, including *Environment and Resource Policies for the World Economy*, and of over three hundred articles.

Ghislain Deleplace is Professor of Economics at the University of Paris 8. He co-authored (with M.-T. Boyer-Xambeu and L. Gillard) *Private Money and Public Currencies: The 16th Century Challenge* and *Bimétallisme, taux de change et prix de l'or et de l'argent (1717–1873)*. He is the co-editor of *Money in Motion: the Post-Keynesian and Circulation Approaches* and has published articles on the monetary theory of Steuart, Ricardo, and Keynes.

Marc Flandreau is a researcher at Centre Nationale de la Recherche Scientifique and at Observatoire Français des Conjonctures Economiques, Paris. He was a Fulbright Scholar at the University of California, Berkeley. His area of research is the theory and history of international monetary regimes, and he is the author of *L'Or du monde: La France et la stabilité du système monétaire international 1848–1873.*

Lucien Gillard is Senior Researcher in Economics at the Centre National de la Recherche Scientifique, Paris. He co-authored (with M.-T. Boyer-Xambeu and G. Deleplace) *Private Money and Public Currencies: The 16th Century Challenge* and *Bimétallisme, taux de change et prix de l'or et de l'argent (1717–1873)*. He is the co-editor of *Simiand et les normes sociales* and has published articles on the monetary theory of Condorcet, Tooke, and Simmel.

Maria Cristina Marcuzzo is Associate Professor of Economics at the University of Rome, La Sapienza. A specialist in classical monetary theory and in the Cambridge School of economics, she is the co-author (with A. Rosselli) of *Ricardo and the Gold Standard* and co-editor of *The Economics of Joan Robinson*. She has published articles in *Economica*, *Revue d'Economie Politique*, *Cambridge Journal of Economics*, and *Review of Political Economy*.

Robert A. Mundell is Professor of Economics at Columbia University. His previous positions include Visiting Professor of Economics, Graduate Training Center, Renmin University of China, Beijing; Professor of Economics, University of Chicago; and Editor, *Journal of Political Economy*. His awards include the Jacques Rueff Prize and Medal, and he has received an honorary doctorate from the University of Paris-Dauphine. His publications include fourteen books, most recently *Inflation and Growth: China and the Other Transition Countries*, and over one hundred articles.

Lawrence H. Officer is Professor of Economics at the University of Illinois, Chicago. He has been Visiting Professor of Economics at the Graduate School of Business at the University of Chicago, Research Consultant at the Bank of Canada, and Consultant at the International Monetary Fund. His academic specialties are monetary history and international economics, and his most recent book is *Between the Dollar–Sterling Gold Points: Exchange Rates, Parity, and Market Behavior*.

Agustín Llona Rodríguez is Professor of Economics at Universidad Carlos III de Madrid. His previous positions include National Project Coordinator, Ministry of Economics, Public Works and Public Utilities, Buenos Aires, Argentina; international consultant, International Labor Office; and Professor of Economics, Universidad de Alcalá, Alcalá de Henares, Spain. He has published papers in development economics, macroeconomics, and income distribution.

Annalisa Rosselli is Associate Professor of Economics at the University of Rome, Tor Vergata. She graduated in mathematics and studied at the London School of Economics. Her publications center on the history of economic thought and on economic history. She is the co-author (with C. Marcuzzo) of *Ricardo and the Gold Standard*.

Massimo V. Rostagno is economist at the Research Department of the Bank of Italy, Public Finance Division. A Ph.D student at the University of California, Los Angeles, he is the author of publications in monetary economics, history of economic thought, international monetary economics, and public finance.

Giuseppe Tattara is Professor of International Economics at the University of Venice. He received a Master of Science in Economics from the London School of Economics and Political Science. He has published articles on international monetary history, international trade, and technical progress.

Mario Volpe is Research Fellow and Lecturer in Economics at the University of Venice. He did graduate study at New York University, where he worked with Nobel Laureate Wassily Leontief. His specialties are applied economics and open-economy macroeconomics.

INTRODUCTION

Maria Cristina Marcuzzo, Lawrence H. Officer and Annalisa Rosselli

In March 1995 a workshop on "Monetary Standards and Exchange Rates" took place in Perugia, Italy. The workshop was organized by Maria Cristina Marcuzzo and Annalisa Rosselli, two of the editors of this volume, and was financed by a research grant provided by the Italian National Research Council in collaboration with the Research Division of the Bank of Italy. A distinguished group of economists and economic historians from Europe and the United States attended the workshop.

After the conference, the two organizers met with a third participant, Lawrence Officer, to discuss producing a book based on the theme of the conference: understanding the workings of monetary regimes based on metallic standards. It was decided to include a selection of papers from the workshop, constituting most of the volume, and, in addition, to invite a few other researchers to provide chapters, the better to ensure a comprehensive treatment of the topic. The result is this volume, which has the same title as the workshop that began it all.

The term "monetary standard" has both a domestic and international connotation. Domestically, the monetary standard pertains to the basis of the currency and the backing of the money supply. Here a commodity standard is contrasted with a paper standard or fiat money. Metallic standards, a subset of commodity standards, involve gold and/or silver (the "precious metals") as the standard; and metallic standards are the focus of this volume. Internationally, a metallic standard at home and abroad is associated with a "fixed" exchange rate, meaning an exchange rate bounded by specie points.

However, the distinction between a metallic and paper standard (or, to put the matter simply, a country "on" or "off" gold) is not clear-cut. For analytical purposes, a floating rate can be converted to the corresponding rate that would occur under a specie standard, as is done by Officer (Chapter 8 in this volume). Empirically, the legal and actual standards can diverge. A country can be nominally on a metallic standard but actually on a paper standard. Examples are the United Kingdom and United States during World War I. The opposite is also true: a metallic standard might be in effect without a legal basis. An example is the Italian "shadowing of the gold standard," discussed by Tattara and Volpe (Chapter 9).

This book is concerned with the economic history of metallic standards and fixed exchange rates, whereas the present system around the world is a paper standard and largely floating exchange rates. As recently as the early 1970s, most countries were on a fixed exchange-rate system. It is quite possible that this situation might recur. Indeed, the European Union has such a system as an explicit goal. Further, discussion of a reversion to the domestic gold standard has a tendency to reappear in the popular press and political debate. The lessons of economic history should not be forgotten, so that informed decisions can be made by policy-makers (or at least informed evaluations of these decisions can be made by scholars).

Metallic regimes are characterized by the fact that the anchor of the monetary system is provided by one or both of the precious metals. The currency unit is fixed and equal to a given weight of gold and/or silver of specified fineness. It follows that the behavior of the monetary system is intertwined with the conditions of demand and supply of the metal or metals chosen as the standard. This is in contrast to the case of a pure fiat monetary regime, in which monetary authorities and market behavior are not subject to this constraint.

The chapters in Part I are concerned with the evaluation of monetary systems. How well do metallic regimes perform compared with the other monetary systems that human history has experienced? Criteria such as growth, inflation, and general economic stability are utilized by the authors.

Robert Mundell (Chapter 1) offers a broad overview of international monetary systems from the end of the Napoleonic Wars through the present to a predicted future. He faces at the outset the question of how to classify international monetary regimes. His taxonomy rests on a double classification: the chosen monetary standard (for example, gold, bimetallism, the dollar) and the degree of flexibility of the exchange rate (fixed, adjustably fixed, floating). For Mundell, there is a correlation between the two arrangements: whenever a monetary standard existed, the system worked as a fixed exchange-rate regime, providing price stability and growth. However, he maintains that the converse is not true. A fixed exchange-rate system, to be effective, must contain a mechanism to discipline the center country; in particular, to allow the peripheral countries to influence the inflation rate selected by the center country. This is precisely what a metallic regime does.

In fact, Mundell shows that, compared with the experience of flexible exchange rates or fixed exchange rates unanchored to a monetary standard, metallic regimes have a good historical record. While the desirability of fixed exchange-rate systems for economic stability is demonstrated, Mundell is careful to note that the exchange-rate levels must be correctly chosen. As for the future, both past anchors of such a system (gold, silver, national currencies) and a world currency are viewed as unrealistic – even though the experienced anchored dollar system was a relative success. The predicted outcome for the near future is regionalism, although a multilateral system based on a world currency would be preferable.

Mundell pays scant attention to bimetallism, viewing it as simply a way-station on the road to the international gold standard. He notes that bimetallism is the least understood system, a reason why the whole of Part II is devoted to bimetallism. Also, nothing is said regarding pre-1815 standards, the subject of Rostagno's contribution in Part II.

Though the volume does not emphasize floating rates, one might comment that Mundell's castigation of the 1970s experience with floating rates does not distinguish between a free and managed float. That experience was decidedly in the latter category. In early history, floating rates were genuinely free and they often only temporarily dethroned a metallic standard – for example, the Bank Restriction Period, discussed by de Cecco.

Chapter 2, by Richard Cooper, was originally published in 1989 but is not widely known. Yet it is extremely relevant to the theme of the book and so appears here (in slightly revised form). Cooper has broadly comparable views to Mundell on the need for an anchor for exchange rates, but is more skeptical about its functioning. Indeed, he challenges the possibilities of an anchor – given not only by a metallic standard but alternatively by a physical commodity or a basket of commodities – in maintaining price and (real and nominal) exchange-rate stability.

Cooper's argument is twofold. First, he argues that in order to stabilize the price level, the price of the standard (the chosen metal or basket of commodities) must be adjusted any time that a change occurs in the terms of trade between the monetized commodity and the other goods and services – a very likely event. In fact, changes in technology and productivity are never of the same magnitude, nor do they occur at the same time, in the industry producing the monetized commodity and in the industries producing all the commodities. Conversely, if the price of the standard is kept fixed, oscillations in the price level are bound to occur. Cooper notes that during the gold-standard era there were long periods of price decline as well as long periods of rises in prices.

Second, he distinguishes two cases: (a) two or more countries choose the same monetary standard linked to the same commodity, (b) the countries choose different standards. In case (a) the source of instability of the exchange rate, both real and nominal, lies in the rate of change of the ratio between the price of tradable goods and the price of nontradable goods. Because changes in productivity occur at different rates in different countries, the terms of trade between tradables and nontradables change at different rates in the two countries. Moreover, the price level in each country is not affected in the same way by changes in the tradable/nontradable price ratio, because the weight of the tradable sector in the economy is not the same. The larger the gap between the incomes of the two countries, the greater the difference.

Consequently, it is impossible to obtain the stability of both the price level and the nominal exchange rate. If the price levels are stabilized, the nominal exchange rate has to be adjusted. This in turn implies a change in the price of the standard or the abandonment of the commodity-standard (or metallic-standard) regime. If the nominal exchange rate is kept fixed, it is the real exchange rate (the nominal exchange rate adjusted by the ratio of the countries' price levels) which fluctuates, imposing severe cost on the real sector of the economy.

In case (b), in which two or more countries choose different standards, the rate of exchange obviously cannot be kept fixed, because it depends on the market price ratio between the two standards, which varies.

It is not a surprise, therefore, that for Cooper the gold standard "did not perform very well – indeed it was a source of consternation and controversy to those who lived through it." He does not want to return to past historical commodity standards or variant (multiple commodity standard). Indeed, Cooper's endorsement of a fixed exchange-rate regime is much weaker than Mundell's, although for both the preferred regime for the future is a multilateral system based on a world currency.

Marcello de Cecco's contribution (Chapter 3), originally published in *The New Palgrave*, can be legitimately described as a "recent classic" and fits very well into the theme of the volume. The dependence of gold monometallism on the bimetallist periphery is an interesting concept, and leads into Part II. De Cecco argues that a clear choice in favor of gold or silver was never actually made and that the monetary system which prevailed during the first three-quarters of the nineteenth century needed the stocks of both metals for its smooth working. Even Britain, which was the first country in Europe to adopt gold as the standard for its currency, relied on the bimetallic French reserve earlier, and on Indian silver and South African gold later, to manage the system. Given its lean gold reserves, it was vital for Britain to be able to draw gold to London.

A theme of Mundell is the importance of checks and balances in any international monetary system. De Cecco – referring to the British-led international monetary system of the pre-World War I period – discusses the situation of instability: when such checks and balances run amok, or the opposite situation – unstable forces are present. While de Cecco shares Mundell's view that the gold standard was not a monometallic system but rather a bimetallic one, he sides with Cooper in claiming that the classical gold standard was beset with forces making for instability. However, Cooper and de Cecco see the source of instability differently, the former in the changing pattern of the terms of trade among trading partners, the latter primarily in the changing distribution of the stocks of gold and silver among countries.

Indeed, de Cecco views the classical gold standard as beset with forces making for instability. The United States is interpreted as a prime destabilizing element. The United States suffered recurrent crises and lacked a central bank; it also had destabilizing government policy. Unlike France, India, and South Africa, the United States was helped by the Bank of England rather than helping the Bank. The domestic financial structure within Britain was also destabilizing.

We observe that good indicators of the *instability* of an international monetary regime based on a metallic standard are either how long such a regime can be maintained before the standard itself has to be abandoned or how many times the system is forced off the chosen exchange rate. The experiences of the center, not peripheral, countries are pertinent in this respect. Also, metallic regimes, *even when in effect*, are not synonymous with fixed exchange-rate systems, and fluctuations in exchange rates within, and occasionally even outside, specie-point bounds are an observed feature of international monetary regimes based on monometallic and bimetallic standards.

In Part II the behavior of exchange rates under the metallic regimes as we know them from history is looked at in detail. Maria Cristina Marcuzzo and Annalisa Rosselli (Chapter 4) discuss and compare two-country cases in which (a) the same metal is adopted as standard in each country, (b) different metals are used as standard in the countries, and (c) a bimetallic standard reigns in each country. In each case a different definition of the "official exchange rate," or "official parity," is required.

Deviations of the market rate of exchange from the official parity reflected both the conditions prevailing in the market for bills of exchange – which in turn reflected the conditions of the balance of payments – and the conditions prevailing in the market for gold and silver, the latter being influenced by the employment of the two metals in monetary and non-monetary uses.

Marcuzzo and Rosselli present a framework to distinguish between these two components. Taking the London–Paris exchange rate from 1821 to 1870 as an empirical case, they compute a measure – the deviation of the exchange rate from real (commercial) par – that indicates whether the balance of payments (market for foreign exchange) is favorable or unfavorable for the domestic currency and therefore whether an inflow or outflow of bullion is likely to occur. Left for future research is testing the indicator empirically, that is, correlating their indicator measure with England's gold flow.

Although Marcuzzo and Rosselli do not so state explicitly, what they do is to systematize and extend the concepts of the English bullionists writing during the Bank Restriction Period – the floating pound of 1797–1821 – an episode discussed in de Cecco's Chapter 3.

The issue of the stability of the exchange rate when two different standards are involved requires consideration of additional constraints on the rate, which is the subject of Chapter 5 in Part II. Marie-Thérèse Boyer-Xambeu, Ghislain Deleplace, and Lucien Gillard construct a "bimetallic snake" for the London–Paris exchange rate for the first three-quarters of the nineteenth century, and claim that this was the pertinent constraint on the rate. Their constraint is in contrast to the conventional gold-point spread or even the gold-point snake. Their innovations are the use of market rates for bullion (gold and silver) and the explicit inclusion of both metals in their modeling, incorporating the silver market in London even though this metal was demonetized.

To the general discussion of the characteristics of commodity-standard regimes, Boyer-Xembeu, Deleplace, and Gillard introduce the point that these regimes cannot possibly be classified in the fixed-exchange-rate category, since what matters is not the fixed legal par of exchange but the variable market par of exchange, which reflected the changing prices of gold and silver in the London and Paris markets.

The authors' empirical result is that the exchange was favorable to the pound during most of the period after the resumption of convertibility (subsequent to the Bank Restriction Period). The use of data on bullion flows in testing their model is commendable.

Their study can be compared with that of Marc Flandreau (Chapter 6), who adopts a different methodology to examine bimetallism within France. The focus of Flandreau's contribution is to challenge two conventional wisdoms associated with bimetallism: the idea that the system is unstable, and the role in it of gold–silver arbitrage. According to the traditional view, bimetallism is intrinsically unstable, because the gold–silver price ratio is market determined and therefore bound to change as the conditions of demand and supply of gold and silver change. Attempts by government to fix a legal price ratio are ineffective. Whenever there is a slight divergence between the legal and market ratio, the public uses the overvalued metal as money to discharge debt, while arbitrageurs buy the undervalued with the overvalued metal at the legal ratio and sell the latter at the market ratio at a profit. Thus the undervalued metal disappears from circulation and is withdrawn from monetary use. It follows that bimetallism as such cannot exist, and what we have instead is an alternation of *de facto* gold and silver standards, with the other metal disappearing from circulation.

Flandreau challenges the traditional view on two grounds, theoretically and empirically. The first criticism is that the demand for gold and silver is composed of the demand for monetary and for nonmonetary uses; so that there results a degree of flexibility in relative prices compatible with a given legal price ratio. Second, the traditional view ignores the costs involved in gold and silver arbitrage. Flandreau produces evidence that these costs were relatively high, so there was in fact around the legal ratio a wide interval within which the market ratio could vary without making the buying and selling of one metal against the other profitable. Given these high arbitrage costs, according to Flandreau, the stabilizing role of gold–silver arbitrage has been overstressed in the literature.

His conclusion is that France-led bimetallism was extremely stable during the period 1851–70, with the market gold–silver price ratio always within the gold–silver arbitrage points. In principle, arbitrage activity diverts the overvalued metal from nonmonetary to monetary uses, raising its market price and narrowing the gap between the market and legal ratio. In practice, Flandreau concludes, metal-specific arbitrage *in the same metal* between coin and bullion was less costly and more efficient than arbitrage between gold and silver in stabilizing the gold–silver market-price ratio within the gold–silver points.

However, bimetallism need not be interpreted as represented solely by the classical gold–silver regime of the French type. There is the case explored by Massimo Rostagno (Chapter 7) in his modeling of pre-Napoleonic (*Ancien Régime*) monetary systems in Europe. In this regime there are two types of money within the economy. One money is for the wealthy (nobles and merchants), and it is composed of essentially full-weight gold and silver coins. The other is for the poor, and it consists of copper and debased gold or silver coins. The dichotomy of the monetary system was a reflection of the separation of the internal sector (mainly consumption at subsistence level) from the external sector of the economy (international trade engaged in by merchants), and was efficient in insulating the former from the perturbations arising in the latter.

This peculiar type of bimetallism was asymmetric, as convertibility between the higher and lower order of the metallic circulation worked mainly down the scale (for example, from gold to copper) and hardly upward. This is explained by the different level of seigniorage (reflected in the degree of fineness of the metal embodied in coin) that the two types of money could bear. The discipline imposed on the sovereign in the case of money used in international transactions was much tighter than in the case of money used only for internal circulation. The latter performed only the role of medium of exchange and it was never hoarded, because the public knew that its face-value could be altered by decree at sovereign will. Thus seigniorage was also a way of conducting monetary policy.

The monetary system of the *Ancien Régime*, Rostagno argues, was able both to economize the costs of the currency and to provide a certain amount of flexibility, two goals that the gold standard achieved much later, through the introduction of paper money and discretionary monetary policy. Though the other authors in the volume concentrate on the post-Napoleonic period, it should be noted that the regime considered by Rostagno lasted a long time – a thousand years – so it warrants attention.

Part III of the volume examines an important aspect of metallic regimes, the different behavior of the system at center and at periphery.

Lawrence Officer (Chapter 8) investigates the extent to which the American foreign-exchange market was integrated (the degree of perfection of the market) over a long time span – from 1791 to 1931. The existing literature on the issue of exchange-market integration under a metallic standard has two strands. The first approach is to compute the amount of variation of the exchange rate, and observe how the magnitude of the variation changes over time. The second approach looks at the gold-point spread. What Officer does is to present a formal model by means of which the two approaches are integrated. Also, his model distinguishes between the external and internal components of integration.

Although the time span examined includes periods in which the United States and Britain were off the gold standard, an adjustment is made so that it can be pretended that the countries were on the gold standard, as long as a free gold market was in operation. Officer's computations show how the integration of the American foreign-exchange market varied over time, especially the trend improvement.

At the other extreme of the spectrum are the peripheral countries, which often were unable to maintain convertibility. Giuseppe Tattara and Mario Volpe (Chapter 9) argue that Italy, from 1861 to 1913, was on the gold standard more informally than formally, as convertibility of banknotes was enforced only initially, for a five-year period. However, during the whole period under scrutiny Italy maintained a remarkably stable exchange rate and stable prices, effectively "shadowing" the gold standard. In other words, the Italian real exchange rate was stationary over time.

This is different from Officer's examination of the American case, in which the paper standards of the United States and Britain did not "shadow" the gold (or silver) standard but rather were genuine periods of inconvertibility. In Italy monetary circulation was expanded, and yet stability was achieved. Tattara and Volpe explain the puzzle by arguing that the increase in the money supply was required by the remarkable growth in output throughout the period.

The authors maintain that the gold standard worked mainly through capital movements in an integrated financial market, so that an excess demand for money in one country led to a portfolio adjustment, which was largely independent of relative price levels and commodity flows. In emphasizing the role of international capital mobility in permitting Italy to adhere essentially to the gold standard, they denigrate the traditional price specie-flow mechanism. Their time-series analysis confirms that the Italian "shadowing" of the gold standard was a genuine phenomenon.

Agustín Llona Rodríguez (Chapter 10) deals with the experiences of Portugal and Spain, two "dependent economies," to provide an explanation of the difficulties of these peripheral countries in maintaining the gold standard in the nineteenth century. His argument is that there were three sources of such difficulties. The first is the variability and volatility of the terms of trade, due to the structure of the "dependent economy," the exports of which are chiefly primary products and the imports manufactured goods, prices of primary products being more subject to fluctuations. The second source of difficulties is the rigidity of prices in the nontradable sector.

These two elements constitute an obstacle to maintenance of convertibility, because variable terms of trade make the balance of trade unstable, and in order to keep the economy in equilibrium, prices of nontradables should be as flexible as those of tradables – a rare occurrence. However, according to Llona Rodríguez, Portuguese adherence to the gold standard from 1854 to 1891 was made possible not by flexibility in domestic prices but by capital inflows and surpluses in the invisible balance due to remittances from Portuguese *émigrés.*

Capital inflows helped Portugal to remain on the gold standard for a long period, but capital movements also forced Portugal to abandon it. In order to remain on the gold standard, the peripheral countries had to adjust their interest rates on the basis of the interest rate ruling in the center country (Britain). This was a third source of difficulties: a sudden rise in Bank rate in London could draw gold from anywhere in the world, depriving poorer countries of their gold.

Spain was a different case. It never officially adopted the gold standard. In the years before 1868 the country was on a bimetallic standard, then switched to a *de facto* silver standard until 1883, when convertibility was abandoned. Spain experienced large variability and volatility in its terms of trade and therefore high fluctuations in its real exchange rate. Llona Rodríguez's main point is that although the real exchange rate in each country did not behave as required to remain within a commodity-standard regime (or, more generally, any fixed-exchange-rate system) as a peripheral country, inconvertibility did produce stability in the real exchange rate and favored some export growth, although the price paid was a deterioration in the terms of trade.

Returning to the volume at large, its title, *Monetary Standards and Exchange Rates,* manages to convey the idea that by monetary standard or regime is meant something more than just the system of exchange rates. A monetary regime is strongly characterized by what nineteenth-century economists called the "standard" and in modern language we refer to as "international reserves."

Contrary to a commonly held view, monetary regimes where the standard was gold and/or silver – "metallic regimes" for short – were characterized by a certain amount of flexibility in the exchange rate and occasionally were able to overcome the quantity constraint on their reserves by relying on the stock of the metal which was standard in other countries. Moreover, suspension of convertibility of banknotes into gold or silver, as long as coins remained in circulation, can be interpreted as not sudden abandonment of the regime but rather a temporary widening of the interval of variation of the exchange rate. With the anchor gone, the system became less stable, but more flexible in its ability to accommodate fiscal or monetary expansions and real shocks. Certainly in the center countries, convertibility would invariably be restored, and at the former parity.

The discipline of the gold standard was circumvented in all the circumstances in which it threatened the pursuit of more urgent policy objectives. Metallic regimes are no more immune to discretionary intervention and change of priorities than are monetary regimes in which the reserve money is simply the debt of the hegemonic country. Such experience shatters the myth of the discipline of the commodity anchor. Historically, gold and silver indeed exercised some restraint, as a reserve which is not the debt of a single country always does. This discipline worked, however, only so long as the regime was believed to be everlasting or at least only temporarily abandoned. As for all myths once shattered, it will never be trusted again.

ACKNOWLEDGEMENTS

We wish to express our gratitude to Dr. Pierluigi Ciocca, former Head of the Research Division, now Director of the Bank of Italy, for his support in all stages of the project. We thank also Dr. Matteo Russo of the Bank of Italy for helpful assistance in various matters.

We wish to thank the *Rivista di Politica Economica*, where Mundell's chapter was originally published in Italian (n. 6, 1995), *Cato Journal*, where a previous version of Cooper's chapter appeared (vol. 8, n. 2, 1988), and Macmillan Publishing Company for permission to reproduce De Cecco's chapter, originally published as the entry "Gold Standard" in *The New Palgrave: A Dictionary of Economics*, edited by John Eatwell, Murray Milgate and Peter Newman (London, 1987).

Part I

MONETARY SYSTEMS

1

EXCHANGE-RATE SYSTEMS AND ECONOMIC GROWTH

Robert A. Mundell

INTRODUCTION

My topic is "Growth and the Exchange-Rate System." What is the relationship between the exchange-rate system and the rate of growth?

This topic can be analyzed from different perspectives. One approach would consider the topic from the standpoint of a single country making the inescapable choice of an exchange-rate regime, and thus evaluate the merits of alternative exchange-rate policies in particular situations. Another approach would consider the interactions between countries and study alternative ways of managing the currency interdependences that are an inevitable feature of international economic relations. Yet a third alternative is to consider the topic from a global-historic-theoretic vantage and evaluate the success or failure of alternative exchange rate systems in promoting or inhibiting growth of the economy. It is from this third perspective that I shall approach my subject.[1].

To avoid tedious pedantry, I shall adopt the pragmatic approach of restricting my attention to situations that have actually occurred in the past and are likely to occur in the future. It is therefore useful to begin by studying how historical international exchange-rate systems have promoted or impeded economic growth in the world economy.

OVERVIEW OF THE INTERNATIONAL MONETARY SYSTEM

It is convenient to begin a modern history of international monetary systems after the Napoleonic Wars. Table 1.1 summarizes the international monetary systems over time: past, present, and possible future. From 1815 to 1873 there was a bimetallic standard, characterized by a fixed price of gold relative to silver and therefore a fixed exchange-rate system, for all countries in the world that adhered to gold (like Britain), silver (like most countries), or both metals (like France and the United States).

The breakup of the bimetallic standard in the early 1870s disrupted the

Table 1.1 Summary of international monetary systems

System	*Time period*	*Reserve assets*	*Key countries*
Bimetallism	1815–73	gold and silver	France, US, UK
International gold standard	1873–1914	gold, £	UK, US, France
Anchored dollar standard	1915–24	gold, $, £	US
International gold-exchange standard	1925–36	gold, $, £	US, UK, France
Anchored Dollar standard	1936–71	gold, $, £	US, UK
Unanchored dollar standard	1971–3	$, gold	US
Flexible exchange rates	1973–9	$, gold	US
Currency areas	1979–85	$, gold, DM	US, Germany
Coordinate dollar system	1985–93	$, DM, gold	US, Germany, Japan
Currency areas	1994–2005?	$, DM, gold	US, Germany, Japan
Hard-SDR standard?	2005?–?	$, hard SDR, ECU	US, Europe, Japan

monetary unity of the world economy and led to a contracting silver bloc, an expanding gold bloc, and a group of inconvertible paper currencies. By 1900 all the major countries except China were on the gold standard.

With the outbreak of World War I in 1914, the gold standard broke down. For a decade, the main currency was the dollar, anchored to gold. In the 1920s, however, European countries initiated a return to the international gold standard, creating new demand for gold with no accompanying increase in supply.

Deflationary monetary policies led to deflation and the great depression, in the process of which all countries either devalued their currencies or left gold completely.

After 1936, when France had finally devalued the franc, the dollar resumed its position as the key currency in the international monetary system. Increasingly, countries pegged their currencies to the devalued dollar, as refugee capital and war preparations centralized monetary gold in the United States.

The anchored dollar standard continued after the war, but postwar inflation had again lowered the real value of gold and made it scarce. Increasingly, the gold convertibility of the dollar was placed in doubt, and it eventually was ended when President Nixon took the United States off gold in 1971.

The demise of the anchored dollar standard led to a regime of floating exchange rates which, however, was soon replaced by a new try at exchange rates fixed to an inconvertible dollar. The dollar standard broke up into flexible exchange rates in June 1973.

Unhappy with flexible exchange rates and a depreciating dollar, the European countries created the European Monetary System (EMS) in 1979 and, within it, the exchange-rate mechanism (ERM) which constructed a joint float *vis-à-vis* the dollar and other currencies. Meanwhile, disinflation in the United States combined with tax-cut fiscal expansion led to a soaring dollar in the early 1980s, only to be reversed in the latter half of the 1980s. During the 1980s, the ERM came to be seen as a DM standard which, however, almost broke down after the unification shock, creating renewed sentiment for a broader-based regional system along the lines of the Maastricht plans for European Monetary Union. This would lead to a tripolar system of currency areas based on the ECU, the dollar and perhaps the yen.

BIMETALLISM, 1815–73

The bimetallic standard was the least understood of the international monetary systems and has always been the subject of great controversy.[2] It had the great advantage over monometallic systems of providing for a monetary unity in most of the world, whether a country adhered to gold or silver or to both. It is for this reason that Sir Roy Harrod referred to it as a "high-brow" standard, despite its bad reputation in the academic world.[3]

Bimetallism requires that one (or more) countries fix the domestic currency price of both metals (normally gold and silver); this country is normally the one with the largest economy. The bimetallic standard up to 1870 had been kept stabilized by France, the largest economy in the first half of the nineteenth century, with the United States in a backup position. From 1815 until the middle of the century, there was generally deflation in the world economy as economic growth exceeded the production of the precious metals and money substitutes (such as paper notes and bank deposits).[4]

Bimetallism imposes on the pivot country the role of buffer-stock agency. The gold discoveries in the middle of the century in New South Wales and California, which reversed the earlier deflation, led to a fall in the relative price of gold. Gold was therefore brought to the French mint and silver was exported, an exchange that cushioned the impact of increased gold production on prices and made gold the dominant means of payment in France.

With the US Civil War in the early 1860s, the dollar became inconvertible and stability of the bimetallic ratio rested on France alone. But the opening of the Franco-Prussian War forced France to suspend specie payments, bringing the bimetallic era to a close. From 1870 until 1914, the world was divided between an expanding gold bloc and a contracting silver bloc.

In the struggle before the forces of silver and the forces of gold, the latter was gradually becoming dominant in the world economy. Gold had been selected, already at the Paris Conference of 1867, as the "modern" metal, and countries like Prussia that were on the silver standard gave notice of their intention to shift to gold. When, in the early 1870s, the German Empire, bulging with gold from French reparations (and followed by the Scandinavian countries) moved onto the gold standard, it dumped silver on world markets. In 1874, the countries of the Latin Union (France, Belgium, Italy and Switzerland in 1865, later joined by Greece, Romania and the Church States) suspended the free coinage of silver. The bimetallic ratio then began to diverge from its "parity" between 15 silver = 1 gold and 16 silver = 1 gold, a range that had held since 1815, reaching 17: 1 in 1876 and 18: 1 in 1879 (it would fall to 20: 1 and above in the late 1880s). Fearing that a return to bimetallism would force it to exchange all its gold currency for silver, France elected, in 1878, to join the gold brigade.[5]

The breakdown of the bimetallic system led to flexible exchange rates between gold and silver countries. The excess supply of silver and excess demand for gold led to appreciation of the gold standard currencies relative to the silver standard currencies, bringing on deflation in the former and inflation in the latter.

The breakup of the bimetallic system led to severe depression in the 1870s and to two decades of deflation in gold standard countries, combined with inflation and instability in the silver standard countries. The movement to flexible exchange rates between silver – and gold – standard countries was not conducive to economic growth.

INTERNATIONAL GOLD STANDARD, 1873–1914

Exactly when "the" gold standard started, it is impossible to say. Strictly speaking, there was both a gold and a silver standard, as well as a group of inconvertible currencies, between 1873 and 1914. By 1880, however, the four important "core" countries – Britain, the United States (*de facto*), Germany and France adhered to gold. Russia, Austria-Hungary, Italy, Japan, China and India were still on silver.

The turning point in the battle of the standard came with the discovery of gold in the Witswatersrand in 1885 and the application of new techniques shortly after. This supply shock would change the course of the twentieth century. More than two-thirds of all the gold ever produced has come from the mines of South Africa.

The increase in gold supply in the early 1890s could normally have been expected to reverse the deflationary trend in the world economy that had set in after 1873. But simultaneously, new demands for gold appeared on the scene. Countries formerly on silver jumped onto gold after 1880: Italy in 1884, Greece in 1885, Russia and Austria-Hungary in 1892, and Japan in 1897. This continuing shift to gold held up demand and prolonged the deflation in the gold countries. The new gold supplies brought about a rise in prices only after a long lag.

The 1890s witnessed a long depression in the United States and much of Western Europe. The trauma of industrialization, unemployment, gold losses, and labor strife left its stain on this period, putting the gold standard under attack as a wagon of deflation. It was in the election campaign of 1896 that presidential candidate William Jennings Bryan electrified his audiences with the charge that the "American farmer had been crucified on a cross of gold." Yet that very year was a year of resurrection! By 1896 new gold supplies had caught up with increased demand, transforming two decades of mild deflation into almost two more decades of mild inflation.

The gold standard era, say from 1880 to 1913, was successful in maintaining long-run price stability; the price level in 1880 was approximately the same as that in 1913. There were, however, systematic trends first of deflation, arising from the shift to the gold standard, followed by inflation, arising from the impact of new gold production and metallurgical discoveries. Both the deflation and inflation were serious causes for concern, and the depression of the 1890s presented a significant check to economic growth.

ANCHORED DOLLAR STANDARD, 1915–24

With the outbreak of World War I, the European countries engaged in deficit finance, imposed exchange controls, and left the gold standard.[6] Gold was exported to those countries still on gold, especially the United States.[7] With the excess supply of gold in the world caused by the departure from the gold standard, and its monetization in the gold-importing countries, the value of gold fell in half and the price level in the United States doubled. After the end of the war, only the United States, of the major countries, was still on the gold standard. Most of the other European currencies were fluctuating with respect to the dollar or stabilized with the device of exchange controls.[8]

The decade from 1914 to 1924 was, for all practical purposes, a dollar standard anchored to gold; the dollar was the only major currency on gold. The anchored dollar gave a cohesion to the international monetary system that would have been absent under a system of flexible exchange rates. It could be interpreted as an equilibrium system (which countries had not before experienced) provided that no new demands were placed upon the stock of gold reserves by a re-introduction of the international gold standard.

The anchored dollar standard was a stop-gap system arising from a confluence of two factors: World War I and the dominating strength of the US economy. The anchored dollar standard was, however, successful in providing a reference point for currency stabilization after the war and might have been a useful and long-lasting expedient had it been politically acceptable to the former great powers.

INTERNATIONAL GOLD-EXCHANGE STANDARD, 1925–36

Unfortunately, the major countries hankered for a return to gold, an international monetary system they had identified with the golden age of Europe that World War I had obliterated. But a return to the gold standard made sense only if the conditions were right. The supply of gold was sufficient for an anchored dollar standard, but not for a return to an international gold standard on the scale that existed before the war. During World War I, prices had doubled in the United States, the only major country still on gold. Prices fell substantially during the postwar recession of 1920–1, but the dollar price level was still 35 per cent higher than in the prewar period. The real value of gold reserves was substantially lower, even after taking into account increased supplies, than in the prewar period.

That gold was scarce was a fact acknowledged by the major powers. An attempt was made by international officials to economize on gold by using foreign-exchange reserves as a substitute.[9] Nevertheless, despite the scarcity, the major powers restored a version of the international gold standard. Germany, after a successful stabilization of its currency following the great hyperinflation, reintroduced the gold mark in 1924.[10] Sweden soon followed in the same year. Britain, despite wartime and postwar inflation higher than that in the United States, restored the pound to its old parity in 1925. France went back to gold *de facto* the following year and *de jure* in 1928. Other countries followed the lead of the major countries: the Netherlands, Australia and Chile in 1925; Canada, Belgium and Finland in 1926; Italy, Denmark, Brazil and Argentina in 1927; Norway and Greece in 1928; Switzerland in 1929; and Japan in 1930.

The rush to the gold standard from 1924 to 1930 at a time when there was an acknowledged shortage of gold was an economic blunder of the first magnitude.[11] The return to the gold standard sowed the seeds of the great depression and its corollaries of economic nationalism, mass unemployment, and world war.

My views on this differ from the conventional wisdom, which usually focuses on the abortive return of sterling to its old parity. I agree, of course, with Keynes' argument (and now the general consensus), that Winston Churchill and Montagu Norman erred in going back to gold at the old prewar parity. That was a serious error as far as Britain was concerned, overvaluing British labor and dooming Britain, as Keynes argued, to the stagnation and high unemployment of the late 1920s.[12] But it is a mistake to blame the great depression on that event. Keynes thought the pound was overvalued by 10 per cent. But conduct the thought experiment of restoring the pound at $4.40 or even $4.20. Britain's position would have been better and sterling might not have been forced off gold as early as it was. But the great depression would not have been avoided on that account.

It is fatuous to believe that the international monetary system is so fragile that a 10 per cent error in the exchange rate of an important (but not the most important) country is sufficient to bring about a collapse of the system.[13] The problem in the interwar period that set in motion the great depression was not the overvaluation of sterling but the overvaluation of all currencies – given the return to the gold standard – in terms of gold. The gold scarcity had come about as a result of three factors: (a) the higher postwar price level, which lowered the real value of gold reserves, (b) the increased demand for gold as a result of increased uncertainty, aggravated by fluctuating exchange rates, and (c) the increased requirements for gold due to the return to the gold standard. Even if there were enough gold at the prevailing price level for the anchored dollar standard when other countries were not on gold, there was not enough to meet the requirements of a pre-1914 type international gold standard. As a result, the abortive restoration of the international gold standard in the late 1920s laid the basis for the deflation that was to follow.

The tragedy of the early 1930s is that the deflation of the early 1930s could have been prevented by an early increase in the price of gold in terms of all currencies. As it was, the price of gold was raised sporadically as one country after another went off the gold standard often only to restore it – or the dollar parity – at a higher price. Even before Britain left gold in September 1931 in the wake of the failure of the Creditanstaldt, Argentina and Australia had already left gold in 1929 and Brazil was to follow in 1930. Following hard on the heels of the British departure from gold were Germany, Japan, Canada, Portugal, Denmark, Norway, Sweden and Finland in 1931, and Greece in 1932.

The United States left gold in March 1933, in the wake of the national banking collapse brought on by the depression.[14] The dollar floated and, for a short period, the "gold bloc," the rump of the gold standard including France, Italy, the Netherlands, Belgium and Switzerland, was the only formal connection of the international monetary system to gold. France was able to outlast the Anglo-Saxon countries on the gold standard, because the franc had been restored to gold at a parity that undervalued it relative to the pound and even the dollar and because France had a tolerance for deflation greater than its neighbours.[15]

Little more than a year after taking the United States off gold, in April 1934, President Roosevelt, using prior congressional authorization, devalued the dollar. The official price of gold was raised from its old parity of $20.67 to $35.00 an ounce. This price would last for 37 years – until 1971. The devaluation was combined with dirigiste measures to emasculate the internal gold standard: the dollar was no longer redeemable into gold; US citizens were required to turn over all their gold coins to the government; and US citizens were forbidden to hold any gold at home or abroad.[16] The

Federal Reserve, however, was required to keep 40 per cent of its liabilities in the form of gold certificates (claims on gold held by the US Treasury).[17]

For two years after the United States set its new parity, a vestige of the international gold standard remained: the United States, France, Italy, Belgium and Switzerland were all on some version of a gold standard. But the currencies of the gold-bloc countries were now recognized to be seriously overvalued with respect to gold and the dollar. Belgium was the first to devalue, in March 1935. By the end of 1936 the other countries had also devalued, putting *finis* to the restoration experiments of 1924–36.

The international gold exchange standard as it developed in the 1920s was probably the worst international monetary system ever developed as far as its relation to economic growth is concerned. It created an excess demand for gold and forced countries to follow monetary policies that led to the deflation and depression of the 1930s. The transition period away from the international gold exchange standard took place during one of the worst periods in modern economic history; it was a story of escaping from an oppressive international monetary system. The countries which, like the sterling-area countries, left the system early were the first to recover; those which, like the gold bloc countries, hung on the longest, suffered the most.

ANCHORED DOLLAR STANDARD, 1936–71

After the US devaluation of 1934, the US balance of payments position became exceptionally strong. After the French devaluation of 1936, it became apparent that the dollar was now the master currency. The new position of the dollar was manifested in the sudden awareness in markets that it was the dollar that gave value to gold, not vice versa. Had the United States withdrawn from the gold market, the price would have plummeted. Reflecting this possibility, there was a gold scare based on an unfounded rumour that the United States, deluged with gold imports, might withdraw its commitment to gold.

The gold scare is the origin of what later became known as "the dollar shortage." The dollar was as good as gold, but was gold as good as the dollar? The new position of the dollar was reflected in the new exchange-rate arrangements by which the other leading countries, including the United Kingdom and France, managed their exchange rates: not by intervention in the gold market but by intervention in the foreign-exchange market against dollars. This system harked back to the system prevailing between 1914 and 1924. It was again a dollar standard anchored to gold. This was especially true after the Tripartite Agreement signed by the United States, the United Kingdom and France, following the devaluation of the franc. It required countries to give notice to one another in advance of any change in exchange-rate policies. It can be interpreted as the first agreement setting out a mechanism for managing the interdependence imposed by separate currencies and independent central banks.

The agreements at Bretton Woods in 1944 did not set up a new international monetary system. Both before and after the conference, the international monetary system was a dollar standard, anchored to gold. In the postwar system, the US dollar was the only currency convertible into gold and this only for foreign monetary authorities.

As a result of capital inflows to the United States – refugee capital and rearmament spending – and wartime spending, gold had again become concentrated in the United States after World War II, with about 70 per cent of the world's monetary gold reserves. Not only in this respect, but also in another did the situation resemble that after World War I. As a result of wartime and postwar inflation, prices had doubled in the United States.[18] Whatever benefit in terms of international liquidity was achieved by the devaluation of the dollar in 1934 was more than offset by wartime-related inflation.

Was gold undervalued and the dollar overvalued as a result of the US inflation? The answer depends on what is meant by "overvaluation." The dollar was not overvalued with respect to foreign currencies; many writers still wrote of a "dollar shortage." But whether or not gold was undervalued (and the dollar and all other currencies overvalued with respect to gold) depends on the demands put on gold by the international monetary system.

The quick answer to the question about the appropriate valuation of gold is that gold was not undervalued if countries chose to accumulate dollars rather than gold in their international reserves and refrained from cashing them in for gold. But under the anchored dollar standard, other countries had a right to exchange dollars for gold; the United States was absolved of its exchange-rate commitments under the Articles of Agreement of the International Monetary Fund (IMF) only because it declared that it was "buying and selling gold freely." The other countries were required to intervene in their foreign exchange market to fix exchange rates, and adjust their monetary policies to achieve balance-of-payments equilibrium, but the United States was exempt from the requirement because of its commitment to stabilize the price of gold.[19]

Given the fact that other countries were fixing their currencies to the dollar rather than gold, they did not need to hold gold for intervention purposes. But they had other reasons for holding gold. One was the possibility that the price of gold might be raised and that they could reap capital gains; this would be more likely the lower the US gold stock relative to its liabilities and the higher the US rate of inflation. Another was a reluctance to hold dollars because it seemed to imply a superior status for the dollar conferred on the United States. A third (related) reason was that gold gave a country a more-independent status. A fourth reason is that the exchange of dollars for gold could be used to discipline the United States if its monetary policies were too expansionary and pushed too much of the burden of adjustment onto surplus countries.

US gold losses began with a substantial decline in 1950 and minor losses in a few of the following years. These losses were at first looked upon as a healthy redistribution of the world's gold stock. But by the late 1950s, that Panglossian view was no longer credible. In the early 1960s the United States was in the process of losing 60 per cent of its gold stock. The US gold stock fell from 664 million ounces at the end of 1952 to 311 million ounces in 1968 and 276 million in 1972.[20]

During the 1960s there was some sentiment in favor of raising the official dollar price of gold. Sir Roy Harrod had long advocated doubling the price, a solution that had been provided for in the Articles of Agreement of the International Monetary Fund. Such a policy, however, was strongly opposed by the Kennedy and Johnson administrations. The two big gold producers in the world were then perceived as pariahs: South Africa, because of its policy of apartheid; and the Soviet Union, because it was NATO's adversary in the Cold War.

Instead of relieving the scarcity of gold by raising its price, the international monetary authorities chose the path of finding a substitute for gold in the form of "paper gold" Special Drawing Rights. SDRs were given a gold guarantee and could have, in principle, eliminated the gold shortage. But this imaginative solution was implemented too late and was introduced in too-small amounts to create confidence that the excess demand for gold would be met by the new gold substitute.[21] The system therefore broke down during a period when the dollar was weakened by the 1970–1 recession and there was a large capital outflow to Europe, embarrassing the surplus countries. The Bank of England (followed by other countries) detonated the collapse by asking to convert excess dollars into gold. On August 15, 1971, President Richard M. Nixon said no, the gold window was closed, and the postwar international monetary system broke up.[22]

The other surplus countries let the dollar fall. At first there was some attempt on the part of the major European countries to float jointly against the dollar, hoping to avoid flexible exchange rates between the European currencies. But this first attempt at a joint float was premature. There was no agreement on a center currency – the pound, the franc or the mark – and it was not yet so obvious that the mark had superseded the pound as the most important European currency. Nor would it have been politically attractive for French politicians to fix on either the mark or the pound. Consequently, Europe got unstable exchange rates.

Over the history of the anchored dollar standard, from 1936 to 1971, with currencies fixed to the dollar, the major European countries had achieved a high degree of monetary convergence: this was reflected in narrow differentials between inflation rates and interest rates in different countries.[23] At the same time, inflation rates were comparatively low, budgets were in approximate balance, growth rates were substantial, and, to some most important, unemployment rates were low. The economic performance of the European countries under the anchored dollar standard was far superior to their performance since, even after the formation of the EMS and ERM.

The anchored dollar standard that existed from 1936 to 1971 should be divided into three periods. The first period, from 1936 to 1950, incorporated the war and early-postwar adjustment; like most war periods, it had the defect of weak financial discipline. More relevant is the second period, from 1950 to 1967, when the balance-of-payments problem of the United States, associated with the dollar-reserve mechanism and gold losses, became apparent; this was a period of relative price stability and solid economic growth, especially in Europe, with remarkably low levels of unemployment. The third period, from 1964 to 1971, was also a period of rapid growth, marred, however, by the Vietnam War and the threatened breakup of the system. Overall, the period gets high marks compared to its successors, making due allowance for the inevitable inflationary excesses brought about by its three wars.

UNANCHORED DOLLAR STANDARD, 1971–3

Fluctuating exchange rates were anathema to most countries in Europe, and they soon took steps to revert to a system of fixed exchange rates. The major countries met at the Smithsonian Institution in December 1971 and went back to fixed exchange rates, again anchored to the dollar. But this time the dollar was no longer anchored to gold. The other countries fixed their rates to the dollar, but the dollar was now inconvertible. The system was for all practical purposes, as the Bundesbank conceded, a pure dollar standard.

The weakness of a fixed-exchange-rate system anchored to a major currency is that it does not contain a mechanism for disciplining the center country. If the center country deflates, the rest of the currency area is stuck with deflation; if the center country inflates, the rest of the currency area has to inflate. It is a quasi-imperial system in which the outer countries delegate to the center country the power to determine the inflation rate of the currency area as a whole.

Contrast this fixed-exchange-rate system to that where the center country, to which the other currencies are fixed, is itself anchored to something else – such as a commodity like gold. When the rest of the currency area holds both the reserve currency and gold in its reserves, it has a mechanism for influencing the inflation rate of the center country. If, in the view of outer countries, acting individually or in concert, the center country is deflating excessively, the outer countries can sell gold to the center country and hold more of the reserve currency; this would increase the gold reserves of the center country and encourage it to expand. If, on the other hand, the outer countries believe the center country's policies are too inflationary, it can sell the reserve currency for gold, forcing the center country to tighten.

This was the situation with the anchored dollar standard of the postwar period. Countries built up dollar balances in the 1940s and 1950s, when they were inflating more than the United States. But after they had achieved an adequate level of reserves, they became concerned about their composition and wanted to accumulate fewer dollars than the United States was supplying, and to buy more gold than that available from new production. Their policy of dollar conversions could be interpreted as sending a message to the United States that its monetary policies were too expansionary for the interests of the new surplus countries of Western Europe.

It is true, of course, that Europe's dollar conversions and US gold losses were insufficient – in the midst of the Vietnam War – to prevent inflationary policies in the United States and it did not prevent the system from breaking down. But for twenty years it did serve the purpose of keeping the United States from inflating more than it did. Whenever the United States lost gold in the 1950s and 1960s, the reserve base of the system would diminish automatically. The Federal Reserve would then turn around and neutralize the monetary effects of these gold losses by selling government bonds – sterilization. Nevertheless, the massive gold losses kept monetary policy tighter, and the US and world inflation rate lower, than it would have been in the absence of the convertibility requirement on the United States. Just compare US monetary policy in the 1950s and 1960s under the convertibility regime with that after the dollar became inconvertible in 1971!

If the anchored dollar standard suffered from the defect that it was too inflationary – at least for the surplus countries – the *unanchored dollar standard* that replaced it had the potential to be worse. The outer countries were subject to the balance-of-payments discipline, but the United States was no longer required to convert unwanted dollars into gold. The unwanted dollars were referred to as the "overhang."

The US balance-of-payments deficit was jointly determined by the United States and the rest of the world. On the one hand, the Federal Reserve controlled the reserve base for the system and could determine the increase in that base – available not only for the United States but also for the rest of the world. Given fixed exchange rates, the outer countries had to accumulate any reserves spilling over from US requirements and allow bank reserves and money supplies to expand, increasing expenditure and creating the potential for increased inflation.[24]

This flaw would soon be seen in the dollar standard erected at the Smithsonian Institution, and it would later have its counterpart in the breakup of the ERM system in September 1992 (although Germany erred in the opposite direction). Exempted from its balance-of-payments constraint, the Federal Reserve expanded the money supply and aggravated the inflationary pressures in Europe. In February 1973, the US devalued the dollar again, raising the non-operative official price from $38 per ounce to

$42.22 per ounce. This silly devaluation merely whetted the appetites of speculators and set in motion the forces that ended with the collapse of the system.

In the spring of 1973, Europe again tried to arrange a joint float, but again no agreement could be reached on how to bring it about. The result was that in June 1973, the Committee of Thirty scrapped the international monetary system and suggested that countries should try to control inflation on their own under a regime of flexible exchange rates.

The fatal flaw of an unanchored currency area is that it throws the burden of adjustment to disequilibrium onto the outer countries. The center country (in this case, the United States) determines the rate of inflation in the world as a whole. If this does not suit the interests of the other countries, they are reduced to the expedient of (a) moral exhortation, (b) pressure for multilateral monetary reform, or (c) leaving the system. The first two options (a) and (b), did not work, so the result was (c). The basic problem of the unanchored system is not that it is in theory unworkable, but that its success depends on the willingness of the center country to take some account of the interests of its partners; this problem (with different actors) would recur in the ERM crisis of 1992.

FLEXIBLE EXCHANGE RATES, 1973–9

If the step from an anchored to the unanchored dollar standard organized at the Smithsonian Institution in December 1971 represented a relaxation of international monetary discipline, how much more so was the complete abandonment of the system represented by the movement toward flexible exchange rates in June 1973. This step represented a degree of folly on the part of international monetary officials comparable only to the fatal restoration of the international gold-exchange standard in the 1920s. But whereas the latter restoration brought about deflation and mass depression, the movement to flexible exchange rates opened the doors to the greatest inflation the world has ever experienced.[25]

What keeps monopolies (of goods or labor) from tripling prices in a common-currency area? Why don't, say, the United Auto Workers (UAW) triple or quadruple wage demands in Michigan? The obvious answer is that they would be rejected by employers or, if they were not rejected, the companies would go bankrupt and workers would lose their jobs; labor competes with labor all around the world. For this reason, such excessively unreasonable wage demands are never made.

But what would happen if the UAW knew or thought that the Federal Reserve system would rapidly expand the money supply to accommodate the wage demands? Then, even though general inflation would follow, the auto workers would gain from getting their tripled wages a step ahead of the increase in prices. Given such anticipated laxity on the part of the Federal Reserve, labor-union leaders would have to exercise their fiduciary authority to push for the higher wages. The workers would win out, if there were no monetary discipline.

The situation is analogous in the international monetary system after the movement to flexible exchange rates in 1973. The world money supply was no longer anchored (even if indirectly) to gold as before 1971, and there was no longer even the discipline of fixed exchange rates. The door was opened, not to the UAW, but to the Organization of Petroleum-Exporting Countries (OPEC). Within nine months of the shift to floating rates, OPEC had quadrupled oil prices.[26]

Under a gold standard, or even under the anchored dollar standard, such an aggressive increase in the price of any key commodity would have quickly brought about a reduction in oil receipts to the oil-exporting countries and a recession in the West. The result would have been moderation of the price demands and a restoration of equilibrium at a somewhat higher price.

This re-equilibration process did not occur, because the new international money-supply function had become highly elastic. Even if domestic monetary policies had been restrained, there was a potential for a multiplied expansion of liquidity in offshore centers, particularly in the Eurodollar market; low-powered demand deposits in US banks could become high-powered reserve money in Europe. The Eurodollar market exploded as Eurobanks recycled petrodollars to the deficit importing countries. From $263.8 billion at the end of 1972, it rose to $379.1 billion in 1973, $480.3 billion in 1974, $579.2 billion in 1975, $721.8 billion in 1976, $891.4 billion in 1977, $1,183.1 billion in 1978, $1,486.9 billion in 1979, $1,822.6 in 1980, $2,182.9 in 1981 and $2,362.1 billion in 1982. In ten years the Eurodollar market multiplied 13.7 times!

The inflationary excesses of the 1970s brought about a reaction against flexible exchange rates, at least in Europe. Continuing inflation stemming both from US monetary policy and the explosion of the Eurodollar market had brought in its wake the depreciation of the dollar. Europe reacted by seeking to form an international monetary system of its own.

The regime of flexible exchange rates was tried in the 1970s and was found wanting. Hardly any of the forecasts made by advocates of flexible exchange rates had turned out to be correct. Advocates had argued that foreign-exchange reserves would not be necessary under flexible rates: the reality was that they were more necessary than before, and foreign-exchange reserves – and the value of gold stocks – exploded.[27] *A second prediction, that depreciation of the currency would act as just as strong or stronger a deterrent on monetary expansion as a loss of reserve assets proved equally incorrect. As far as inflation, economic growth, and employment are concerned, the period of flexible exchange rates in the 1970s was greatly inferior to the earlier periods of fixed exchange rates.*

CURRENCY AREAS, 1979–85

The falling dollar led to the proposal, at the Bremen meeting in 1978, for a sequel to the earlier, but unsuccessful attempt, to promote European monetary integration. The European Monetary System came into being in March 1979, and soon after, the exchange rate mechanism (ERM) within the system was established to engineer a joint float against the dollar.

Although the exchange-rate "grid" gave the appearance of symmetry in the relations between the currencies in the ERM, the reality was very different. The level of transactions in exchange markets determines which currency dominates, and the level of transactions roughly corresponds to involvement in international trade.[28] In the 1980s Germany's exports were almost twice those of France and an even larger proportion of those of Britain or Italy. The ERM was, and came to be recognized as, a DM standard.

The case for a DM standard was not just that Germany's was the largest economy; Germany also had the tightest monetary policy and the strongest balance-of-payments position. German fears of inflation – inherited from the hyperinflation of the 1920s and the currency conversions of 1923 and 1948 – were backed up by a commitment providing for a Bundesbank (a) that is independent, (b) does not finance government expenditures, and (c) adopts price stability as its sole (or main) target. Since 1950, Germany had the best inflation performance of any of the large powers.

There is, of course, also a case against a DM standard. It is in theory the same as the case against a pure dollar standard; (1) the monetary policy of the center country determines the inflation rate of the area, (2) there is no mechanism by which the other countries can discipline the center country if inflation preferences clash, (3) it is an asymmetric imperial system, the "Roman" solution, rather than a shared sovereignty.

These defects were to emerge in the working out of the ERM in the late 1980s and early 1990s. France at first thought it had sufficient monetary independence in the system to expand its economy on its own. The failure of these policies in the early years of the Mitterrand government were at first blamed on Germany, then subsequently acknowledged by President Mitterrand himself.[29] Under the DM standard, countries outside Germany were no longer able to pursue independent macroeconomic policies. France moreover acknowledged, under the Basle–Nyborg accord, that countries whose currencies were under attack would follow the "rules of the game" and raise interest rates.

Meanwhile, Britain, a member of the EMS like all the member countries, had not yet decided in favor of joining the ERM, waiting until the time was "ripe." Such an opportunity arose in November 1985 and most of the Cabinet were in favor of joining. Relying, however, on the advice of Sir Alan Walters, Prime Minister Thatcher vetoed the prospect.[30] It would come up again later at a less favorable occasion, and the answer would be different. Had Britain joined in 1985, France and Britain together might have been able to exert some influence on the German financial anchor.

Uncomfortable with the position *vis-à-vis* Germany, France sought two alternative routes to exercise influence over German policy. One was the establishment of the Franco German Economic Council, the other was a resumption of consideration of plans for a European Central Bank and European currency. The first initiative was resisted by the Bundesbank, which took steps to preserve its monetary autonomy; the second led to the Delors Report and, subsequently, to the Treaty of Maastricht. The DM standard, like the dollar standard, had the advantage of providing a focus for convergence of monetary policies, inflation, and interest rates. The weakness in any national-currency standard, however, is the monetary unilateralism of the center country. The dollar standard broke up because the center country was too inflationary. The DM standard came close to breaking up, in 1992, because the DM standard, following the unification shock, imposed currency appreciation and deflation on its partner countries. By contrast, the anchored dollar standard had a mechanism for disciplining the center country: dollar conversions into gold. This deterrent had the effect of checking excess monetary expansion of the United States. However, after the United States had lost two-thirds of its gold reserves, the deterrent no longer worked, and the system gravitated to a *de facto* dollar standard.

COORDINATED DOLLAR SYSTEM, 1985–93

Meanwhile, during the experience with the ERM in Europe, new developments were unfolding in the global sphere. In 1981, under the new Reagan administration, there was a dramatic shift in the policy mix from easy money with fiscal creep, to tight money, tax cuts, and a stronger military posture. The Economic Recovery Act of 1981 slashed tax rates, increased the efficiency of the economy, and, in conjunction with the Federal Reserve's tight money, brought about disinflation and, after a sharp recession, a strong economic expansion. The "seven fat years" – so called in Robert Bartley's book of that title – of the Reagan-Bush expansion, from the end of 1982 to the middle of 1990, initially brought about a strong dollar; the dollar doubled against the DM from late 1980 to early 1985, when it reached a high of DM 3.4. By late 1984, the fundamentals had changed. The US recovery was showing and the Federal Reserve gunned the money supply. By February 1985 the dollar reached a peak and started to tumble throughout the spring and summer. To help it down – and to create the impression that the descent was being managed – the US administration convened, at the Plaza Hotel in New York in September 1985, a G-5 meeting, wresting a commitment from its partners to help in coordinating a further depreciation of the dollar. The dollar did depreciate after monetary policies in Japan and elsewhere were tightened somewhat, but a more important factor was the subsequent collapse of oil prices, which benefited Europe and Japan more than the United States. The second half of the 1980s was characterized by a falling and/or low dollar. By February 1987, when the G-7 met at the Louvre in Paris, it was agreed that the dollar had fallen far enough and should be stabilized "around current levels." Thus the Louvre Accord marks the end of the belief that the free market necessarily results in a desirable exchange-rate equilibrium.

After the Louvre Accord, the subject of international monetary reform, dormant since 1973, was revived. Given the desire to keep rates stable at the Louvre, the question turned on the mechanism for keeping them stable. Whose monetary policies should change: should countries with strong currencies expand, or should countries with weak currencies contract? Who should bear the burden of adjustment? Elsewhere, I have referred to a variant of this degree of freedom as the "redundancy problem."[31]

When currencies are anchored to a common asset, such as gold, the problem is solved automatically; the burden is distributed in inverse proportion to the size of country – measured by international reserves and banking reserve ratios.[32] Under an automatic system (such as the gold standard or adjustment between different regions of a common-currency area), the distribution of the burden of adjustment between surplus and deficit countries is resolved automatically, but under a discretionary system, an artificial mechanism must be set up. The basic idea under consideration at the Venice summit that followed the Louvre Accord was to use an index. If there is general inflation in the world at a given level of stable exchange rates, then the deficit countries should contract; if there is deflationary pressure in the world, then the surplus countries should expand. If there is neither inflation nor deflation, the burden should be distributed between the countries.

At the IMF meetings, in September 1987, Secretary James A. Baker III stunned his audience with the proposal for a commodity-price index – *including gold*, he emphasized – as a means of allocating the distribution of the burden of adjustment. However, the use of the four-letter word – a word that had become taboo since the Second Amendment to the IMF Articles of Agreement – created the impression that Secretary Baker might have some new plans for gold up his sleeve.[33] There was some support for the use of an index, but the issue got sidetracked in the following month with the stock-market crash on October 19–20, 1987, induced by continuing weakness in the dollar and uncertainty over monetary policy.

Since the days of Secretary Baker, there has been no talk of international monetary reform. Under President George Bush and Secretary Brady, there was no consideration of international monetary reform; attention was rather shifted to the Brady Plan approach to coping with the international debt crisis.

Under President Clinton there was no leadership in the field of international monetary reform; and no prospect of any is in sight. Nor are there any plans or pressures for reform coming from the opposition parties. There is not likely to be any leadership in the field of international monetary reform coming from the United States over the next few years.

The need for the coordinate dollar system arose out of the sharply differing monetary and fiscal policies followed by the United States. In the late 1970s US monetary policy was too expansionary, leading to inflation, tax bracket creep, a depreciating dollar, and a second oil shock. These policies were reversed in the early 1980s, with a tax-cut-led fiscal policy, an expanding economy, and a soaring dollar. The appreciation of the dollar served US interests in the early 1980s, because it fostered the disinflation policy; but it no longer served after the disinflation had been achieved and growth had begun to stall. The reversal of the appreciating dollar achieved or fostered by the Plaza accord thus helped to prolong the Reagan boom into first half of the Bush years.

The negative aspect of the coordinated dollar was that Europe's problems with rising unemployment were augmented by the currency appreciations of the late 1980s. From the standpoint of unemployment, Europe's interests would have been better served with a higher value of the dollar.

GROWTH AND EXCHANGE-RATE SYSTEMS

Ideally, it would be desirable to compare the performance characteristics of different international exchange-rate systems measured against the challenges faced during that time period. This methodology, however, is particularly difficult to implement. International monetary systems are not independent of political events, and vice versa. Which determines which is an open question. Political events can change the international monetary system, and economic events can cause political changes. A less sophisticated approach, looking at economic performance during the different periods, is probably necessary.

Are fixed exchange rates more conducive to growth than flexible exchange rates? Let us start with the United States and compare two time periods for which the data are readily on hand: 1947–67, the 20-year heyday of the anchored gold dollar; and 1968–93, a 25-year period under the paper dollar.[34]

It is clear from Table 1.2 that the first period dominates the second in all respects. Real growth, productivity, and real wage growth were higher; inflation, unemployment, and interest rates were unambiguously lower. *Prima facie* evidence suggests that the gold-anchored dollar standard was a superior system to those that succeeded it.

What about Europe and Japan? Table 1.3 gives some evidence about key features for these countries and the United States for three decades. The

Table 1.2 US economic performance, 1947–93

	Average annual rates (%)	
	gold dollar 1947–67	*paper dollar 1968–93*
Real GDP growth	3.6	2.6
Productivity	3.3	1.4
Real wage growth	1.8	−0.5
Inflation rate	2.6	5.2
Unemployment rate	4.7	6.5
Treasury Bond yield	3.8	8.6
Treasury-bill rates	2.4	7.0

Source: *Economic Report of the President* (1994)

Table 1.3 Growth rates, 1963–92

	1963–72	*1973–82*	*1983–92*
United States	3.8	1.6	2.6
Japan	9.7	3.5	4.1
EC	4.5	1.9	2.5
Other Europe	4.4	2.1	2.5
Canada	5.3	3.0	2.7

Source: *WEFA World Economic Service*, July 1993

first decade, when exchange rates were fixed, was a decade of considerably higher growth than either of the other decades for every group of countries. It is also true, however, that, except for Canada, the decade of the 1970s was worse than the following one. By this criterion, the anchored dollar standard before the 1970s comes out on top; this is followed by the currency-area systems of the 1980s, which had a superior performance to the decade of the 1970s.

Growth figures represent only one facet of economic performance. If instead we studied unemployment rates, we would find the results in Table 1.4. Once again we find that performance judged by unemployment is vastly superior in every area in the first period, i.e., that under fixed exchange rates. But there is now a difference with respect to the second period. Measured by unemployment rates, the second period, under flexible rates, is superior to the third period, under currency areas, in every area except the United States.

What about inflation rates? Table 1.5 provides information for the same time periods. Again, the evidence is clear. The first period dominates the second by far. However, the third period dominates the first! The period of the 1980s was a period in which wholesale prices rose at a slower rate than the period of not only the 1970s but also the 1960s.

Table 1.4 Average unemployment rates, 1963–92

	1963–72	*1973–82*	*1983–92*
United States	4.7	7.0	6.8
Japan	1.2	1.9	2.5
EC	2.5	5.4	10.1
Other Europe	3.9	5.8	7.3
Canada	4.7	7.5	9.7

Source: *WEFA World Economic Service*, July 1993

Table 1.5 Inflation rates: rate of change of wholesale price indexes, 1963–92 (%)

	1963–72	*1973–82*	*1983–92*
United States	2.6	9.3	1.6
Japan	2.3	10.7	1.9
EC	1.3	7.0	−1.5
Other Europe	4.4	2.1	2.5
Canada	2.7	9.2	2.8

Source: *WEFA World Economic Service*, July 1993

CONCLUSIONS

This chapter has examined the relation between performance characteristics of the world economy, measured by growth, stability, employment and inflation, and the exchange-rate system, prevailing at different time periods. Starting with bimetallism and the gold standard in the nineteenth century, through the modern system of currency areas separated by flexible exchange rates, I have argued that periods of exchange rate instability have been associated with periods of low performance of the world economy; and that periods of exchange-rate stability have been associated with periods of high performance of the world economy.

The instability of the interwar period, including the great depression, was caused by the restoration of the gold standard on a gold base that had been eroded by World War I inflation. The mistake led to the worst period of growth the world economy has ever experienced.

The dollar standard anchored to gold inaugurated a period of quasi-fixed exchange rates that was characterized by moderate inflation, rapid growth, and remarkably low unemployment. The anchored dollar standard endorsed at Bretton Woods broke down because, as after World War I, gold had been undervalued and because of the struggle that developed between the United States and Europe (reflected in the management of dollar liabilities and European gold conversions), for control over the right to determine the common global rate of inflation.

The breakdown of the anchored dollar standard in 1971 inaugurated another period of instability and low growth, though not as severe as in the 1930s. The abandonment of international monetary discipline led to the flexible exchange rates, soaring oil prices, and mounting unemployment of the 1970s.

Overly expansionary US monetary policies in the late 1970s prompted Europe to defend itself from the avalanche of dollars by instituting its own regional monetary system, the EMS. This system helped to stabilize the European currencies when the dollar recovered in the early 1980s under the Reagan administration, and made the coordinated dollar system easier to manage; at the same time, it was a retreat toward regionalism from the multilateral approach that had characterized the Bretton Woods arrangements.

The low dollar of the late 1980s helped the United States to prolong the Reagan-Bush boom, and at the same time it contributed to the difficulties experienced in Europe with mounting budget deficits and rising unemployment. Europe reacted to the low dollar again by a renewed push for European monetary integration, reflected in the Delors Report.

The ERM crisis in 1992, arising in the aftermath of the German unification shock, allowed some countries (e.g., Britain and Italy) in fundamental disequilibrium to leave the ERM. It appeared as a clash between the inflation preferences of Germany and its partners; because German monetary policy was tied to the narrow German basket, its monetary policy was too deflationary for the region as a whole.

A system of stable exchange rates produced by a quasi-independent European Central Bank producing a common European currency, dedicated to the stability of an index of prices that represented a wide European basket of goods, comprising over 20 per cent of the world economy, would be an alternative to the DM-standard that would be more compatible, with both growth and stability of the world economy. In Table 1.1 this system is suggested for Europe as a potential currency area for the years 1994–2005.

The conclusion of this chapter is that fixed-exchange-rate systems have, historically, been associated with stability and solid growth; by contrast, flexible exchange rate systems have been associated with instability and uneven growth. Exchange-rate stability is associated with monetary discipline, instability with indiscipline. Monetary instability leads to inflation and unemployment.

It would be incorrect to conclude, however, that fixed rates are desirable *per se*. *Incorrect* fixed rates are worse than flexible rates. The restoration of the gold standard in the 1920s was a case in point. Had the European countries not restored the gold standard, there would have been no great depression and it is even arguable that there would have been no World War II. The instability of the 1930s was the deadly aftermath of an incorrect fix.

The best periods for the world economy, over the past century, from the standpoints of inflation, growth, and unemployment, were the period of the gold standard up to 1914; and the post-Bretton Woods era, up to 1971. The 1915–45 and 1973 to present periods contrast unfavorably with these two periods. Unfortunately, the international monetary options of the former period – one resting on gold, the other on the dollar – are no longer politically feasible options for the world economy. A restoration of fixed-exchange-rate multilateralism must now go through the route of currency-area regionalism.

International monetary regionalism is only a second-best alternative to international monetary multilateralism, but it may be the only feasible route to a more desirable and better-balanced internationalism. European success with EMU could be cheered if it were accompanied or succeeded by a suitable global monetary agreement to minimize instability of the European Currency *vis-à-vis* the dollar and other major currencies.

Such a global monetary agreement, however, would have to solve the difficult problem of choosing or establishing an anchor. It is unlikely that the anchors that have served in the past – silver, gold, sterling, dollars, marks – will be satisfactory in and of themselves. Nor is the existing SDR of much use.[35] It is possible that at some future time a world currency could be created, based perhaps on a stable international asset, say, a "hard-SDR" standard, which in Table 1.1 is suggested as a possibility for 2005 and thereafter. In the mean time, however, there is a little demand for such an instrument and no chance of reaching agreement on a world currency. The most likely outcome, therefore, in the foreseeable future is that the existing system of currency areas will continue to evolve with changes in the power configuration of the world economy.

NOTES

1 An exchange rate is the price of one currency in terms of another. It is unambiguous when there are only two countries and currencies in the world. But if there are three or more currencies, no country has a single "exchange rate." There is a whole complex of exchange rates that have to be defined. To simplify, it is often helpful and not too unrealistic to focus on a single exchange rate on an important country. For example, most countries in Latin America use "the" exchange rate to refer to the domestic currency price of the dollar. Because the dollar is the most important international currency at this time, the exchange rate on the dollar is often sufficiently representative of exchange rates in general. In Europe, however, the exchange rate on the mark is also important, as, in Asia, is the exchange rate on the yen.

Because an exchange rate is the price of one currency in terms of another, it is frequently necessary to have a third currency for use as a reference currency. If, for example, the lira price of the mark (DM) rose suddenly, it would not be clear immediately whether the German currency had strengthened or the Italian currency had weakened. To make the distinction, it would be necessary to note the exchange rate also on the dollar. If, when the lira had weakened against the DM the lira price of the dollar had stayed constant, and the DM had risen also against the dollar, it would be possible to reach the tentative conclusion that the origin of the exchange-rate change was in Germany, not Italy. If, on the other hand, the lira had depreciated against *both* the DM and the dollar, it would appear likely that the problem had originated in Italy.

It is more relevant to consider the relation between economic growth and *changes* in the exchange rate. Changes in the exchange rate can occur because of disturbances that (a) are real or monetary; (b) stem from demand or supply shocks; (c) originate abroad or at home; (d) are temporary or permanent; or (e) are a hybrid of these possibilities. Short of a long treatise on the subject, it would be sterile to try to discuss all possible combinations, however relevant a few may be.

2 A good illustration of the confusion concerning bimetallism and the gold standard is Anna Schwartz's dating of the beginning of the "gold standard era" in 1821 when Britain resumed specie payments at the old parity. The gold standard era could be dated from this period only if "gold standard era" is defined as the period in which Britain is on the gold standard, to the neglect of all the other countries! Yet this seems to be what Schwartz (1984: 1) has in mind, because she dates its end in 1931, when Britain left the gold standard, ignoring the fact that the United States, France and some other countries remained, for a time, on gold.

3 Harrod (1952).

4 The British price level reached a peak of 182.5 in 1813 (1930 = 100), fell to a trough of 77.3 in 1851, rose to a peak of 114.4 in 1873, fell to a trough of 62.9 in 1896, and rose to 87.6 in the first year of World War I.

5 In what became criticized as the "crime of '73" the United States government (under President Ulysses S. Grant) failed to make a provision for minting the silver dollar, in effect making bimetallism unprofitable in the United States when that country resumed specie payments in 1878. The United States did not adopt the gold standard *de jure* until 1900.

6 Britain however, kept up the pretence of a gold standard throughout the war; even the United States imposed restrictions on gold outflows.

7 World War I marks the period when the United States emerged as a dominant power and the leading country in the international monetary system. Already by 1880, with a rapidly growing population of 50 million the United States had the biggest economy in the world. By 1914 the population had doubled and the United States had become a supereconomy with the largest stock of monetary gold. Throughout the nineteenth century, indeed up until 1914, the United States had run substantial current account deficits financed by capital inflows, building up a substantial debtor position in the world economy. From 1850 to 1873, the United States had a trade deficit, but from 1874, the trade balance turned sharply positive, financing outward interest and amortization payments like a mature debtor country. The outbreak of World War I signalled a turning point, when the United States quickly emerged as the leading creditor and lending country.

8 The departure from gold during World War I was by no means restricted to the European belligerents. For example, Argentina and Brazil both suspended gold payments in 1914, as did the four Scandinavian countries; Japan suspended gold payments in 1917.

9 The Gold Delegation of the League of Nations met in Genoa in 1922 to endorse a British recommendation that countries use foreign exchange (read "sterling") reserves in lieu of gold in their international reserves.

10 One gold mark replaced 1 trillion paper marks.

11 To be precise, what was lacking was not a physical shortage of gold, but rather an economic scarcity arising from the fact that gold was underpriced. The scarcity could have been eliminated at one blow by a once-for-all increase in the price of gold had anyone thought of it. Among well-known economists, only Ludwig von Mises and Gustav Cassel seemed to be aware that a return to the gold standard would bring on a deflation of the first magnitude. Mises in the second edition of his *Theory of Money and Credit* thought, however, that restoring gold may be worth doing even if it caused deflation; otherwise, how would central banks be prevented from inflating? Cassel, writing in 1928, was worried about how to "prevent a permanent fall of the general price level and a prolonged and world-wide depression which would inevitably be connected with such a fall in prices" (Cassel 1928). Cassel thought the solution would have to lie in steps to economize on gold.

12 Britain's price level, based on 1930 = 100 stood at an index of 87.6 in 1914; 143.3 in 1924, the year before Britain returned to gold; 100 in 1930; and 85.6 in 1931, at which it remained stable over the next five years. It is clear that Britain's return to gold imposed severe deflation on the British economy and was the major culprit in the Britain's stagnation in the interwar period. My point, however, is that even had Britain restored the pound at a lower parity relative to the dollar (as recommended by Keynes and others), the world economy would still have suffered deflation.

13 This point should be especially clear to present-day economists who followed the gyrations of the exchange rates of major currencies in the 1970s and 1980s.

14 US deflation began shortly after the rest of the world returned to the gold standard and the magnitude of the deflation corresponded to the magnitude of the prior inflation since the outbreak of war. Again, with 1930 = 100, the US index of wholesale prices was 78.7 in 1914, 119.7 in 1925, 110.1 in 1929, 100 in 1930, 84.3 in 1931, 75.3 in 1932 and 76.2 in 1933. This lends some plausibility to the view expressed above that the restoration of the gold standard was the cause of the deflationary depression and that an increase in the price of gold in the late 1920s would have prevented it.

15 Nevertheless, the franc was, even in 1926, probably somewhat overvalued with respect to gold. Its overvaluation with respect to gold became more apparent after the devaluation of the dollar.

16 This prohibition was removed in 1975 during the presidency of Gerald Ford.

17 The Federal Reserve gold reserve ratio was reduced to 25 per cent in 1945 at the time the United States formally joined the International Monetary Fund.

18 With the wholesale price index at 100 in 1940, it reached 135 in 1945 and 205 in 1948: thus most of the open inflation occurred after price controls were lifted.

19 The basis for the asymmetrical system was Article IV-4(b), which only the United States adopted.

20 In 1994, the US gold stock was 262 million ounces, not much changed from 1972.

21 The authorities had to balance the possibility of too little with the possibility of too much SDR creation which had the risk of undermining monetary discipline and causing inflation.

22 August 15 was a sad day for US economic policy. Drawing on a preposterous

bouquet of economic theories, the United States imposed a 10 per cent surcharge on imports, raised interest rates, and introduced an elaborate machinery for price controls. Although the surtax was lifted a few months later, price controls were to continue, at least on oil, throughout the remainder of the 1970s. Controls, as usual, caused shortages and even greater inflation.

23 Oddly enough – but not surprisingly – the monetary convergence between the European countries and the United States was superior under the anchored dollar standard to that which would emerge under the ERM.

24 Many countries operated under the illusion that they could sterilize the domestic monetary effects of an influx of reserves. For example, a central bank could sell other assets (such as government bonds) so that the central bank kept its total assets (and thus high-powered reserve money) constant. This, however, except in the very short run, is an illusion, both because the bond sales will keep interest rates high, attracting more arbitrage capital, and because the reserve increases will attract more speculative capital.

25 How does one measure "large" and "small" inflations in order to compare them? The best way is probably to weight the average rate of inflation per time period (say, per decade) by the basket of goods and services to which it applies. The US wholesale price index rose 2.7 times between 1971 and 1983; and it tripled between 1967 and 1983. Taking into account the fact that the US inflation over this period was lower than in all except a few countries (Germany, Switzerland, Austria, the Netherlands, Belgium-Luxembourg, and Japan); that the United States at the time accounted for one-third of world output, that price levels more than doubled in even the seven mentioned low-inflation countries, the decade of the 1970s was by far the most inflationary period in world history.

26 There will be those who will insist that the cause of the rise in oil prices lay not in the inflation potential of the international monetary system nor in the rising price of gold, but in the political circumstances associated with the Egyptian–Israeli War. I can recall at the time officials from the OECD and other institutions proclaiming at various conferences that the rising inflation rates in different countries all had unique explanations and that they were not in any way connected to monetary policies! A typical assumption on the part of officials at the time was that OPEC economists were unsophisticated and did not understand the implications for inflation of the collapse of the international monetary system. This, however, is belied by the evidence, which shows that, as early as January 1972, at the OPEC meeting at the Intercontinental Hotel in Geneva, OPEC took account of the devaluation of the dollar arranged at the Smithsonian meeting (which raised the price of gold to $38 an ounce) to raise the price of oil by an equivalent amount. This minor change was but a foretaste of the much more significant increase in oil prices two years later.

27 Between 1950 and 1960, foreign exchange reserves rose by 39 per cent; between 1960 and 1970, by 145 per cent; and between 1970 and 1980, by 546 per cent! The rate of expansion slowed down in the next decade, reserves rising by 102 per cent between 1980 and 1990.

28 More correctly, dominance is based on the size of the economy and particularly the size of monetary assets; large economies adjust to shocks more slowly than small economies and thus have greater stability. For a reference, see note 32 below.

29 "C'est une loi à laquelle nul n'échappe: un pays dont la hausse des prix dépasse celle des ses voisins est condamné à dévaluer d'une façon ou d'une autre. Telle

est la vérité. Je devais vous la dire sans chercher d'excuses trompeuses". ("It is a law that no one escapes: a country in which inflation is higher than that of its neighbors is condemned to devalue in one way or another. This is the truth. I cannot avoid telling you this.") *Le Monde* March 25, 1983; quoted in Szàsz (1992).

30 See Howe (1994: 448–53).

31 See Mundell and Swoboda (1969). It is a redundancy problem, because there are only n−1 exchange rates in an n-currency world, providing a degree of freedom for "independence" that might be given to one country (as to the United States under the dollar standard and to Germany under the mark standard) or it could be shared by some cooperative solution.

32 See Mundell (1965), reprinted (with a mathematical appendix) in Mundell (1968: 187–98).

33 The Second Amendment, which adopted the "system" of managed flexible exchange rates, recommended that measures be taken to reduce the role of gold and enhance the role of the SDR.

34 The 1967 break in the data can be justified by some criteria: (a) the sterling devaluation of 1967, (b) the Gold Communiqué of March 1968, freeing the market price of gold, (c) the decision to create SDRs in 1967, (d) the changes in the franc and mark exchange rates in 1968, and (e) the withdrawal of France from the gold pool in 1967 and its disbandment in 1968.

35 Only four countries at present use the SDR as an anchor: Libya, Myanmar, Rwanda, and the Seychelles.

REFERENCES

Cassell, G. (1928) *Post-war Monetary Stabilization*, New York: Columbia University Press.

Harrod, R.F. (1952) *The Dollar*, London: Macmillan.

Howe, G. (1994) *Conflict of Loyalty*, London: Macmillan.

Mundell, R.A. (1965) The Proper Distribution of the Burden of International Adjustment, *National Banking Review* 3: 81–7.

——(1968) *International Economics*, New York: Macmillan.

Mundell, R.A. and Swoboda, A.K. (eds) (1969) *Monetary Problems of the World Economy*, Chicago: University of Chicago Press.

Schwartz, A.J. (1984) Introduction, in M.D. Bordo and A.J. Schwartz (eds) *A Retrospective on the Classical Gold Standard*, Chicago: University of Chicago Press.

Szàsz, A. (1992) Towards a Single European Currency: ECU, franc-fort, question-mark, *Journal of Foreign Exchange and International Finance* 6: 274–87.

2

TOWARD AN INTERNATIONAL COMMODITY STANDARD?[1]

Richard N. Cooper

Determination of the basis for a national currency is one of the foremost attributes of national sovereignty. At irregular intervals over the past half-century, countries have been urged to link their currencies by more or less rigid formulae to a variety of commodity baskets, with contents varying from one (gold) to several dozen commodities, and even beyond to an index of prices of goods and services, with varying intermediate combinations. Usually the stated aim is to ensure stability of the real value of money or, what is not the same, to reduce uncertainty in the real value of money. These objectives are typically assumed to be sufficient unto themselves, but sometimes they are justified as reducing uncertainty for business and household decisions that involve allocation of resources over time, and thereby contributing to national well-being.

This chapter will discuss the desirability of basing an international monetary system – encompassing the formal rules and conventional practices governing payments among residents of different nations – on a basket of commodities. To anticipate the conclusion, it finds that such a move, while technically workable, would not have much to recommend it and it offers an alternative suggestion for improving the international monetary system: a common currency among the industrialized democracies, with a common, jointly agreed monetary policy, which could be targeted either on some measure of price stability or on a broader array of economic objectives.

But as background it will be helpful first to review briefly the various suggestions that have been made over the years to tie a given national currency to commodities – to tie money to the real economy so as to "anchor" the price level in some way. We then turn to international monetary systems both in theory and in practice.

NATIONAL COMMODITY-BASED MONETARY SYSTEMS

Commodity money

The most straightforward way to link a national currency to the real side of the economy is to have a commodity *be* the currency or, closely related, to require the money-issuing authority buy and sell the currency for the commodity at a fixed price (perhaps with a mint charge between buying and selling price), as was done under the metallic standards (usually based on gold or silver, occasionally copper) of bygone times. But unless the commodity in question is an unusual one, representative of the whole collection of goods and services in which producers and consumers have an interest, this procedure will lead both to fluctuations over time in the growth of the money supply and to fluctuations in the general price level measured in terms of currency and of the monetized commodity. These fluctuations are simply a manifestation of changes in the commodity terms of trade, for any commodity in terms of others, that will occur in any economy undergoing continual changes in technology and in the level and composition of final demand. If P is an index of money prices of a broad and relevant collection of goods and services, P_G is the money price of the monetary commodity (e.g. dollars per ounce of gold), and T is an index of the terms of trade between the monetized commodity and the other goods and services, then

(1) $P = P_G \times T$

A commodity standard fixes P_G by law or convention, but that is not sufficient to assure the stability of P, the widely accepted objective, so long as T is not also fixed. T will vary in response to variations in the relative supply and demand for the monetized commodity relative to other goods and services. If P_G is fixed, P will vary with T. Moreover, not only will P be variable, but also it will be unpredictable except insofar as future movements in T can be predicted with confidence. More will be said below about the stability and the predictability of P under the historical gold standard.

Commodity-convertible money

The foregoing problem can be mitigated by enlarging the contents of the monetized commodity basket. Alfred Marshall suggested a century ago that a basket comprising fixed weights of gold and silver, with the price between them free to vary, would offer a more stable monetary medium (measured in T or P) than would gold or silver alone. Edgeworth dubbed it a symmetallic standard to differentiate from a bimetallic standard, based on gold and silver at a fixed price, which ran the risk under Gresham's Law of evolving into a monometallic standard as one or the other became more valuable as a commodity than as money. (Isaac Newton had undervalued newly reminted silver coins relative to gold in 1717, and thus inadvertently put Britain on the gold standard as silver was exported; a similar development occurred in the United States in 1834 when legislation designed to correct an undervaluation of gold in terms of silver overdid it by altering the mint ratio from 15: 1 to 16: 1, and full-bodied silver ceased to circulate as money.)

A logical extension of Marshall's symmetallism would be to enlarge the basket of commodities, fixed in quantities, in which money is defined and against which it is issued. Such a proposal was put forward by Benjamin Graham (1937) in the 1930s.[2]

Graham proposed that the dollar be defined in terms of a fixed-weight basket of 23 commodities, and that the Federal Reserve issue notes against warehouse receipts for the basket thus defined. He selected his commodities on the strength both of their economic importance and their storability, and they included the standard list of such commodities, varying from coal to wood pulp. Graham was motivated in large measure by antidepression considerations; his idea was first advanced in 1933. He felt that support for commodity prices in times of economic slack would help stabilize overall economic activity. By the same token, sale of the commodity basket (demonetization) would limit inflationary pressure in booms, both by supplying commodities out of stocks and by contracting the money supply. His scheme in effect would provide perfectly elastic demand for the commodities (taken as a group their individual relative prices were free to vary) in the monetary unit in times of depressed economic activity, and it would provide perfectly elastic supply (so long as physical stocks lasted) in times of boom.

Graham envisioned that his scheme should supplement the then-existing monetary system. His unrelated namesake Frank D. Graham (1942) carried the proposal further. He would have included a much longer (but unspecified) list of commodities in his basket, and he would have required all future money growth to be based solely on purchases of warehouse receipts for these commodities, in the stipulated proportion. This proposal would have tied money growth directly to production of the monetized commodities, in this respect much like a metallic gold standard but with an enlarged basket.

Stabilizing the price level of a basket of storable commodities will stabilize the general price level only if the term of trade between the monetized commodities and other goods and services is unchanging over time, an improbable event. Broadening the basket from a single commodity may help, but the problem in equation (1) remains: fixing P_G will not in general stabilize P. For instance, over the period 1947–86 the US price index for crude materials, which includes all the items in Graham's list plus some, increased by 177 per cent. Prices of finished manufactured goods rose by 291 per cent over the same period of time, and prices of services in the consumer price index rose by 684 per cent. Reducing the 40-year price increase of crude materials to zero would have reduced but would not have eliminated inflation in a broader index.

Apart from this problem and from the fact that real resources are tied up in warehoused monetary commodities (proponents have placed the annual costs at 3–4 per cent of the outstanding value), it is unclear why there has not been more enthusiasm for commodity-reserve proposals. While they could not stabilize the general price level, these proposals might make its movements more predictable, insofar as prices of finished goods and services have a reasonably stable relationship to commodity prices, about which more will be presented below. Yet these proposals have found little interest beyond intellectuals. I suspect that conservatives really want gold, for reasons of history and sentiment, whereas nonconservatives prefer managed fiat money.[3] Also, the schemes are too complicated to appeal to a wider public.

The tabular standard

In the mid-1960s Albert Hart, Nicholas Kaldor, and Jan Tinbergen revived the idea of commodity-reserve currency in an explicitly international context, and their proposal will be taken up below. But before doing so, it is worth mentioning the logical extension of the commodity-money idea in the context of a national currency to the entire basket of goods and services which is deemed to be the relevant price level for purpose of stabilization. This is known as the "tabular" standard, described by W. Stanley Jevons in 1875, advocated by Irving Fisher in 1920, and revived by Robert Hall in 1982.

Fisher, writing during the gold standard period, proposed that the definition of the dollar in terms of gold should be indexed to the cost of living. In this way not only contracts written in nominal terms but also currency itself in effect would be indexed so as to stabilize their real value over time, except during the intervals between adjustments.[4] If, for instance, the cost-of-living index fell, the number of grains of gold that defined the dollar as a unit of account would be reduced by a corresponding amount. For purposes of settling debts, the real value of the dollar would be preserved, since more gold would be required to settle a given dollar debt. The reverse adjustment would take place if the relevant price index rose. In terms of equation (1), P_G would be adjusted exactly to compensate for movements in T, thus stabilizing P over time.

This scheme amounts to the full indexation of all contracts, including gold convertible paper money, against changes in the value of gold, with gold remaining the formal basis of the dollar. Fisher would also have adjusted the gold money supply in parallel with adjustments in the gold value of the dollar. If the price level fell, for instance, the dollar price of gold would be raised, and gold would flow into the Treasury (against the issuance of gold certificates) from private holdings, from abroad, and eventually from new production. The reverse would occur if the price level rose. Fisher would have reinforced this natural influence by issuing new gold certificates against the capital gains on existing Treasury stocks of gold, or by retiring gold certificates in the event of rising prices.

Robert Hall (1982) has revived the idea of a tabular standard (without endorsing it), but he suggests substituting for gold a fixed-weight basket of four commodities (ammonium nitrate, copper, aluminum, and plywood – ANCAP for short) whose index tracked well the US consumer price index over 30 years. The dollar would be defined in terms of the ANCAP basket, and the basket would be legal tender in settlement of debts. Bank notes could be issued freely and would be fully redeemable in ANCAPs. When the consumer price index rose, the dollar would be redefined to contain more ANCAPs. In this way, dollar contracts with deferred payment would involve repayment that was constant in terms of purchasing power, as measured by the consumer price index. Unlike Fisher or the Grahams, Hall would not require or even permit the government to engage in purchases or sales of the commodities composing ANCAP. He would simply define the dollar in terms of ANCAPs and endow them with the attribute of legal tender, so that debts could be settled in ANCAPs or paper claims on them. Private arbitrage, which would involve some physical storage of the commodities in the ANCAP basket, would be relied upon to ensure that a paper dollar or dollar demand account remained equal in value to the current ANCAP definition of the dollar.

Price-level target

Storage costs could be avoided by dropping the intermediary commodities (gold in Fisher's proposal, the ANCAP basket in Hall's) and simply gearing monetary action to a target price level. If the price level rose above the target, the monetary authorities would take steps to reduce some definition of the money supply (relative to trend), or to raise interest rates; and the reverse if the price level fell below its target. The action could be governed by formula. Since this approach would not involve the direct purchase and sale of commodities, however, the linkage between changes in monetary policy and prices would be an indirect one, which would be mediated by the full economy and by the responsiveness of the public to, say, additions or subtractions from some measure of the money supply. How close and how reliable is the linkage between money and prices is a deeply controversial question. It has been known for years, moreover, that when there are response lags in any dynamic system, maintaining steadiness in one variable (the price level) by controlling another variable (the money supply or short-term interest rates) in the face of diverse and not directly observable shocks is not an easy task, and indeed if improperly formulated, even well-intended policy actions may lead to less, rather than greater, stability (Phillips 1954).

Futhermore, if the response lags themselves are unknown and variable, simple formula-based control will be suboptimal, and might even be destabilizing. This observation points to discretionary control of monetary policy, aimed at a well-defined target such as stability in some measure of the price level. This conclusion presupposes, of course, that the complex and not fully articulated "feeling" of the monetary authorities in a variety of circumstances will yield superior results to a formula-based response. This presupposition is and will continue to be a source of continuing controversy involving as it does a comparison of discretionary responses, which will always (ex post) be suboptimal except by sheer good luck, with a formula-based response, which can always (ex post) be made optimal with sufficient imagination. But of course that is not the relevant comparison for assessing alternative regimes with respect to future disturbances and responses.

If a price level is to be targeted, a *specific* measure of the price level must be chosen. What should it be? The consumer price index is the obvious choice, but that involves certain problems when considered in the context of an international monetary system (taken up below). Moreover, in an open economy the consumer price index contains imported items; it thus may be strongly and directly influenced by prices of imported goods, a problem that is less acute for value-added deflators.[5] The appropriate choice requires careful consideration of exactly what ultimate objectives are to be served by price-level stability.

Even the notion of price-level stability, on any particular measure, requires more careful specification if it is to be targeted. Do we mean by stability constancy over time (i.e., an expectation of return to a particular level)? Or do we mean that it should not change from where it is now (i.e., a zero expected rate of change)? These definitions are not the same, and they have quite different implications for policy if the price level is altered by some unforeseen event or is unexpectedly altered by a foreseen event. Should bygones be bygones, or should the price level be forced back to its earlier level? Finally, when we talk about the desirability of *stability* in the price level, that may really represent a loose way of expressing a desire for *predictability* in the price level. Most of the costs that economists have been able to attribute to price-level "instability" arise from unpredictable movement rather than from predictable movement. Again, a more precise statement of ultimate objectives is required to sort out these various possibilities. A steady and predictable rate of inflation of, say, 5 per cent a year, if it could be achieved, might be superior to no secular drift in the price level but with 2 or 3 per cent short-run variations up and down.

Again, a more precise statement of ultimate objectives is required to sort out these various possibilities.

Once this necessity is acknowledged, and active manipulation of monetary policy is countenanced, whether by formula or discretion, the question naturally arises whether stability of some measure of the price level is, or should be, the sole economic objective of society and, if not, whether monetary policy should be directed solely toward that objective rather than, say, to reducing unemployment, to increasing home ownership, or to fostering investment in plant and equipment.[6]

Since stability of the price level is manifestly not society's only economic objective, what is the case for directing monetary policy solely toward that objective? It must rest on one or another of several possible assumptions:

1 Price stability is a necessary condition for the attainment of other objectives, so there is no real conflict or "trade-off" among objectives.[7]
2 Monetary actions cannot influence any other objectives. This view, often adopted in the formal theorizing of professional economists, is clearly erroneous in the short run. Moreover, it is unlikely to be true in the long run, for any given definition of money (Tobin and Buiter 1976).
3 Monetary actions have a comparative advantage in influencing the price level, and other instruments are better suited to the pursuit of other objectives.
   This proposition may have some validity, but runs up against William Brainard's (1967) observation that optimal policy formulation in an uncertain world would require that all objectives influence the choice of all policy instruments.
4 While monetary actions might usefully help to attain other objectives, attempts to use them for this purpose, and disagreements over which objectives should be emphasized, are likely to reflect inconstancy of purpose and lead to instability in real activity and in the price level, or even neglect of the latter objective.

This observation, while possibly valid, takes economists out of their role as economic analyst and prescriber of economically optimal policies, and into the realm of political and social analysis. That is fair enough, but consistency requires that a similar perspective be taken on other proposed policy regimes as well, and on the political prospects for their survival in the form proposed under the impact of serious disturbances and social strains.

AN INTERNATIONAL COMMODITY-BASED MONETARY SYSTEM

The world has over 160 distinct national monies. The collection of national choices concerning the basis for these monies determines the character of the international monetary regime. The regime may (but need not) involve formal and explicit undertakings by national authorities with regard to their monetary relationships with other countries, and may (but need not) involve formal multilateral agreement on the main features of the international monetary regime. Some observations on the relationship between national monetary bases and the international regime are in order.

First, if two or more countries choose the same national standard, linked to the same basket of goods and services (e.g., gold), by so doing they also fix the exchange rate between their national monies, which to that extent determines the international standard as well. A special case involves the choice by one country to peg its currency to the currency of another country. It thereby indirectly chooses the same standard as the other country, whatever it may be.

Second, if two or more countries choose different standards (i.e., a different basket) as bases for their currencies, then all but inevitably the exchange rate between those currencies will have to be altered from time to time, if not continuously. In particular, this proposition is true even if the countries select the same principle, such as stabilizing the national consumer price index. A corollary is that if a country chooses to peg its currency to that of another country, it will not, in general, stabilize its national price level except by coincidence. The reason has to do with the presence of nontradable goods and services, combined with the proposition that over time there is likely to be an upward drift in the price of (mostly nontradable) services (P_N) with respect to the price of (generally tradable) goods (P_T). This drift will occur at a rate that will vary from country to country, depending largely on the differences in *per capita* income and in growth rates.

The secular rise in P_N/P_T occurs in part from a slower growth in productivity in services than in tradable goods, and in part because we have much greater difficulty in measuring productivity growth in services than in goods, leading to a tendency to overstate price increases in services. Indeed, for a number of services the national statistical authorities identify outputs with inputs (e.g., an hour of a physician's time) so that by assumption there can be no increase in measured productivity. Under these circumstances, the secular upward drift in P_N/P_T will be a positive function of the national growth in productivity, and this in turn will be especially rapid in low-income, rapidly growing countries such as Japan in the 1950s or South Korea in the 1980s.

When we speak of a national price level, we usually mean a weighted average of P_N and P_T in which the weights must be adjusted from time to time, generally giving more weight over time (at least for high-income countries) to the service component of consumption. If $P = a(t)\,P_N + (1 - a(t))P_T$ is successfully targeted for constancy in each of two countries that differ in *per capita* income, that will require a secular decline in P_N in both countries, but more sharply in the poor than in the rich country. That in turn will require a secular appreciation of the currency of the poor country, provided tradable goods in the two countries are in close competition. Alternatively, if the exchange rate is fixed between the two currencies, *P* will increase more rapidly in the poor but rapidly growing country than in the rich one, and that indeed conforms with general experience.[8]

The alteration in exchange rates need not take place continuously, but failure to do so will generate a transitory misallocation of resources – toward tradable goods in the low-income, growing countries and away from tradable goods in the high-income countries. Moreover, discrete changes in exchange rates, or the prospect of them, provoke substantial international movements of speculative capital, unless prevented by exchange controls. So these characteristics also affect the international monetary regime, pushing it toward floating exchange rates, or at least toward managed flexibility, whether by formula or not. The general point is that national consumer price levels and exchange rates cannot both be stabilized over time; one or the other must sooner or later be given up. The strains become less severe, however, as the ratio of tradables to nontradables in national output grows (a function of trade barriers and of transport and communication costs) and as the dispersion among nations in per capita income declines.

If nations choose to target their exchange rates, instead to fix their currencies to other currencies, that action will anchor individual currencies, but it will not anchor the international monetary system as a whole. That can be accomplished in one of two ways:

1 A collective agreement to some common target, such as the price of tradables ($e\ P_T$, where e is each country's exchange rate fixed to a numeraire currency), or some average of national consumer price indices, or some other common basket.
2 An explicit or implicit agreement that the country whose currency is used by others as an anchor will target some basket of goods and services. If the basket is its consumer price index and if P_N/P_T rises over time, the money price of tradables will fall both in the anchor country and in all countries whose currencies are tied to it; the consumer price index will also fall in those countries where the upward drift of P_N/P_T is slower than in the anchor country.

INTERNATIONAL MONETARY STANDARDS AS PROPOSED

There has been much less systematic discussion of the international monetary standard than of national standards. Historically, the international standard has simply been the resultant of national standards. There have, however, been several exceptions to this generalization.

The Genoa Conference of 1922

The Genoa Conference was called after World War I to deal explicitly with the international standard, and concretely to address the shortage of monetary gold that would emerge as countries resumed – as it was taken for granted they would – convertibility of their currencies into gold. Exchange rates among currencies were floating at the time, but that was assumed to be an unsatisfactory and therefore a temporary condition. The problem was that national price levels had greatly increased since 1914 and could not be supported by the available gold; yet to require monetary contraction sufficient to restore convertibility was recognized to require a substantial and prolonged depression in economic activity.

The proposed solution was to economize on monetary gold in two ways: (1) to call in gold from circulation, to be held by central banks (this was largely an accomplished fact outside the United States); and (2) to encourage central banks to hold in their reserves "bills of exchange" on foreign financial centers in partial substitution for gold reserves. Thus a multiple reserve currency system was formally sanctioned, along with exchange rates fixed by gold convertibility. Under a simple monetarist model, the world price level could then ultimately be determined by the world's monetary gold stock, plus the willingness of central banks to hold in their reserves financial claims in other currencies. Without specifying the latter component quantitatively, however, the price level would strictly be indeterminate. But at the time, the problem was assumed to be that central banks would hold too little foreign exchange reserves, not too much, and that the gold holdings of the countries whose currencies were held (combined with a commitment to gold convertibility) would limit the expansion of foreign exchange holdings – and thus also of domestic currencies and the price level.

The significance of the Genoa Conference lies mainly in its attempt to view the international monetary system as a whole.

Bretton Woods

British and American authorities negotiated a plan for the international monetary system during World War II, whose purpose was to foster trade and growth and to avoid a repetition of the economic disasters of the interwar period. The regime that emerged was structurally similar to the regime envisaged at Genoa: fixed exchange rates determined by a gold parity for each currency, convertibility into gold or into a currency that was convertible into gold (the US dollar), and the holding of foreign exchange as international reserves. There were two important additions: the regimen of the system was not to prevent the pursuit of national employment policies; and if the combination of commitments and policies became irreconcilable, a country could, with international permission, change the parity of its currency (i.e., devalue or revalue against gold and other currencies).

In practice, after some postwar adjustments, major currencies rarely changed their parities; and the US dollar came to play a much greater role in reserves than had originally been envisioned. Gold provided a *de jure* anchor for the system, except for a somewhat mysterious provision for a "uniform change in par values" (i.e., a change in the price of gold). In fact, the system relied for its anchor on the prudence of US economic policies, disciplined as necessary by conversion of dollars into gold.

The world economy grew much more rapidly in the 1950s and 1960s than anyone dared anticipate in the late 1940s, and the demand for reserves grew with it. They were supplied in part from the large US gold stock but in larger part by an accumulation of dollar balances. This development led to the dilemma posed by Triffin (1960): if dollar balances continued to grow, the gold-convertibility of the dollar would cease to be credible; if they did not, the growth in world trade might be constrained by insufficient internationally acceptable monetary medium.

The dilemma was resolved in 1968 by the decision to create a new international fiat money, the SDR – now defined as a fixed-weight basket of the five leading currencies – to be created by the International Monetary Fund at not less than five-year intervals with the aim

> to meet the long-term global need, as and when it arises, to supplement existing reserve assets in such manner as will promote the attainment of [IMF] purposes and will avoid economic stagnation and deflation as well as excess demand and inflation in the world.
>
> (IMF Article XVIII(1a))

In 1976 it was agreed that IMF members should strive to make the SDR "the principal reserve asset in the international monetary system" (IMF Article XXII). In principle, the SDR could be issued to satisfy the secular growth in demand for international reserves, subject to the general guideline of avoiding both inflation and economic stagnation. Thus was introduced a fully discretionary monetary system at the international level, which, in fact, mirrored the practice at the national level in virtually all countries with the exceptions of Liberia and Panama (which use US dollars), the CFA (African Financial Community) franc zones of west and equatorial Africa, and a few British colonies which still use fully backed currency boards for local issue. There have, however, been only two decisions to allocate SDRs over a 20-year period, totaling 21 billion SDRs (a sum that accounts for less than 5 per cent of existing official foreign exchange reserves and even less if officially held gold is included in reserves).

In short, neither national monetary systems nor the international monetary system is anchored to the world price of goods and services, except by the prudence of monetary authorities. In addition, the international monetary system at present is extremely permissive with regard to exchange rates, requiring only that nations notify the IMF of their exchange arrangements and that these conform with the objectives of fostering "orderly economic growth with reasonable price stability" and of promoting economic and financial stability. Member nations are enjoined to "avoid manipulating exchange rates or the international system in order to prevent effective balance of payments adjustment or to gain an unfair competitive advantage over other members" (IMF Article VIII(1)), and cannot introduce discriminatory exchange rate practices.

An international commodity-reserve currency

When discussion of the Triffin dilemma was in full swing, Albert Hart, Nicholas Kaldor, and Jan Tinbergen (1964) proposed that it be resolved by creation of an international commodity-reserve currency (ICRC), an international version of the Graham proposal. The proposal was updated in a post-SDR context by Hart (1976). Hart suggests that the goods in question should be both standardized and storable, and offers an illustrative list (reproduced in Table 2.1) of 31 commodities which might make up the basket. He suggests that annual storage and turnover costs on the commodities selected should not exceed 5 per cent. He would leave some operational flexibility for the final list of goods to be included in the ICRC, and their weights, which would be necessary if the initial accumulation period is to have a fixed time period of, for example, five years.

The IMF would purchase the basket of commodities, aiming at an amount equal to, say, 25 per cent of world trade in these commodities,

Table 2.1 Standardized and storable commodities for possible inclusion in an international commodity-reserve currency

Wheat	Pork bellies, frozen	Cotton
Maize	Orange juice, frozen	Wool
Rice	Butter	Jute
Soybeans	Lard	Hard fibers
Oats	Milk, dried	Silk
Linseed		Rubber
Peanuts	Copper	
Sugar	Lead	Plywood
Coffee	Zinc	Lumber
Tea	Tin	Woodpulp
Cocoa	Silver	Newsprint

Source: Hart (1976: 6)

issuing SDRs in exchange.[9] The SDRs so issued would be the principal source of new international reserves. Increases in monetary gold and in foreign exchange reserves would not be allowed once the scheme was in full swing, although Hart would permit the IMF to engage in open-market operations in SDRs to provide some monetary flexibility beyond purchases of the commodity basket.

The commodity basket would be bought or sold as a unit, by telegraphic instruction to the different markets and storage areas in which the various goods were physically held around the world. The IMF would have a 10 per cent buy–sell spread on its purchases and sales of the basket to cover costs and to gain a bit of seigniorage. The gross costs of managing the scheme would involve storage costs plus interest plus the costs of turnover, since some of the commodities deteriorate physically over time and would have to be changed occasionally. Hart reckons annual storage costs for most of the commodities at 1 per cent or less of their value, although for wheat and maize it approaches 6–7 per cent. It is noteworthy that the interest costs, from a social point of view, might be negligible if the stocks are acquired mainly in times of economic slack, when the future opportunity cost of producing now is low, a point that Hart fails to mention. He does note that net social cost would be lower than gross cost to the extent that the existence of public storage of these commodities permits some reduction in private stocks, and to the extent that his scheme headed off various proposals for export-restricting commodity schemes that were under discussion at UNCTAD in the mid-1970s.

Hart makes the interesting suggestion that the IMF might occasionally substitute future contracts for physical holdings of individual commodities in the basket, thereby releasing those commodities into the market under conditions of an emergency.

Under this conception of an international currency, individual nations would be free to set national monetary standards as they chose, and to allow their currencies to float against one another and against the SDR. But individual countries would be permitted to peg their currencies to the SDR, and in all likelihood many would do so, just as many peg their currencies to some other currency or to a basket of currencies today.

In sum, this proposal involves an international unit of account and the creation of an international money which is anchored in a basket of economically significant commodities. The unit of account would over time maintain a stable value in those commodities through purchases or sales of the basket within a margin of plus or minus 5 per cent. The omission of oil and coal from the basket is noteworthy: both were included in Graham's list in 1937. Moreover, this scheme obviously would not stabilize a more general price level if there is secular drift between the average prices of the ICRC commodities and other prices. The problem of a secular increase in prices of services, as we measure them, has already been discussed.

The question of whether there is secular drift in the prices of primary products relative to the price of manufactured goods has long been debated. The view of David Ricardo, revived in the 1970s by the Club of Rome, is that the price of manufactured goods must decline secularly relative to the price of primary products in a world of growing population and income, due to the increase in rents on agricultural land and natural resources in limited supply. Under these circumstances, stabilizing the value of the monetary unit in terms of primary products would result in a secular decline in the price of manufactured goods, although that would perhaps be offset in whole or in part by the rise in the measured price of services.

In the early 1950s, Raul Prebisch took the opposite view, widely held in many developing countries, that there is a secular rise in the price of manufactured goods relative to that of primary products due in part to a higher income elasticity of demand for manufactures than for primary products. If the monetary unit is stabilized in terms of the prices of primary products and if the Prebisch view is correct, the ICRC scheme will generate secular inflation. In fact, the historical evidence is ambiguous on very long-term movements in the ratio of primary product to manufactured goods prices (Spraos 1980). There do seem to be swings in one direction or the other for periods of a decade or longer, such as the swings that took place under the gold standard, but those swings are less pronounced than for gold alone.

THE INTERNATIONAL MONETARY SYSTEMS IN PRACTICE

The gold standard

The pre-World War I gold standard does not fall into the category of carefully worked out international monetary systems. It was a historical consequence of national choices, strongly influenced by the political, military, and economic successes of Britain, plus the historical accident of Britain being on the gold standard. It was, moreover, a period of great economic tension and considerable instability both in prices and in output (Cooper 1982).

An idealized version of the gold standard was, to be sure, a self-correcting mechanism that could both stabilize the world price level and generate the right amount of international liquidity. For a single country with an insufficient monetary base to support its desired activities, the national price level would fall, a trade surplus would develop, gold would flow into the country from the rest of the world, and this process would continue until price level equality was restored with sufficient additions to gold money to support the higher desired economic activity. This mechanism was described by David Hume clearly and concisely in 1752.

For the world monetary system, inadequate gold would lead to a decline in the world price level, thus increasing the real value of money and satisfying the need for money in that way. But a longer-term adjustment would also be set in motion. With gold more valuable in real terms, gold production could be expected to increase, and the total supply of money in physical terms would thus be augmented. This process would assure long-run stability of the price level, provided technological improvements in ore extraction and new discoveries could be assumed to offset exactly the gradual exhaustion of known gold supplies and to thwart the emergence of Ricardian rents, which otherwise would require a trend decline in the general level of prices measured in gold money so long as the world economy was growing.

Unhappily, this idealized version was not readily observable in reality. The lags in the adjustment process were so long that large swings in prices could be observed as a result of periodic surpluses or shortages of gold relative to commodities. Table 2.2 records the changes in wholesale prices that occurred during a century under the gold standard, roughly parallel movements in all four countries listed, with amounts between 30 and 70 per cent. This experience is certainly not a record of price stability.

It is conceivable that, despite these long swells, economic agents expected an eventual return to a "normal" price level. Certainly a striking feature of the nineteenth century is that there were long periods of price decline as well as long periods of inflation.

If the relevant public expected the long-term price level to be stable, long-term interest rates should be *negatively* correlated with the price level. High levels would give rise to expectations of a subsequent fall in prices, which should lower nominal long-term interest rates; and vice versa for a lower-than-normal price level. In fact, long-term nominal interest rates were *positively* correlated with prices – rising as the price level rose, falling as it fell: a phenomenon dubbed the Gibson Paradox by Keynes (1930), and a puzzle to analysts already in the 1920s.

The movements in long-term interest rates in the nineteenth century are

Table 2.2 Wholesale price changes under the gold standard, 1816–1913 (percentage change)

	US	*UK*	*Germany*	*France*
1816–49	−45	−41	−29	−33
1849–73	67	51	70	30
1873–96	−53	−45	−40	−45
1896–1913	56	39	45	45

Source: Cooper (1982: 9)

more easily interpreted by assuming that the relevant public expected the contemporary price level to remain unchanged regardless of where it is relative to past levels, perhaps adjusted slightly in the direction of recent changes. That is, if prices have fallen recently, the public expected them to fall a bit more, and then remain unchanged.

But if this was the public's expectation – and it fits best the observed relationship between the price level and long-term interest rates – they were constantly fooled. We now know that, at least for a 20-year holding period (this was the maturity of many bonds), ex post real interest rates varied much more sharply than did nominal interest rates, and both series were positively correlated with the price level. This is not a record of intertemporal constancy in contract values.

It is conceivable too that despite long-term swells in prices, and apparently erroneous expectations about the real value of long-term contracts, short-term predictability was quite high despite the high variability both of short-term prices and of short-term interest rates. Lawrence Summers (1983) has shown, however, that short-term nominal interest rates did not, in fact, adjust well to compensate for short-term fluctuations in the price level. More recently, Allan Meltzer (1986) has shown that quarterly prediction errors (on a simple forecasting model relying only on past data of each series) were much higher in the gold standard era both for prices and for real output than they were in the 1950–80 period. Table 2.3 records the forecast errors for quarterly forecasts of US GNP and prices for each of six monetary periods as characterized by Meltzer. (He distinguishes between a gold standard with and without a Federal Reserve System, and he separates the period of fixed long-term interest rates during the 1940s; he does not exclude the two world wars.)

A comparison of the first two rows with the last two rows shows a

Table 2.3 Variance of quarterly forecast errors, 1890–1980 (thousands)

	US nominal GNP	*US price level*	*US real GNP*
Gold standard			
1890 (1)–1914 (4)	2.98	0.25	2.83
1915 (1)–1931 (3)	1.80	0.60	1.41
No clear standard			
1931 (4)–1941 (4)	5.64	0.24	4.02
1942 (1)–1951 (1)	0.67	0.60	0.78
Bretton Woods			
1951 (2)–1971 (3)	0.13	0.02	0.11
Fluctuating rates			
1971 (4)–1980 (4)	0.13	0.02	0.14

Note: Quarterly forecasts are made using a Kalman filter with respect to expected level and expected rate of change on past data for each series
Source: Meltzer (1986: 141)

dramatic improvement in quarterly predictability on moving from the gold standard to either the managed monetary system under Bretton Woods or the period of fluctuating exchange rates since the early 1970s. The forecast errors decline relative to price and output variability as well as in absolute terms, and they decline sharply on expectations with respect to level and rate of change of the variables as well as with respect to general background noise (Meltzer 1986: 141–4). It is likely, furthermore, that an extension of Meltzer's analysis through the present would show, by these standards, a marked superiority of the Bretton Woods system over the full period of fluctuating exchange rates, although of course, we could not be sure that the difference was attributable to the change in international monetary arrangements.

In sum, the historical gold standard did not perform very well – indeed it was a source of consternation and controversy to those who lived through it – except with respect to fixing exchange rates among currencies.

The present non-standard

The present mixed arrangement of fixed and fluctuating exchange rates also does not reflect a considered collective judgment on what the international monetary system should be. Rather, present arrangements are a jumble reflecting national choices and evasion of choices. They are not "anchored" in anything, neither a commodity basket nor even (except for the United States) the prudence of US macroeconomic policy. This lack of an anchor is a source of uneasiness to some. Neither national price levels nor the SDR-denominated price level are determined in the "logic" of the arrangements, although they are determinate at every moment of time. The lack of a clear anchor may suggest that there is no foundation for long-term expectations about the price level, although, as we have seen, such expectations were not very accurate under the historical gold standard either.

There are two further problems with present international monetary arrangements. The first concerns unsettled expectations about the future value of real exchange rates among major currencies, over the horizon of one to five years that is appropriate for investment and production decisions. It is noteworthy that while under the gold standard prices moved substantially, price indexes in different countries moved roughly in parallel with one another, suggesting that there may not have been significant variations in national competitiveness arising from the monetary side of national economies, although this is an aspect of the gold standard that deserves to be more closely explored.

Most business people, especially in manufacturing, if they are to be subjected to economic disturbances, place a high value on their competitors being subjected to the same disturbances, so they are not put at a competitive disadvantage. The problem with present arrangements involving flexible exchange rates is that it provides no such assurance in industries operating in a world market. On the contrary, for reasons remote from a firm's activity, often originating in the arcane world of finance, the firm can suddenly find itself facing much stiffer competition (or much less, but that is rarely a cause of concern) as the result of the movement of an exchange rate.

This uneven source of uncertainty will have several consequences adverse to the efficient allocation of resources. First, business people, at the national level, will attempt to blunt the source of supposedly unequal competition by urging an increase in trade barriers of various kinds. This response has been manifest in the United States and may slow import liberalization in Japan. I expect it to become more pronounced in Europe as trade surpluses decline there.

Second, investment will be reduced in the tradable sector as a result of the greater uncertainty arising from fluctuations in real exchange rates – an uncertainty of a more compelling type for investors than uncertainty about the general price level over the period of their investments. The latter influences profitability, but the likelihood that unanticipated changes in the price level will cause bankruptcy is much lower than the likelihood that unanticipated changes in the exchange rate will cause bankruptcy. It is perhaps not a complete coincidence that investment rates in manufacturing have dropped sharply in all major industrial countries since the advent of flexible exchange rates, although there are other explanatory factors as well, most notably the two oil price increases and the associated sharp recessions in economic activity.

Third, firms will adjust their investment behavior to hedge against the offending uncertainty. Since they cannot hedge their future commitments to production through financial markets, they will do so by investing abroad, across currency zones, even if that means giving up some of the advantages of cost and scale associated with exporting from their home bases or some other lowest cost location. One possible consequence, since some of this diversification takes place through takeovers and buyouts, is a greater world concentration in certain industries, leading to a reduction in worldwide competition.

So on all these counts, a regime that reduced uncertainty about the real exchange rate without corresponding increases in costs elsewhere would be an improvement over the present arrangements.

A second problem with current monetary arrangements is that the most important official international reserve continues to be the US dollar, despite a general commitment to make the SDR the principal reserve asset. The dollar is supplemented by holdings of other currencies, most notably the German mark and the Japanese yen. In practice, dollars are likely to provide most of the growth in reserves in the foreseeable future, although the share held in other currencies may grow somewhat. Reserves are necessary, and are thought to be necessary, because the exchange rates of almost all countries are either fixed to something or are subject to managed floating. We have a mixed and permissive system rather than a floating rate system. Moreover, as many countries have now discovered, access to the international capital market is not ensured at all times, especially when a country is seen to be in some external economic difficulty (i.e., just when it needs foreign funds most urgently). So monetary authorities feel that they need owned reserves, and they will want those reserves to grow, on average, over time.

Sometimes countries acquire reserves as the lesser of evils, as a result of exchange-market intervention to keep their currencies from appreciating too rapidly or too far. But, once acquired, the higher level of reserves sets a new expectation: while some decline may be tolerated and even welcome, a decline toward the former level more often than not provokes restrictive action to halt the drop. A rachet is thus introduced into implicit reserve targets.

Over the coming decades, the relative importance of the United States in the world economy is likely to decline – not because the US economy is performing badly, but because others are performing well. Europe and Japan are also likely to experience relative declines as well, and for the same reasons: low population growth rates and productivity that advances only as rapidly as new technology permits. Other countries have more rapid population growth, and they can continue to introduce existing technology from abroad. Of course poor economic policies or political turmoil may retard their growth, but on balance the US share of gross world product is likely to decline over time.

The combination of reduced relative US economic importance with growing use of the dollar as an international reserve will sooner or later put serious strains on US monetary policy. In a certain sense it implies more external "discipline" on the United States. But this discipline will not necessarily conduce toward greater economic or monetary stability, so as to provide a firm anchor for the system. Rather, the Federal Reserve will find itself more frequently having to respond to international financial pressures, whether they are rational in the larger scheme of things or not, and these pressures may sometimes cause less rather than more stability in monetary affairs. Yet the proper role of a monetary system, national or international, is to provide a stable and supportive expectational environment for the wealth-producing sectors of the economy and for the public generally.

AN INTERNATIONAL FIAT CURRENCY

The exceptional importance of real exchange-rate uncertainty suggests that a system should be introduced that can reduce it. Several proposals to accomplish this objective have been made, ranging from target exchange-rate zones which would limit exchange rate movements around a calculated equilibrium real exchange rate (Williamson 1985; Williamson and Miller 1987) to close coordination of monetary policy among the three largest countries with a view both to stabilizing their exchange rates and controlling their collective monetary growth (McKinnon 1984).

But to eliminate exchange rate uncertainty definitively – and sharply reduce real exchange rate uncertainty – requires a single currency. For the international monetary system this objective could be effectively achieved, with much greater prospect of negotiability by introducing the single currency first to the large industrialized democracies of Europe, North America, and Japan, rather than a global currency. A single money requires a single monetary policy. The constitution of the new International Central Bank (ICB), as we may call it, could be modeled on the Federal Reserve System, with changes appropriate to the circumstance that participants would be nations rather than regions within a nation. Representatives of national central banks, whether or not under control of sitting governments, could make up the Board of Governors, with votes weighted by the relative size of national economies. Or finance ministries could be directly represented. Or there could be nationally selected independent appointees, with the number of appointees apportioned by economic size. Whatever its exact constitution, the key point is that decisions on monetary policy would be a collective one; no single government could determine the outcome.

The ICB's powers would be similar to those of central banks today, with a discount window for distress lending and open market operations to influence the monetary base. Governments would share the seigniorage resulting from the issue of central bank money. But no government could finance budget deficits at the ICB beyond its share of the seigniorage; it would have to go to the financial market for that.

Other democratic countries could formally join the system, and of course any nonmember could choose to fix its exchange rate *vis-à-vis* the international kroner,[10] which would permit many of the advantages of fixed exchange rates without the formal commitments.

What principles should guide the actions of the ICB? It would face much the same choices that nations face today, although of course it could not fix the exchange rate, because there would be no plausible currency to which to fix it. The discussion above about various national standards becomes relevant, including the various disadvantages of a commodity-based standard. Nonetheless, the ICB needs some guidelines. The standard could be, as Keynes (1930: 391) suggested, a tabular standard based on an index of wholesale prices of 62 internationally traded commodities, with an implied secular inflation in consumer prices, which Keynes recognized and welcomed. Or it could be a target based on a weighted average of the consumer price indices in the participating countries, with its implied secular decline in commodity prices. Or the standard could be a defined price level but modified in response to movements in unemployment away from some target level, as Hall (1986) has suggested. Or the ICB could even fail to agree on a sharply defined target and muddle through as the Federal Reserve does now. That would not be intellectually satisfying, but Meltzer's findings suggest that we could be much worse off under many alternatives.

NOTES

1 An earlier version of this chapter was published in the *Cato Journal* 8 (1988).
2 The next few paragraphs draw heavily on Cooper (1982: 38–43).
3 It is of interest, though, that F.A. Hayek (1943) viewed commodity money favorably. Keynes and Friedman both opposed it. Keynes, though highly supportive of stabilization schemes for individual commodities, opposed a commodity-reserve currency on the grounds that it would have the same disadvantages as a gold standard in failing to persuade organized labor that it should keep its demands for money wages in line with the increase in efficiency wages (that is, productivity). He considered the risk of excessive money wage demands as one of the major obstacles to maintenance of a full employment economy. See his 1943 letter to Benjamin Graham, reprinted as an appendix to B. Graham in Yeager (1962: 215–17).

Friedman (1953) also opposed a commodity-reserve currency on the grounds that a full commodity-reserve currency, lacking the mystique and historical legitimacy of gold, would in time become financially burdensome because of the real costs associated with it. This in turn would lead in effect to discretionary policy, which he also opposed. It is, therefore, a system dominated both by a gold standard, with its mystique, and by a properly managed fiat money, which Friedman favors.
4 Fisher (1920: 142) suggested an adjustment every two months, with a 2 per cent "brassage fee" to prevent gold speculation at the expense of the Treasury immediately before each adjustment.
5 But not entirely absent, insofar as some domestically produced goods are in close competition with foreign-produced goods.
6 For a proposal for formula-based use of monetary policy to pursue a combination of price stability and employment stability, see Hall (1986).
7 See, for example, the statement by Alan Greenspan on December 18, 1987, testimony before several subcommittees of the House Committee on Banking Finance, and Urban Affairs:

> The mandate for economic policy in the United States and elsewhere should be to maintain the maximum growth in real income and output that is feasible over the long run. A *necessary condition for accomplishing that important objective is a stable price level*, the responsibility for which has traditionally been assigned in large part to the central bank, in our case to the Federal Reserve [italics added].

8 During the 1950s when the Japanese currency was fixed at 360 yen per US dollar, the consumer price index in Japan grew at 4 per cent per annum compared with 2.1 per cent in the United States, even while Japanese tradable goods were becoming more competitive relative to American goods. This

general phenomenon has been emphasized by Balassa (1964) and shows up in a different way in Kravis *et al.* (1982), who show that real purchasing power in poor countries is far higher than is suggested by per capita income converted at official exchange rates.

9 A proposal in Hart (1966) suggests 75 per cent of world trade in the listed commodities. No explanation is given for the lower figure suggested in 1976.

10 It does not matter what the new currency is called. In view of the widespread use around the world of the US dollar, "dollar" would be a natural designation, but that might be politically offensive to some. So it could be called the thaler, or the kroner, or the franc. *The Economist* (January 9, 1988: 9) has suggested the "phoenix."

REFERENCES

Balassa, B. (1964) The Purchasing-Power Parity Doctrine: A Reappraisal, *Journal of Political Economy* 72: 584–96.

Brainard, W.C. (1967) Uncertainty and the Effectiveness of Economic Policy, *American Economic Review* 57: 411–25.

Cooper, R.N. (1982) The Gold Standard: Historical Facts and Future Prospects, *Brookings Papers in Economic Activity* 1: 1–45.

Fisher, I. (1920) *Stabilizing the Dollar*, New York: Macmillan.

Friedman, M. (1953) Commodity-Reserve Currency, in *Essays in Positive Economics*, Chicago: University of Chicago Press.

Graham, B. (1937) *Storage and Stability*, New York: McGraw-Hill.

Graham, F.D. (1942) *Social Goals and Economic Institutions*, Princeton, NJ: Princeton University Press.

Greenspan, A. (1987) Testimony before several subcommittees of the House Committee on Banking, Finance, and Urban Affairs, December 18.

Hall, R.E. (1982) Explorations in the Gold Standard and Related Policies for Stabilizing the Dollar, in R.E. Hall (ed.) *Inflation: Causes and Effects*, Chicago: University of Chicago Press.

Hall, R.E. (1986) Optimal Monetary Institutions and Policy, in C.D. Campbell and W.R. Dougan (eds) *Alternative Monetary Regimes*, Baltimore, MD: Johns Hopkins University Press.

Hart, A.G. (1966) The Case for and against an International Commodity Reserve Currency, *Oxford Economic Papers* 18: 237–41.

Hart, A.G. (1976) The Case as of 1976 for International Commodity-Reserve Currency, *Weltwirtschaftliches Archiv* 112: 1–32.

Hart, A.G., Kaldor, N., and Tinbergen, J. (1964) The Case for an International Commodity Reserve Currency, in N. Kaldor (ed.) *Essays on Economic Policy*, vol. 2, New York: Norton.

Hayek, F.A. (1943) A Commodity Reserve Currency, *Economic Journal* 53: 176–84.

Jevons, W.S. (1875) *Money and the Mechanism of Exchange*,London: D. Appleton.

Keynes, J.M. (1930) *A Treatise on Money*, vol. 2, New York: Macmillan.

Kravis, I., Heston, A., and Summers, R. (1982) *World Product and Income: International Comparisons of Real Gross Product*, Baltimore, MD: Johns Hopkins University Press.

McKinnon, R.I. (1984) *An International Standard for Monetary Stabilization*, Washington, DC: Institute for International Economics.

Marshall, A. (1926) *Official Papers by Alfred Marshall*, New York: Macmillan.

Meltzer, A.H. (1986) Some Evidence on the Comparative Uncertainty Experienced under Different Monetary Regimes, in C.D. Campbell and W.R. Dougan (eds) *Alternative Monetary Regimes*, Baltimore, MD: Johns Hopkins University Press.

Phillips, A.W. (1954) Stabilization Policy in a Closed Economy, *Economic Journal* 64: 290–353.

Spraos, J. (1980) Statistical Debate on the Net Barter Terms of Trade, *Economic Journal* 90: 109–25.

Summers, L.H. (1983) The Non-Adjustment of Nominal Interest Rates: A Study of the Fisher Effect, in J. Tobin (ed.) *Symposium in Honor of Arthur Okun*, Washington, DC: Brookings Institution.

Tobin, J., and Buiter, W. (1976) Long-Run Effects of Fiscal and Monetary Policy on Aggregate Demand, in J.L. Stein (ed.) *Monetarism*, Amsterdam: North-Holland.

Triffin, R. (1960) *Gold and the Dollar Crisis*, New Haven, CT: Yale University Press.

Williamson, J. (1985) *The Exchange Rate System*, 2nd edn, Washington, DC: Institute for International Economics.

Williamson, J., and Miller, M.H. (1987) *Targets and Indicators: a Blueprint for the International Coordination of Economic Policy*, Washington, DC: Institute for International Economics.

Yeager, L.B. (ed.) (1962) *In Search of a Monetary Constitution*, Cambridge, MA: Harvard University Press.

3

THE GOLD STANDARD[1]

Marcello de Cecco

EARLY MONETARY STANDARDS

For nearly three thousand years coined weight of metal has been used as money and for just as long, gold, silver and copper have been the preferred metals for minting coins. Currencies consisting of coins whose value is expressed by the weight of the metal contained in them at market prices, however, have seldom been used.

Until the inception of metallist reforms, the necessary amounts of the metals required for coinage were brought to the Mint by the sovereign or by the public. The sovereign's monetary prerogative consisted in fixing the Mint price of the metal, that is how many coins of a certain denomination could be coined from a given weight of metal. The Mint price was established with reference to a money of account, and it could diverge, and very often did, from the market price of the metal. When the sovereign deemed it necessary to devalue the coinage, he or she could change the parity between the coins and an "ideal" currency, usually one which had circulated in the past. This made it unnecessary to resort to recoinage operations. The latter were also available but were considered as more radical policies, while changing the relative value of coins in terms of the ideal currency was a more gradual instrument, which could be used almost daily if need be. But it was only very rarely that the sovereign would renounce the prerogative of giving coins a face value by law. Indeed, for many students of money this sovereign prerogative was that which transformed a coined metal into money. Theodor Mommsen (1865, vol. 3: 157) wrote some unforgettable passages on Emperor Constantine's decision, in the fourth century AD, to resort to free minting of gold coins whose value was given by their weight at market prices. To Mommsen this was the lowest point reached in the degradation of Roman monetary sovereignty. A Roman coin had always been taken at its face value, whatever its weight. Indeed, this had been the chief testimony of the credibility of the Roman state.

After the fall of the Roman Empire, none of the successor states can be said to have enjoyed, in the following centuries, an equivalent degree of monetary sovereignty. The plurality of successor states implied a plurality of currencies, with ample possibility of speculating and arbitraging between currencies. Citizens learned to defend themselves when the sovereign's privilege became exorbitant. Seignorage tended to be inversely correlated with the commercial openness of states. The less truck subjects had with foreigners, the greater the divergence between the legal and intrinsic value of coins could be. A trading nation very soon found that it had to have a currency whose value corresponded to its metallic content. With the rise of the absolute state, the sovereign's monetary privilege tended again to become exorbitant. The ratio of internal to international trade increased, in spite of the rise of mercantilism, and the fiscal use of money by the state became greater. It is obvious that this sovereign's prerogative, when it became exorbitant, made life very difficult for the sovereign's subjects, who could defend themselves only by changing prices, provided that had not been declared illegal by the sovereign. Metallist reforms were an expression of the new power acquired by the subjects *vis-à-vis* the state. At the core of these reforms was the actual coinage of the "ideal" money as a real full-bodied coin, whose weight and fineness was decreed, and this coin became the "standard" of the national monetary system. By these reforms, sovereigns saw their monetary prerogatives diminished to those of a keeper of weight and measures. In the intentions of the reform's advocates, it was a way of constitutionalizing sovereigns, so that they would be compelled to resort openly to their fiscal powers, which had been constitutionalized long before.

ORIGIN OF GOLD STANDARD

The Gold Standard was just one of the possible metallic standards. It was adopted in England, while the French preferred to choose a silver standard. In the course of the following centuries intellectual debate centered around the choice of metal, and economists, statesmen, intellectuals, declared themselves in favor of or against silver or gold, in favor of or against bimetallism or monometallism. But the basic choice in favor of a pure metallic standard, where an actual coin whose value as given by the weight of its metal content at market prices was the only money of account available, was not seriously discussed again for a long time, until the development of banking and the integration of world commodity and financial markets gave reason to challenge existing institutions.

The great metallist reforms were the outcome of the intellectual movement which would later take the name of "political economy." This is now used to define an academic subject, taught in universities, but between the second half of the seventeenth century and the first decades of the nineteenth century, it became an intellectual, almost a political movement. It was composed of people who, in many countries, believed that human society was organized according to natural principles, which could be studied by the same methods used to inquire into the world of nature. By scientific inquiry the laws which governed society could be discovered and the action of the state could be made to agree with them. In particular, the laws governing the production and distribution of commodities could be discovered, and the principles according to which value was conferred upon goods and services. The political economists soon found themselves considerably disturbed by the existence of a human institution, Money, which continually interfered with the progress of commodity valuation. As hinted above, they tried to devise a solution which would allow society to enjoy the advantages of using money while being spared the problems which the creation and use of money entailed. The solution was a commodity money, a monetary regime whose standard would be a coin made of metal of fixed weight and fineness. They hoped that a commodity money would free the economic world from the uncertainties induced by the raids of those who exercised or usurped monetary sovereignty. A pure metallic money would be subject to the same laws of value to which other commodities were subject; its demand and supply would be determined strictly by the needs of trade.

By advocating the adoption of a pure metallic standard, the political economists were thus killing two birds with one stone. They were putting a stop to exorbitant privilege of the state, which used its monetary prerogative to tax people without asking for the powers to do so, and were also recommending a type of money which would not disturb the functioning of economic laws, since it obeyed those laws. By the adoption of a pure metallic standard, a truly neutral money could be relied upon.

If the desires of political economists were important in actually pushing forward the adoption of metallic standards, however, it was more because both governing circles and public opinions were anxious to put an end to the previous system, which was based on uncertainty and sovereign's privilege, than because of a widely felt need to put economic theory on a sounder theoretical footing.

In this respect British experience is different from the French. In England, a metallic standard had been in use since soon after the great recoinage of the end of the seventeenth century. At the turn of the next century, Sir Isaac Newton, the Master of the Mint, had established the canonical weight for the pound sterling in gold, at 123.274 grains of gold at 22/24 carats (corresponding to 7.988 grammes at the title of 0.916). Free minting remained possible but, as very little silver was coined, silver coins were soon demoted by the public to the role of subsidiary currency, as they were still of the old sort, without milled edges, and were badly worn, because of the repeated clipping. Thus, early in the eighteenth century, England went on the Gold Standard.

In France, metallist reform had to wait until the Revolution. After an early attempt to introduce the Gold Standard, and a gigantic outflow of gold under the Terror government, in the year XI of the Revolution the free minting of both gold and silver was declared. One franc was given a weight of 5 grammes of silver at 9/10 title. A fixed parity was also established between gold and silver, although the French legislators, in the report of the Comité de Monnayes in 1790, had declared that a permanently fixed parity between the metals was impossible, and had quoted Newton and Locke to corroborate their declaration. Bimetallism was thus instituted in France, and would last almost as long as the Gold Standard in England, but from the beginning it was understood that the parity between gold and silver would have to be changed when necessary, even if it was to be done by law each time. The French lawmakers gave life, therefore, to a system which we would call today of fixed but adjustable parity between gold and silver.

Contemporary literature devoted much attention to the relative virtues of mono- and bimetallism. Modern economic literature, however, starting from the end of World War I, has almost exclusively focused on gold monometallism. From the point of view of monetary history this is a pity, because what commonly goes under the name of the International Gold Standard was, on the contrary, a complex system composed of a monometallist and a bimetallist part, where the importance of the former was not greater, for the functioning of the whole system, than that of the latter. We shall see, in what follows, how the smooth functioning of the Gold Standard essentially required the existence of a bimetallist periphery which surrounded the monometallist center.

RESUMPTION AFTER SUSPENSION

Let us first concentrate on the British Gold Standard. After it had been in existence for close to a century it had to be suspended in 1797, because of the difficulties which the Napoleonic Wars entailed for monetary management. In the period of over 25 years in which cash payments remained suspended, a very lively debate took place among political economists, politicians, bankers, and industrialists on how suspension affected internal and international economic relations. Some of the best pages in the history of political economy were written as contributions to that debate.

Specie payments had been suspended by an Order in Council in February 1797. The same decree had undertaken that they be resumed, at par, six months after a definitive peace treaty had been signed. In the intervening period of open hostilities, the currency had depreciated, the government had incurred a huge debt which was largely in the hands of City financiers, and war demand for all sorts of commodities had favored the amassing of great fortunes by a bevy of *homines novi.* As peace approached, it was found that a resumption at the old parity would enhance the postwar slump which already appeared after Waterloo. This prospect united landowners and industrialists, who had been natural enemies heretofore, against creditors, government debt holders and, in general, people with fixed incomes. Because of its huge debt, the government ought to have been on the same side as the debtors. It had, however, muddled through the war by putting up a system by which it held bond prices up and kept the financial market favorable to new debt issues. The system consisted of redeeming old long-term debt and replacing it by floating debt. Pascoe Grenfell and David Ricardo were quick to chastise the government's debt management policy. In 1816 and 1817 the government's balancing act was successful but in 1818 it came unstuck, as the government had to buy stock dear and sell it cheap. Meanwhile, the ratio of funded to floating debt had fallen, and this precluded the possibility of reducing the main debt.

Resumption was as highly political a measure as Restriction had been. The Whig opposition railed against Restriction, calling the government a committee of the Bank of England. And, indeed, the Bank did its best to make the accusation credible. It tried to blackmail the government into a continuation of Restriction by threatening to stop its support of the government's debt management policy. It also threatened to stop accommodating Meyer Nathan Rothschild, who was the principal holder of government stock. But Resumption had also its advocates within the Cabinet; Huskisson, for instance, who with Parnell, Henry Thornton, and Francis Horner, had drafted the Bullion Report in 1810 and had thus permanently alienated traditional City interests. He had advocated a prompt resumption in a memorandum he submitted in 1816, and again, early in 1819, he submitted a memorandum calling for prompt resumption accompanied by fiscal deflation. The government then appointed a Secret Committee to consider resumption, which soon became dominated by opinion in favor. When the committee's report was discussed in Parliament, Ricardo's vehement advocacy of resumption definitively swung parliamentary opinion. Payments were resumed, at the old parity, in May 1819. Ricardo called the decision to resume "a triumph of science, and truth, over prejudice, and error." It certainly was a triumph of new City blood over old financial interests, who had thrived in the easy days of inflationary finance, lending to financially weak governments, at rates they themselves pushed up by manipulating the money market.

After resumption at the old parity, a shock wave went through all British economic circles. The Gold Standard did seem to have no advocates left among manufacturers and financiers. The Bank of England had been against it all along, and so menacing had been its representations that the government had been driven by such impudence to breaking its useful wartime alliance with it, which had rested, it now appeared, on easy money. Landowners, on the contrary, were pleased. A measure that made them poorer in capital values, gave them, at the same time, a greater real value for their rents. It also represented a restoration of old values against the encroachment of industry and its social evils, which had occurred during Restriction. If the Gold Standard was bad for industry, which had flourished under the paper pound, there the relative power of the Old Order, which agriculture represented, would grow again.

The bullionists, who had campaigned for a resumption at the old parity, believed that a deflation would purge society of the most glaring speculators, of unsound industrialists, and, more generally of upstarts who had grown rich on easy money. At the same time they believed that the Gold Standard would transform Britain – and we have Huskisson's testimonial to this belief – into the chief bullion market of the world. London would become the "settling house of the money transactions of the world." The intention, was thus to favor the New City, to be "mart and banker" to the world, rather than its workshop.

Finally, Resumption was seen as an instrument of social justice. Deflation would give back to creditors, who had lent their money to their country in wartime, the full value of what they had lent. To politicians, an automatic Gold Standard looked like a relief from the heavy responsibilities of managing the economy. It would restore them to true political activity, and mark the final transition to peace.

The French monetary reform was very different. It was aimed directly against the *Ancien Régime*, seen however in its fiscal capacity, and not as an unholy alliance of politicians and financiers. It ended up by establishing a long-lasting bimetallic system, which did not overlook the interests of those whose prices were fixed in silver, like wage earners and petty traders. The Reform thus did not represent a clearly determined social choice, like the Resumption in Britain. A more neutral system was devised, which tried to accommodate both the third and the fourth estate. The revolutionary experience was too recent to invite, by a deflationist monetary regime, new social disorders. It is somewhat ironic to see how the country, on the verge of defeat, opted for a regime much less radically deflationist than the one the victorious country would choose. In both countries money was constitutionalized, but in Britain, the coalescence of interests of the New City and the landowners made the country the world pivot of monetary radicalism. It is fair to say that the expectations of those who had favored the Gold Standard in Britain were not fulfilled. Deflation brought in its wake unemployment and social disorder. It also induced British industrial producers to invade world markets, as home demand shrank. The benefits the New City interests had expected did indeed materialize, but only a few decades later. The Gold Standard induced export-led growth in Britain, and to become "mart and banker" to the world it first had to become the workshop of the world. The mechanisms the bullionists had set working thus functioned in reverse. But it would be unfair to say that Huskisson's expectations were representative of those of all bullionists. David Ricardo, for one, expected the Gold Standard to bring about industrial expansion.

And he wanted industrial growth to employ the labor made available by the working of the Law of Population, in which he firmly believed.

FUNCTIONING OF GOLD STANDARD

The Gold Standard was supposed to check the power of the Bank of England, which seemed to have become so great under the paper pound as to represent a threat to a truly constitutional institution like Parliament. But its actual functioning enhanced that power even further. As Britain became the workshop of the world and sterling was more and more widely used as an international currency, the importance of London as a financial center grew apace. The Bank of England thus became pivot of an international payments system founded on Britain's industrial and financial supremacy. The Bank of England's importance as a commercial bank was enhanced by its monopoly position as a joint stock bank. Just as it had flourished as the chief source of government finance under restriction, the Bank flourished as a commercial bank as a result of Britain's ascent to industrial and commercial leadership.

Its international pre-eminence was always dependent on its domestic primacy. Under the auspices of the Bank's monopoly, the centralized reserve system, which remained for a long time unique to Britain, was developed. It was a very lean and efficient system, which minimized the amount of cash needed to oil the wheels of the domestic payments network. But it was also highly unstable, since its leanness did not tolerate any serious obstacle which might appear in the national and international flow of cash and capital. The fact that it could carry on for such a long time, until World War I, is explained by a series of fortunate circumstances which occurred in succession. We shall examine them in some detail.

We must, however, strongly underline the fact that, under the Gold Standard, Britain experienced very strong cyclical swings. The hundred years after resumption were marked by commercial and financial crises which recurred about every ten years, even if the last part of the period saw crises appear at longer intervals than before. The regularity of crises gave rise to much monocausal theorizing, and the Gold Standard was often indicted as one of the chief culprits. It was, by contemporary opinion, accused of being a monetary regime too inflexible to allow for the smooth growth of the economy. Critics invariably quoted the French and then the German monetary systems as preferable, since they were supposed to possess a greater degree of flexibility and made possible better management of the economy.

Yet, in spite of a very lean centralized reserve, and of recurrent financial crises, Britain never abandoned the Gold Standard. One of the most important reasons why it was not compelled to do so under the pressure of crises must be found, as we noted earlier, in the peculiar features the international financial system possessed in the combination of a monometallic and bimetallic part. Since oldest antiquity, silver was the metal preferred by the Far East for coinage. And for almost as long as history goes, the Western trade balance with the Far East has shown a deficit. A structural trade imbalance with the Far East meant a continuous export of silver towards the East. Around the middle of the nineteenth century, this structural trend combined with gold discoveries to depress the price of gold. In the last 30 years of the century, however, the trend was reversed, as silver started to be abandoned by most developed countries as a monetary standard. The gold–silver parity rose accordingly.

Throughout the century, London retained a quasi-monopoly of gold and silver transactions. And it maintained, without any interruption, a free gold market. It is certain that it could not have afforded to do so, had not first France and, later on, the Indian Empire come to the rescue.

The Anglo-French financial connection is one of the most fascinating, and least researched, features of the nineteenth-century international payments system. From what we know, however, it appears that the much greater liquidity the French monetary system retained throughout the nineteenth century was skilfully exploited by Britain. Bank rate would be raised when pressure was felt on the Bank of England's reserve, but the expectation was that gold would flow mainly from Paris. Why did it flow? First of all, because there was a lot there, because of both the wealth of the French economy and of the underdevelopment of the French banking system, which rendered the use of gold coins for large transactions necessary (whereas in Britain cheques were commonly used). We must not forget, however, the essential role played by the House of Rothschild in connecting the French and British money markets. The archival evidence available shows that, in most British financial crises, the reserves of the Bank of England were refurbished with gold procured by Rothschild from France. The House of Rothschild intermediated between the gold and silver sides of the international monetary system. They were the super arbitrageurs who had the huge reserves and prestige necessary to play successfully a role which remains to be described in full detail, but whose importance it is possible to detect even in the present state of research. They were the 'protectors' of Bank Rate. It is not without importance that a Rothschild sat in the Court of Directors of the Bank of England and a French Rothschild occupied an equivalent position in the Directorate of the Banque de France.

Towards the end of the century, however, the precipitous fall of silver, induced by and in turn determining the abandonment of silver as a monetary standard in the whole developed world, reduced the role played by the French monetary system as a stabilizer of the Gold Standard. France had itself to close the mints to silver, to avoid being flooded by a metal nobody seemed to want any more. In the remaining period, commonly referred to as the "heyday of the Gold Standard," the Bank of England's balancing act could continue with the help of two other shock absorbers, the Indian monetary system, still based on silver, and South African gold production. The Empire of India was kept by the British on a silver standard even when silver was fast depreciating against gold. This made export of primary commodities and raw materials easy and was undoubtedly responsible to a large extent for the large export surplus India earned in the last part of the prewar period. It is in the management of this surplus in a way conducive to the stability of the Gold Standard that the British financial elite proved most imaginative and successful. The Indian surplus was invested in London, in government bonds or in deposits with the banking system. The "Council Bills" system, which had been devised to effect financial transfers between India and the Metropolis, was managed so as to keep the Rupee's value stable. The whole system, called the "Gold Exchange Standard," was extolled as a paragon of skill and efficiency by J.M. Keynes (1913), in the book that first gave him notoriety. Indeed, the young Keynes was right, as far as the functioning of the Gold Standard was concerned. Whether it was also efficient from the point of view of promoting Indian economic development, is entirely another matter, and one with which Indian economic historians have seldom concerned themselves.

South African gold production also helped to stabilize the Gold Standard. All the gold mined there was commercialized in London, and the proceeds invested there, at least in the short run. It is easy to imagine how important the British monetary authorities considered the control of that huge flow. This became evident, after World War I, when an attempt was made to revive the Gold Standard. Following Professor Kemmerer's advice, South Africa decided in favor of the Gold Standard, and against pegging its currency to sterling. The connection with London was cut, to the great discomfort of Montagu Norman, who saw one of the main props of sterling suddenly disappear.

ROLE OF UNITED STATES

If France, India and South Africa contributed to making the Gold Standard stable, the United States represented throughout the century in which the Gold Standard lasted, one of the great, perhaps the single greatest, disturbing elements to its smooth functioning. After the political and economic forces which stood for an orderly financial development of the Republic had been routed in the first decades of the nineteenth century, the growth of the American economy took the spasmodic features it would keep until World War II. The United States was deliberately deprived of the Central Bank that Alexander Hamilton, imitating the Bank of England, had designed. Banks proliferated everywhere, following a model of wildcat finance which, if it promoted the phenomenal growth of the US economy, also gave it a very strong cyclical pattern. For the whole Gold Standard period, the Bank of England was called to play the difficult role of being the lender of last resort to the American financial system. The growth of American farm exports, coupled to local industrial growth and the peculiar development–underdevelopment of the US banking system, gave rise to a notorious seasonal pattern of financial difficulties, which was called the "autumn drain." This recurred every year, when American crops were sold on world markets and the proceeds disappeared into the entrails of the completely decentralized American banking system, and, more generally, into the hands of American farmers. A gold drain was felt first in New York, the main US financial center. Interest rates rose violently, as there was no centralized banking reserve in New York, and the US Treasury, which kept a very large gold reserve, knew only very imperfectly how to use it for stabilization purposes. The rise of New York rates would thus be transmitted to London, which kept the only free gold market. Gold would thus flow to New York and it would be months before it could be seen again, as farmers spent the proceeds of crop sales and US local banks recycled the money back to New York.

To this seasonal drain, to which the Bank of England was never able to find a remedy, other sudden drains would be added, when the peculiar American banking system went into one of its recurrent panics. After the most violent of them had, in 1907, brought chaos to the whole international economy, the US Congress decided to move and the Federal Reserve System was established, in 1913. But it took another 20 years, and another huge crisis, that of 1929–33, before it really began to work as a central bank.

We have dedicated considerable space to a summary of US financial history because it must be fully appreciated what the peculiar structure of American finance meant for the world financial system in the age of the Gold Standard. What by the end of the century had become both the largest industrial producer and largest agricultural exporter, was still importing huge financial resources from the rest of the world. It lacked a central bank and had developed a thoroughly decentralized banking system which, if it was functional to rapid economic growth, had also a strong vocation for recurrent instability. The US Congress and government also did their part to enhance instability, by unwise and partisan policies concerning, for instance, silver prices, and the management of fiscal revenues.

OTHER EXTERNAL DIFFICULTIES

In the last decade of the nineteenth century the crisis of silver induced a veritable stampede by governments and Parliaments, in most countries, to adopt the Gold Standard. More than the undirectional movement of silver, it was its wild oscillations, made deeper by the inconsiderate silver policies of the United States, that convinced most interested parties to opt for gold.

Even European farmers, who were fighting a desperate war against cheap New World imports, were reduced to favoring the Gold Standard by the impossibility of forecasting a price for their harvest at sowing time. Industrialists in developing countries who had started import substitution activities were in favor of a strong currency, to repay foreign loans without problems, and preferred protection as a means of keeping out foreign industrial products. Most countries, when they went on the Gold Standard, also started a centralized gold reserve, which they intended as an exchange stabilization fund. Very often they surrounded this reserve by an outward layer of foreign currency reserves, which they called upon under pressure in order to keep their gold reserve intact.

Contrary to what British monetary authorities thought and did after World War I, their prewar predecessors were extremely worried by the universal trend in favor of Central Banking and of the Gold Standard. They very correctly understood that Britain had succeeded in staying at the center of the system as long as it remained a free-flow system, where the only stock of gold was the one kept by the Bank of England. French gold accumulation had been seen favorably, as it enhanced the *masse de manoeuvre* of the Bank of England at almost no cost. But already German gold accumulation was a threat, as Germany did not believe in a free gold market and Bank Rate found obstacles in attracting gold from there. That German pattern was, unfortunately for Britain, the one that found the largest number of followers among countries that established a Central Bank, and a central reserve to manage the Gold Standard. The result was the increasing seclusion of previously free-flowing gold into large stocks, over which the British traditional control instrument Bank Rate scarcely exercised any leverage and which dwarfed in size the reserves of the Bank of England.

DOMESTIC DIFFICULTIES

To these external difficulties with which British monetary authorities were greatly concerned, others of a more domestic nature had to be added.

The British financial system had emerged from the turmoil of the Napoleonic Wars apparently unscathed. It was formed by a cluster of merchant banks and other financial institutions, like the discount house, and by the great commodity and service exchanges, and it had the Bank of England at its center. The composition of the governing body of the Bank of England ensured that most City voices would get a fair hearing. It is impossible to exaggerate its internal homogeneity and cohesion (especially at a time like the present, when the system is definitively being demolished). A good study of the City in the years of the Gold Standard ought to be conducted by structural anthropologists, rather than by economists. A very serious threat to this semi-tribal system, which had succeeded in controlling world trade and payments for many decades, was developing fast in the late years of the Gold Standard. It was represented by the rapid concentration of British deposit banking, which resulted in the survival of only a handful of giant joint-stock banks. The Clearing Banks – as they came to be called – provided the City with a large part of the short term funds which were used as raw material to finance world commodity trade. They had huge branch networks which channelled savings from the remotest corners of Britain to London, and thence to all parts of the world through City intermediation. Thus the Clearing Banks provided the base for the whole British financial system. But their power was not constitutionalized by any matching responsibility. They had no say in the conduct of monetary policy. They were not represented in the Court of Directors of the Bank of England. Moreover, as concentration increased, the Clearing Banks thought they might as well invade some of the markets traditionally reserved to merchant banks, and in particular, they started invading the field of commodity trade financing. Finally, they began to lay the foundations for their own centralized gold reserve, alternative to that kept by the Bank of England.

Speaking more generally, a trend can be noticed in the last 25 years of the prewar Gold Standard, away from homogeneity and towards decentralization, in the British financial system. The Clearing Banks increasingly balked at being disciplined by the Bank of England. Often, especially in times of crisis, they pulled the rug from under the financial establishment, by withdrawing their short-term deposits with City houses. By this behavior they showed their muscle and demanded recognition. This pattern is clearly detectable in the 1890, 1907 and 1914 crises. It was a trend that greatly disturbed the financial elite and contributed, with the exogenous factors we have mentioned before, to making the Gold Standard more unstable. It could even be said that the loss of cohesiveness and homogeneity of the British financial system brought the Gold Standard to its demise, in July 1914. The system collapsed long before Britain entered the conflict.

THE GOLD STANDARD AND THE ECONOMISTS

The development of Gold Standard theory coincides with the development of economic theory. We have already mentioned the role played by commodity money in the theoretical apparatus of the classical economists. A commodity money would obey the rules dictated by Nature (of which even human behavior was part) as far as its supply, demand, and price were concerned. Thus a monetary economy based on a pure metallic standard would enjoy all the advantages afforded by the presence of money, without being subject to the many disadvantages induced by a synthetic currency not tied to a metal. For David Ricardo, the recommendation to adopt the Gold Standard not only meant preventing the Bank of England from usurping monetary sovereignty, which he recognized as a parliamentary prerogative, but also meant giving the economic system a standard, like gold, which had the virtue of being a good approximation to his invariant measure of value. He wanted to see the price system uninfluenced by political power, so that Nature would be free to play her game and gold would be distributed among the "different civilized nations of the earth, according to the state of their commerce and wealth, and therefore according to the number and frequency of the payments which they had to perform" (Ricardo [1811] 1951: 52). If freedom of gold movements existed, this redistribution would soon bring about a state of rest, when gold had been allotted to each nation according to its need and would not move again. If all countries promoted metallist reforms, fixing a gold weight for their currencies, arbitrageurs would operate, within the gold points, to keep gold prices uniform. Gold would function as the numeraire of the gold economic system and it would be enough to ensure gold arbitrage to guarantee uniformity of all the world price systems. There would be no need for arbitrage to involve other, bulkier, commodities, whose transportation would imply greater costs. This of course, did not mean that international trade would not take place. Commodities would move across countries according to the Law of Comparative Advantage, and the Gold Standard would make sure that this law did not suffer perturbations because of "unregulated" money supplies. "Regulation," of course, meant that fiduciary money would depend, for its supply, on the dynamics of the gold reserve of the issuing agency. Ricardo's view of how the world economy worked, based on his analysis of commodity currency systems, rapidly conquered not only the economics profession but also politicians and intellectuals. It was a scientific system of political economy, whose core was the Gold Standard. John Stuart Mill and Alfred Marshall were to refine and qualify that world view.

Mill analysed with great care the implications of a commodity money, whose exchange value would be equal to its cost of production. He did, however, clearly point out the importance of the existing stock of gold relative to its current or even potential flow. The gold stock/flow ratio made full adjustment a lengthy process, so that, in the short run, the price level would be determined by the demand for, and supply of, money. He never doubted, however, that a commodity money would not be able to change the international production relations as they existed under barter. To him money was, like oil in the wheels of moving mechanism, "a contrivance to reduce friction." He fully trusted that David Hume's adjustment mechanism would have only nominal consequences in the case of a discovery of a hoard of treasure in one country. This would raise prices there, discourage exports and induce imports. The resulting balance of payments deficit would redistribute the hoard to the rest of the world and lower prices in the original country to their previous level. In Mill's opinion, real effects would, however, result in the case of a loan from one country to another. Then a real transfer would have to be effected.

Neither Mill nor Marshall considered the Gold Standard a perfect system. Both of them opposed bimetallism at fixed rates. They believed that relative changes in the costs of production of the two metals would be likely, and that would involve a scarcity of the dearer metal and a shift in favor of the monetary use of the cheaper one. Instability was therefore built into the bimetallist system. Mill preferred a "limping" Gold Standard, where gold would be the only legal tender, and silver would be coined at market prices. John Locke's tradition obviously lived on.

Marshall's creative thinking in the field of monetary standards included symmetallism and the Tabular standard. According to the first scheme, vaguely reminiscent of the oldest currency, the Lydian Elektron, if the public wanted to give paper currency and receive metals it could only get gold and silver together, in bars of fixed proportions. Marshall thought this would link the paper currency to the mean of the values of the two metals and make possible, by this more stable currency, a world monetary area including both the gold and silver countries. It is easy to recognize in Marshall's scheme a forerunner of the contemporary European Monetary System's ECU.

Marshall's Tabular standard, on the other hand, reintroduced the concept of a money of account separate from the medium of exchange. The money of account would serve for long-term contracts and would be tied to an "official index number, representing average movements of the prices of important commodities" (Marshall 1923: 36).

As far as the adjustment mechanism under a gold standard regime was concerned, Marshall clearly saw the growing integration of capital markets replacing traded goods, arbitrage and gold movements as the chief instrument of adjustment. This of course meant recognizing the importance of interest rate differentials and interest arbitrage. And, in turn, giving a great role to play to banks and Central Banks.

With J. S. Mill, Marshall, and, in particular, Irving Fisher, we begin to get out of the "naturalist" world view which permeates the writings of Ricardo, his inspirers, and his followers. The world is not run solely according to forces of nature, which it is the economist's role to discover and which cannot be violated without meeting an inevitable punishment. The Gold Standard is not a "scientific method" of organizing a monetary regime. Like Marshall, Irving Fisher thinks of it more in historical rather than scientific terms. It is something the world embraced by historical accident. Supply and demand conditions for gold and silver are unstable. The system is not perfect and is perfectible, justifying proposals to make it work better.

As we advance toward what has been called the "heyday of the Gold Standard," in the eyes of contemporary economists its virtues seem to pale and its vices to come into relief. To Knut Wicksell, under a commodity standard there is no guarantee that a causal link will be able to exist between money supply and price level movements. Such a link can be seen to exist only if we take a very long view. Like the practitioner-theorists who staffed the British Treasury before 1914, Wicksell noticed that central banks, by keeping large gold reserves, had interposed themselves between gold supply and price movements. The price stabilization function of central banks is recognized and the new institutional set-up is in any case superior to a pure metallic standard, which in Wicksell's eyes would be totally at the mercy of the vagaries of demand for and supply of gold.

The "heyday of the Gold Standard" which (as we hope to have shown above) was in historic reality the beginning of its decline, were thus also days of decline as far as Gold Standard theory was concerned. A growing scepticism begins to engulf Hume's price-specie flow mechanism. Commodity arbitrage is seen as prevailing over gold arbitrage. Adjustment must involve real, not just nominal changes. International capital movements are brought increasingly into the picture. Stock adjustment in all sorts of markets is a phenomenon which fascinates the economic theorists of this age. From recognizing stock adjustments to advocating stock management is a short intellectual distance and most of these theorists cover it at great speed.

Ironically, in the theoretical cycle the pendulum had swung in the 25 years before World War I, away from Ricardo and Locke and towards Lowndes and Thornton. The pure metallic standard has lasted only *l'espace d'un matin* both in theory and practice. Economists had not been able to ignore the giant strides of banking and of world economic and financial integration. From Ricardo's golden rules, simple and infallible, we move to Mill, Marshall, Wicksell, and Fisher and their inventive recipes for national and international monetary management. Doubts prevail over certainties. We cannot accept J.M. Keynes's postwar strictures about the prewar perception of the Gold Standard. It was not seen as immutable, frictionless, as automatic by its contemporaries. The seeds of postwar criticism and disenchantment were firmly sown before the war. In fact, we might go as far as to say that prewar learned opinion was much less apologetic of the pure metallic standard than would be the postwar economists and politicians. Prewar observers had realized that the Gold Standard was a game which had become increasingly hard to play, precisely because everybody had learned – and wanted – to play it.

NOTE

1 Previously published as the entry "Gold Standard" in *The New Palgrave: A Dictionary of Economics*, J. Eatwell, M. Milgate and P. Newman (eds), London: Macmillan, 1987.

REFERENCES

Keynes, J.M. [1913] (1971) *Indian Currency and Finance*, in D. Moggridge (ed.) *The Collected Writings of J.M. Keynes*, vol. 1, London: Macmillan.
Marshall, A. (1923) *Money, Credit and Commerce*, London: Macmillan.
Mommsen, T. (1865) *Histoire de la monnaie romaine*, Paris: Rollin et Feuardent.
Ricardo, D. [1811] (1951) *The High Price of Bullion: A Proof of the Depreciation of Bank Notes*, in P. Sraffa (ed.) Works and Correspondence of David Ricardo, vol. 3, Cambridge: Cambridge University Press.

Part II

METALLIC STANDARDS

4

METALLIC STANDARDS AND REAL EXCHANGE RATES[1]

Maria Cristina Marcuzzo and Annalisa Rosselli

INTRODUCTION

In the late eighteenth and early nineteenth centuries, the international monetary system relied on the merchants' response to profitability conditions for the import and export of gold and silver to bring about the adjustment mechanism of the monetary system. Price arbitrage in the trade of precious metals gave rise to a unified bullion market and paved the way to the late-nineteenth-century monetary order.

From the merchants' point of view, profitability conditions for the export and import of the precious metals, involved knowledge of the price of gold and silver, at home and abroad, and of the rate of exchange (Marcuzzo and Rosselli 1987, 1991). But what was the right rate of exchange?

The "observed" variable was the market rate of exchange, which was the price of the domestic currency in terms of foreign currency as established in the market for bills of exchange. For the occurrence of gold and silver flows what mattered was the difference between the market exchange rate and the cost of obtaining the same amount of foreign currency through exporting gold (or silver).

Variations in the price of bills of exchange reflected both the conditions prevailing in the market for bills of exchange – which in turn reflected the conditions of the balance of payments – and conditions prevailing in the market for gold and silver; the latter being influenced by the employment of the two metals in monetary and nonmonetary uses.

It follows that behind any variation of the market rate of exchange two different sets of forces were at work: excess demand of bills and changes in the price of gold and silver. In this chapter we present a general framework of analysis which will allow us to distinguish between the two causes of changes in the exchange rates and thus offer a contribution to the interpretation of the working of the gold standard in its early history.

MONETARY STANDARDS AND MONETARY REGIMES

In addressing the issue of the causes of changes in the exchange rates, the first point to clarify is what the standard of the currency is and which monetary regime it defines. When gold or silver are chosen as standard, there is an official value of the unit of currency in terms of a given quantity of bullion, or – amounting to the same thing – an official price of bullion. Whenever there is a mechanism by which the market price of bullion is brought in line with the official price, the metal chosen as the standard becomes a special commodity in two respects.[2] First, the prices at which the standard metal are bought and sold on the market are relatively stable; second, any outflow or inflow of the standard metal leads to a variation in the quantity of money.

When this mechanism is absent or becomes ineffective – because, for example, convertibility is suspended – the price of the standard metal is not bounded and there may be no change in the quantity of money for any outflow or inflow of the metal. In these circumstances, however, the standard metal may retain its function as standard of money (i.e., the purchasing power of the currency over the standard measures the variations in the value of money) although, in all other respects, it does not differ from any other commodity.[3]

When both countries have a monometallic regime, either the standard is single and the same in each country (i.e., both are on either a gold or a silver standard) or the standard is single but different in the two countries (i.e., one country is on gold and the other on silver). When the standard is single, the other metal may be entirely demonetized, i.e., there is no coinage in other metal than the standard. Otherwise, the regime may be only *de facto* monometallic, because there continues to be an official price of the other metal. For instance, coins of a given nominal value are minted from a given quantity of bullion, but these coins are valued according to their weight and are not legal tender, or are legal tender only for a limited sum.

We shall analyze the two cases of monometallic regimes with the same and with a different standard in turn.

EXCHANGE RATES IN MONOMETALLIC REGIMES: THE CASE OF A SINGLE AND IDENTICAL STANDARD

Let us start with the case of two countries having the same standard, which we assume is gold. The gold parity is then defined as the ratio between the gold content of their respective units of currency. Only when there is a change in the official gold content of a currency does the parity change. Normally it remains constant for long periods of time and becomes the center around which the market exchange rate oscillates.

In pure conditions of "perfect convertibility," namely, when gold can be bought and sold at its official price, the parity represents the cost (net of transport costs) of making international payments by remitting gold. When there are coins in circulation, "perfect convertibility" requires – besides the condition that the Mint be open to the public – that two very special conditions hold.

First, there must be no coinage expenses, not even in the form of loss of interest during the time required to have the coins delivered. Thus the price of a given quantity of gold could never fall below the nominal value of the coins made out of that bullion, because no seller of gold would accept a price lower than that which could be obtained from the Mint.

Second, melting of coins is not prohibited, and is costless. Thus the market price of a given quantity of gold could never rise beyond the nominal value of the coins of equal weight, because any buyer of gold would always have the option of melting the coins to obtain bullion.

Moreover, when convertible paper-money also exists, conditions of "perfect convertibility" require that the buying and selling price of gold in paper money both coincide with the official price of gold.

Historically, perfect convertibility has never existed. There has always been a difference between the buying and selling price of gold at the central bank (say, the Bank of England) and there have always been coinage and melting expenses. Consequently, the market price of gold has diverged from the official price. Besides the "official" parity, it is therefore necessary to take into consideration the effective cost of exchanging domestic currency for foreign currency on the basis of the respective market gold prices. The latter was known as "real" or "commercial" parity (British Parliamentary Papers 1819).

The "official" gold parity, X_g, when the rate of exchange is defined in terms of foreign currency for one unit of domestic currency, can be expressed as

$$X_g = \frac{p_M^*}{p_M}$$

where

p_M^* = official (Mint) price of gold abroad
p_M = official (Mint) price of gold at home.

The "real" or "commercial" gold parity, R_g, can be expressed as

$$R_g = \frac{p^*}{p}$$

where

p^* = market price of gold abroad
p = market price of gold at home.

Let us consider the percentage deviations of the market price of gold bullion from the official price at home (**p**) and abroad (**p***) and of the market rate of exchange, determined by supply and demand of bills of exchange, from the official gold parity (**e**) and from the "real" gold parity ($\mathbf{t_g}$). We define the following (bold letters always stand for percentage deviations)

$$(1) \qquad \mathbf{p^*} = \frac{p^* - p_M^*}{p_M^*}$$

$$(2) \qquad \mathbf{p} = \frac{p - p_M}{p_M}$$

$$(3) \qquad \mathbf{e} = \frac{E_m - X_g}{X_g}$$

$$(4) \qquad \mathbf{t_g} = \frac{E_m - R_g}{R_g}$$

where E_m is the exchange rate on the domestic market and $\mathbf{t_g}$ represents those variations in the exchange rate that reflect the conditions prevailing in the market for foreign bills of exchange. The value of $\mathbf{t_g}$ is bounded by the so-called "gold points," i.e., by transaction and transport costs of remitting gold to the foreign country.

To what extent does commercial parity differ from official parity? From the definitions given above, it follows that **e**, the percentage deviation of the market rate of exchange from the official parity, X_g, is given by[4]

$$(5) \qquad \mathbf{e} = \mathbf{t_g} + \mathbf{p^*} - \mathbf{p}$$

As long as market mechanisms are at work at home and abroad to enforce the equality of the market to the official price of gold, **p** and **p*** are close to zero. When domestic convertibility is suspended or coins are debased, however, the market price of bullion can be significantly higher ($\mathbf{p} > 0$), because it is not possible to obtain gold at the official price by melting coins of legal weight or by converting banknotes. In contrast, when seignorage is high, $\mathbf{p} < 0$, because coined gold fetches a premium over bullion that can be as high as seignorage.

The divergence between the official and the market price of gold represents either a loss or a gain for the bullion merchant, which must be distinguished from the other transaction costs of a gold remittance for at least two reasons. First, unlike transport and transaction charges, which tend to remain constant through time, it is a variable and not a relatively fixed cost, depending on the conditions of demand for bullion. Second, the amount of loss or gain involved is a function of the difference between the market and the official price of the standard. In this respect, it is a rough measure of how far Gold Standard differs in practice from its pure and ideal form.

EXCHANGE RATES IN MONOMETALLIC REGIMES: THE CASE OF A SINGLE BUT DIFFERENT STANDARD

The relevant parity

Let us turn now to the case of two countries on a single but different standard, such as gold and silver. It is necessary to modify equation (5) in order to incorporate a modified concept of parity. Since in each country the unit of currency is officially equivalent to a given quantity of bullion, we can still define an "official" parity on the basis of the official price of the respective standard. As we shall see, it is not a fixed parity, since it varies with every variation in the market ratio between gold and silver, both at home and abroad. Moreover, given that there are two standards, we have two parities, one for gold and the other for silver. We shall label each of these parities as the "true par" (Officer 1985: 566), corresponding to what the classical authors called the "computed exchange" (Marcuzzo and Rosselli 1991: 104–13).

The purpose of defining an "official parity" in the case of two different standards is threefold. First, to indicate that in each country there is an official price of either metal; second to compare this monetary regime with others in which the price of one or both metals is fixed; third, to be able to distinguish between two different causes of variations in the market exchange rate. By comparing the market rate of exchange with an official parity, we do not confine ourselves only to the conditions prevailing in the market for bills, but allowance is made for a "monetary" cause of the movements of the exchange rate due to the difference between the market and the official price of either metal.

Let the parity be defined with respect to gold as E_g and the parity defined with respect to silver as E_s and, furthermore, let us assume that the domestic country is on the gold standard and the foreign country on the silver standard.

In order to define E_g, we know that the quantity of gold which is officially equivalent at home to one unit of currency is given by $\frac{1}{p_M}$. This quantity of gold can buy abroad the quantity of silver given by $\frac{1}{p_M}\frac{p^*}{q^*}$, where q^* equals market price of silver abroad. By multiplying the latter by the foreign official price of silver, q^*_M, we obtain E_g units of foreign currency, that are equivalent to 1 unit of domestic currency, so that

$$(6) \quad E_g = \frac{q_M^*}{p_M} \frac{p^*}{q^*}$$

Similarly, one unit of foreign currency is officially equivalent abroad to $\frac{1}{q_M^*}$ units of silver, which – when sold on the domestic market – obtains $\frac{1}{q_M^*} \frac{q}{p}$ units of gold. By multiplying the latter by the domestic official price of gold, we obtain $\frac{p_M}{q_M^*} \frac{q}{p}$ units of domestic currency. So that, given our definition of the rate of exchange as units of foreign currency per one unit of domestic currency, we get

$$(7) \quad E_s = \frac{q_M^*}{p_M} \frac{p}{q}$$

Adopting the same notation as in the previous section, we define

$$(8) \quad \mathbf{q} = \frac{q^* - q_M^*}{q_M^*}$$

Denoting $\mathbf{e_g}$ the deviation of the market rate of exchange from E_g, we obtain from (6) and (8)

$$(9) \quad E_m = E_g\ (1 + \mathbf{e_g}) = \frac{p^* q_M^*}{q^* p_M} (1 + \mathbf{e_g}) = \frac{p^*(1 + \mathbf{e_g})}{p_M(1 + \mathbf{q^*})}$$

By definition we have

$$(10) \quad E_m = R_g\ (1 + \mathbf{t_g}) = \frac{p^*(1 + \mathbf{t_g})}{p_M(1 + \mathbf{p})}$$

Neglecting second order terms, by comparing (9) and (10), we obtain

$$(11) \quad \mathbf{e_g} = \mathbf{t_g} + \mathbf{q^*} - \mathbf{p}$$

In other words, although the parity is no longer fixed, in the difference between the market rate of exchange and parity we can still distinguish that component due to the condition of the market for bills of exchange, $\mathbf{t_g}$, from the components due to the conditions of circulation, $\mathbf{q^*}$ and $\mathbf{p}$.

Similarly, defining $\mathbf{e_s}$ as the deviation of the market rate of exchange from E_s and $\mathbf{t_s}$ as the deviation of the market rate of exchange from the "real" silver parity R_s we have

$$(12) \quad E_m = R_s\ (1 + \mathbf{t_s})$$

and we obtain

$$(13) \quad \mathbf{e_s} = \mathbf{t_s} + \mathbf{q^*} - \mathbf{p}$$

There is only one case in which the two parities, E_g and E_s, coincide, namely when $\frac{p}{q} = \frac{p^*}{q^*}$; in this case obviously also $\mathbf{t_g}=\mathbf{t_g}$ and $\mathbf{e_g}=\mathbf{e_s}$. However, in general, the gold/silver ratios differ and to this case we now turn.

The gold/silver ratios

When the gold/silver ratios are not equal in every country, we may have larger differences between them than those between the foreign and domestic individual prices of gold or silver. In fact, arbitrage opportunities offered by the difference in the gold/silver ratios are fewer, since they imply transaction costs double those implied in the arbitrage in one bullion market alone. For example, an arbitrage operation may involve the purchase of gold, the shipment and sale of gold abroad, the purchase of foreign silver, the shipment and sale of foreign silver in the domestic country. This can immediately be seen if we denote the transaction costs involved in a gold shipment (as percentage of the total value) by c_g and the transaction costs involved in a silver shipment by c_s, assuming that costs are the same in both directions. So that, when all arbitrage opportunities have been exploited, the variation interval of the ratio is given by[5]

$$(1 - c_g)(1 - c_s)\frac{p}{q} < \frac{p^*}{q^*} < \frac{p}{q}(1 + c_g)(1 + c_s)$$

or, if $c_g = c_s = c$

$$(1 - 2c)\ \frac{p}{q} < \frac{p^*}{q^*} < \frac{p}{q}\ (1 + 2c)$$

Thus, the difference between the gold/silver ratios, although constrained by the level of transaction costs, could still be relevant.

The divergence of $\frac{p}{q}$ from $\frac{p^*}{q^*}$ gives rise to different profitability conditions for the remittance of precious metals. Thus, unlike the case in which both countries are on the same standard, we must here find out which is the relevant $\mathbf{t}$ (i.e., whether $\mathbf{t_g}$ or $\mathbf{t_s}$) as indicator of the conditions prevailing in the market for bills of exchange.

It is always the metal undervalued at home, relatively to the other country, to be preferred in making an international payment, since it yields a greater amount of foreign currency in exchange for the bullion corresponding to one unit of domestic currency.[6] If the most economical means to obtain foreign currency for a domestic merchant is shipping gold, then the relevant parity – to ascertain the most profitable alternative to buying a bill of exchange – is the gold parity and the merchant who wants to purchase foreign currency must choose between buying a bill of exchange and shipping gold. Conversely, whenever gold is undervalued at home, the merchant who wants to sell foreign currency must choose between importing silver or selling a bill of exchange in the domestic market. In this case, the relevant parity to ascertain the most profitable alternative to selling a bill of exchange is the silver parity. Obviously, if $\frac{p}{q} > \frac{p^*}{q^*}$, the opposite applies.

However, unlike the case in which both countries are on the same standard, the maximum and minimum levels that the market rate of exchange can reach have to be defined accordingly. The maximum depreciation is a situation in which the export of bullion represents the alternative to the purchase of a bill on the foreign currency, while the maximum appreciation is a situation in which the import of bullion represents the alternative to the sale of a bill on the foreign country. In fact, as shown by equations (11) and (13), the minimum and maximum values of the exchange rate depend on the maximum values of $\mathbf{t_g}$ and $\mathbf{t_s}$.

It is clear that this maximum value is determined only by transportation and transaction costs, since coinage and melting expenses are included in the calculations of the deviations of the market price of the standard from its official price.[7] The reason for excluding coinage and melting expenses from the calculation of the "gold points" is that they represent the maximum deviation of the market price of the standard from its official price, whereas in fact that deviation can be less than its maximum value, according to the conditions prevailing on the bullion market.

Given that $E_g \leqslant E_s$ if and only if $R_g \leqslant R_s$, there are two ways to find out whether $\mathbf{t_g}$ or $\mathbf{t_s}$ apply and to calculate their value. The first is to calculate the deviations of the market exchange rate from the official parities, E_g and E_s, then to add algebraically the deviations of the market price of the standard from its official price, according to (11) and (13). The second, which is exactly equivalent, is to calculate the deviations of the market exchange rate directly from the commercial pars, R_g and R_s.

However, the official and the commercial parities have a different role in our search for the forces which explain the behavior of the exchange rate on the basis of historical evidence. The parities most used in practice were the official parities, because they represented a widely accepted term of reference. The market rate of exchange was always compared with the official parities – computed by taking into account the deviations of the market prices of the standard from their official prices, when the purpose was to ascertain whether the currency was depreciating or appreciating.[8]

On the contrary, the parities which were relevant to decide whether gold or silver are more profitable than bills of exchange in transacting foreign currency on the basis of gold/silver ratios, transaction and transportation costs, were the commercial pars, R_g and R_s.

Finally, in order to find out the maximum and minimum value of the exchange rate we must distinguish two cases: first, when $\frac{p}{q} < \frac{p^*}{q^*}$, second when $\frac{p}{q} > \frac{p^*}{q^*}$.

If $\frac{p}{q} < \frac{p^*}{q^*}$ – and therefore $E_g > E_s$ and $R_g > R_s$ – that is to say, when gold is less valued at home than abroad, then the market rate of exchange finds its lower limit (maximum depreciation) in R_g, diminished by the costs of shipping gold (see Figure 4.1). In fact, nobody would be prepared to obtain fewer units of foreign currency than those that could be obtained by remitting gold. When the rate of exchange reaches this minimum level, it is profitable for the resident in the domestic country to export gold instead of buying a bill of exchange.[9]

The upper limit (maximum appreciation) is given by R_s augmented by the costs of shipping silver, because as soon as the exchange rate rises to higher levels, it becomes profitable to import silver. So that

(14) $R_g(1 - c_g) \leq E_m \leq R_s(1 + c_s)$

Conversely, if $\frac{p}{q} > \frac{p^*}{q^*}$, the profitability conditions are reversed: $E_g < E_s$ and $R_g < R_s$. The upper limit of the exchange rate (maximum appreciation) is set by the gold parity, while the lower limit (maximum depreciation) is set by the silver parity.

Thus we have

(15) $R_s(1 - c_s) \leq E_m \leq R_g(1 + c_g)$

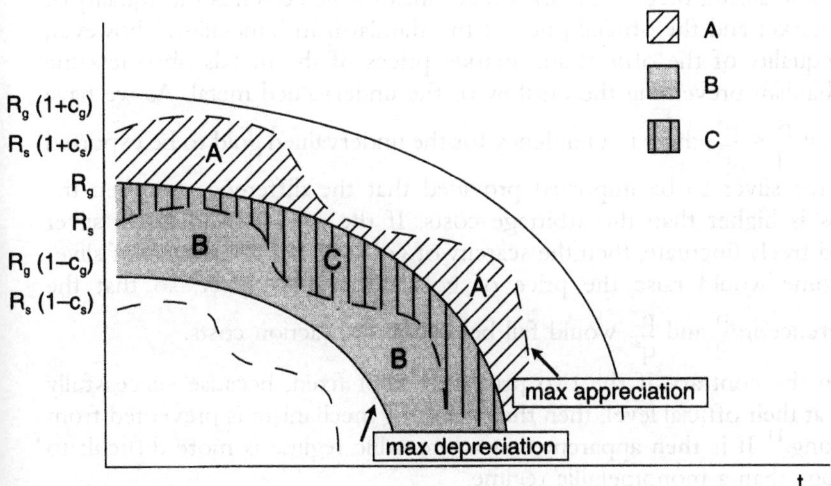

Figure 4.1 Range of variations in the market rate of exchange when p/q < p*/q*

If transport costs for gold and silver are equal, then the fluctuation margins of the market rate of exchange are narrower than in the case of a single standard in both countries, given that $R_g \neq R_s$.[10]

In summary, when two countries have a single but different standard, variations in the market ratios between gold and silver in the two countries are relevant for three reasons. First, because they alter the gold or silver parity, which varies as the gold/silver ratio varies, as shown by (6) and (7). Second, they make either gold or silver parity the relevant parity to ascertain the profitability conditions for shipping one of the two metals. Third, they set the fluctuation margins of the exchange rate.

EXCHANGE RATES IN A BIMETALLIC REGIME

In a bimetallic regime both gold and silver are standards of money. Historically, this meant that both silver and gold coins circulated as money and/or banknotes were convertible into either metal.

In the bimetallic case we have two official parities. Besides X_g, the official gold parity, we have an official silver parity, X_s:

$$X_s = \frac{q^*_M}{q_M}$$

From the above definitions it follows that $X_g = X_s$, if and only if the official gold/silver ratio is identical in both countries.

Bimetallism works when the official gold/silver ratio is such that there are no gains to be made from the exportation of either of the two metals. Otherwise one metal alone would become the standard. As in the case of monometallism, there is a market mechanism which ensures the equality of the market and the official price of the standard. In bimetallism, however, the equality of the official and market prices of the metals obstructs the mechanism preventing the outflow of the undervalued metal. As we have seen, if $\frac{p}{q} < \frac{p^*}{q^*}$, there is a tendency for the undervalued gold to be exported and for silver to be imported provided that the difference between the ratios is higher than the arbitrage costs. If the prices of gold and silver could freely fluctuate, then the scarcity of gold and the abundance of silver at home would raise the price of gold, relative to silver, so that the difference in $\frac{p}{q}$ and $\frac{p^*}{q^*}$ would fall below the transaction costs.

On the contrary, if the two prices are kept fixed, because successfully kept at their official level, then the equalizing mechanism is prevented from working.[11] It is then apparent that a bimetallic regime is more difficult to manage than a monometallic regime.

Conceptually, however, the framework of analysis of the oscillations of the market rate of exchange around parity does not differ from what we illustrated in the previous section, and we need only to substitute X_g for E_g and X_s for E_s.

Here too the oscillation margins of the market exchange rate are set by the export and import points of the standard, the transportation charges relative to one metal defining the upper limits, and the transportation charges relative to the other metal the lower limit. To find out which is the relevant metal in setting the upper and lower limit, we must know the relationship between $\frac{p}{q}$ and $\frac{p^*}{q^*}$. The same applies to the choice of the metal to ship rather than selling or buying a bill and the price of which enters into the calculations of the merchants in trading on the market for bills of exchange.

However, unlike the previous case, the relevant parities, X_s and X_g, are fixed and reflect only the ratio between the official prices of the two standards in both countries.

COMPUTATION OF t_g AND t_s

Deviations in the market rate of exchange from gold or silver parity can be employed as significant indicators of conditions in the market for bills of exchange if allowance is made for that part representing the deviations in the market price from the official price of the respective standard. We defined $\mathbf{t_g}$ and $\mathbf{t_s}$ as the deviation of the market rate of exchange from the "commercial" gold and silver par, respectively. In order to employ $\mathbf{t_g}$ and $\mathbf{t_s}$ as indicators of the conditions prevailing in the market for bills and therefore of the state of the balance of payment between the two countries, we have to solve the question of which is the relevant $\mathbf{t}$.

The assumption that equilibrium in the market for foreign bills of exchange is characterized by $\mathbf{t_g} = 0$ (or $\mathbf{t_s} = 0$) needs some justification. As noted by Viner (1937: 379) for the Gold Standard, any exchange rate within the gold points – whenever $\mathbf{t_g}$ is less than the transaction costs of shipping gold – is an equilibrium rate. According to this view, the market can be said to be out of equilibrium only when gold flows occur, since the equality between supply and demand would require a level of the exchange rate which is beyond the gold points and therefore unattainable. Clearly, the rate of exchange at which $\mathbf{t_g} =0$ (or $\mathbf{t_s} =0$) is not the only equilibrium rate, within the gold points, that is the only rate at which demand is equal to supply, but is the relevant exchange rate which, in our model, provides the unifying term of reference. This is a homage to the tradition which views the normal ratio between two currencies as determined by their purchasing power over their respective standards.

However, by normal value it is not meant the average value of the market rate of exchange under the assumption of a uniform distribution within the interval of the gold points (as in Officer 1985; see also Chapter 8 in this volume). In fact, the latter coincides with the condition $\mathbf{t} = 0$ only when transaction costs are equal in both directions.

In the case of a monometallic regime in which both countries have the same standard (say gold), a value of $\mathbf{t_g}$ greater than zero means an excess supply of foreign currency in the home market; conversely a value for $\mathbf{t_g}$ less than zero means an excess demand for foreign currency and therefore an "unfavorable" rate of exchange for the domestic currency.

In the case of a bimetallic regime, in which each country has a different standard, as we have seen, the metal which is more profitable to export is not the one which is more profitable to import. Once more, we assume that there are two countries and that the domestic country is on the gold standard while the foreign country is on the silver standard. The profitability conditions for the domestic merchant in deciding which is the most economical way to remit a payment to the foreign country are not the same as those confronting the seller of a bill denominated in the foreign currency in the domestic exchange market.

We shall start by assuming that we have the situation depicted in Figure 4.1, that is to say that $\frac{p}{q} < \frac{p^*}{q^*}$ (the shape of the two curves could be any).

For the buyer of a bill denominated in foreign currency, the term of reference is the gold par, because shipping gold is the alternative to buying a bill, while for the seller of foreign currency the term of reference is the silver par. In these circumstances, we have then three occurrences.

(I) $\mathbf{t_g} > 0$ and $\mathbf{t_s} > 0$

The market rate of exchange lies within the area A of Figure 4.1, corresponding to an appreciation. We know for sure that there is an excess supply of the foreign currency and therefore $\mathbf{t_s}$ is a measure of the appreciation of the domestic currency.

(II) $\mathbf{t_g} < 0$ and $\mathbf{t_s} < 0$

The market rate of exchange lies within the area B of Figure 4.1, corresponding to a depreciation. We know for sure that there is an excess demand for the foreign currency and therefore $\mathbf{t_g}$ is a measure of the depreciation of the domestic currency.

(III) $\mathbf{t_g} < 0$ and $\mathbf{t_s} > 0$

The rate of exchange lies in the area C, that is to say it is bounded from above by R_g and by R_s from below. The very concept of a favorable rate of exchange becomes meaningless, since in this case – given that the rate of exchange is lower than the gold par but higher than the silver par – it implies that it is favorable to both buyers and sellers of foreign currency.

To give meaning to the concept of a favorable exchange, it would be necessary to take one parity arbitrarily as the term of reference, or an average between the two. We discarded the idea of taking an average between the two parities for two reasons. First, because it was not a term of reference for merchants and brokers; second, because it requires *ad hoc* assumptions. In fact, when there are two parities, a gold par and a silver par, the midpoint of the interval bounded by the "bullion points" – which is equal to the average value of the exchange rate under the assumption of its uniform distribution in the interval – coincides with the average between the two parities only when the transaction costs involved in shipping either metal are equal in both directions when measured not in percentage but in absolute value.

Thus, lacking any argument to choose one par rather than the other, we are left with the only option of labeling the corresponding values as indeterminate.[12]

AN EXAMPLE: LONDON ON PARIS 1821–70

We shall employ the conceptual framework set out above to study the behavior of the market exchange rate in London on Paris for the 50 years that saw the official beginning of the Gold Standard in England and the *de facto* end of bimetallism in France, when convertibility of banknotes was suspended.[13] The aim of our chapter is to show that behind the fluctuations of the exchange rate there may be two types of forces at work. By employing equations (5) and (13) we can interpret the market signal of the exchange rate, imputing its variations partly to the conditions of circulation ("monetary factors", **p** and **q***) and partly to the conditions of the balance of payments ("real factors", **t**).

In the period under consideration Great Britain was on the Gold Standard. The official price of gold was £3 17s 10½d., per oz. troy (equal to 31.1 grams) of standard gold (22 carats). Since 1816 silver had not been legal tender for any sum above 500 shillings. There were gold coins in circulation and banknotes were convertible in gold coins at the Bank. Gold could also be sold to the Bank at a price slightly lower, or coined at the Mint at no cost beyond the interest involved in the time span before coins were delivered.

In France, since 1803, the franc (FF) had been convertible both in gold and in silver. The official price of gold was 3444.44 FF per kg. Gold could then be sold to the Banque de France at the buying price of 3434.44, or be coined at the Hotel de la Monnaie, obtaining 3444.44 FF from which 10 F had to be deducted to cover coinage expenses. Similarly, the Banque de France's buying price for silver was 218.89 FF per kg and its selling price 222.23, the difference being imputed to coinage expenses of 3.33 FF per 1 kg of silver.

Although the prices at which gold and silver could be sold were fixed and generally known, this did not apply to the prices at which gold and silver could be bought. The Banque de France had the right to choose the metal in which to convert its banknotes. It followed that the price of the other metal could rise on the market, since the prospective buyer who did not succeed in obtaining it from the Bank, in principle, was willing to pay up to the sum corresponding to the nominal value of the coins plus the cost involved in melting them.

Figure 4.2 shows, for Paris, yearly averages of the deviations of the market price of silver from the official price and the yearly averages of the deviations of the market price of gold from its Mint price. The data are taken from Schneider, Schwarzer and Zellfelder (1991, henceforth SSZ), who give the first quotation available for each month and a yearly average, derived from contemporary sources such as commercial bulletins and newspapers.

A certain degree of flexibility in gold prices facilitated the task undertaken by France of maintaining a bimetallic regime with no preference for either metal. In fact, flexibility in the price of gold allowed the gold/silver ratio in France to be brought in line with the international ratio. Moreover, the task of pursuing a bimetallic regime was facilitated by the choice, made by France in 1803, to set its official gold and silver prices so that the $\frac{p^*_M}{q^*_M}$ ratio, set at 15.5, was an average value of those prevailing in its neighbouring countries: 14.5 in the Netherlands, 15.21 in England, 16 in Spain and Portugal (Thuillier 1983: 117), the consequence being that a country, for instance Spain, that could gain from an undervalued silver, shipped silver to the Netherlands rather than to France, thus leaving the gold/silver ratio in the latter country unaffected.

As we pointed out earlier, there are two pars of exchange in London on Paris. The first is the gold parity, defined as the ratio between the official gold prices, being equal to

$$X_g = 25.22 \text{ FF} / £$$

if we follow the traditional way of quoting francs per pound.

The second is the silver parity, E_s (see equation 7) which can be calculated through the gold/silver price ratio in London, which in turn is derived from the prices of gold and silver in that market. The latter were regularly published in London twice a week in the Lloyd's and Wetenhall's Lists, on the basis of "Average Amount of Sales and Purchases of the Bank of England, or Merchants on Tuesday and Friday in each week."[14] They were based on actual transactions, the minimum amount being £1500 and their source was the House of Goldsmid, brokers for the Bank of England. (In fact most of the transactions were carried out at the Bank.) Although

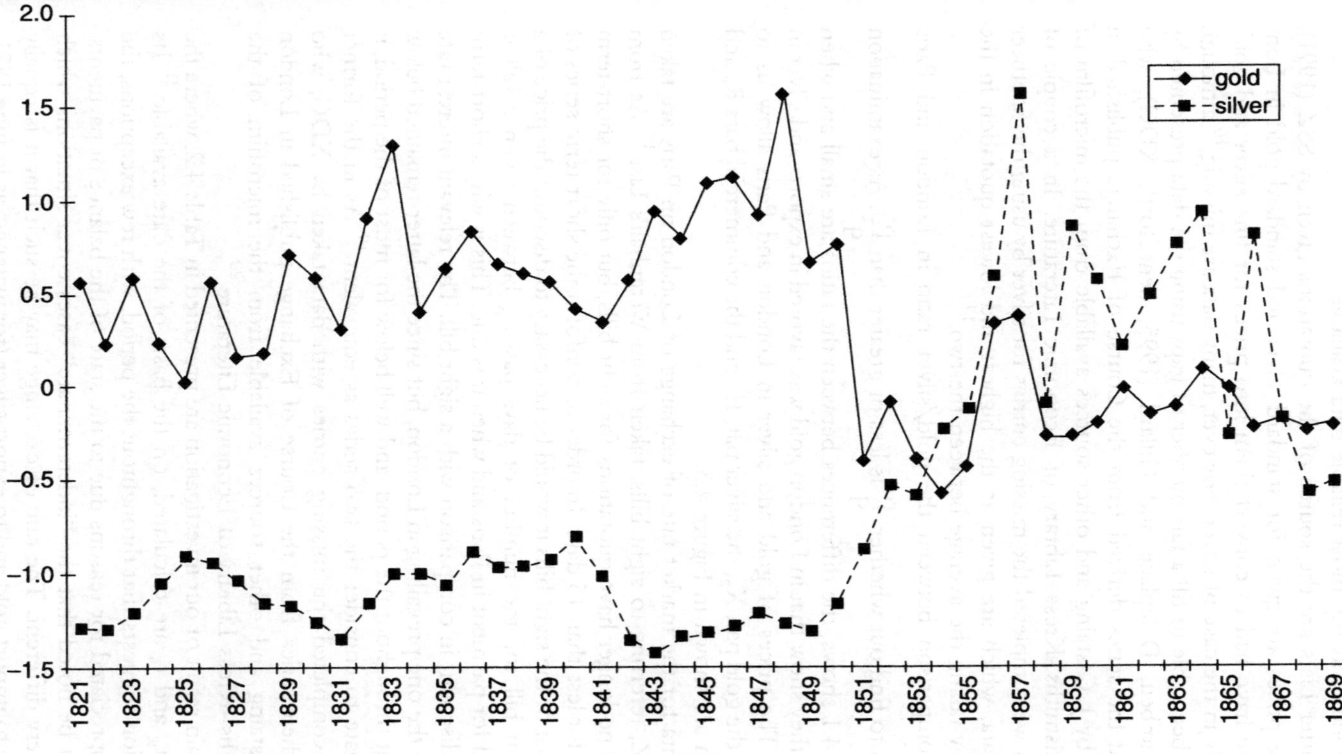

Figure 4.2 Percentage deviations of the market price of gold and silver from the official price, Paris 1821–70
Source: Our elaboration from Schneider, Schwarzer and Zellfelder (1991)

they did not appear as official publications, those quotations were taken by contemporaries as the most reliable data available.

The latter Lists are the source of the quotations given by SSZ (1991). Since the prices are given for standard silver and standard gold in London,[15] we have had to convert them into prices for fine silver and gold. Especially in the case of silver, however, many data are missing,[16] although we have been able to fill a fair number of gaps using the data presented by Boyer-Xambeu, Deleplace and Gillard (1995, henceforth XDG), who employed the series derived from the Course of Exchange published in London by J. Castaing and other sources available from the microfilm of the Goldsmiths'-Kress Library of Economic Literature. In a couple of instances we completed the missing entries for silver by using the Soetbeer (1880) data, which are given as the highest and lowest quotation in the month, by taking the average between the two.[17]

The comparison between the gold/silver ratio in London and Paris allows us to find out whether $\frac{p}{q}$ is less or greater than $\frac{p^*}{q^*}$. As examination of Table 4.1 shows, the differences between the ratios are small and when negative they show that in London gold was favored in exports and silver in imports. The prices of gold and silver in London and Paris allow us to calculate the gold par, X_g, the silver par, E_s, and the commercial pars R_g and R_s, which are shown in Figure 4.3.

The data for the market rate of exchange of London on Paris are taken from SSZ, referring to sight bills, taken from Wetenhall's List.[18] As from 1834, we no longer have quotations for sight bills, but only for short-term bills, i.e., for less than 15 days. In order to conform the short-term series of bills to that of the sight bills it would be necessary to discount the price of a short-term bill for the number of days passing between when a bill is presented for payment in Paris and when it is due. This is why a short-term bill is at discount in comparison with a sight bill. The relevant interest rate would be the one prevailing in London, but since the latter remained below 5 per cent throughout the period, and well below for most of the period, it is legitimate to consider the two series as equivalent.[19] As in the former case we completed the missing entries with data taken by XDG, who derived their series from the Course of Exchange published in London by J. Castaing and other sources available from the microfilm of the Goldsmiths'-Kress Library of Economic Literature.[20]

The main result of our investigation are presented in Table 4.2, where the relevant $\mathbf{t_g}$ and $\mathbf{t_s}$ are calculated, on the basis of the date available.[21] Its examination suggests that throughtout the period, with few exceptions, the pound appreciated for reasons due to the state of the balance of payments.

It must be noted that the "indeterminate" cases cover situations which may be very different. The rate of exchange may be such that it is equally profitable to import gold and to export silver (for instance, as in June 1821,

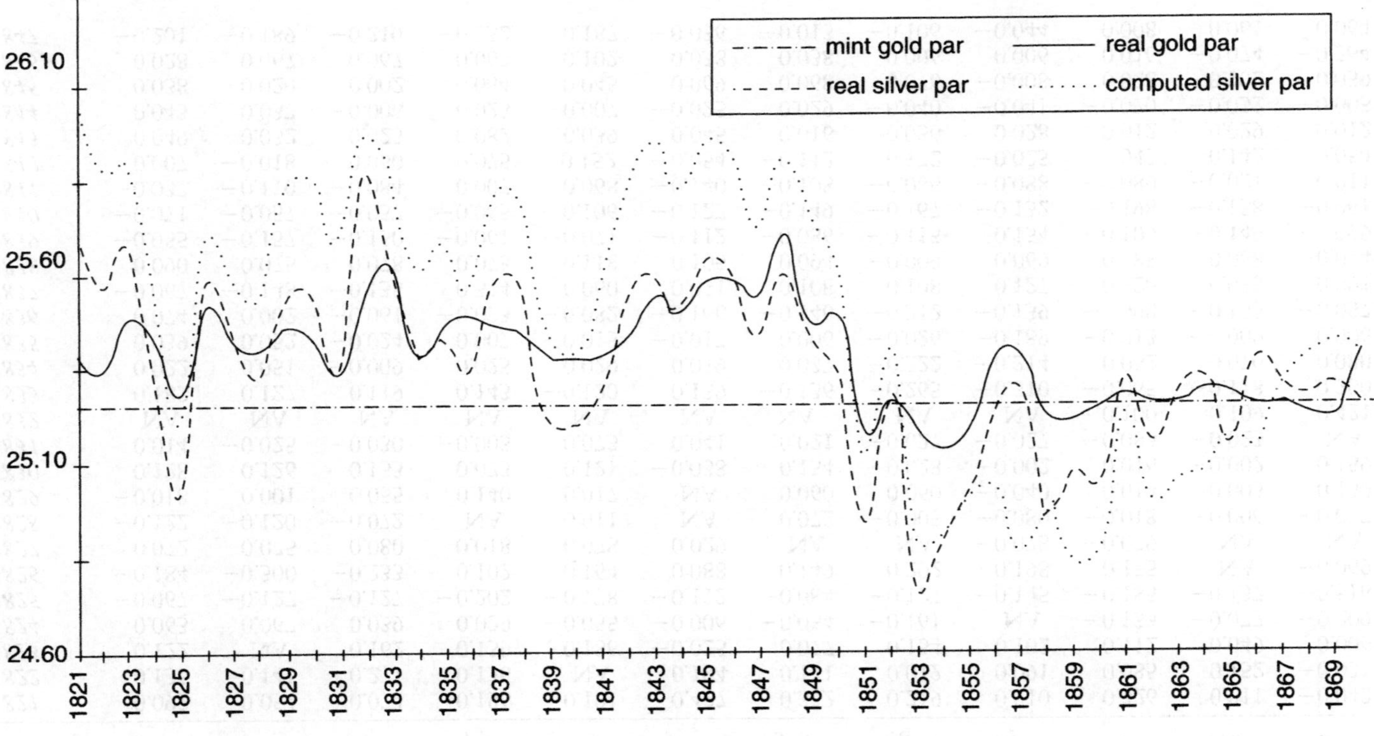

Figure 4.3 London/Paris parities, 1821–70 (FF per £)

Source: Our elaboration from Boyer-Xambeu, Deleplace and Gillard (1994); Schneider, Schwarzer and Zellfelder (1991); Soetbeer (1880)

Table 4.1 Differences in gold/silver ratios in London and Paris (monthly data), 1821–69

	Jan	*Feb*	*March*	*April*	*May*	*June*	*July*	*August*	*Sept*	*Oct*	*Nov*	*Dec*
1821	0.092	0.054	0.074	0.196	0.191	0.427	0.332	0.219	0.210	0.326	0.211	−0.042
1822	0.135	0.141	0.271	0.136	NA	0.194	0.171	0.012	0.091	0.085	0.152	−0.031
1823	0.122	NA	0.162	0.139	0.186	−0.025	0.077	0.154	0.102	0.112	0.049	0.006
1824	0.063	0.067	0.039	0.029	−0.055	−0.006	−0.054	−0.161	NA	−0.133	−0.077	−0.209
1825	−0.067	−0.127	−0.127	−0.202	−0.178	−0.112	−0.084	−0.127	−0.145	−0.185	−0.137	−0.516
1826	−0.184	−0.300	−0.233	0.102	0.164	0.088	0.149	0.202	0.198	0.155	NA	−0.069
1827	0.072	0.075	0.080	0.018	0.078	0.029	NA	NA	−0.078	−0.079	NA	NA
1828	−0.122	−0.120	−0.072	NA	0.011	NA	0.072	−0.005	−0.080	−0.018	−0.006	−0.077
1829	−0.018	0.001	0.055	0.140	0.017	NA	0.060	0.060	−0.040	0.014	−0.005	0.130
1830	0.128	0.126	0.133	0.073	0.121	−0.038	0.154	−0.028	−0.002	0.016	−0.002	0.159
1831	0.014	−0.025	−0.030	−0.005	0.073	0.041	0.021	−0.027	−0.027	−0.083	−0.023	NA
1832	NA	NA	NA	NA	NA	NA	NA	NA	NA	0.100	0.109	0.421
1833	0.182	0.127	0.119	0.143	−0.120	0.139	−0.136	−0.265	−0.310	−0.065	−0.118	0.200
1834	0.022	0.051	−0.009	0.025	0.029	0.019	0.037	−0.222	−0.214	0.052	0.070	0.080
1835	0.039	0.052	−0.024	0.007	−0.015	−0.017	0.006	−0.026	−0.189	−0.013	−0.009	0.006
1836	0.074	0.002	−0.061	−0.023	−0.082	−0.166	−0.146	−0.212	−0.139	−0.098	−0.155	−0.057
1837	−0.067	−0.148	−0.135	0.514	0.060	0.071	0.108	0.108	0.127	0.120	0.058	0.091
1838	0.090	0.075	0.078	0.078	0.118	0.105	0.094	−0.009	0.069	0.088	0.088	−0.014
1839	−0.055	−0.157	−0.150	−0.061	−0.071	−0.112	−0.086	−0.115	−0.154	−0.109	−0.149	−0.099
1840	−0.071	−0.057	−0.057	−0.065	−0.106	−0.127	−0.149	−0.167	−0.132	−0.198	−0.158	−0.061
1841	−0.037	−0.110	−0.084	0.007	−0.068	−0.140	−0.108	−0.085	−0.088	−0.089	−0.021	0.011
1842	0.007	−0.018	0.060	0.075	0.152	−0.054	−0.112	0.172	−0.025	0.043	0.142	0.054
1843	0.049	0.032	0.023	0.082	0.039	0.045	0.016	0.036	0.028	0.012	0.029	0.012
1844	0.043	0.037	−0.006	0.023	0.007	−0.025	0.029	−0.040	−0.041	−0.070	−0.032	−0.005
1845	0.038	0.020	0.002	0.064	0.045	0.069	0.068	0.076	−0.008	0.028	−0.102	0.059
1846	0.028	0.067	0.067	0.067	0.102	0.038	0.038	0.006	0.006	0.016	−0.074	−0.264
1847	−0.201	−0.189	−0.210	−0.252	0.187	−0.036	−0.013	−0.106	−0.044	0.008	0.061	0.064

Table 4.2 Measure of excess demand in the London market for bills of exchange denominated in French francs, 1821–70

	Jan	*Feb*	*March*	*April*	*May*	*June*	*July*	*August*	*Sept*	*Oct*	*Nov*	*Dec*
1821	1.73%	1.50%	1.84%	1.75%	1.72%	indet.	indet.	2.12%	indet.	indet.	indet.	0.53%
1822	1.32%	indet.	indet.	indet.	NA	indet.	1.20%	0.12%	0.76%	0.72%	indet.	0.25%
1823	1.62%	NA	2.02%	2.27%	1.66%	0.89%	1.07%	indet.	1.21%	1.48%	1.34%	0.67%
1824	0.84%	0.68%	0.64%	0.57%	0.38%	0.20%	0.63%	indet.	NA	indet.	indet.	indet.
1825	indet.	indet.	indet.	indet.	indet.	0.79%	indet.	indet.	1.13%	1.40%	1.21%	indet.
1826	indet.	indet.	2.38%	1.26%	1.06%	0.60%	indet.	indet.	indet.	indet.	NA	indet.
1827	0.84%	0.86%	0.68%	0.81%	0.63%	0.72%	NA	NA	0.70%	0.58%	NA	NA
1828	0.95%	indet.	indet.	NA	0.17%	NA	indet.	0.10%	indet.	0.14%	0.37%	indet.
1829	indet.	0.08%	indet.	indet.	0.79%	NA	0.67%	0.78%	1.03%	0.74%	0.86%	2.79%
1830	1.55%	1.33%	1.08%	1.14%	1.16%	0.87%	indet.	1.26%	0.67%	0.66%	0.09%	indet.
1831	−0.63%	−0.59%	−0.82%	−0.46%	−0.63%	−0.43%	−0.53%	−0.38%	indet.	indet.	0.20%	NA
1832	NA	NA	NA	NA	NA	NA	NA	NA	NA	0.83%	0.82%	indet.
1833	indet.	indet.	0.84%	1.06%	1.81%	1.05%	1.96%	2.16%	2.17%	0.71%	indet.	1.76%
1834	−0.32%	0.40%	−0.21%	indet.	0.21%	indet.	indet.	indet.	1.49%	0.57%	0.63%	indet.
1835	0.26%	indet.	0.41%	0.85%	0.10%	0.71%	0.55%	0.71%	1.71%	0.59%	0.37%	0.31%
1836	0.47%	0.35%	0.82%	0.29%	0.60%	indet.	1.11%	indet.	indet.	0.76%	indet.	0.54%
1837	0.82%	indet.	0.90%	indet.	0.57%	−0.54%	0.71%	indet.	indet.	indet.	0.43%	indet.
1838	1.17%	indet.	0.68%	indet.	0.76%	indet.	indet.	0.38%	indet.	indet.	indet.	−0.11%
1839	indet.	indet.	indet.	indet.	indet.	indet.	indet.	indet.	indet.	0.98%	indet.	indet.
1840	0.51%	indet.	indet.	indet.	indet.	indet.	indet.	indet.	indet.	1.33%	indet.	indet.
1841	indet.	0.72%	0.78%	0.32%	0.47%	indet.	1.06%	0.73%	2.03%	0.91%	0.47%	0.59%
1842	0.55%	0.56%	0.72%	0.73%	indet.	0.69%	0.95%	indet.	0.63%	0.73%	indet.	0.79%
1843	0.91%	0.43%	0.56%	0.67%	0.66%	0.60%	0.62%	0.48%	0.54%	0.63%	0.44%	0.54%
1844	0.58%	0.32%	0.50%	0.49%	0.24%	0.35%	−0.19%	0.58%	0.68%	0.78%	0.81%	0.78%
1845	0.56%	0.62%	0.87%	0.81%	0.70%	0.63%	0.69%	0.48%	0.69%	0.76%	1.45%	0.89%
1846	0.66%	0.92%	0.92%	1.31%	1.01%	0.50%	0.32%	0.50%	0.50%	0.46%	−1.98%	indet.
1847	indet.	indet.	indet.	indet.	1.53%	0.49%	0.86%	indet.	−0.28%	−0.23%	0.50%	indet.

1848	0.080	0.066	−0.347	−0.252	0.209	−0.111	−0.133	0.039	−0.094	−0.138	−0.187	0.091
1849	−0.026	−0.066	−0.017	0.007	−0.103	−0.066	−0.043	−0.053	0.083	−0.003	−0.032	−0.025
1850	−0.053	−0.080	−0.090	−0.098	−0.157	−0.089	−0.017	−0.060	−0.048	−0.074	−0.020	−0.271
1851	−0.347	−0.347	−0.287	−0.254	−0.254	−0.098	−0.067	−0.088	−0.014	0.079	−0.028	−0.067
1852	−0.059	0.009	0.040	0.033	0.110	0.109	−0.008	0.043	0.124	−0.078	−0.170	0.042
1853	−0.326	−0.289	−0.266	−0.254	−0.254	−0.107	−0.208	−0.238	−0.415	−0.270	−0.171	−0.232
1854	−0.192	−0.138	−0.222	−0.219	−0.189	−0.100	−0.111	−0.126	−0.115	−0.069	−0.104	−0.134
1855	−0.166	−0.166	−0.134	0.022	0.090	−0.104	−0.134	−0.175	−0.195	−0.146	−0.071	−0.151
1856	−0.132	−0.114	0.003	−0.027	−0.087	−0.090	−0.103	−0.163	0.007	0.019	−0.167	−0.167
1857	−0.219	−0.130	−0.085	−0.079	0.008	0.153	0.032	−0.086	0.032	−0.086	−0.086	−0.092
1858	−0.130	−0.180	−0.060	−0.142	−0.131	−0.190	−0.190	−0.051	−0.041	−0.101	−0.288	−0.208
1859	−0.105	−0.054	−0.075	−0.227	0.310	−0.114	−0.114	−0.231	−0.054	−0.114	−0.114	−0.114
1860	−0.139	−0.220	−0.153	−0.060	0.001	−0.108	−0.136	−0.146	−0.165	−0.133	−0.135	−0.002
1861	−0.104	−0.033	0.019	−0.007	0.088	0.046	0.113	0.089	0.028	0.052	0.037	−0.086
1862	0.013	−0.138	0.060	−0.169	−0.108	−0.070	−0.060	0.036	−0.113	−0.059	−0.157	0.054
1863	0.016	0.076	0.024	0.114	−0.045	−0.026	0.095	0.029	−0.016	0.012	−0.027	−0.036
1864	0.040	0.116	0.056	0.116	0.189	0.116	0.095	−0.079	−0.139	−0.035	−0.087	−0.200
1865	−0.200	−0.140	−0.146	−0.026	−0.022	−0.026	0.044	−0.030	0.032	−0.091	−0.151	−0.212
1866	−0.126	−0.051	0.050	−0.071	−0.010	−0.189	−0.007	0.301	0.239	0.551	0.178	0.125
1867	−0.005	−0.010	0.051	−0.010	0.051	0.077	0.051	0.052	0.113	0.043	−0.008	−0.019
1868	0.020	0.020	0.020	−0.041	0.020	−0.041	0.020	0.029	0.076	0.075	0.075	0.012
1869	0.028	0.098	−0.018	0.044	0.028	0.152	0.090	0.099	0.024	0.013	0.026	0.030

Source: Our elaboration from Boyer-Xambeu, Deleplace and Gillard (1994); Schneider, Schwarzer and Zellfelder (1991); Soetbeer (1880)

1848	indet.	indet.	−2.57%	2.37%	−2.70%	indet.	indet.	−0.74%	indet.	indet.	indet.	−0.90%
1849	−0.38%	0.53%	−0.17%	−0.28%	indet.	indet.	indet.	indet.	indet.	−0.04%	0.23%	0.23%
1850	indet.	indet.	indet.	indet.	indet.	indet.	0.20%	indet.	indet.	indet.	−0.33%	2.49%
1851	indet.	indet.	indet.	indet.	indet.	indet.	−0.55%	indet.	indet.	0.55%	0.42%	indet.
1852	−0.60%	0.38%	0.48%	0.53%	indet.	−2.07%	indet.	0.41%	indet.	0.64%	indet.	−0.29%
1853	indet.	indet.	indet.	indcet.	indet.	indet.	indet.	indet.	indet.	1.80%	indet.	indet.
1854	indet.	indet.	indet.	−2.42%	indet.	indet.	indet.	indet.	indet.	0.52%	indet.	2.24%
1855	indet.	indet.	indet.	0.15%	indet.	0.93%	indet.	indet.	1.64%	1.67%	0.72%	indet.
1856	indet.	indet.	0.49%	0.49%	0.88%	0.80%	indet.	indet.	−0.14%	−0.72%	indet.	indet.
1857	indet.	indet.	indet.	indet.	−0.40%	−1.28%	−0.51%	indet.	−0.71%	indet.	indet.	1.00%
1858	1.08%	indet.	−0.48%	indet.	indet.	indet.	indet.	−0.38%	indet.	indet.	indet.	indet.
1859	indet.	indet.	indet.	indet.	−2.45%	indet.	indet.	indet.	indet.	indet.	indet.	indet.
1860	indet.	indet.	indet.	indet.	−0.21%	indet.	indet.	indet.	indet.	indet.	indet.	−0.15%
1861	indet.	indet.	0.54%	0.58%	−0.67%	0.55%	indet.	indet.	0.64%	0.63%	0.36%	0.61%
1862	0.26%	−2.36%	−0.72%	1.44%	0.86%	0.51%	0.75%	indet.	0.84%	indet.	indet.	−0.56%
1863	−0.28%	indet.	−0.23%	−0.76%	indet.	0.25%	indet.	0.36%	0.36%	0.15%	0.26%	0.45%
1864	indet.	indet.	indet.	−1.10%	indet.	−0.80%	−0.83%	0.77%	1.06%	0.61%	indet.	indet.
1865	indet.	indet.	indet.	indet.	−0.37%	−0.35%	indet.	indet.	indet.	0.72%	1.06%	indet.
1866	indet.	indet.	indet.	0.56%	−0.07%	indet.	0.09%	−2.08%	indet.	indet.	−1.25%	indet.
1867	−0.05%	−0.25%	−0.53%	indet.	−0.58%	−0.53%	indet.	−0.38%	indet.	−0.33%	−0.35%	−0.45%
1868	−0.28%	−0.23%	−0.33%	0.27%	−0.28%	0.27%	indet.	−0.23%	indet.	indet.	−0.53%	−0.13%
1869	indet.	−0.73%	0.12%	indet.	−0.23%	indet.	indet.	indet.	indet.	−0.13%	−0.22%	−0.29%
1870	indet.	indet.	−0.40%	indet.	NA	−0.08%	indet.	indet.	−0.67%	NA	NA	NA

Source: Our elaboration

probably as a consequence of the return to gold by Great Britain). This case is "indeterminate" because the market rate of exchange lies between the silver and the gold par. However, in this case, it is higher not only than the gold par, but also than the gold import point and it is lower not only than the silver par, but also than the silver export point. This, in general, does not apply to all other "indeterminate" cases.

Finally, Table 4.2 could offer a way of testing how many times the gold and silver points were reached throughout the period, if we had a more detailed knowledge of the transaction costs involved in shipping gold and silver.[22]

CONCLUSIONS

The purpose of this chapter is twofold. The first is to provide a general framework of analysis of exchange-rate variations and profitability conditions in bullion trade under monometallic and bimetallic regimes. The second is to offer an example of its application, by constructing the series of the relevant indicator for the London-Paris markets during 50 years of the early history of the Gold Standard.

We show that the variation in the market rate of exchange from the relevant parity is a good indicator of the conditions prevailing in the bills market and, therefore, of the state of the balance of payments, provided two conditions are met: first, the parity from which the deviations of the market rate of exchange are calculated must be the parity assumed as the term of reference by economic agents engaged in actual transactions; and second, allowance must be made for the component due to the conditions of the demand for bullion, which can fluctuate widely, as we saw on p. 84.

In this chapter we provide, as an example, computation of an indicator which is the measure of the deviation of the market rate of exchange from the real par, which satisfies *both* requirements. While its sign tells us whether the market is favorable or unfavorable to the domestic currency, its value – compared with the costs of shipping bullion – tells us whether an outflow or an inflow of bullion is likely to occur.

NOTES

1 The first version of this chapter was presented at the Cliometric Session of the Eleventh International Economic History Congress, Milan 1994. We are indebted to D. McCloskey for helpful comments. The second version was presented at the workshop on "Monetary Standards and Exchange Rates," held in Perugia in 1995. We are grateful to M. Flandreau, L. Officer and G. Tattara for comments and to G. Deleplace for stimulating criticism. Financial assistance from the Italian National Research Council is gratefully acknowledged.

2 The most obvious mechanism is the convertibility of banknotes into coins or

bullion. Generally, the same mechanism exists when the circulation is made up only of coins or of coins and paper, regardless of whether paper money is convertible or inconvertible (see Marcuzzo and Rosselli 1991: 123–8).

3 On the function of the standard as measure of the variations in the value of money see Marcuzzo and Rosselli (1994).

4 By rearranging (3) and (4) we have:

$$\text{(3b)}\quad E_m = X_g (1 + e) = \frac{p^*_M}{p_M} (1 + e)$$

and

$$\text{(4b)}\quad E_m = R_g (1 + t_g) = \frac{p^*}{p}(1 + t_g)$$

Substituting (1) and (2) in (4b), we obtain

$$E_m = \frac{p^*_M}{p_M} (1 + e) = \frac{p^*}{p^*} (1 + t_g) = \frac{p^*_M (1 + p^*)(1 + t_g)}{p_M(1 + p)}$$

and by neglecting second order terms we obtain (5).

5 In fact, if $\frac{p}{q} < \frac{p^*}{q^*}$, namely if gold is undervalued at home, it is profitable to buy gold at home, ship and sell it abroad, buy silver abroad and ship it home, if and only if

$$\frac{qp^*}{p(1 + c_g)\, q^* (1 + c_s)} > 1$$

or

$$\frac{p^*}{q^*} > \frac{p}{q} (1 + c_g) (1 + c_s)$$

where $\frac{1}{p(1+c_g)}$ is the amount of gold that can be bought and shipped abroad with one unit of domestic currency. This amount of gold, when sold abroad at the price p*, enables the merchant to buy $\frac{1}{p(1+c_g)} \frac{p^*}{q^*(1+c_s)}$ amount of silver, whose value at home is obtained by multiplying it by its price q. Therefore when the left-hand side of the above inequality is greater than one, this means that there is a positive gain in the arbitrage.

Similarly, if $\frac{p^*}{q^*} < \frac{p}{q}$, namely when silver is undervalued at home, it is profitable to buy silver at home and exchange it for gold abroad to be shipped back home, if and only if

$$\frac{q^*p}{q(1 + c_s)\, p^* (1 + c_s)} > 1$$

or, by rearranging terms:

$$\frac{p^*}{q^*} < \frac{p}{q} (1 - c_g)(1 - c_s)$$

6 Given that $\frac{p}{q} < \frac{p^*}{q^*}$ implies $\frac{q^*}{q} < \frac{p^*}{p}$, the amount of gold purchased by one unit of domestic currency $\frac{1}{p}$, fetches abroad a higher price than $\frac{1}{q}$, the amount of silver purchased by one unit of domestic currency.

7 Transportation and transaction costs include freight, insurance and commission.

8 See, for instance, Ricardo (1951: 31–3).

9 When transportation costs of shipping gold and silver widely differ, it is theoretically possible that R_s, diminished by transport costs, be higher than R_g, diminished by the transport cost, if transportation costs for silver are lower than for gold. However, this is a case that does not seem to be empirically relevant. For instance, in 1819 transport costs for gold and silver from London to Paris were approximately the same. See Evidence of Richard Page, General Merchant, to the Resumption of Cash Payments Committee of the House of Lords (British Parliamentary Papers 1819: 150). However, later on there seem to have been slight differences (see Flandreau 1995: 104).

10 The same point is made in greater detail by Boyer-Xambeau *et al.* (1994) and in Chapter 5 in this volume.

11 Historically, we have examples of either metal in turn being left to fluctuate relative to its official value or of banknotes being converted into the metal chosen by the Bank and not by the public.

12 The case of $\frac{p}{q} > \frac{p^*}{q^*}$ is perfectly analogous: in case (I) $\mathbf{t_g}$ is the measure of the excess supply in the market for foreign bills of exchange and in case (II) $\mathbf{t_s}$ is the measure of the excess demand.

13 From the end of bimetallism to full adherence to the Gold Standard in France, gradual steps were taken: first the suspension of convertibility in 1870; then 5 Francs silver coin was no longer coined as from 1875 (Thuillier 1983: 330); finally silver was no longer coined as from 1876 (Shaw 1967: 196).

14 Evidence of Robert Mushett, First Clerk to the Master of the Mint, to the Committee on Resumption of Cash Payments of the House of Lords (British Parliamentary Papers 1819: 205).

15 In SSZ there is an apparent slip in the reference to the relevant gold and silver prices. They are quoted as "Feingold" and "Feinsilber" respectively, but in correspondence with the authors of the present paper it was confirmed that they are quotations of prices for *standard* gold and silver.

16 For the reason why the series of silver prices in London is incomplete see Flandreau (1995: 103).

17 Data for September 1839 and November 1867.

18 According to the Evidence given by Isaac Goldsmid to the Resumption of Cash Payments Committee, the Wetenhall's List reported the quotations made at the fixing of the exchanges on Post day and were not the "result of actual transactions, but a guide for the transactions to take place." The actual price of bills drawn on the Houses of the utmost credit could differ as much as 0.5 per cent from the quoted price (see British Parliamentary Papers 1819: 205).

19 The price of a short-term bill is higher than a sight bill, but for a 15 days bill, at a rate of interest lower than 5 per cent, the difference can never be more than 0.2 per cent.

20 The data are for Oct.–Nov.–Dec. 1833 and July 1840.

21 In fact, the calculation requires that five data be available: the market rate of exchange and the prices of gold and silver in London and Paris. We calculated

the $\mathbf{t_g}$ and $\mathbf{t_s}$ utilizing also the data provided by XDG. Differences in the results were insignificant.

22 Between London and Paris, transportation and transaction charges were never, for most of the period under consideration, above 1 per cent. See Evidence of R. Page to the Resumption of Cash Payments Committee of the House of Lords (British Parliamentary Papers 1819: 149); Evidence of I. Goldsmid (*ibid.*: 258); Evidence of G. Gurney to the Committee of the Bank of England Charter (British Parliamentary Papers 1831–32: 253–4). See also Flandreau (1995: 105) and Chapter 6 in this volume.

REFERENCES

Boyer-Xambeu, M.T., Deleplace, G. and Gillard, L. (1994) Régimes monétaires, points d'or et "serpent bimetallique" de 1770 à 1870, *Revue Économique* 45: 1139–74.

Boyer-Xambeu, M.T., Deleplace, G. and Gillard, L. (1995) Bimétallism, taux de change et prix de l'or et de l'argent 1717–1873, *Économies et Sociétés* 7–8.

British Parliamentary Papers (1819) *Reports from the Secret Committees of the House of Commons and of the House of Lords on the Expediency of the Resumption of Cash Payments*, vol. III, London.

British Parliamentary Papers (1831–32) *Report from the Committee of Secrecy on the Bank of England Charter* (1832), vol. VI, London.

Flandreau, M. (1995) *L'Or du monde: La France et la stabilité du systéme monétaire international 1848–1873*, Paris: l'Harmattan.

Marcuzzo, M.C. and Rosselli, A. (1987) Profitability in the International Gold Market in the Early History of the Gold Standard, *Economica* 54: 367–80.

Marcuzzo, M.C. and Rosselli, A. (1991) *Ricardo and the Gold Standard: The Foundations of the International Monetary Order*, London: Macmillan.

Marcuzzo, M.C. and Rosselli, A. (1994) The Standard Commodity and the Standard of Money, *Cahiers d'économie politique* 45: 19–31.

Officer, L.H. (1985) Integration in the American Foreign-Exchange Market, 1791–1900, *Journal of Economic History* 45: 557–85.

Ricardo, D. (1951) *Works and Correspondence*, in P. Sraffa (ed.) vol. VI, Cambridge: Cambridge University Press.

Schneider, J., Schwarzer, O. and Zellfelder F. (1991) *Währungen der Welt I. Europäische und nordamerikanische Devisenkurse 1777–1914*, vols I-III, Stuttgart: F. Steiner Verlag.

Shaw, W.A. (1967) *The History of Currency 1252 to 1896*, New York: Kelley.

Soetbeer, A. (1880) Edelmetall Produktion, "Ergänzbugsheft 5," Gotha: Petermann's Geographisches Mitteneilungen.

Thuillier, G. (1983) *La Monnaie en France au début du XIX siècle*, Geneva: Librairie Droz.

Viner, J. (1937) *Studies in the Theory of International Trade*, New York: Harper.

5

"BIMETALLIC SNAKE" AND MONETARY REGIMES

The stability of the exchange rate between London and Paris from 1796 to 1873[1]

Marie-Thérèse Boyer-Xambeu, Ghislain Deleplace and Lucien Gillard

> The precise magnitude of the stretch between the gold points deserves more scientific consideration than it has yet received.
>
> (Keynes 1930, vol. 2: 296)

The nineteenth century prior to 1873 presents remarkable properties for the history of money and exchange in Europe. Three monetary zones coexisted: England was on the gold standard (*de facto*, and from 1816 *de jure*); France was on bimetallism; and the Northern European countries were on the silver standard. These zones had their respective centres in London, Paris and Hamburg, where three key currencies were freely exchanged: the pound sterling, the franc and the mark (or the schilling, before 1828). And finally, there was in each of these zones, side by side with the circulation of specie, a circulation of banknotes convertible into specie; exceptional (though persistent) circumstances even led to the inconvertibility of Bank of England banknotes.

These characteristics make the period in question an interesting subject for a historical study for at least three reasons. First of all, there were fundamental debates going on at the time about the theory of money and exchange, and the effects on the exchange of the existence of two standards instead of one were variously understood. For Tooke, the comparison between a country with a monometallic standard and a country with a bimetallic one shows that the movements of the exchange with a third country (whatever its standard) are always larger in the latter one (Tooke 1848, 3: 217). Goschen maintains that the movements of the exchange rate between a country with a monometallic standard and a country with a bimetallic one are circumscribed to a band determined by the standard they have in common (Goschen 1861: 82). Juglar states that the band of exchange variations of a country with a bimetallic standard is narrower against a country with a monometallic standard than against a country with a bimetallic one (Juglar 1874: 211). Our analysis will cast doubts on the rightness of these opinions.

A second reason to study that period is to put in a different perspective the accepted theories on exchange rates under a metallic standard, which were chiefly influenced by the observation of the generalized gold-standard period after 1873.[2] And third, the study of this tripolar international monetary system may contribute to a more detailed analysis of monetary and exchange regimes.[3]

We shall limit our present investigations to the state of exchange between London and Paris from 1796 to 1873. To our knowledge, there exist no published series of prices of precious metals and exchange rates in London and Paris that appeared more than once a week, as would be required for the analysis of the adjustment processes. We therefore had to construct these long series on the basis of the original data. The first results of our analysis were published in Boyer-Xambeu, Deleplace and Gillard (1994b). In Boyer-Xambeu, Deleplace and Gillard (1995), we publish these figures with detailed commentaries.[4]

This chapter is divided into four sections. We first present the methodology of our study of pre-1873 exchange rate between London and Paris, stressing the differences between our approach and the conventional gold-points theory. In the second section, we suggest a form of interaction between the exchange markets and the gold and silver markets, which we label "bimetallic snake," and which we substitute for the traditional gold-points mechanism. The study of the stabilizing properties of this bimetallic snake for the rate of exchange combines two types of analysis: a static one and a dynamic one. In the third section, static analysis and historical observation of the width of the snake converge to show that using two metals rather than one to settle the balances was indeed more stabilizing, because it narrowed the range of exchange variations at a moment of time. In the fourth section, the introduction of dynamics suggests that the bimetallic snake has probably limited the long-run tendency of the pound to appreciate against the franc and that the rules embedded in the English monometallic and the French bimetallic monetary regimes significantly contributed to the stability of the rate of exchange in that period, because they limited the undulations of the bimetallic snake over time. We conclude by stressing that the history of pre-1873 exchange rates should concentrate more on the nature of monetary and exchange regimes than on exogenous shocks in the quantities of the precious metals. In that perspective, it appears necessary to extend the analysis to the relations between exchange rates, gold and silver prices, and interest rates.

METHODOLOGY

The stability of the pound

The stability of the external value of the leading pre-1914 currency, the pound sterling, has been well documented. It is, however, unclear whether this stability should be attributed to the automatic working of a particular monetary and exchange regime, the gold standard, or to a deliberate policy of the Bank of England. At any rate, both explanations can be offered only for the period between 1873 and 1914, when the gold standard had spread over most of the industrialized countries, and when the discount policy of the Bank of England was concerned with foreign as domestic issues.

Before 1873, the operation of the gold standard as a domestic monetary regime was restricted to England, and the settlement of balances with silver-standard or bimetallic countries involved both metals. Hence at least the need to reformulate the analysis of the gold-points mechanism, in order to extend it to two metals. The interplay between this mechanism and interest-rates differentials (and consequently the discount policies of the central banks) will be studied in another work.

But is it worthwhile to inquire about the stability of the external value of the pound before 1873? The raging debates of the "bullionist controversy" in the early years of the century, and the repeated need to lift Peel's Act in the middle of it could convey the impression that the internal and external stability of the currency were not enough achieved to reveal the existence of a stabilizing process. As far as the external value of the pound is identified with the short exchange rate with the French franc, this impression is misleading. If Figure 5.1 confirms wide movements of the exchange rate in London (LPV) during the period of inconvertibility, Figures 5.2 and 5.3 show that, with two limited exceptions, the exchange rate was confined between 25 F and 26 F from 1820 to 1870, which yields a range of variation of 4 per cent.

The rough insight provided by these graphs is ambivalent. On the one hand, the movements of the exchange during half a century are not large enough to exclude any stabilizing process.[5] On the contrary, the observation of limited but alternate upswings and downswings suggests that bouncing-back effects may be operating. Moreover, this operation is even strong enough to resist a sudden shift of the exchange, like the downward one in 1850–1 (3.4 per cent in seven months).[6] On the other hand, the range of variation is twice the one which would be expected according to the then often mentioned cost of remitting gold (1 per cent above and below par). As a consequence, the computation of the gold points on the basis of this cost and the legal gold-par of 25,225 F leads to frequent violations of them, during convertibility and inconvertibility periods as well, as shown by the graphs (the gold-points "tunnel" being in grey).[7]

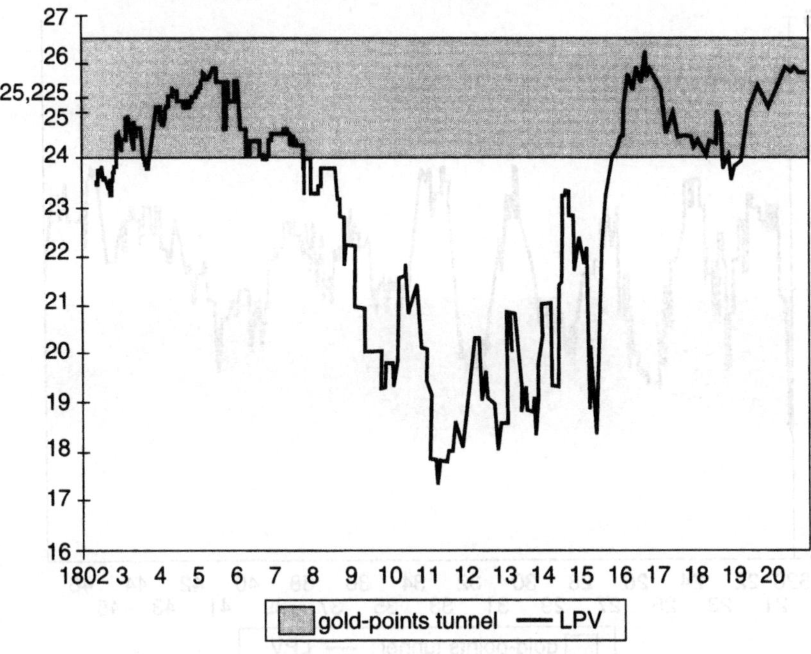

Figure 5.1 Exchange rate of the pound in francs in London (LPV) and the gold-points tunnel, 1802–20

This last observation should not, in fact, be a surprise.[8] As early as the middle of the eighteenth century, the remittance of metal by arbitrageurs involved bullion markets.[9] In these markets the price of uncoined bullion may differ from the legal price of coined metal. This occurs when the current internal value of the currency (which, in a metallic monetary regime, is the reciprocal of the market price of bullion) does not correspond to its legal value (the reciprocal of the official price of the metal coined in the standard specie).[10] Hence the relevant gold-par between England and France is not the legal one, equal to the ratio of the official prices of gold coined respectively in napoleons and in sovereigns, but the commercial par, equal to the ratio of the market prices of gold bullion in Paris and London.

At any moment in time, for given prices in both markets, arbitrage should not allow the exchange rate to deviate from the par by more than the cost of remittance of the metal. But from one moment to another, changes in the market prices of the metal, hence in the par, may lead to wider movements of the exchange rate. The exchange is no longer constrained by a "tunnel" but by a "snake," whose width and undulations determine that constraint. We shall see below (Figures 5.12, 5.14 and 5.16)

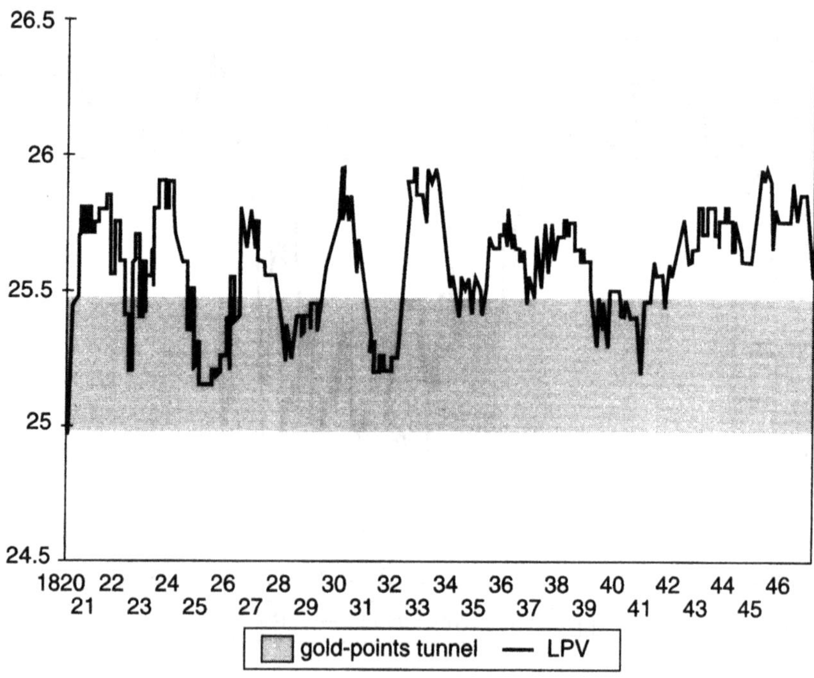

Figure 5.2 Exchange rate of the pound in francs in London (LPV) and the gold-points tunnel, 1820–46

that the "gold snake" constructed in that way encompasses the movements of the exchange somewhat better than the conventional "gold tunnel."

Bullion markets and monetary regimes

The analysis of the stability of the external value of a national currency raises the question of its relation with the internal value of that currency. In a metallic standard regime, this amounts to considering the relation between the exchange rate and the bullion price of the metal chosen as monetary standard, which are expected to vary inversely. This was the central issue of the "bullionist controversy," with bullionists favoring an analysis of the depreciation of the pound in terms of causation from the internal value of money to the external one, and anti-bullionists the other way round.

Statistical observation of that relation for England is quite puzzling, as shown by Table 5.1.[11]

Although silver is no longer a monetary standard after 1816, the correlation between its market price and the exchange rate has been computed to

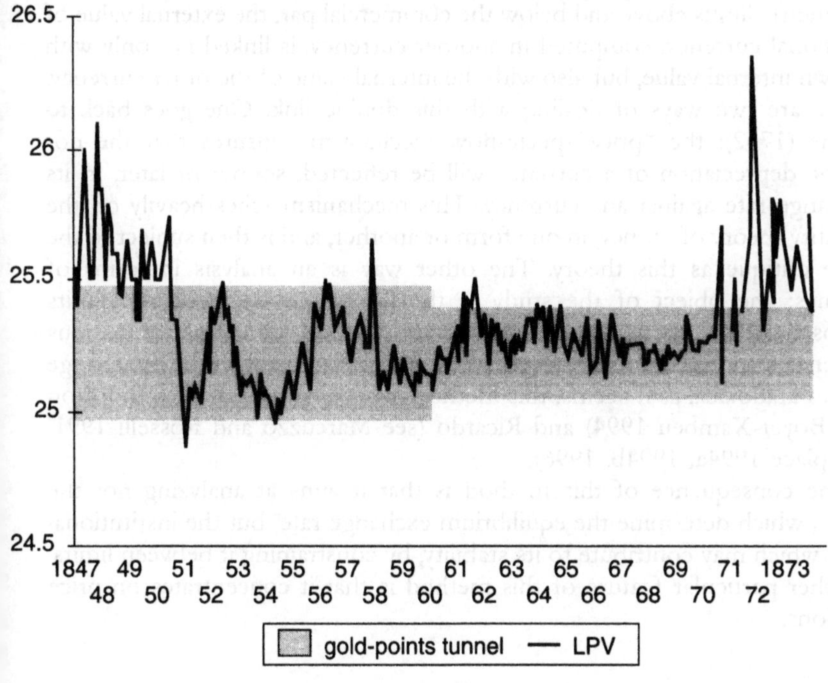

Figure 5.3 Exchange rate of the pound in francs in London (LPV) and the gold-points tunnel, 1847–73

Table 5.1 Correlation between the exchange rate of the pound in francs and the bullion prices of gold and silver in London, 1796–1873

	1796–1820	*1821–46*	*1847–73*
Gold	−0.882	−0.116	+0.154
Silver	−0.790	−0.795	−0.703

offer a comparison with gold. It appears that the expected correlation exists (although not very good) with both metals during the period of inconvertibility and with silver alone after the resumption of convertibility in 1821. In contrast, there is no correlation between the exchange rate of the pound and the market price of the standard after 1821. This suggests that the existence of institutional rules defining a monetary regime, such as the mintage of a standard metal and the convertibility of banknotes, disconnects the internal value of a currency (constrained by these rules) and its external value (determined in the exchange market).

Monetary rules are not, however, the only factor of disconnection between the internal and external values of a currency. Varying between parametric limits above and below the commercial par, the external value of a national currency, computed in another currency, is linked not only with its own internal value, but also with the internal value of the other currency. There are two ways of dealing with this double link. One goes back to Hume (1752): the "price specie-flow mechanism" ensures that the domestic depreciation of a currency will be reflected, sooner or later, in its exchange rate against any currency. This mechanism relies heavily on the quantity theory of money, in one form or another, and is then subject to the same critique as this theory. The other way is an analysis in terms of regimes: the object of the study is the interaction between the limits imposed by the monetary regimes on the internal values of the various currencies and the limits imposed by the bullion markets on their exchange rates. Paradoxical as it seems, this method may be traced back to Thornton (see Boyer-Xambeu 1994) and Ricardo (see Marcuzzo and Rosselli 1991; Deleplace 1994a, 1994b, 1996).

One consequence of this method is that it aims at analyzing not the forces which determine the equilibrium exchange rate, but the institutional rules which may contribute to its stability, by constraining it between limits. Another particular feature of this method is that it concentrates on price relations.

Price relations and quantity adjustments

The relation between the exchange rate of two currencies and the prices of the standard metal in both countries is twofold: the latter determines bullion points which constrain the former, and they are affected themselves by bullion flows implemented when the exchange rate hits the export or the import point. Therefore, the exchange rate and the bullion prices influence one another.

A general-equilibrium approach would determine simultaneously the equilibrium level of these three prices, corresponding to the absence of bullion flows, and would leave to the "price specie-flow mechanism" the task of explaining how they are reached. But the interaction between exchange and bullion markets may exist only when arbitrage between them operates, i.e., when the exchange rate hits a bullion point. As long as the exchange rate stays inside the "snake," away from its "skins," no arbitrage is taking place: there is no relation between the exchange market and the bullion markets, and their levels are determined by factors of their own. Therefore a general-equilibrium approach should be discarded for the analysis of the relation between the exchange rate and any bullion point: strictly speaking, there is only such a relation when they are equal, i.e., precisely when the exchange rate is *not* at its equilibrium level.

An alternative approach consists in using a sequential analysis which separates the two effects: one has a static nature, and concerns price relations occurring in one period of time; the other effect has a dynamic nature, and concerns quantity adjustments occurring interperiodically. This is the approach that we have chosen, for two reasons, one theoretical and one practical.

The theoretical reason is the complexity of adjustment through time, which involves various sorts of quantity flows: bills of exchange, monies, metals, short-term and long-term capital, commodities. The precise impact of each is not easy to ascertain. So it may be useful to isolate the relations which will hold in any case, whatever the other effects. Arbitrage is a relation of that sort. The canonic gold-points model teaches that when the exchange rate hits a gold import (export) point, supply of (demand for) the foreign currency stops, and the exchange rate of the domestic currency stops increasing (decreasing). Whatever the consequences of the gold flows then implemented, the exchange rate is bound between limits during that period of time. If some institutional rules can narrow these limits, this is valuable information to have.

Of course, this will not tell what the equilibrium exchange rate is going to be and how to reach it, but it may help in stabilizing the current exchange rate. To put it another way: *arbitrage is not equilibrium*. More precisely, arbitrage assumes an individual behavior which compares the advantages of alternative solutions; in that sense, it refers to *individual equilibrium*. But it is free from any assumption about *market equilibrium*: arbitrage does not necessarily imply that individual behaviors will be compatible in a market-clearing way. It is therefore worthwhile to understand how arbitrage works, and how the range in which it operates can be narrowed, thanks to an appropriate institutional framework. This does not mean that one is able to demonstrate the existence of an equilibrating mechanism on the exchange market. But it will provide a robust result upon which to elaborate further.

The second reason is practical. Exchange rates and prices of gold and silver in bullion or in coins have been published regularly as early as the end of the seventeenth century, and series of them over a long historical time can therefore be constructed.[12] Estimates of quantities are far more controversial. A famous example is the magnitude of the flows of American gold and silver in the sixteenth and seventeenth centuries. The estimates made by Hamilton (1934) have greatly influenced the understanding of inflation in Europe for that period. But today they are no longer considered as reliable (see Morineau 1985), and a previous work of ours on sixteenth-century Europe shows that another explanation of inflation, based entirely on price relations, may be given (Boyer-Xambeu, Deleplace and Gillard 1994a). The situation is not much better for the nineteenth century, and authors like Juglar and Nogaro frequently complain that the statistics are not reliable. Then if a model is built to fit the data – which is the purpose of historical economics – it is better to start with relations which deal with the least unsatisfactory ones – prices.

Gold points and silver points

As noted above, gold was not then the only metal arbitraged with bills of exchange. This means that silver points existed along with gold points.[13] This may look strange because, if coined silver was legal tender in France, it was no longer the case in England, legally since 1816, in fact already before then. But, as soon as arbitrage relies on market prices, any commodity may be arbitraged with bills of exchange. The one which is effectively chosen is the "cheapest exportable" one,[14] and one would expect, the one which is likely to vary less in market price, in order to avoid adverse movements during the time of remittance. The criterion of being cheaply exportable favors gold and silver as well.[15] Being monetized has an influence on the low variability of the market price of a commodity, but, although it was no longer monetized in England, silver was not disfavored according to the second criterion. The reason for that is the existence of a specific monetary regime in France: bimetallism.[16]

The existence of silver points along with gold points means that the exchange is constrained not only by a gold snake, but also by a silver one. If the cost of remittance of both metals is roughly the same, these two snakes either coincide (when the pars of gold and silver are equal), or interweave (when they differ). In the last case, exchange is constrained by an import point of one metal and an export point of the other, what we shall call a "bimetallic snake." It should be observed that this result not only still holds when the remittance costs on gold and silver differ, provided their difference is not greater than the spread between the gold-par and the silver-par (this point is demonstrated in the appendix), but also is the consequence of arbitrage between bills of exchange and two metals (instead of one), and not of the existence of a bimetallic monetary regime in one of the countries involved. Such a regime may contribute to the stabilization of the prices of the two metals, and help making them both eligible for arbitrage. Then it influences the properties of the bimetallic snake (which we shall study below), but it should not be confused with the existence of the latter.

To sum up, our methodology emphasizes the constraint imposed on the exchange rate by a "snake" rather than by a "tunnel," the institutional rules defining monetary and exchange regimes rather than automatic equilibrating mechanisms, price relations rather than quantity adjustments, the interplay of gold and silver rather than the pre-eminence of gold. This kind of approach seems to us appropriate to deal with the two questions raised by the observed stability of the pound between 1821 and 1873: Was bimetallism superior to monometallism? Was the existence of institutional monetary rules superior to the unconstrained working of markets?

THE "BIMETALLIC SNAKE"

Gold-par, silver-par and "bimetallic par": a simple model

As mentioned above, arbitrage between bills of exchange and two metals, gold and silver, means that the movements of the exchange in London are constrained by a "snake," whose "skin" "above" (at the import point) and "below" (at the export point) is made of one metal or the other. Whenever the silver-par differs from the gold-par, the snake is bimetallic. In London, which quotes Paris certain, the import point is the bullion point first reached by the exchange rate when it changes upward, and the export point is the bullion point first reached by it when it changes downward, which is necessarily in a different metal from the first one when the remittance costs are equal. The relevance of the bimetallic snake, as opposed to a gold one, depends on how often (and how much) the two pars diverge.

Let us call T the exchange rate of the pound against the franc:

(1) 1£ = T F

The par of exchange is defined as the exchange rate T = R which equalizes the prices of one and the same weight unit of pure metal in both places, expressed in the same unit of account.[17] Consider the following abbreviations: L = London, P = Paris, B = bullion, G = gold, S = silver, I = import, X = export, RB = bullion ratio (market par). If one unit weight of bullion has a market price LB in London (expressed in £) and PB in Paris (expressed in F), the market par RB is as follows:

PB = LB . RB

therefore

(2) RB = PB / LB

Let RGB and RSB be the market pars of gold and silver. The market prices of gold in London and Paris are LGB and PGB, and the prices of silver LSB and PSB. By definition,

(3) RGB = PGB / LGB

(4) RSB = PSB / LSB

If LGS and PGS are the relative prices of gold in terms of silver in the London and Paris markets, then by definition

(5) LGS = LGB / LSB

(6) PGS = PGB / PSB

A comparison of equations (3) to (6) shows that if PGS is higher than, equal to or lower than LGS, a corollary is that RGB is (respectively) higher than, equal to or lower than RSB. So it is equivalent to reason in terms of the difference between the relative prices of gold and silver in Paris and London or in terms of the difference between the market pars of gold and silver.

The possibility of divergence between the two bullion pars creates a problem, because the concept of par (or parity) traditionally fulfils two roles in exchange rate determination. One has a *microeconomic* character: as the ratio of bullion prices in two places, it allows one to compute how much one will receive (or pay) in foreign money when remitting one unit of domestic money worth of metal. Subtracting (adding) the remittance cost gives the export (import) bullion point. The other role has a *macroeconomic* character: the comparison between the exchange rate and the par allows one to compute how much the domestic currency is appreciated (or depreciated) in respect to a foreign currency, and therefore to infer a positive (or negative) balance of payments.

As early as 1767, James Steuart had observed that the state of the English balance could be wrongly assessed if the exchange rate of the pound in French *livres* was compared to the legal, instead of the commercial, par.[18] In contrast with the legal par, the market par is subject to variations. Therefore, at a moment of time, the exchange may look favorable or not according to the way it is assessed. Moreover, a decline in the exchange rate through time, while the legal par remains unchanged, does not necessarily mean a deterioration of the balance of payments: if the market par decreases more, it might well correspond to a situation where the exchange rate moves from below to above par, revealing a balance becoming positive.

Things are still more complex when there is not one bullion par, but two, which generally diverge. Whereas the microeconomic behavior of the dealer in bullion is only slightly affected (the dealer just has to extend the calculations to additional bullion points), the macroeconomic conclusion of the economist becomes perplexing, because the exchange may look unfavorable when assessed with the market gold-par and favorable when assessed with the market silver-par (or the other way round). If each metal acts as the specific standard for each currency (as between the pound and the mark), or if both metals act as standards for one currency (as between the pound and the franc), there is no reason to prefer one diagnosis to the other. A typical example is given in Table 5.2 by the sub-period 1796–1820. During the two other sub-periods, the choice of the criterion appears of secondary importance in the average, but may lead to opposite conclusions at particular moments.

Logic then suggests that one ascertain the state of the exchange by comparing the exchange rate and the "bimetallic par," i.e., the simple arithmetic average of the market gold-par and silver-par. The reason is that the concepts of "bimetallic par" and "bimetallic snake" complement each other, as may easily be seen.

Let us denote by 2r the difference between the pars of gold and silver, in percentage of the simple arithmetic average of them. In other terms, r is the percentage deviation of the gold-par from the bimetallic par

(7) $r = (RGB - RSB) / (RGB + RSB)$

with r positive or negative according to whether the gold-par is higher or lower than the silver-par.

Let c be the cost of remittance of metal between London and Paris, in percentage of the par.[19] If IG and XG are, respectively, the import and export gold points in London, while IS and XS are the silver points, we obtain the following definitions

(8) $IG = RGB\ (1 + c)$

(9) $IS = RSB\ (1 + c)$

(10) $XG = RGB\ (1 - c)$

(11) $XS = RSB\ (1 - c)$

Let us denote by RGSB the bimetallic par, equal to (RGB + RSB) / 2. By definition of r, we have

(12) $RGSB = RGB / (1 + r)$

As stated above, the relevant import and export points depend on the sign of r. Let us denote by SC the simple arithmetic average of them: SC is the "spinal column" of the bimetallic snake, equidistant from the "skin above" (at the import point), made of one metal, and the "skin below" (at the export point), made of the other metal. Apart from the case when $r = 0$ (then RGB = RSB = RGSB = SC), two cases may appear:

- the gold-par is higher than the silver-par ($r > 0$): the bullion points are IS and XG. Combining equations (7),(9), and (10) gives $SC = RGB\ (1 - rc) / (1 + r)$.
- the gold-par is lower than the silver-par ($r < 0$): the bullion points are IG and XS. Combining equations (7), (8), and (11) gives $SC = RGB\ (1 + rc) / (1 + r)$.

As a consequence, we obtain

(13) $SC = RGB\ (1 - |r|c) / (1 + r)$

From equations (12) and (13) we derive

(14) $(SC - RGSB) / RGSB = - |r|c$

Since r and c are close to zero, RGSB and SC may be considered as identical: the bimetallic par is the spinal column of the bimetallic snake.[20] The exchange rate being constrained between limits around SC, it is then logical to assess whether it is favorable by comparing it to SC, therefore to the bimetallic par.

Thus the bimetallic par is the appropriate macroeconomic tool to ascertain the state of the exchange when arbitrage involves gold and silver. But one should note that it does not play the microeconomic role which is also usually attributed to the par by bullion dealers. The reason is simple. By definition, the spread between the gold import (or export) point and the gold-par is equal to a parameter: the cost of remittance of the metal. The bimetallic par is equidistant from the relevant import and export points but, as we shall see in the next section, this distance is variable and generally smaller than the remittance cost. Hence it is not possible to compute the relevant bullion points by adding a parameter to the bimetallic par; the arbitrageurs must still calculate the gold points and the silver ones separately. It is probably the reason why this notion does not show up in exchange manuals. The bimetallic par is then a purely macroeconomic tool, which may be used by the economist to give transparency to the state of the exchange, but is useless for the dealer in bills and in bullion.

The historical relevance of the bimetallic par

Table 5.2 compares the average values of the different pars for various periods.

One striking feature of Table 5.2 is the exact equality between the gold-par and the silver-par (hence the bimetallic par), when computed on the average from 1821 to 1873. But this conclusion is misleading, because positive and negative spreads may cancel out. When considered in absolute terms, the spread 2 | r | appears to be above six in a thousand during this period, i.e., far more than the minimum quoted variation of the exchange

Table 5.2 Average values of the pars and the exchange rate of the pound in francs, 1796–1873

	1796–1820	*1821–73*	*1821–46*	*1847–73*
Exchange rate in London (LPV)	22.97	25.45	25.58	25.31
Gold-par (RGB)	23.18	25.37	25.43	25.30
Silver-par (RSB)	22.54	25.37	25.47	25.25
Bimetallic par (RGSB)	22.86	25.37	25.45	25.275
2 | r |	3.00	0.64	0.60	0.67
r	+1.40	+0.02	−0.08	+0.10

Notes: 2 | r |: percentage spread between gold-par and silver-par (in absolute terms)
r: percentage deviation of the gold-par from the bimetallic par

rate (two in a thousand until 1850, one after). There lies an additional reason to use observations twice a week, as illustrated by Figures 5.4 and 5.5 (where a surface in grey above the horizontal axis denotes that the gold-par is higher than the bimetallic par, and the reverse if the grey surface is below).

From 1796 to 1820, the gold-par is nearly always above the silver-par, the deviation (r) from the bimetallic par going as high as 5 per cent. From 1821 to 1850, both cases are observed, with the deviation most often below 0.5 per cent. From 1851 to 1866, the gold-par is again the higher, sometimes deviating by 1 per cent. From 1867 on, the silver-par is the higher, by a lower margin. In conclusion, cases when the two pars diverge significantly are by far the most frequent ones. To reverse a famous phrase, the gold-points theory – considered as stressing the exclusive role of gold – might well be 93 per cent false.

The usefulness of the bimetallic par as a macroeconomic tool may be illustrated for two sub-periods by Figures 5.6 and 5.7, which show the premium (or discount) on the exchange rate of the pound against the franc in London (LPV), when computed in respect to the bimetallic par (p_b), the legal gold-par (p_L), or the market gold-par (p_m). Between 1802 and 1820,

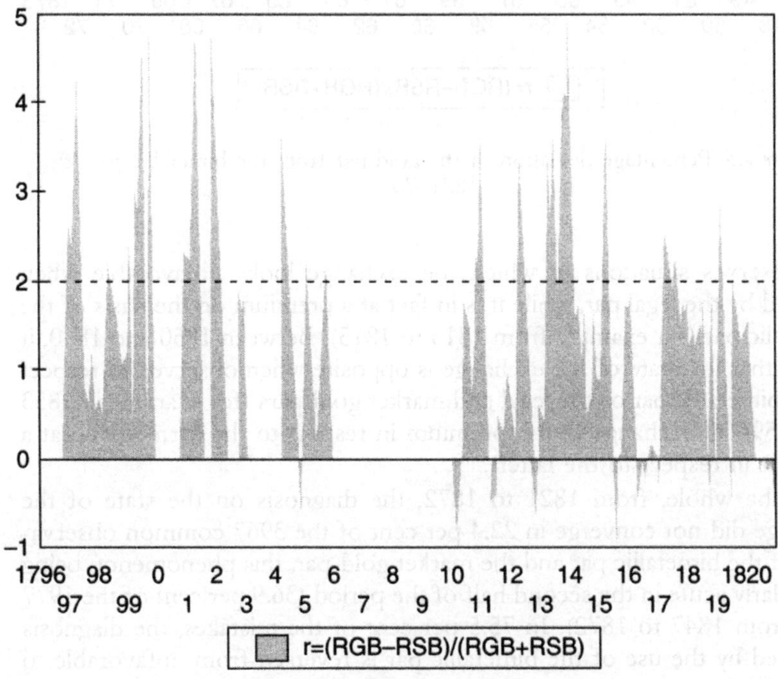

Figure 5.4 Percentage deviation of the gold-par from the bimetallic par (r), 1796–1820

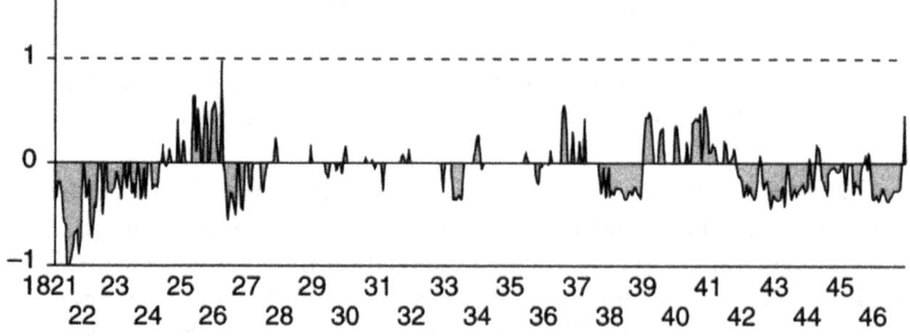

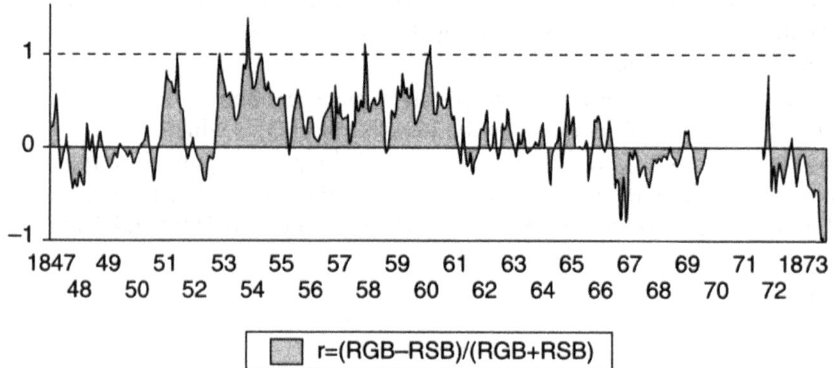

Figure 5.5 Percentage deviation of the gold-par from the bimetallic par (r), 1821–73

one observes situations in which the exchange looks unfavorable when assessed by the legal par, while it is in fact at a premium on the basis of the bimetallic par (for example from 1813 to 1815). Between 1850 and 1860, it occurs that the state of the exchange is opposite when observed in respect to the bimetallic par or the legal and market gold-pars (for example in 1853 and 1859–60, exchange is at a premium in respect to the former, and at a discount in respect to the latter).

On the whole, from 1821 to 1872, the diagnosis on the state of the exchange did not converge in 22.4 per cent of the 3967 common observations of the bimetallic par and the market gold-par, this phenomenon being particularly acute in the second half of the period (36.9 per cent of the 1977 cases from 1847 to 1872). In 75.5 per cent of the mistakes, the diagnosis corrected by the use of the bimetallic par is reversed from unfavorable to favorable. As a consequence, reference to the bimetallic par reinforces the fact that the exchange has been favorable to the pound during most of the period after the resumption of convertibility: from 1821 to 1872, it is so in

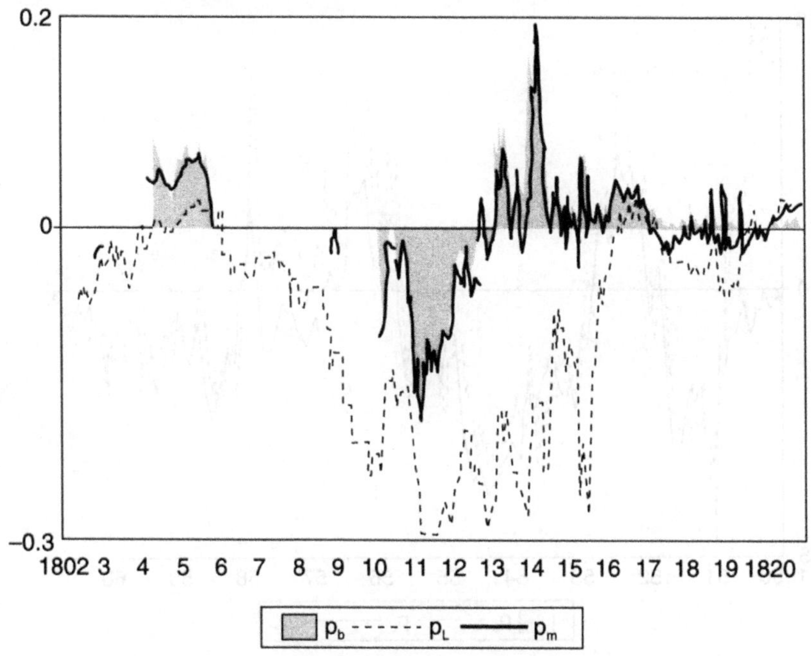

Figure 5.6 Premium (or discount) on the exchange rate of the pound in francs in London, in percentage of the bimetallic par (p_b), the legal gold-par (p_L), or the market gold-par (p_m), 1802–20

80.7 per cent of the cases when assessed by the bimetallic par, and only 69.3 per cent when assessed by the market gold-par.[21]

Now we may go back to the original question: What was the contribution of the bimetallic snake to the stabilization of the exchange? As noted above, the movements of the exchange rate depend in statics on the width of the snake, and in dynamics on its undulations. Lets us examine these two factors successively.

THE STABILIZATION OF THE EXCHANGE IN STATICS

The width of the bimetallic snake

As seen above, the specific feature of the bimetallic snake is that the import and export points are of different metals, because they are computed on the basis of different pars. Hence the spread between them is not a fixed magnitude equal to twice the cost of remittance, as in a monometallic snake. It depends on this cost *and* on the spread between the pars.

Let us denote by 2s the relative width of the bimetallic snake, i.e., the

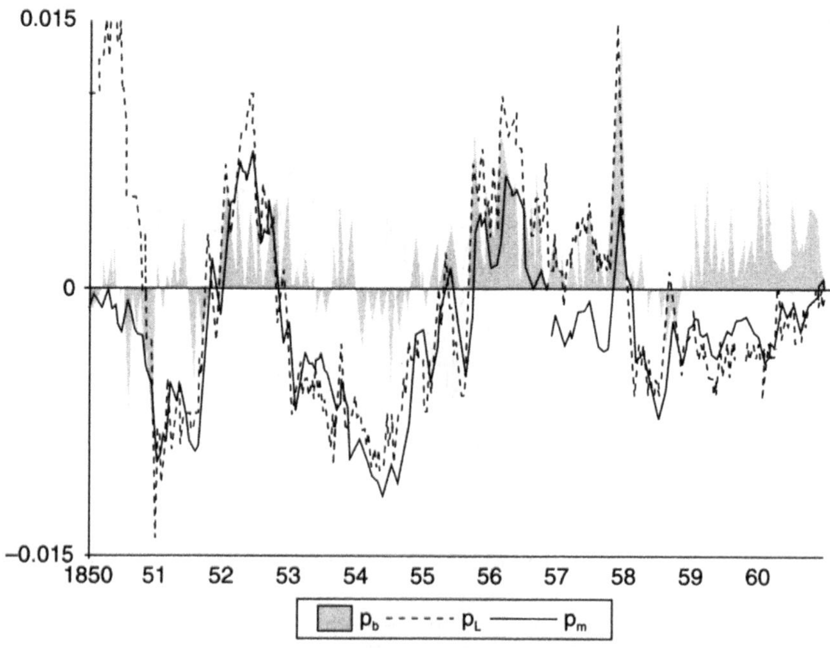

Figure 5.7 Premium (or discount) on the exchange rate of the pound in francs in London, in percentage of the bimetallic par (p_b), the legal gold-par (p_L), or the market gold-par (p_m), 1850–60

spread between the relevant bullion points, as a percentage of the bimetallic par. In other words, s is the percentage margin by which the exchange rate may deviate from the bimetallic par, if arbitrage is fully operative. By definition[22]

(15) $s = (1 / 2)$ [Min (IG, IS) − Max (XG,XS)] /RGSB

Again, two cases have to be distinguished:

- the gold-par is higher than the silver-par ($r > 0$): the bullion points are IS and XG. Combining equations (7), (9), (10), and (12) gives $s = c - r$.
- the gold-par is lower than the silver-par ($r < 0$): the bullion points are IG and XS. Combining equations (7), (8), (11), and (12) gives $s = c + r$.

As a consequence, we obtain:

(16) $s = c - |r|$

The bimetallic snake allows a margin of variation (s) of the exchange rate around the (bimetallic) par, which is a linear function of half the spread (r) between the gold-par and the silver-par (i.e., of the deviation of the gold-par from the bimetallic par). This function is increasing with the negative values of r and decreasing with its positive values, as illustrated in Figure 5.8.

The possibility of arbitrage between bills and two metals will therefore shrink the margin of variation of the exchange rate (as compared with arbitrage involving only one metal), provided that the pars on these metals differ: this shrinkage is in percentage equal to $(c - s)/c$. For a given level (c) of the remittance cost of the metals, the greater the spread between the pars, the smaller the margin of variation of the exchange rate will be. This margin is maximum when the two pars are equal; the bimetallic snake then coincides with the gold one, and the cost of remittance is the only factor limiting the movements of the exchange at a moment of time. The margin goes to zero when the spread between the pars is equal to the cost of remittance both ways (2c); the bimetallic snake is then reduced to a single line: at a moment of time, arbitrage prevents the exchange from moving at all.[23]

It should be observed that this stabilizing property of the bimetallic snake in statics has nothing to do with the flexibility often attributed by advocates of bimetallism to the availability of appropriate quantities of two metals instead of one.[24] In accordance with the methodological principles stated above, this bimetallic effect is simply a consequence of price relations produced by arbitrage between bills and two metals, and requires no assumption about their quantity flows.

We have seen in Table 5.2 that the gold-par and the silver-par diverged most of the time between 1796 and 1873. Equation (16) suggests that

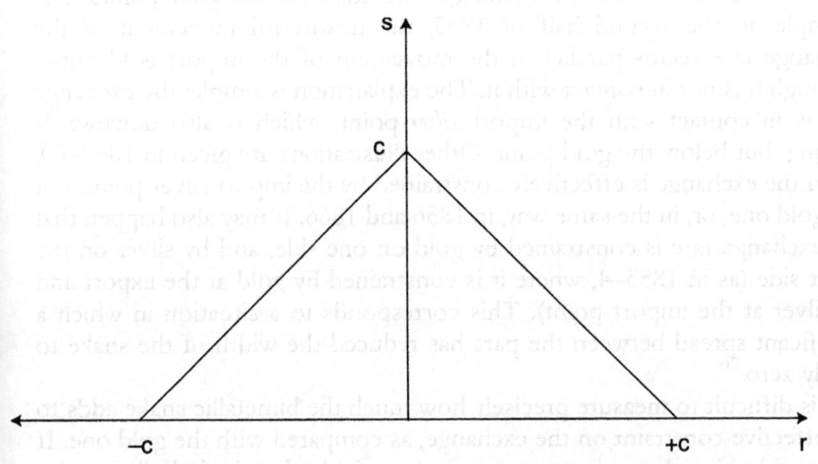

Figure 5.8 Relation between the margin of variation of the exchange rate around the bimetallic par (s) and half the spread between the gold-par and the silver-par (r)

historical observation will then show that the bimetallic snake has provoked a significant shrinkage in the margin of variation of the exchange rate, as compared with the traditional margin given by the parametric cost of remittance of gold. On the average, this shrinkage is equal to 30.0 per cent from 1821 to 1873, with a striking difference between the first half-period (25.1 per cent) and the second (35.0 per cent).[25] Figure 5.9 illustrates the evolution of this shrinking effect (in grey on the graph), which appears to be significant as early as the end of the 1830s.

The gold snake and the bimetallic snake

As noted above, gold points computed on the basis of the legal gold-par do not appear to constrain the exchange rate significantly, because they are frequently violated. A gold snake performs better, as shown by Figures 5.10, 5.12, and 5.14. However, the absence of violations does not mean that the constraint imposed on the exchange rate by the bullion points was always effective: the exchange rate may move inside the snake without hitting one of its "skins", hence without triggering arbitrage. Therefore it may be interesting to focus on the situations in which the exchange rate is in the neighborhood of a bullion point. The fact that the bimetallic snake is narrower than the gold snake suggests that there should be more cases like that with it, hence that the constraint imposed by the bullion points should appear effective more often. The reason is simply that a silver point may be close to the exchange rate, whereas a gold point is not.

The comparison of Figures 5.11, 5.13, and 5.15, where the bimetallic snake has been represented, with Figures 5.10, 5.12, and 5.14 illustrates that it constrains more the exchange rate than do the gold points. For example, in the second half of 1833, the downward movement of the exchange rate seems parallel to the movement of the import gold point, although it is not in contact with it. The explanation is simple: the exchange rate is in contact with the import *silver* point, which is also downward-sloping, but below the gold point. Other illustrations are given in 1839–40, when the exchange is effectively constrained by the import silver point, not the gold one, or, in the same way, in 1856 and 1866. It may also happen that the exchange rate is constrained by gold on one side, and by silver on the other side (as in 1853–4, where it is constrained by gold at the export and by silver at the import point). This corresponds to a situation in which a significant spread between the pars has reduced the width of the snake to nearly zero.[26]

It is difficult to measure precisely how much the bimetallic snake adds to the effective constraint on the exchange, as compared with the gold one. If we consider that the exchange rate is in the neighborhood of a bullion point when the difference between them is less than or equal to 5 *centimes* (two in a thousand, i.e., the minimum variation in the quotation of the exchange rate

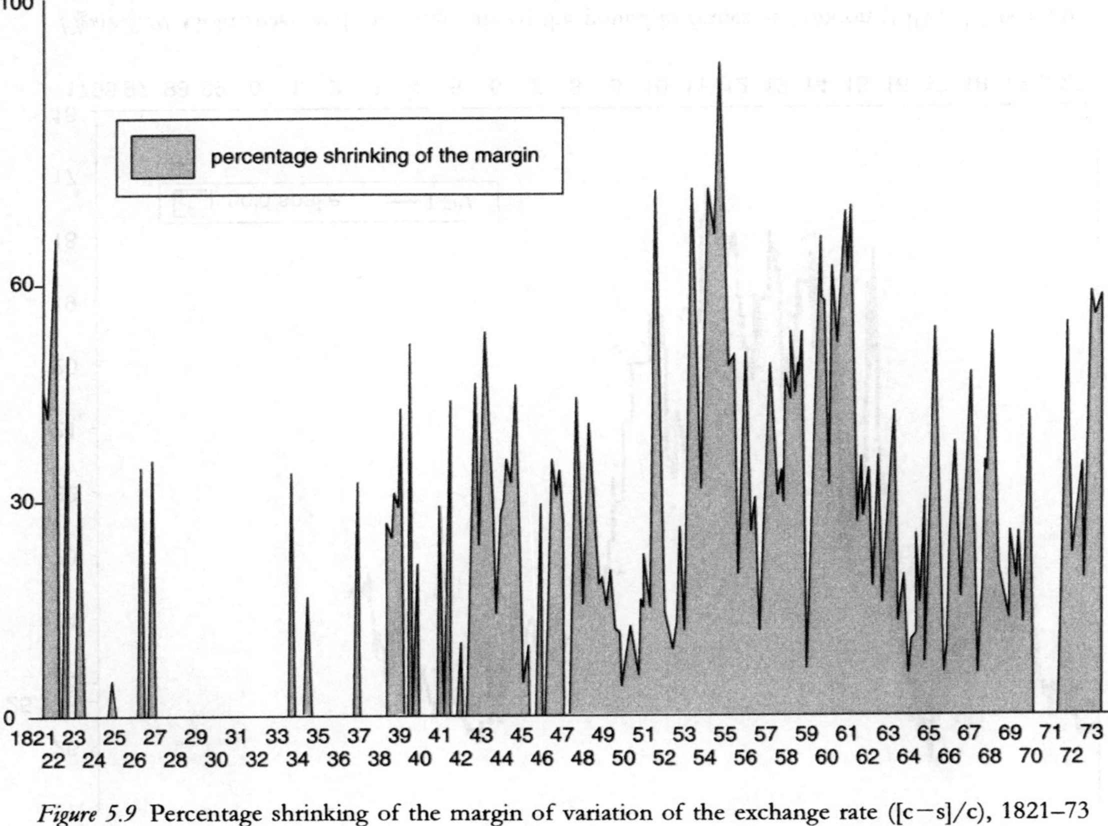

Figure 5.9 Percentage shrinking of the margin of variation of the exchange rate ([c−s]/c), 1821–73

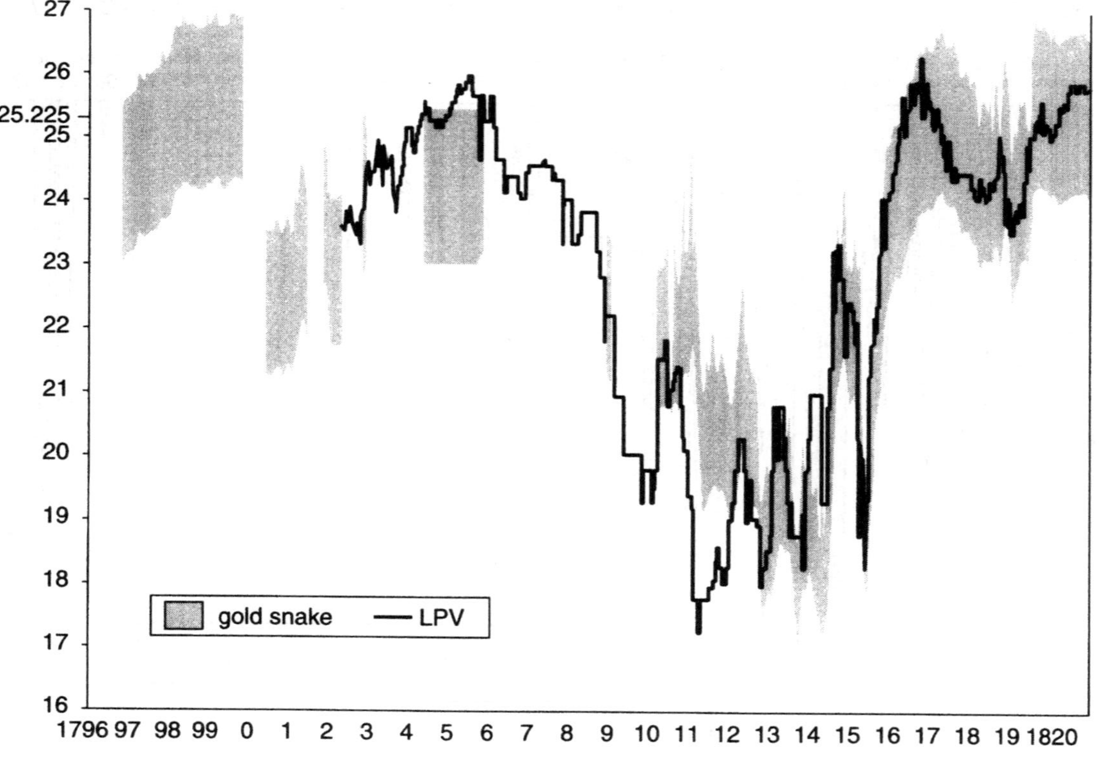

Figure 5.10 Gold snake and exchange rate of the pound in francs in London (LPV), 1796–1820

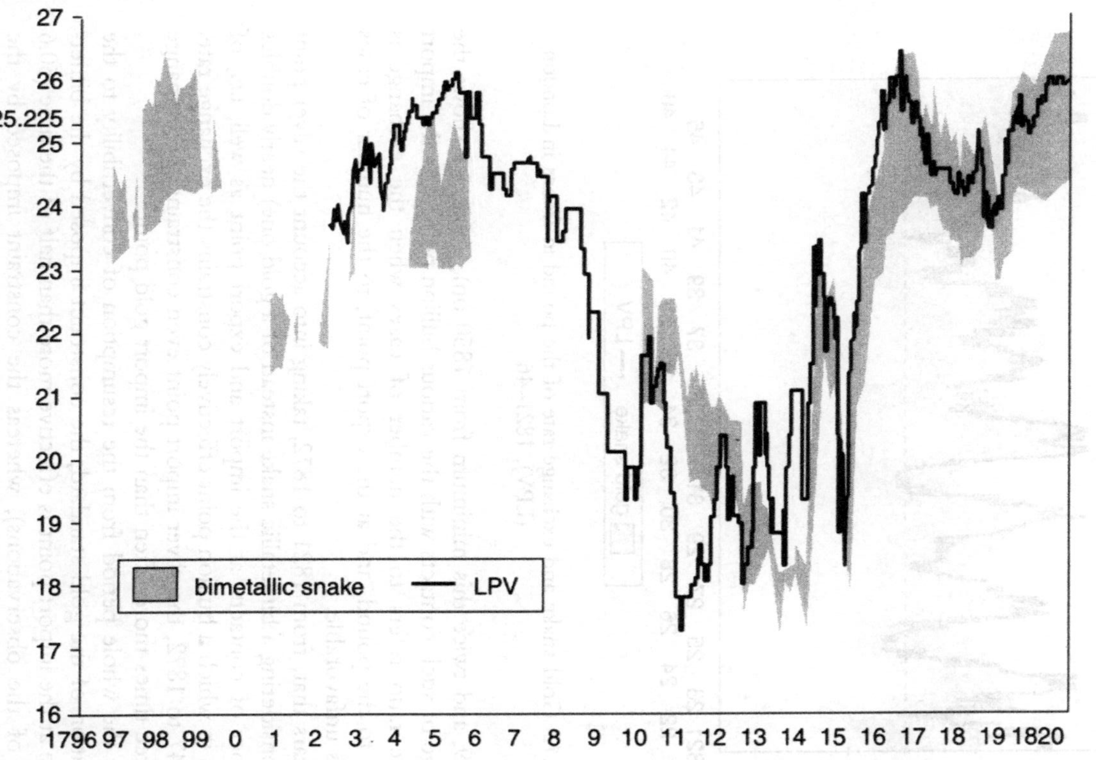

Figure 5.11 Bimetallic snake and exchange rate of the pound in francs in London (LPV), 1796–1820

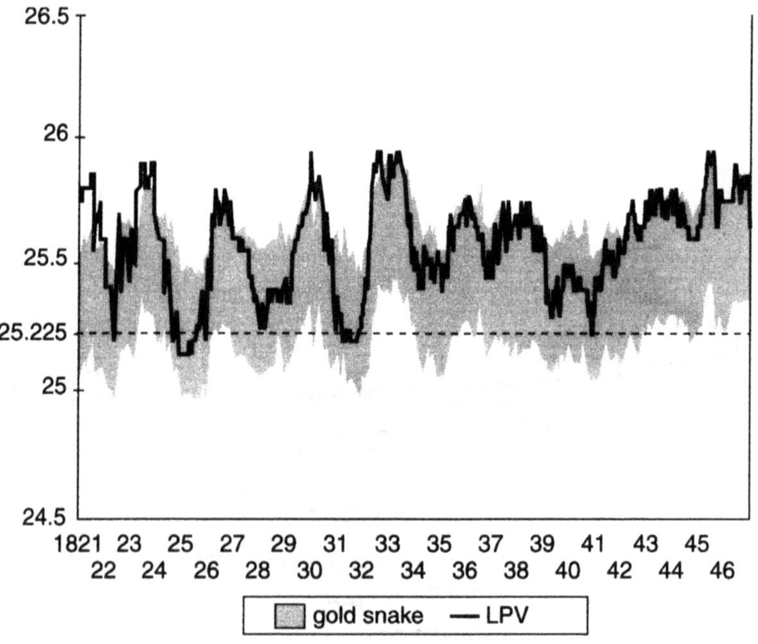

Figure 5.12 Gold snake and exchange rate of the pound in francs in London (LPV), 1821–46

until 1849, and twice this minimum from 1850 on), Table 5.3 shows the percentage of such contacts with the various bullion points. At the import point, the ratio refers to the number of cases when the exchange is favorable to the pound, and at the export point, to the number of cases when it is unfavorable.

It appears that, from 1821 to 1872, taking into account the silver point (hence considering a bimetallic snake instead of a gold one) nearly doubles the number of contacts, at the import and export point as well, i.e., of situations in which a bullion point effectively constrains the exchange rate. From 1847 to 1872, the silver import point even constrains the exchange nearly three times more often than the import gold point.

During the whole period from the resumption of convertibility to the generalization of the gold standard, the constraint imposed by the bimetallic snake at the import point is effective more than half of the time (50.6 per cent of the observations), whereas the constraint imposed by the import gold point would show up only a little more than one-fourth of the time (28.0 per cent of the cases). The effectiveness of that bimetallic constraint may be observed in the two half-periods as well, whereas the import gold point is only poorly effective during the second one. At the export point, the constraint imposed by the bimetallic snake is effective

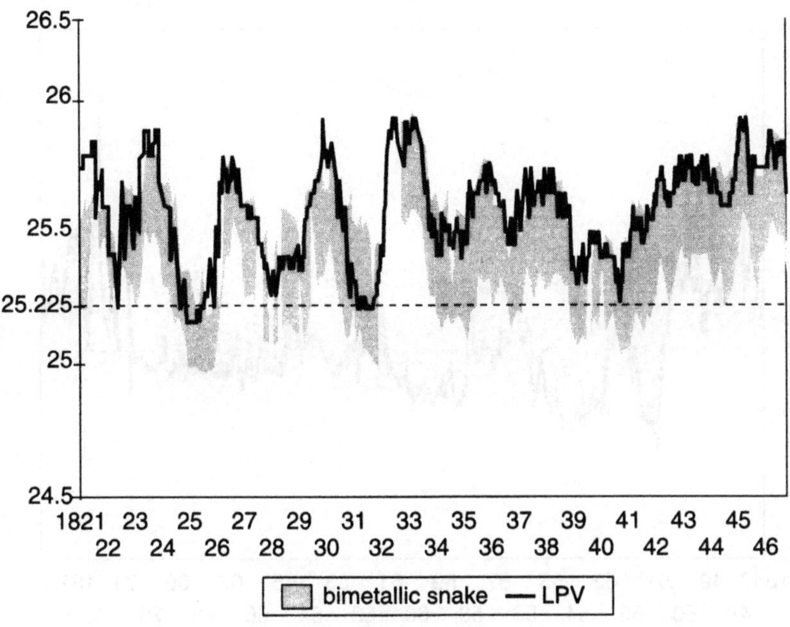

Figure 5.13 Bimetallic snake and exchange rate of the pound in francs in London (LPV), 1821–46

Table 5.3 Percentage of contacts between the exchange rate and the bullion points, 1821–72

	1821–46	*1847–72*	*1821–72*
LPV and IG alone	34.0	12.3	24.9
LPV and IS alone	13.9	34.8	22.6
LPV and IG and IS	3.2	3.0	3.1
LPV and XG alone	1.4	10.7	9.3
LPV and XS alone	10.5	7.2	7.7
LPV and XG and XS	0.0	0.0	0.0
Contacts at the import point	51.1	50.1	50.6
Contacts at the export point	11.9	17.9	17.0
Total contacts	48.6	39.7	42.7

only one-sixth of the time (and less than one-tenth for the export gold point). The reason is probably that the general tendency of the pound to appreciate (we have seen that the exchange was favorable in 80.7 per cent of the cases) rendered less necessary at the export point the bouncing back effects produced by the bullion points.

These observations can be made with greater detail in Figures 5.16 to 5.19. Because a contact between the exchange rate and a bullion point

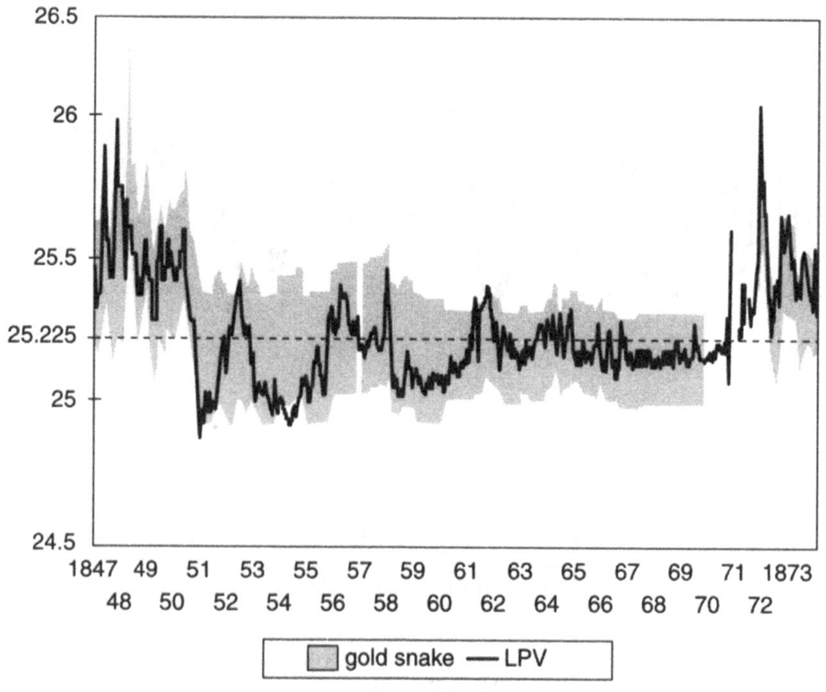

Figure 5.14 Gold snake and exchange rate of the pound in francs in London (LPV), 1847–73

triggers flows of one or the other metal, the frequency of occurrence of these flows in London may be derived. Whereas outflows occur during limited periods of time (e.g., gold in 1851 and 1854 and silver in 1867), inflows are more frequent, mainly of gold from 1822 to 1833, alternatively of gold and silver from 1834 to 1847, and mainly of silver from 1851 to 1870.

During the period of suspension of convertibility, the impact of the bullion points appears only from 1813 on, but, here again, the bimetallic snake seems more effective than the gold snake. Conclusions are less reliable, however, because of the problems mentioned above and connected with the estimation of the remittance costs.

In conclusion, on the stabilization of the exchange produced by the bimetallic snake in statics, one may say that theoretical analysis and historical observation do not contradict the role traditionally ascribed to bullion points as constraining the exchange rate. On the contrary, this role is strengthened: where the gold points may appear to operate only a weak constraint, the bimetallic snake constrains the exchange effectively when

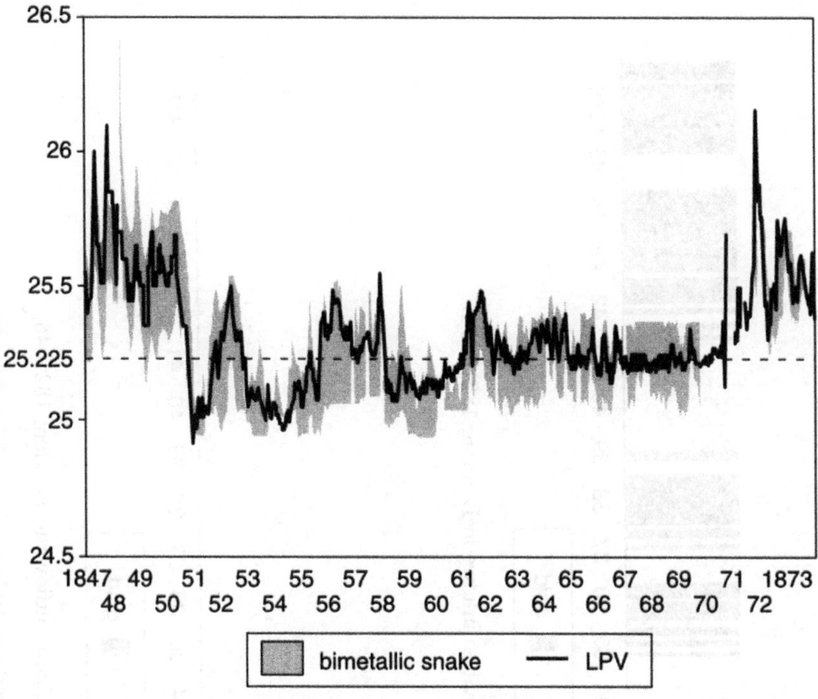

Figure 5.15 Bimetallic snake and exchange rate of the pound in francs in London (LPV), 1847–73

the exchange rate has a definite tendency (upwards, in the case of the pound against the franc).

THE STABILIZATION OF THE EXCHANGE IN DYNAMICS

We have just seen that, from 1821 to 1872, silver effectively constrained the exchange rate as often as gold. More precisely, gold and silver did constrain the exchange, but not at the same time: it was either one metal or the other. This is the reason why the bimetallic snake stabilized the exchange more than the gold one: it was always the lower of the two import points and the higher of the two export points which were limiting. This means that the import point was sometimes gold and sometimes silver, and the same (but symmetrically) for the export point. Each time the sign of the spread between the gold-par and the silver-par changes, a "switching" of metals occurs. For example, when r changes from a positive to a negative value, IS switches to IG and XG to XS; at the "switching point" (r = 0), both metals are equally limiting the exchange rate.

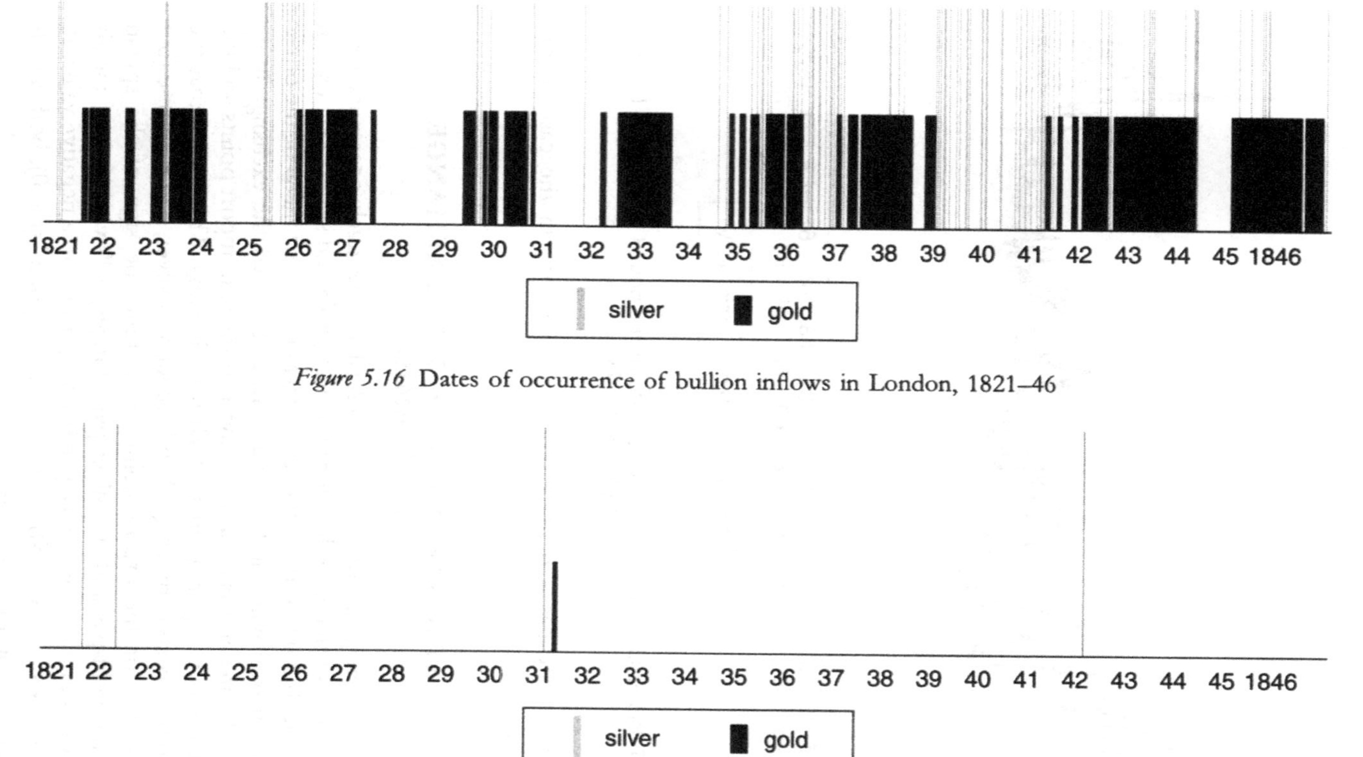

Figure 5.16 Dates of occurrence of bullion inflows in London, 1821–46

Figure 5.17 Dates of occurrence of bullion outflows in London, 1821–46

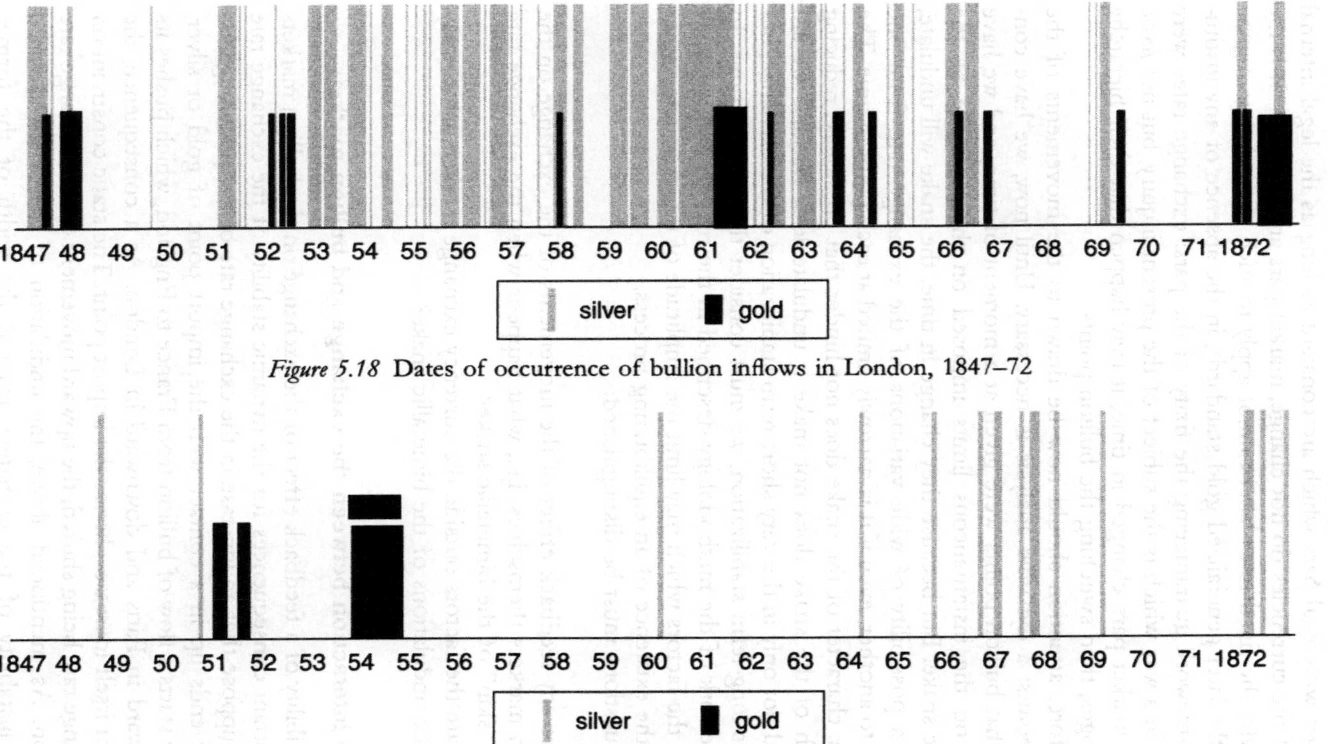

Figure 5.18 Dates of occurrence of bullion inflows in London, 1847–72

Figure 5.19 Dates of occurrence of bullion outflows in London, 1847–72

The existence of switching of metals is the consequence of the fact that, in contrast with legal pars which are constant as long as the legal internal values of the currencies do not change, market pars are not fixed. It is the reason why the fixed rates-label cannot apply to such an exchange regime (and to the later generalized gold standard), in the absence of any institutional framework guaranteeing the fixity of the pars: exchange rates were *stabilized* in a way which is the subject of the present inquiry, but not *fixed*. Because market pars changed in time, it may happen that their hierarchy also changes, then switching the bullion points.

Therefore, attention should now be drawn to the movements of the bullion points: a dynamic analysis is necessary. Until now, we have considered that bullion points were given at a moment of time, and we have focused on the instantaneous limits imposed on the exchange by the bimetallic snake. But because they change in time, the snake will undulate, opening a possibility of wide variations of the exchange rate from one moment to another, even if it is narrowly limited at each point in time. The bimetallic character of the snake does not hinder that possibility: reducing the width of the snake does not make it undulate less. Because we are interested not only in the very short-term stabilization of the exchange, but also in its long-term stabilization, we must consider these undulations. In the framework of the methodology described in the first section, we shall focus on the factors which may limit the amplitude of the exchange, rather than on the existence of an equilibrating process.

Two questions must be distinguished:

- Is there any feedback effect of the movements of the exchange on the bullion markets themselves, i.e., what happens when the exchange rate hits a "skin" of the bimetallic snake?
- What are the factors outside the currency exchange markets which may limit the undulations of the bimetallic snake?

The interaction between the exchange and bullion markets

The possibility of a feedback effect of the exchange on the bullion markets has important consequences for the dynamic stability of the exchange rate itself.[27] Suppose that an increase in the exchange rate of the pound against the franc ends up in a contact with the import point of gold or silver. Arbitrage starts a flow of bullion from France to England, which pushes its price upward in Paris and downward in London. As a consequence, the market par itself increases, hence the import point. The static constraint on the exchange rate being shifted, the upward movement of the exchange rate will go on. As mentioned above, the undulation of the snake allows a dynamic instability of the exchange, even if the width of the former imposes a static constraint on the latter. The new feature is that here the undulation of the snake is provoked by the movement of the exchange itself (feedback effect).

Does this situation occur frequently in the period under observation (1821–72)? We shall here concentrate on the contacts at the import point which, as seen in Table 5.3 and Figures 5.16 to 5.19, are the more frequent ones. A first approximation to the phenomenon may be given by the proportion of cases in which the relevant import point shifts upward after a contact with the exchange rate. It is obvious that such shifts may be attributed to factors other than arbitrage between the exchange and bullion markets; then this proportion gives the maximum magnitude of the phenomenon. It is 15 per cent, which means that in 85 per cent at least of the cases, the level of the relevant import point is not affected by the arbitrages triggered by a contact with the exchange rate.[28] The undulations of the bimetallic snake may be considered as independent of the exchange.[29]

The situation in which the relevant import point shifts upward after it has been hit by a *rising* exchange rate is more interesting, because it corresponds to the process described above; 19 per cent of contacts occur after an increase in the exchange rate, and among them one-fourth (24.9 per cent) is followed by an increase in the import point (as against 15 per cent of increase after no change in the exchange rate and 4 per cent after a decline). As a consequence, one cannot rule out the possibility of a cumulative process, in which a rise in the exchange rate goes on without limit, because arbitrage pushes upward the alleged limit provided by the import point. However, in three-fourth of the cases, the snake resists an exchange shock, and, on the whole, during the period a favorable exchange leads to a deformation of its above limit in less than 3 per cent of the cases.

These observations suggest that no substantial dynamic feedback of the exchange on the bullion markets was operating. The assumption of an asymmetry between the exchange rate and the bullion points – the latter constraining the former, but being seldom affected by it – appears quite robust. This confirms the initial rejection (see pp. 112–13) of a general equilibrium approach applied to the relation between the exchange and bullion markets, and validates the static analysis of the stabilization of the exchange by the bimetallic snake. But, as we shall see in the conclusion, this does not call for considering the bullion points as exogenous; other factors must be introduced to understand their movements.

In the static part of the analysis, we have shown that a bimetallic snake was more stabilizing than a monometallic one. In dynamics, the relevant bullion points appear to resist the movements of the exchange; but is this so because of the bimetallic character of the snake or because of the relative inelasticity of bullion prices in response to arbitrage with the exchange market? The above observations cannot answer this question, because they focus on the shift in the *relevant* import point, i.e., the lower of the gold and silver points. This encompasses two possible situations. In the first, the same bullion import point remains operative; the crucial feature is then the inelasticity of the bullion prices. In the second, a shift in the import point sets off a switching to the import point in the other metal, which has become the lower one; the resulting resistance is then the consequence of the bimetallic character of the snake.

The switching of metals is therefore important not only because it narrows the width of the snake in response to autonomous movements in the bullion markets, but also because it allows the implementation of a new constraint when a movement of the exchange has shifted the former one. For example, arbitrage with gold triggered by a rising exchange rate may push the gold import point upward, but by definition it does not affect the silver import point, which then substitutes for the defaulting gold in the role of the constraint. This may not be enough to stop the rise in the exchange rate, but it can delay it, the more so each bullion price separately is inelastic to this rise.

The coexistence of two metals in the limitation of the exchange may contribute to its dynamic stabilization in another way. Insofar as the undulations of the bimetallic snake are independent of the exchange, one should examine which other factors influence them. Much attention has been devoted to quantity aspects: the availability of two metals instead of one is supposed to have given more flexibility to the operation of the bullion points mechanism (see Friedman 1990a, and, in another way, Flandreau 1995, 1997). Another factor which involves the use of one or two metals is the monetary regime implemented in each of the countries.

The influence of the domestic monetary regimes

If in both countries involved in exchange, the market prices of gold and silver are stabilized (fixed and nearly equal purchase and sale prices being imposed by each Central Bank for each metal), the market pars themselves will be stabilized. The movements of the exchange rate will then be mainly limited by the width of the snake, and it will suffice to fix the spread between the legal monetary ratios (the official domestic ratios between gold and silver prices) according to the remittance cost of the metals to reduce the range of variation of the exchange as much as is desirable. Such stabilization will evidently require cooperation between the two states (to the exclusion of competitive modifications of monetary ratios), which might come up against problems of "prisoner's dilemma." But, barring such problems, the adoption of a bimetallic standard in each of the countries is more conducive to the stabilization of exchange than that of a monometallic standard in one and/or the other country.

The exchange regime ruling between France and England from 1821 to 1870 does not fulfil this condition: England was on a gold standard, while France was bimetallic. From the 1830s, the market price of gold was constrained in both countries by a legal bracket, and according to our computations it varied less in England than in France. The market price of silver was also legally constrained in France, but not in England, where it went through significant variations (of greater magnitude than those of the exchange).[30]

One might thus expect the silver par to be more variable than the gold par, the hierarchy between the two pars being itself liable to change. It is then normal to observe zones in which the snake differed both in its skins and in its width. In particular, the period after 1850 shows an exogenous increase in the demand of silver to settle some bilateral balances of England (with China, India, the United States, etc.), which pushes up the price of silver in London.[31] The price of gold in terms of silver becomes lower in London than in Paris (at least until mid-1861), and correlatively, the silver-par becomes lower than the gold-par. This corresponds on Figure 5.15 with the long "silver above/gold below" phase from late 1850 to mid-1863. The upward pressure on the silver price in London had another consequence. It resulted in an increase in the positive spread between the pars of gold and silver and thus in reducing the width of the snake. This phenomenon is also observed during the period between 1851 and 1861.

CONCLUSION

This chapter fits in with the revival of the debate concerning the contribution of bimetallism to the stabilization of the system of international payments in the nineteenth century.[32]

As is often the case in monetary subjects, this question of bimetallism is usually approached in terms of *quantities*: the advantages and disadvantages of this regime are considered on the basis of the positive or negative results that the production of monetary metals may have in supplying the market with either one or two metals. The question of the *price* of the monetary standard, and hence of the internal value of money, is then broached only in terms of the influence of the quantity of one or the other metal on its price. The possible superiority of bimetallism over monometallism thus stems from its greater capacity to regulate the flux of metals in accordance with needs, and therefore to lend more stability to the internal value of money.

Characteristic of the approach upheld in this chapter is the postulate that certain rules embedded in a monetary regime render the prices of monetary metals independent of the quantities in which they are produced. This postulate is not arbitrary, and it can at least claim to be backed by David Ricardo[33] and by a French tradition represented in particular by Bertrand Nogaro. What it mainly drives at is that the analysis of a metallic monetary and exchange regime must lay greater stress on the formation of the prices (rather than the quantities) of monetary metals, especially in their relation with those other prices, the exchange rates.

The importance of the concept of the bimetallic snake for the analysis of exchange regimes will have to be pointed out in two ways in the future. On the one hand, the presence of two monetary metals requires the integration of a monometallic silver pole in the configuration already consisting of a monometallic gold pole (London) and a bimetallic pole (Paris). On the other hand, the uncertainties regarding the construction of the bimetallic snake during the period of the revolutionary and Napoleonic wars must not lead to the hasty conclusion that it did not exist in the eighteenth century. A further analysis of the bimetallic snake will then require collecting the pre-1795 series for Paris, Amsterdam, and Hamburg.

These extensions will consequently raise at least three questions. First, did the functioning between 1821 and 1873 of a tripolar regime (London, Paris, Hamburg) significantly differ from that of the bipolar regime presented here? In particular, does it give a better insight in the movements of the bullion points? Second, does the functioning of the bimetallic snake require the presence of a bimetallic pole (such as Paris in the nineteenth century), or can it be the result of the conjunction between different monometallic poles? And third, did the regulation of the prices of monetary metals and of the exchange rates in the eighteenth century depend more on the conditions of public minting of specie or on banking rules other than the convertibility of Bank of England notes, those concerning, for example, the Bank of Amsterdam?

But our analysis also calls for follow-ups for the comprehension of nineteenth-century monetary history. If the year 1873 marks the disappearance of an exchange regime built around the bimetallic snake (which justifies the fact that our study stops at this date), the periodization internal to this regime is still unclear. Apparently, the trend of the exchange rate of the pound against the franc is downward-sloping from 1821 to 1872, but a closer analysis reveals that the trend is upward-sloping from 1821 to 1847 and from 1851 to 1872, these two periods being separated by a sharp drop of the exchange around the middle of the century. This observation raises two questions. First, what was the influence of the bimetallic snake on this trend? Our computations have shown that from 1821 to 1872, the exchange rate was favorable to the pound in 80 per cent of the cases, and among them, half corresponded to a contact with an import bullion point. Our dynamic analysis then suggests that the resistance of the bimetallic snake to an exchange shock limited the long-run tendency of the pound to appreciate against the franc. But this has to be confirmed. Second, what was the influence of the bimetallic snake on the exchange drop of 1847–51? It is tempting to connect this break with the well-known changes in the relative productions of gold and silver. But the important phenomenon appears to be not so much the exogenous and general decline in the relative price of gold in terms of silver, as it is the more rapid decline in London than in Paris, for reasons concerning national monetary regimes.

Moreover, Figures 5.18 and 5.19 show that during the months of sharpest drop in the exchange rate (from May to December 1850), it is not in contact with either skin of the snake, as one would expect if the latter pushed the former downward.

A more detailed analysis of the history of this exchange regime is then necessary. This chapter has focused on relations between the exchange rate market and the gold and silver markets. We have deliberately omitted relations between these markets and the international money market provided by the link between "short" exchange and "long" exchange. The exchange "at usance" (generally three months) offered an opportunity of money investment, and its comparison with short exchange exhibits an "implicit interest rate" (Eagly and Smith 1976), the movements of which are representative of the evolution of the international money market. The observations presented in Boyer-Xambeu, Deleplace, and Gillard (1995) show that the periodization of the exchange regime has to take this evolution into account. A more elaborate model of this regime requires a formalization of the relations between the various exchange rates, the domestic prices of gold and silver, and the domestic interest rates. One may show that the markets for short exchange and long exchange between two countries are constrained by an "interest rate parity", so that it is indifferent for the arbitrageur to make short or long exchange, not considering risk.[34] Our current work is aimed in this direction as well.

APPENDIX
THE CASE OF DIFFERENT COSTS OF REMITTANCE ON THE METALS

The condition for the existence of a bimetallic snake

When the cost of remittance is the same for both metals, the snake is bimetallic whenever the pars of gold and silver diverge. This is no longer true when this cost differs according to the metal. Even with different pars, the import point in one metal may be higher than the import point in the other metal, and the export point lower; then this metal does not constrain the exchange rate, and the snake is monometallic (in the other metal).

Under which condition is the snake bimetallic? The definition of r being unaffected, equation (7) may be rewritten in the following way:

(7′) $RSB = RGB\ (1 - r)\ /\ (1 + r)$

The costs of remittance of gold and silver being denoted cg and cs, equations (8) to (11) become

(8′) $IG = RGB\ (1 + cg)$

(9′) $IS = RSB\ (1 + cs)$

(10′) $XG = RGB\ (1 - cg)$

(11′) $XS = RSB\ (1 - cs)$

It should be recalled that the magnitude of cg, cs, and r is not greater than 1 per cent, which allows one to neglect second-order terms in the calculations.

Two cases must be distinguished:

* $r > 0$: the snake is bimetallic if $IS < IG$ and $XG > XS$

Neglecting second-order terms, the first condition is fulfilled if, combining (7′), (8′), and (9′), $cs - cg < 2r$. The second condition is fulfilled if, combining (7′), (10′), and (11′), $cs - cg > -2r$.

* $r < 0$: the snake is bimetallic if $IG < IS$ and $XS > XG$.

The first condition is fulfilled if $cs - cg > 2r$, and the second one if $cs - cg < -2r$.

In summary, the snake is bimetallic if and only if:

(I) $2 \mid r \mid > cs - cg > -2 \mid r \mid$

The necessary and sufficient condition for the snake to be bimetallic is that the magnitude of the difference between the higher and the lower costs of remittance be smaller than the magnitude of the difference between the pars.

The bimetallic par

The analysis in the text has shown that the exchange rate of the pound is (is not) favorable to England when it is above (below) the spinal column SC of the bimetallic snake, which is equidistant from the relevant import and export points. When the cost of remittance is the same for both metals, equation (14) shows that SC may be considered as identical to RGSB, the simple arithmetic average of the two bullion pars. This is no longer true when the costs of remittance are different. Let us call d the rate of deviation of SC from RGSB, with $d = (SC - RGSB) / RGSB$. Combining (7′), (9′), and (10′) when $r > 0$, or (7′), (8′), and (11′) when $r < 0$, gives

* $r > 0$: $d = [(cs - cg) - \mid r \mid (cs + cg)] / 2$

* $r < 0$: $d = [-(cs - cg) - \mid r \mid (cs + cg)] / 2$

Neglecting second-order terms, the deviation of SC from RGSB is equal to half the difference between the costs of remittance. Using the relation between RGSB and RGB (the gold par) given by equation (12) gives the following formula of the bimetallic par to be used to assess the state of the exchange:

(II) $SC = RGB\,(1 + d) / (1 + r)$

with $d = (cs - cg) / 2$ if $r > 0$ and $d = -(cs - cg) / 2$ if $r < 0$.

The width of the bimetallic snake

SC now has to substitute for RGSB in equation (15) to define the value of s, which is half the relative width of the bimetallic snake (the spread between the relevant bullion points). Neglecting second-order terms, the usual combinations of equations (7′) to (11′) give

* $r > 0$: $s = [-2r + (cs + cg)] / [2 + (cs - cg)]$
* $r < 0$: $s = [2r + (cs + cg)] / [2 - (cs - cg)]$

The comparison between s, cs and cg is shown by the following inequalities (which neglect second-order terms):

$s < cs$ if and only if $cs - cg > -2\,|\,r\,|$

$s < cg$ if and only if $cs - cg < 2\,|\,r\,|$

The necessary and sufficient condition for s to be smaller than cs and cg is therefore

(III) $2\,|\,r\,| > cs - cg > -2\,|\,r\,|$

Condition (III) is identical to condition (I) of existence of the bimetallic snake. We may then draw the following conclusion: whenever the snake is bimetallic, i.e., if the magnitude of the difference between the higher and the lower costs of remittance is smaller than the magnitude of the difference between the pars, the margin of variation of the exchange rate allowed by the bimetallic snake is smaller than the one allowed by the gold points or the silver points.

NOTES

1 This chapter is a much altered version of our contribution to the Bank of Italy workshop on "Monetary Standards and Exchange Rates," held in Perugia on March 24–25, 1995. We wish to thank all the participants to this workshop for their comments, particularly L. Conte, C. Giannini, M.C. Marcuzzo, R. Mundell, L.H. Officer, and A. Rosselli.

2 See, for example, the collected contributions in Bordo and Schwartz (1984) and Eichengreen (1985).

3 For a presentation of the conceptual framework to which the present study belongs, see Boyer-Xambeu, Deleplace, and Gillard (1990).

4 Bi-weekly data have been taken from *Course of the Exchange* for London, *Cours authentique* and *Cours de la banque et de la bourse* for Paris. All the data used in this chapter are published and discussed in Boyer-Xambeu, Deleplace, and Gillard

(1995), to which we refer for all methodological aspects (data sources, indicators, homogeneity of series, etc.).

5 We tested the weak form of market efficiency (in the sense of Fama 1970), by applying ARMA procedures to the log transforms of the quotations of the pound against the franc in London. We distinguished the period May 11, 1802 to April 27, 1821, with inconvertibility and wide movements of the exchange, from the period May 1, 1821 to September 16, 1870, with convertibility and smaller variations. The best ARMA models are respectively (2, 0) and (6, 0) ones, with estimated coefficients of (0.0115, 0.0047) and (−0.005, 0.071, −0.042, −0.029, −0.053, −0.078). A "random walk" can then be excluded, but no other conclusion on the process may be derived.

6 We shall return to this point in the conclusion.

7 Observing violations of the gold points obviously depends on the level assumed for the cost of remittance of the metal. This cost is usually considered as being 1 per cent in the middle of the nineteenth century, but higher at the beginning and lower later on. For example, according to sources quoted by Marcuzzo and Rosselli (1991: 94), it varied from 4 to 7 per cent between London and Hamburg in 1809 and 1810, and was still higher with other places, such as Paris. Conversely, technical improvements were introduced in the 1850s, which lowered the cost, but at a date and in a proportion that are difficult to ascertain. Thus the assumption of the values of this parameter during definite periods is necessarily arbitrary. We have chosen periods which correspond to important changes in the institutional framework (such as 1821, for the resumption of the convertibility of the Bank of England note) and/or in the profile of the exchange rate (such as 1860, when its fluctuations are more and more dampening). As for the level of the cost, we selected 5 per cent before 1821. From 1821 on, we used the following procedure: assuming that the bimetallic snake studied below effectively constrained the exchange, we have retained the maximum margin of variation it allowed (denoted as s in the third section) which encompasses two standard deviations of a Gaussian distribution (i.e., approximately 95 per cent of the observed data). The result happens to be 1 per cent for 1821–59 and 0.7 per cent for 1860–73. The latter figure corresponds to estimates given separately by the banker De Vareux and the dealer Sourdis for a French monetary inquiry in 1865 (Conseil supérieur de l'agriculture, du commerce et de l'industrie 1865: 24th session: 32, 21st session: 73). Seyd (1868: 375) mentions 0.5 per cent, plus interest and commissions. For other estimates, see Flandreau (1995).

8 For a later period, Morgenstern observed that the statistical analysis of rates of exchange in Europe during the last quarter of the nineteenth century showed violations of the margins of variation assumed by the gold-points doctrine in about 10 per cent of the cases. See Morgenstern (1959: 252–62).

9 Arbitrage on the rate of exchange markets have been particularly studied by Eagly and Smith (1976), Officer (1983, 1985), and Schubert (1989), albeit with monthly data. For a critical analysis of these studies, see Boyer-Xambeu, Deleplace, and Gillard (1992).

10 See Deleplace (1994a, 1994b, 1996).

11 For more details, see Boyer-Xambeu, Deleplace, and Gillard (1995). The choice of 1821 as dividing line is explained by the resumption of the convertibility of the Bank of England note (May 1). The choice of 1847 is arbitrary; it allows us to divide the period 1821–73 in two nearly equal sub-periods.

12 See for example MacCusker (1978), Schneider, Schwarzer, and Zellfelder (1994). In Boyer-Xambeu, Deleplace, and Gillard (1995), we list the publica-

tions available for London and Paris, and we provide for each city on Tuesday and Friday two exchange rates of the pound in francs (one short and one long) and the market prices of gold and silver bullion, homogenized on the periods 1717–1873 for London and 1796–1873 for Paris.

13 See Flandreau (1995, 1997).

14 Marcuzzo and Rosselli (1991: 128).

15 The differential against silver in the cost of transportation as a consequence of the difference in weight is compensated by the differential in the other costs (insurance, testing, packaging, etc.). See Seyd (1868: 375). Twenty years before, Tooke considered that the cost of transportation on silver was five per thousand higher than on gold. See Tooke (1848, vol. 3: 212).

16 On the stabilization of the price of silver in the London market, see Boyer-Xambeu, Deleplace, and Gillard (1994b).

17 The calculation of the par thus presupposes a homogeneity of the units of weight and fineness used in both countries. See Gillard (1991).

18 "This, I hope, will be sufficient to satisfy any body that there is a mistake in ascribing the high price paid for the French crown in the London exchange to a wrong balance upon the trade of England with France" (Steuart 1767, vol. 3: 431).

19 Or, more precisely, the magnitude by which the cost of remittance of the metal exceeds the one of the bill. For the sake of simplicity, this cost is supposed identical for both metals and in both directions (when costs of gold and silver differ, see the appendix). Moreover, the divergence between the two pars is not large enough to introduce a bias when c is computed as the percentage of each one.

20 For c equal to 1 per cent and r at its maximum value, equal to c (see pp. 122–3), the divergence between both magnitudes is equal to 0.1 in a thousand, i.e., one-tenth of the smallest quoted variation of the exchange rate.

21 The figure is about the same when computed on all the observations of the market gold-par (even when the market silver-par, hence the bimetallic par, is not available): the exchange then appears favorable in 69.4 per cent of the 5111 cases. Differentiation of the two halves of the period shows that the correction of the diagnosis in favor of the pound is more pronounced in the second half than in the first, precisely when the exchange assessed by the market gold-par appears more often *unfavorable*. The figures are 93.8 per cent instead of 89.5 per cent from 1821 to 1846, and 67.5 per cent instead of 49.1 per cent from 1847 to 1872. The bimetallic snake ceasing to be operative during 1873, we have excluded this year from the computation. For the sub-periods not represented on Figures 5.6 and 5.7, i.e., 1821–49 and 1861–73, see Boyer-Xambeu, Deleplace, and Gillard (1995), graphs 49 and 50.

22 Rigorously, the margin of deviation is the same above and below if it is computed in percentage of the simple arithmetic average of the relevant bullion points (the "spinal column"). Equation (15) is then subject to the above approximation that rc is close to 0. This is the consequence of applying the same *percentage* cost of remittance to a gold-par and a silver-par which differ. When r is not zero, the "spinal column" of the bimetallic snake and the bimetallic par rigorously coincide only if the same absolute cost of remittance is applied to both pars.

23 Figures 5.11, 5.13, and 5.15 show rare cases in which one import bullion point is below the export point in the other metal. Such reversals occur when r is greater than c. But arbitrage between gold and silver normally eliminates such a situation. See Boyer-Xambeu, Deleplace, and Gillard (1994b).

24 For the late-nineteenth-century debates on this question, see Gillard (1991), and for a retrospective conversion to bimetallism on the basis of quantity effects, Friedman (1990a). To our knowledge, the result encapsulated in equation (16) never appeared in the old or recent literature on bimetallism, although it is the plain consequence of the divergence between the gold-par and the silver-par. We have published this equation in Boyer-Xambeu, Deleplace, and Gillard (1994b: 1163).

25 We have not computed this shrinkage for the period 1796–1820, in which the bimetallic snake appears to be often poorly operative, because the evaluation of the cost of remittance is not reliable. See Figure 5.11.

26 More detailed graphs are provided in Boyer-Xambeu, Deleplace, and Gillard (1994b), for the periods 1837–40 and 1852–5, and in Boyer-Xambeu, Deleplace, and Gillard (1995), for each decade from 1820 to 1870.

27 On the importance of this question in the monetary debates of the first half of the nineteenth century, see Deleplace (1994b).

28 In the less numerous (193 instead of 1801) cases of contacts between the exchange rate and the relevant export point, the proportion in which the latter shifts downward is still smaller: 8.8 per cent.

29 The level of the relevant import point does not change in 72 per cent of the cases after contact, as compared with 76 per cent when no contact has occurred.

30 From 1821 to 1869, the maximum variations of the price of silver amounted to 3 per cent in France and 6 per cent in England; for gold they amounted to 1 per cent in France and 0.1 per cent in England. See Boyer-Xambeu, Deleplace, and Gillard (1995).

31 See Nogaro (1908). This author offers an original interpretation for the relative scarcity of silver in comparison with gold from the mid-nineteenth century on, which is usually attributed to the rise in the production of gold caused by the discovery of new mines in California.

32 See Chen (1972), Garber (1986), Bordo (1987), Friedman (1990a, 1990b), Gillard (1991), Flandreau (1995, 1997), Boyer-Xambeu, Deleplace, and Gillard (1994b, 1995).

33 See Deleplace (1994a, 1994b).

34 See Boyer-Xambeu (1997).

REFERENCES

Andreades, A. (1904) *Histoire de la Banque d'Angleterre*, Paris: Arthur Rousseau.

Arnaune, F.A. (1894) *La Monnaie, le crédit et le change*, Paris: Alcan.

Ashton, T.S. (1955) *An Economic History of England: The 18th Century*, London: Methuen.

——(1959) *Economic Fluctuations in England, 1700–1800*, Oxford: Clarendon Press.

Ashton, T.S. and Sayers, R. (eds) (1953), *Papers in English Monetary History*, Oxford: Clarendon Press.

Bagehot, W. (1873) *Lombard Street: A Description of the Money Market*, London: Henry S. King.

Baxter, S.B. (1976) Comment on Paper by Eagly and Smith, *Journal of Economic History* 1.

Bonneville, P.F. (1806) *Traité des monnaies*, Paris: Duminil-Lesueur.

Bordo, M.D. (1987) Bimetallism, in J. Eatwell, M. Milgate, and P. Newman (eds) *The New Palgrave. A Dictionary of Economics*, London: Macmillan.

Bordo, M.D. and Schwartz, A.J. (eds) (1984) *A Retrospective of the Classical Gold Standard 1821–1931*, Chicago: University of Chicago Press.

Borts, G.H. (1960) Review of Morgenstern (1959), *Journal of the American Statistical Association* 1.

Bouchary, J. (1937) *Le Marché du change à Paris à la fin du XVIIIe siècle*, Paris: Hartman.

Bouvier, J. (1973) *Un siècle de banque française*, Paris: Hachette.

Boyer-Xambeu, M.-T. (1994) Henry Thornton et la "bullion controversy": au-delà des bornes, il n'y a plus de limites, *Revue Economique* 45 (5), September.

——(1997) Spéculation et parité des taux d'intérêt sans change à terme dans la *Théorie des changes étrangers* de G.J. Goschen (1861), *Cahiers d'économie politique* 29, Spring.

Boyer-Xambeu, M.-T., Deleplace, G. and Gillard, L. (1990) Vers une typologie des régimes monétaires, *Cahiers d'Economie Politique* 18, September.

——(1992) A la recherche d'un âge d'or des marchés financiers: intégration et efficience au XVIIIe siècle, *Cahiers d'Economie Politique* 20–1, April.

——(1994a) *Private Money and Public Currencies: The 16th Century Challenge*, Armonk, N.Y.: M.E. Sharpe.

——(1994b) Régimes monétaires, points d'or et "serpent bimétallique" de 1770 à 1870, *Revue Economique* 45 (5), September.

——(1995) *Bimétallisme, taux de change et prix de l'or et de l'argent (1717–1873)*, special issue of *Economies et Sociétés*, série AF, 3–4.

Cameron, R. (ed.) (1970) *Essays in French Economic History*, Homewood, IL: Irwin.

Cannan, E. (1919) *The Paper Pound of 1797–1821: The Bullion Report 8th June 1810*, New York: Kelley Reprints, 1969.

Cartelier, J. (1994) Etalon monétaire et mesure de la valeur: monnayage et systèmes de paiement, *Cahiers d'Economie Politique* 23, April.

Chapman, S.D. (1984) *The Rise of Merchant Banking*, London: Allen and Unwin.

Chen, C. (1972) Bimetallism: Theory and Controversy in Prospective, *History of Political Economy* 1.

Clapham, J. (1944) *The Bank of England: A History*, Cambridge: Cambridge University Press.

Condorcet, N. de (1790–92) *Mémoires et discours sur les monnaies et les finances*, B. Courbis and L. Gillard (eds), Paris: l'Harmattan, 1994.

Conseil supérieur de l'agriculture, du commerce et de l'industrie (1865) *Enquête sur les principes et les faits généraux qui régissent la circulation monétaire et fiduciaire*, Paris: Banque de France, Archives du Secrétariat du Conseil.

Cope, S.R. (1942) The Goldsmids and the Development of the London Money Market during the Napoleonic Wars, *Economica* 9.

Corbaux, F. (1802) *Dictionnaire des arbitrages simples considérés par rapport à la France*, Paris: Cropelet, 2 vols.

Corti, E.C. (1928) *The Rise of the House of Rothschild*, New York: Blue Ribbon Books.

Cottrell, P.L. (1980) *Industrial Finance 1830–1914*, London: Methuen.

Coullet, P.J. and Juglar, C. (eds) (1865) *Extraits des enquêtes parlementaires anglaises sur les questions de banques, de circulation monétaire et de crédit*, Paris: Furne.

Courbis, B. (1994) Etalon et moyen de paiement: la disparition de l'unité de compte dans les premiers écrits de David Ricardo (1809–1811), *Cahiers d'Economie Politique* 23, April.

Courtois, A. (1850) *Traité des opérations de bourse et de change*, Paris: Garnier, 1892.

Craig, J. (1953) *The Mint: A History of London Mint from A.D. 287 to 1948*, Cambridge: Cambridge University Press.

De Cecco, M. (1984) *The International Gold Standard: Money and Empire*, London: Frances Pinter, 2nd edn.

——(1987) Gold Standard, in J. Eatwell, M. Milgate, and P. Newman (eds) *The New Palgrave. A Dictionary of Economics*, London: Macmillan.

Deleplace, G. (1994a) Les différents usages de l'étalon monétaire, *Cahiers d'Economie Politique* 23, April.

——(1994b) Aux origines de la pensée monétaire moderne, *Revue Economique* 45 (5), September.

——(1996) Does Circulation Need a Monetary Standard?, in G. Deleplace and E.J. Nell (eds) *Money in Motion: The Post-Keynesian and Circulation Approaches*, London: Macmillan.

Diatkine, S. (1994) A propos de la position de Ricardo concernant la liberté d'émission de la monnaie, *Cahiers d'Economie Politique* 23, April.

Dickson, P.G.M. (1967) *The Financial Revolution in England, 1688–1756*, London: Macmillan.

Duboeuf, F. (1994) Le problème de l'unité de compte dans les écrits monétaires de Ricardo, *Cahiers d'Economie Politique* 23, April.

Duffy, I.P.H. (1982) The Discount Policy of the Bank of England during the Suspension of Cash Payments, 1797–1821, *Economic History Review* 35.

Dutot, C. (1738) *Réflexions politiques sur les finances et le commerce*, The Hague: Prevost.

Eagly, R.V. and Kerry Smith, V. (1976) Domestic and International Integration of the London Money Market, *Journal of Economic History* 1.

Eichengreen, B. (ed.) (1985) *The Gold Standard in Theory and History*, New York: Methuen.

Einzig, P. (1937) *The Theory of Forward Exchange*, London: Macmillan.

——(1962) *The History of Foreign Exchange*, London: Macmillan.

Fama, E. (1970) Efficient Capital Markets: A Review of Theory and Empirical Work, *Journal of Finance* 25, May.

Feaveryear, A. (1931) *The Pound Sterling: A History of English Money*, Oxford: Clarendon Press.

Fetter, F.W. (1965) *Development of British Monetary Orthodoxy (1797–1875)*, Cambridge, MA: Harvard University Press.

Flandreau, M. (1995) *L'Or du monde. La France et la stabilité du système monétaire international, 1840–1878*, Paris: l'Harmattan.

——(1997) As Good as Gold? Bimetallism in Equilibrium, 1848–1870, in this volume.

Fournier de Flex, E. (1887) Le problème monétaire, *Journal de la Société de Statistique de Paris* March.

Friedman, M. (1990a) Bimetallism Revisited, *Journal of Economic Perspectives*, Fall.

——(1990b) The Crime of 1873, *Journal of Political Economy* 98 (6).

Garber, P.M. (1986) Nominal Contracts in a Bimetallic Standard, *American Economic Review* 76 (5), December.

Gillard, L. (1991) La bataille des régimes monétaires à la fin du XIXe siècle, *Economies et Sociétés*, série AF, 16.

——(1994) Change, métal précieux et conventions monétaires dans L'histoire des prix de Thomas Tooke, *Revue Economique* 45 (5), September.

Goschen, G.J. (1861) *The Theory of Foreign Exchanges*, London: Effingham Wilson.

Hamilton, E.A. (1934) *American Treasure and the Price Revolution in Spain, 1501–1650*, Cambridge, MA: Harvard University Press.

Hawtrey, R.G. (1919) *La Circulation monétaire et le crédit*, Paris: Sirey, 1935.

——(1927) *The Gold Standard in Theory and Practice*, London: Longmans, Green, 5th edn, 1947.

——(1938) *A Century of Bank Rate*, London: Longmans, Green; New York: Kelley Reprints, 1965.

Horsefield, J.K. (1977) The Beginnings of Paper Money in England, *Journal of European Economic History* 6.

Hotoi-Phang (1962) L'étalon-or en France de 1820 à 1860, *Revue d'Economie Politique* 6.

Hume, D. (1752) On Money, in E. Rotwein (ed.) *Writings in Economics*, Edinburgh: Nelson, 1955.

Jastram, R.W. (1977) *The Golden Constant*, New York: Wiley.

Jevons, W.S. (1875) *Money and the Mechanism of Exchange*, London: Kegan Paul.

Juglar, C. (1874) La question monétaire d'après les faits observés en France, en Angleterre, aux Etats-Unis, *Journal de la Société de Statistique de Paris* 8.

——(1876) Du rôle de la monnaie et des lingots, *Journal de la Société de Statistique de Paris* 3.

Keynes, J.M. (1930) *A Treatise on Money: The Applied Theory of Money*, in D.E. Moggridge (ed.) *The Collected Writings of John Maynard Keynes*, London: Macmillan, 1971.

Kindleberger, C.P. (1984) *A Financial History of Western Europe*, 2nd edn, Oxford: Oxford University Press.

King, W.T.C. (1936) *History of the London Discount Market*, London: Routledge.

Laidler, D. (1975) *Essays on Money and Inflation*, Manchester: Manchester University Press.

——(1987) Bullionist Controversy, in J. Eatwell, M. Milgate, and P. Newman (eds) *The New Palgrave. A Dictionary of Economics*, London: Macmillan.

Le Touze, C. (1883) *Traité théorique et pratique du change, des monnaies et des Fonds d'Etat*, Paris: Guillaumin et Cie, 3rd edn.

Levy Leboyer, M. and Bourguignon, F. (1985) *L'Economie française au XIXe siècle. Analyse macro-économique*, Paris: Economica.

McCloskey, D.N. and Zecher, J.R. (1976) How the Gold Standard Worked, in J. Frenkel and H.G. Johnson (eds) *The Monetary Approach to Balance of Payments Theory*, Toronto: University of Toronto Press.

McCusker, J.J. (1978) *Money and Exchange in Europe and America, 1600–1775*, Chapel Hill, NC: University of North Carolina Press.

Manuel des agents de change et des courtiers de commerce (1823), Paris: Decle.

Marcuzzo, M.C. and Rosselli, A. (1987) Profitability in the International Gold Market in the Early History of the Gold Standard, *Economica* 54, August.

——(1991) *Ricardo and the Gold Standard*, London: Macmillan.

——(1994a) The Standard Commodity and the Standard of Money, *Cahiers d'Economie Politique* 23, April.

——(1994b) Ricardo's Theory of Money Matters, *Revue Economique* 45 (5), September.

Marshall, A. (1887) Remedies for Fluctuations of General Prices, *Contemporary Review*, March, in A.C. Pigou (ed.) *Memorials of A. Marshall* (1925) New York: Kelley Reprints, 1966.

Mirowsky, P. (1987) What Do Markets Do? Efficiency Tests of the 18th Century London Market, *Explorations in Economic History* 24 (2).

Morgan, E.V. (1943) *The Theory and Practice of Central Banking, 1797–1913*, New York: Kelley Reprints, 1965.

Morgenstern, O. (1959) *International Financial Transactions and Business Cycles*, Princeton, NJ: Princeton University Press.

Morineau, M. (1985) *Incroyables gazettes et fabuleux métaux. Les Retours des trésors américains d'après les gazettes hollandaises (XVIe–XVIIIe siècles)*, London/Paris: Cambridge University Press/Maison des Sciences de l'Homme.

Neal, L. (1990) *The Rise of Financial Capitalism: International Capital Markets in the Age of Reason*, Cambridge: Cambridge University Press.

Nelkenbrecher, J.C. (1844) *Nouveau Manuel des monnaies*, Paris: Renard.

Nogaro, B. (1908) *L'Expérience bimétalliste du XIXe siècle et la théorie générale de la monnaie*, Paris: Sirey.

Officer, L.H. (1983) Dollar–Sterling Mint Parity and Exchange Rates, *Journal of Economic History* 3.

——(1985) Integration in the American Foreign Exchange Market, *Journal of Economic History* 3.

Parieu, M. de (1866–68) *La Question monétaire*, Paris: Bureaux de la Revue Contemporaine.

Plessis, A. (1982–85) *La Banque de France*, Genève: Droz, 3 vols.

Report from Committee on Bank of England Charter (1832), Dublin: Irish University Press, 1968.

Report from the Select Committee on the High Price of Bullion (1810), New York: Arno Press, 1978.

Ricardo, D. (1810) *The High Price of Bullion, a Proof of the Depreciation of Bank Notes*, in D. Ricardo, *Works and Correspondence*, ed. by P. Sraffa with the collaboration of M.H. Dobb, Cambridge: Cambridge University Press, 1951–73, vol. III.

——(1811) *Reply to Mr Bosanquet's Practical Observations on the Report of the Bullion Committee*, *ibid.*, vol. III.

——(1816) *Proposals for an Economical and Secure Currency*, *ibid.*, vol. IV.

Riley, J.C. (1980) *International Government Finance and Amsterdam Capital Market, 1740–1816*, Cambridge: Cambridge University Press.

Rosier, M. (1994) Etre ou ne pas être smithien en 1804: le cas Lord Peter King, *Revue Economique* 45 (5), September.

Schneider, J., Schwarzer, O., and Zellfelder, F. (1991) *Währungen der Welt. Europäische und Nordamerikanische Devisenkurse, 1777–1914*, Stuttgart: Steiner Verlag, 3 vols.

Schubert, E.S. (1988) Innovations, Debts, and Bubbles: International Integration of Financial Markets in Western Europe, 1688–1720, *Journal of Economic History* 2.

——(1989) Arbitrage in the Foreign Exchange Markets of London and Amsterdam during the 18th Century, *Explorations in Economic History* 26.

Schwartz, A. J. (1987) Banking School, Currency School, Free Banking School, in J. Eatwell, M. Milgate, and P. Newman (eds) *The New Palgrave. A Dictionary of Economics*, London: Macmillan.

Second Report from Secret Committee on Expediency of the Bank Resuming Cash Payments (1819), London: British Parliamentary Papers, 1819, 3.

Seyd, E. (1868) *Bullion and Foreign Exchanges, Theoretically and Practically Considered*, London: Effingham Wilson, Royal Exchange.

Simiand, F. (1912) *La Méthode positive en science économique*, Paris: Alcan.

Soetber, A. (1889) *Matériaux pour faciliter l'intelligence et l'examen des rapports économiques*, Paris: Berger-Levrault.

Sperling, J. (1962) The International Payments Mechanism in the Seventeenth and Eighteenth Centuries, *Economic History Review* 3.

Steuart, J. (1767) *An Inquiry into the Principles of Political Economy*, in J. Steuart (ed.) *The Works, Political, Metaphisical and Chronological of Sir James Steuart* (1805), New York: Kelley Reprints, 1967.

Thompson, W. (1919) *Dictionary of Banking*, London: Pitman and Sons.

Thornton, H. (1802) *An Inquiry into the Nature and Effects of the Paper Credit of Great Britain*, New York: Kelley Reprints, 1978.

——(1811) *Two Speeches of Henry Thornton on the Bullion Report, May 1811*, New York: Kelley Reprints, 1991.
Thuillier, G. (1983) *La Monnaie en France au XIXe siècle*, Genève: Droz.
——(1993) *La Réforme monétaire de l'an XI*, Paris: Comité pour l'Histoire Économique et Financière de la France.
Tooke, T. (1848) *History of Prices*, London: Longman, vol. 3.
Trouiller, A. (1912) *La Lettre de change*, Paris: Recueil Sirey.
Van Dillen, J.G. (ed.) (1934) *History of the Principal Public Banks*, The Hague: Nijhoff.
Viner, J. (1937) *Studies in the Theory of International Trade*, New York: Harper.
White, L.H. (1984) *Free Banking in Britain*, Cambridge: Cambridge University Press.
Wilson, C. (1941) *Anglo-Dutch Commerce and Finance in the Eighteenth Century*, Cambridge: Cambridge University Press.
Wilson, C. and Carter, A. (1960) Dutch Investment in Eighteenth Century England, *Economic History Review* 3.
Yeager, L.B. (1976) *International Monetary Relations: Theory, History and Policy*, New York: Harper and Row.

6

AS GOOD AS GOLD?

Bimetallism in equilibrium, 1850–70[1]

Marc Flandreau

INTRODUCTION

> [C'est la supposition de Jevons] que le système bimétallique est essentiellement un système à étalon alternatif en ce sens qu'il ne laisse jamais qu'un seul métal dans la circulation: tantôt l'or, tantôt l'argent. Or, il est positif que c'est là une erreur. Notre raisonnement a établi et l'expérience montre que le bimétallisme peut être effectif.[2]
>
> (Léon Walras, Théorie Mathématique du Bimétallisme, 1881)

The Ancient Greeks used to tell that humankind had gradually decayed from the almost divine golden race that was unaffected by age to a silver race, physically and morally inferior to the former. Then came the third race, of bronze, the fourth, and the fifth, of iron, the most degenerate one. Economists and historians have an opposite story about the evolution of the world monetary system during the nineteenth century: the classical gold standard gradually emerged from the imperfections of earlier ages which used less precious metals. It is said that the final struggle opposed gold to its main opponent, silver. But gold, being better, eventually triumphed. This chapter is an attempt to re-examine this myth.

Before the 1870s, the various national monetary systems can roughly be divided into three groups.[3] The members of the first group (United Kingdom, Portugal, Turkey, Brazil, Australia, and several British colonies) were on the gold standard. The members of the second (most of the German states, Austria, The Netherlands, Sweden, Norway, Denmark, Mexico, China, India, Japan) were on some form of silver standard. The members of the third (the United States, France, Switzerland, Italy, Belgium) were on a dual standard, often called at the time "double standard," and later known as "bimetallism."[4] In these regimes both gold and silver could be used as monies, were freely coined, and had a fixed legal relative purchasing power.

Until about 1873, the exchange rate between gold and silver on international bullion markets remained remarkably stable (as illustrated in Figure 6.1), modestly fluctuating around a ratio of 15.5. This implied that the exchange rate between gold-standard, silver-standard, and dual-standard

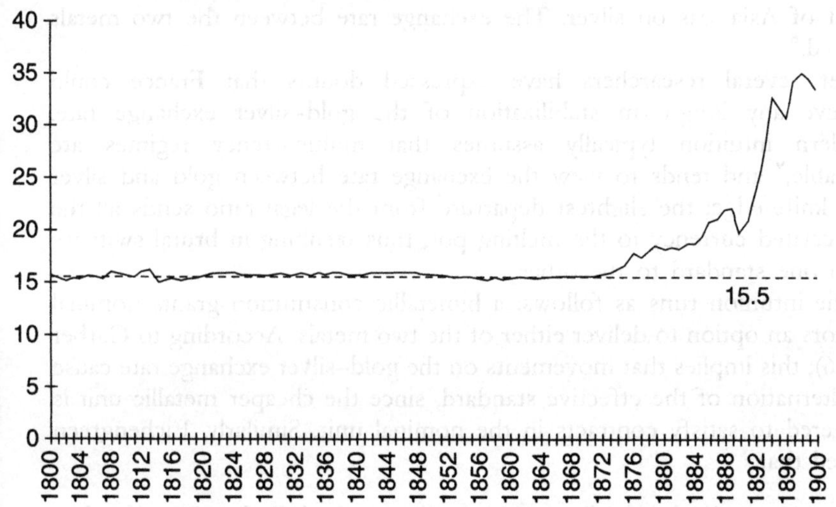

Figure 6.1 London commercial ratio, 1800–1900
Source: Flandreau (1995b: 341)

countries was essentially constant. Hence, the international monetary system of the pre-gold standard era roughly displayed the main characteristics of a national bimetallic regime: throughout the world, gold and silver monies were coined, used, and had an approximately constant relative purchasing power. This suggests calling it an *International Bimetallism*. One should bear in mind, however, that this system was not the result of any kind of international agreement.[5]

One may identify, in the literature to date, two main views on the period prior to 1873. Some scholars argue that the maintenance of the dual standard in France was not irrelevant to the stability of the gold–silver exchange rate. In fact, the 15.5 ratio had been defined in 1803 by the so-called *Loi de Germinal*. According to Yeager,

> the ratio of 15,5 to 1 ruled on world gold and silver markets because of the dominance of France's bimetallic system. . . . Being in effect on both the gold and silver standard at the same time, France was standing ready to deal in the two metals in unlimited quantities and at fixed prices.[6]

Similarly, Friedman (1990b) takes the observed stability of the gold–silver ratio as conclusive evidence that France succeeded in maintaining "a bimetallic standard at a legal ratio of 15.5."[7] Indeed, a proof may be given in the events that took place after 1873, when France decided to limit the coinage of silver: the price of silver collapsed, and the world monetary system split into two parts. Industrialized countries were on gold, while most of Asia was on silver. The exchange rate between the two metals floated.[8]

Yet several researchers have expressed doubts that France could achieve any long-term stabilization of the gold–silver exchange rate. Modern intuition typically assumes that multicurrency regimes are unstable,[9] and tends to view the exchange rate between gold and silver as a knife-edge: the slightest departure from the legal ratio sends all the appreciated currency to the melting pot, thus resulting in brutal switches from one standard to the other.

The intuition runs as follows: a bimetallic constitution grants nominal debtors an option to deliver either of the two metals. According to Garber (1986), this implies that movements on the gold–silver exchange rate cause an alternation of the effective standard, since the cheaper metallic unit is delivered to satisfy contracts in the nominal unit. Similarly, Eichengreen argued that

> France remained officially on a bimetallic standard. By law, [it] offered to convert [its] currency into specified amounts of either gold or silver. In effect it attempted to operate a commodity price stabilization scheme, using reserves of gold and silver as buffer stocks to stabilize the relative prices of two metals. [The] experience illustrates the pitfalls of attempting to use small buffer stocks to stabilize prices in large markets.[10]
>
> (Eichengreen 1985: 4)

Contrary to this latter view, we believe that bimetallism, during the period 1848–73 on which we focus, can be adequately described as being "in equilibrium." In this chapter, we explore the conditions and implications of France's instrumental role in the stabilization of the gold–silver exchange rate. In two variations around that theme – one theoretical and the other one empirical – we argue that bimetallism could work and did work.

The remainder of the chapter is organized as follows: the second section surveys the theory of bimetallism and identifies the constraints under which it can work. We show that there is a one-to-one correspondence between the level of the market ratio (i.e., the gold–silver exchange rate) and the effective regime (joint circulation of gold and silver, *de facto* gold standard or *de facto* silver standard) in which a bimetallic system may find itself at a given date. In the third section, we construct a test which leads us to accept the null hypothesis that effective bimetallism prevailed in France between 1850 and 1870. Finally, the conclusion indicates some directions for future research.

BIMETALLISM IN THEORY: CONSISTENCY, EQUILIBRIUM, AND STABILITY

Two metaphors on bimetallism

Bimetallism is a system of commodity monies. Hence, to determine the relative prices of gold and silver, we may ask whether we should treat them as goods or as currencies. Two metaphors exist in the literature. The first treats them as commodities. In this view (which is probably the most conventional), the relative price of gold and silver should be defined by the market. There is no room for government legislation. De Cecco, for instance, argues that there is a contradiction between the "variations of the free market of precious metals [and the] official conception that the value of money is fixed by law."[11] In other words, a dual-standard regime is inconsistent.

On the other hand, the alternative metaphor considers gold and silver as monies. A currency is valued according to what it may purchase, implying that the exchange rate between two monies is a pure matter of convention. In this case, the government is welcome to suggest a price that will be used by agents to coordinate their actions. This analysis, related to the theory of competing currencies (Kareken and Wallace 1981), received an early proof in the works of Walras (1881) and Fisher (1894). In Fisher's words:

> The user of money . . . must first inquire on the relative circulating value of gold and silver before he can know at what price he himself prizes them. To him, the ratio of substitution is identically the price ratio, and therefore can have no influence in fixing that ratio. *The case of two forms of money is unique: they are substitutes without a ratio of substitution.*
>
> (Fisher 1894: 528, original italics)

To decide which metaphor is more appropriate, we consider the transitory equilibria of an exchange economy with money where gold and silver are used as both currency and commodity (the framework we use is adapted from Grandmont 1983). In this economy, there exists a collection of m goods, in addition to bullion, which are exchanged and consumed. Let p = ($p_1, p_2, \ldots, p_m, p_G$, 1) be the price vector of the m goods, gold, and silver (without loss of generality, the price of silver is set equal to 1 so that p_G is the gold–silver exchange rate). Define $f^j_i(p)$, $g_i(p)$, and $s_i(p)$ as the excess demand of individual i for (respectively) good j ($j \in [1, m]$), commodity gold, and commodity silver (excess demand is the difference between demand and initial endowment). In this economy all the gold and silver that is not demanded for non monetary use is coined.[12] This defines the supply of monetary gold $G^s_m(p)$ (or silver $S^s_m(p)$) as being equal to the aggregate excess supply of nonmonetary gold (silver).[13] We can now write the equations that characterize the general equilibrium of this economy. We have the following system:

Equilibrium in the m goods, gold, and silver markets

(1a) $\sum_i f_i^j (p) = 0; \forall j \in [1, m]$

(1b) $\sum_i g_i (p) + G_m^s (p) = 0$

(1c) $\sum_i s_i (p) + S_m^s (p) = 0$

Equilibrium in the money market

(2) $\sum_i m_i^d (p) = p_G G_m^s (p) + S_m^s (p)$

where $m_i^d (p)$ is the demand of individual i for money.

Positive amounts of both monies held in equilibrium

(3) $G_m^s (p) > 0, S_m^s (p) > 0$

Substituting equations (1b) and (1c) in equation (2) and dropping equation (2) (due to Walras Law), finally yields the following system, which should characterize bimetallic equilibria:

(4a) $\sum_i f_i^j (p) = 0, \forall j \in [1, m]$

(4b) $G_m^s (p) > 0, S_m^s (p) > 0$

It is clear from an inspection of the last system that, provided that there is no binding constraint,[14] we only have m equations to determine m+1 equilibrium prices. In other words, Bimetallic Equilibria (BE) are indeterminate. For a given level of resources in gold and silver, and for given preferences, *there exists a priori a set of possible equilibria which are compatible with equations 4a and 4b, so that the market is unable to determine uniquely* (among other things) *the gold–silver price ratio.* Hence, from the point of view of pure theory, there is no intrinsic contradiction between the operation of a bimetallic regime and the attempt by the government to legislate the gold–silver exchange rate: the government ratio is not necessarily superimposed on a well-defined market equilibrium.

To interpret this result in the light of the two metaphors described above, we consider two limiting cases of the model. First, assume that the monetary uses of gold and silver are small relative to their non-monetary uses. At the limit, our economy behaves as a pure exchange economy with no money. In this case, the equilibrium is fully defined by the following m+1 equations:

(5a) $\sum_i f_i^j (p) = 0, \forall j \in [1, m]$

(5b) $\sum_i g_i (p) = 0$

In other words, a *unique* gold–silver exchange rate is determined by the market, and there is of course no room for government intervention. This is the situation which is implicitly considered by "knife-edge" theorists. For instance, Giffen, who believed that bimetallism was doomed to fail, argued:

> The precious metals, it is admitted on all sides, have an extensive non-monetary use. They are merchandises as well as money. But few people perhaps realize that probably this nonmonetary use is *preponderant* over the monetary use itself.
>
> (Giffen 1892: 56)

By contrast, consider now the opposite circumstance where the demand for commodity gold and silver is small relative to the monetary uses of bullion. At the limit, gold and silver are demanded only for transaction purposes: they become fiat monies. In this case, the exchange rate between gold and silver is defined in the same fashion as the exchange rate between, say, "yellow" banknotes and "white" banknotes: it is only a matter of convention. Formally, we have m equations, m+1 relative prices, and no constraint, implying that *any* gold–silver price ratio can be an equilibrium exchange rate as demonstrated by Kareken and Wallace (1981):

$$(6) \quad \sum_i f_i^j (p) = 0, \forall j \in [1, m]$$

The implication of the previous analysis is straightforward: actual bimetallic systems are located somewhere on a string the ends of which correspond to the two "polar" cases discussed above. To clarify their functioning it is thus useful to characterize in some detail the locus of bimetallic equilibria.

The locus of bimetallic equilibria

In what follows, we use a linear specification of the general model presented above, which allows a simple derivation of the main propositions discussed here.[15] The m commodities considered before are now treated as a composite good. Hence gold, silver, and one consumption good are traded in every period. They are available in quantities that are exogenously given. Due to Walras' Law, we can drop one market (e.g., the market for the consumption good) and focus on the commodity gold, commodity silver, and money markets. The aggregate demands for commodity gold and silver (G_n and S_n) are given by (Y being real income)

$$(7a) \quad G_n = m_G (p/p_G) Y \text{ and } S_n = m_S \, p \, Y$$

where m_G and m_S are positive constants, and p, p_G are respectively the general price level and the price of gold. The price of silver is set equal to 1. The demand for money is given by the quantity theory

(7) $p_G\, G_m + S_m = k\, p\, Y$

where k is a positive constant, and G_m and S_m denote, respectively, gold and silver monetary stocks. Finally, we have the equilibrium relations (where G and S are, respectively, the total outstanding stocks of gold and silver):

(7c) $G_m + G_n = G$ and $S_m + S_n = S$

The model is solved in Figure 6.2, which displays the equilibrium gold–silver (log) price ratio as a function of the relative resources of the economy (the (log) ratio of the silver stock to the gold stock). Line GG′ corresponds to the gold standard equilibria (S_m=0), and line SS′ is the locus of the silver standard equilibria (G_m=0). For a given ratio of resources (R_0), the silver standard equilibrium is represented by point S_0 (associated with the equilibrium price p_G^{min}) and the gold-standard equilibrium is represented by point G_0 (associated with the equilibrium price p_G^{max}). Finally, the segment [S_0, G_0] is the continuum of equilibria compatible with R_0, and for which strictly positive amounts of both monies are held. Hence [S_0, G_0] is the set of possible equilibria associated with R_0.

Figure 6.2 illustrates the indeterminacy result. Suppose that we start from the bimetallic equilibrium B_0 associated with the legal ratio p_G. At this level, the economy is holding strictly positive amounts of gold and silver monies. Assume that the authorities decide on a marginal rise in the gold–silver exchange rate. With gold slightly more expensive, agents are willing to decrease their demand of commodity gold, and increase their demand of commodity silver. This is achieved by marginally increasing the quantity of monetary gold, and marginally reducing the quantity of monetary silver:

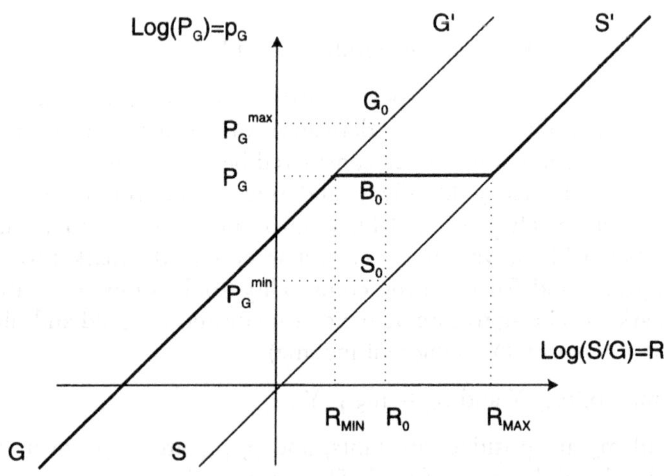

Figure 6.2 Bimetallic equilibria

this substitution eventually checks the initial imbalance. In the new equilibrium, gold holdings have slightly increased, and silver holdings slightly decreased, but the economy is still on a bimetallic regime. Hence there exists, around p_G, a continuum of legal ratios that determine a continuum of bimetallic equilibria.

We can read Figure 6.2 in two different ways. First, we may look at the range of legal gold–silver price ratios which are compatible with a given level of resources. For any given level of gold and silver stocks, the set of possible bimetallic ratios is located between the silver-standard and the gold-standard price ratios. This result (due to Walras 1881 and Fisher 1894) may be interpreted as follows: for given stocks of gold and silver, the aggregate amount of gold available for consumption will be smaller in a gold-standard regime than in a silver-standard regime because part of the total stock must be used as money. Commodity silver, by contrast, will be scarcer in a silver standard than in a gold standard. Thus, if aggregate demand is a decreasing function of price, the gold–silver price ratio will be higher in a gold-standard regime, and lower in a silver-standard regime. A bimetallic constitution, by allowing for a joint use of both metals, uses less monetary silver than a silver-standard regime, and less monetary gold than a gold-standard regime.[16] Hence it is associated with price ratios that must lie *above the silver-standard* and *below the gold-standard price ratios.* This interval defines the range in which the government has to set the legal ratio for a given level of gold and silver resources.[17]

Conversely, Figure 6.2 may be used to define the range of gold and silver stocks compatible with any given price ratio. For instance, if the ratio is p_G, the relative stocks of gold and silver must lie between R_{MIN} and R_{MAX}. In this case the market ratio is identically the legal ratio, and positive amounts of gold and silver monies are held in equilibrium. In contrast, if there is “too much” gold or “too little” silver (R smaller than R_{MIN}), the economy is on a *de facto* gold standard. Finally, if there is “too much” silver or “too little” gold (R larger than R_{MAX}), the economy is on a *de facto* silver standard.

The bold line in Figure 6.2 describes the equilibrium gold–silver price ratios as a function of the economy’s resources. It shows that, for a given legal ratio, a bimetallic system has in fact *three different regimes*, depending on the level of outstanding resources in gold and silver. Since in practice the legal ratio is set for a long period, while gold and silver resources can change, the stability of the gold–silver exchange rate depends on the range of outstanding resources with which effective bimetallism is compatible. Again, this range is a function of the various parameters of the economy, suggesting that the ability of bimetallism to accommodate variations in the stocks of gold and silver is a question *that can be answered only on empirical grounds.*[18]

The important implication of the previous analysis is that, provided that the gold and silver resources remain within a range which is compatible with the legal ratio, joint circulation of gold and silver will prevail. When bimetallism is feasible, agents arbitrage out any potential discrepancy between the price ratio and the legal ratio. Suppose, for instance, that on bullion markets one metal happens to appreciate relative to the other. In this case, someone can sell monetary holdings of the appreciating metal, use the proceeds to purchase the depreciating one, and coin it. This operation is referred to as a *bimetallic arbitrage*, and results in bringing the economy back to equilibrium.

Several conclusions emerge from this section. First, there is no intrinsic contradiction between the government's definition of a legal ratio and the operation of a bimetallic regime. Second, we found that the legal ratio has to be set in a range which is constrained by a combination of exogenous structural factors – chiefly preferences and resources of bullion. In other words, it may turn out that for *some* levels of production, and *some* parameters of consumption and money demand, a given legal ratio is incompatible with the operation of an effective bimetallic regime: in this case the system will collapse to a *de facto* gold or silver standard. Hence, from an empirical perspective, the actual behavior of the commercial ratio is of extreme importance, because it may constitute the basis of a test through which one can assess the compatibility between the 15.5 ratio and the evolution of the gold and silver stocks. While it is very difficult to observe directly whether a regime is or is not "effectively bimetallic," it is possible, by looking at the variations of the commercial ratio, to determine the effective regime prevailing at a given date. As illustrated in Figure 6.2, a commercial ratio above the legal ratio reveals a situation of *de facto* silver standard while a commercial ratio under the legal ratio is consistent with a *de facto* gold standard.

EFFECTIVENESS, EFFICIENCY, AND BIMETALLIC ARBITRAGES

Assessing gold–silver points

The question at hand is to assess whether, during the period 1850–70, the gold–silver commercial ratio remained "close enough" to the legal ratio to be compatible with effective bimetallism or, instead, whether variations in the stocks of gold and silver resulted in successive moves from one regime to the other one.

Although we argued on the basis of Figure 6.1 that the commercial ratio remained remarkably stable until 1873, other authors have reached a different conclusion. Indeed, a closer look reveals successive episodes where the (London) commercial ratio remained *slightly* above (before 1850, after 1865) or below (between 1850 and 1865) the legal ratio. The transition from a stable position above the legal ratio to a stable position under it could be rapid and has been characterized by De Cecco (1990) as "drastic." This has led Oppers (1992) to argue that bimetallism repeatedly switched from a *de facto* silver standard before 1850 to a *de facto* gold standard in the 1850s, and back to a silver standard in the 1860s.

This line of reasoning, however, is not rigorous. Bimetallic arbitrage involved a number of costs: the coins of the appreciating metal had to be melted down and sold, while bars of the depreciating metal had to be purchased and coined. The question, then, is not to determine whether the commercial ratio remained pegged *at* 15.5, but *whether the commercial ratio remained within boundaries reflecting the opportunity cost of arbitraging.* If so, we may deem the commercial ratio "close" to the legal ratio, implying that bimetallism was effective. Hence our null hypothesis is that throughout the period under study variations of the gold–silver exchange rate took place within the arbitrage boundaries, which Friedman dubbed "gold–silver points."[19]

One way to perform the test is to rely on the accounts of contemporary professional brokers and bullion dealers. Since they had on a rather complex mechanism arguably more information than what we may gather today (indeed, we are bound to second-guess the market), their opinion is of importance. According to Seyd, a leading authority for bullion matters in the City, the commercial ratio between gold and silver, until 1873, was nothing else than the indication of a constant ratio between the two metals: "It is mathematically true", he argued, "that the slight variations that have occurred . . . merely resulted from accessory costs."[20] Similarly, Alphonse de Rothschild, who had run the bullion department in his father's bank, claimed: "I do not quite know what a depreciated metal is. There may be exceptional demand for gold or silver as commodities, but *the ratio between the two metals as monies is constant*."[21]

In the recent literature, there have been only two, loose, attempts to further or reject their claims by evaluating more systematically the "gold–silver points." Friedman (1990a) suggested, without much explanation that gold–silver points corresponded respectively to 15.3 and 15.89. He then compared these figures to variations of the average commercial ratio in London. This led him to conclude that – despite slight violations around 1859 – effective bimetallism did prevail.

An opposite conclusion was reached by Oppers (1992), who claimed that the only cost involved in arbitrage was the expense associated with coining the depreciating metal. This gave him a very narrow range of 15.47 to 15.66 determined by the Mint charge. His approach, biased towards rejection (it overlooks transportation, wear and tear, etc.), led him to conclude that during most of the period under study (i.e., between 1853 and 1865), bimetallism repeatedly switched from a *de facto* gold standard to *de facto* silver standard with very short-lived transitions through effective bimetallism. Both Oppers and Friedman tests are represented in Figure 6.3, which is a blow-up of Figure 6.1.

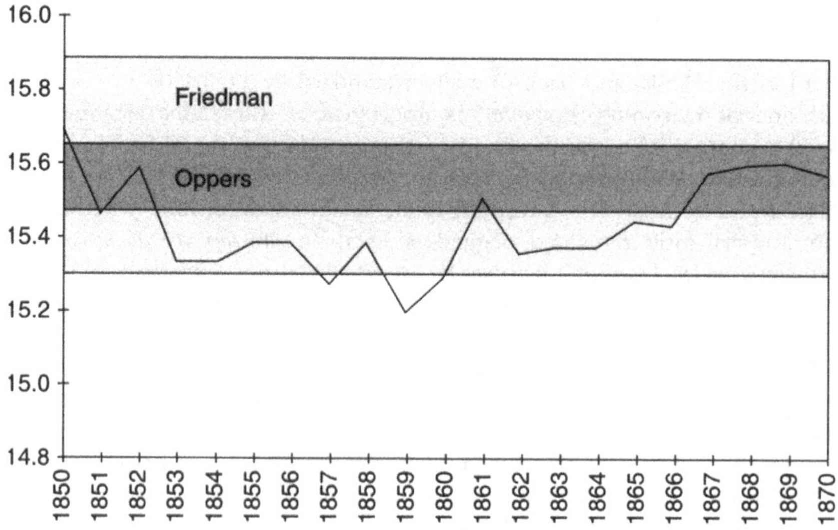

Figure 6.3 Gold–silver points and the London ratio according to Friedman and Oppers
Source: Flandreau (1995b: 341)

Obviously, both approaches are insufficient. In order to construct proper bands for bimetallic arbitrage, it is necessary to go beyond these rough calculations and derive gold–silver points from a careful examination of the market structure in which they took place. As suggested by Officer (1986) in the context of gold points, the best strategy is to "start from first principles," that is to understand exactly how they were computed.

Gold–silver points and the Paris bullion market

A matter of geography

In what follows we focus on a "typical" arbitrage. We consider the situation of an agent located *anywhere* in France and having holdings in both currencies. We then derive the agent's opportunity cost for arbitraging variations of the Paris commercial ratio (bullion being quoted in Paris).

The opportunity cost of "bimetallic arbitrage" involves the following:[22] (1) transportation to Paris of the coins made of the appreciating metal, (2) loss in weight (compared to the nominal value of the coins) due to abrasion, (3) transaction costs on the Paris market implied by exchanging one metal for the other, (4) coinage charge;[23] (5) transportation from Paris of the coins made of the depreciating metal, (6) interest loss associated with items (1), (4), and (5).[24]

In this framework, geography matters: arbitraging will be cheaper in places from which bullion markets can be easily reached, and where large amounts of the appreciating metal are concentrated. This gives an advantage to Paris over the provinces, and to provincial towns well related to Paris over the countryside, for which railway was not always available. Hence the relevant arbitrage cost will be determined by the location of the "marginal arbitrageur," i.e., the one who can arbitrage at the lowest expense. For this agent, the cost of arbitrage will exactly compensate for the benefit. Obviously, the location of the marginal arbitrageur is determined by path dependent effects. Consider, for instance, the economy represented in Figure 6.4. Agents are located along the [A, B] line. We assume that at the beginning all agents hold both gold and silver coins. Moreover, we consider that the arbitrage cost (which includes a fixed charge and transportation costs) is an increasing function of the distance from the bullion market located at the center of the economy. Assume now that gold is discovered and shipped (from abroad) to the bullion market. This will drive down the price of gold until arbitrage occurs. Obviously, the agents located near the bullion market will intervene first. This will drive silver out of the bimetallic economy *from the center* until more distant regions are contaminated. In Figure 6.4, segment [M, M′] has been emptied but silver still remains in segments [AM] and [M′B].

Hence we should observe that, as gold kept arriving in France during the 1850s and most of the 1860s, the distance between the Paris market and the "marginal arbitrageur" kept increasing. Indeed agents located close to the Paris market (where the bullion market was located) did arbitrage until

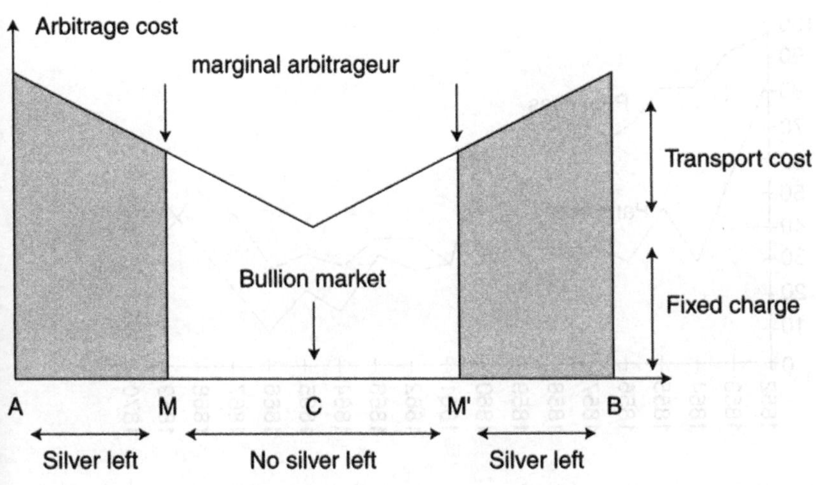

Figure 6.4 The geography of arbitrages: theory

they ran short of silver. Agents located marginally further from Paris did arbitrage next, and so on.

There is strong evidence that this mechanism did actually operate. For instance, it was reported that by 1854, gold had become the main component of the circulation in Paris. This is illustrated by the evolution of the proportion of silver in the reserves of the Bank of France, which may be thought of as a sample of the Parisian circulation (Figure 6.5). The arbitrage then extended to the Paris suburbs and in 1856, to the surrounding towns. In 1857, a survey conducted by the French Administration provided extensive insights about the regional effects of bimetallic arbitrages.[25] At this date, the arbitrage was concentrating on the main provincial cities related to Paris by train (such as Lyons), or on the regions from which silver could be easily shipped to silver-standard countries, which had a large demand for this metal, or to other bullion markets. Hence, ports (such as Marseilles or Nantes) or Eastern departments (close to silver standard Germany) were primarily targeted, as illustrated in Figure 6.6 But more distant regions, where railways were not yet developed, had not even heard of the arbitrage. In Clermont-Ferrand, for instance, it was said that no silver exports had been experienced so far.[26]

After 1860, gold became the main component of the monetary circulation in most of the provincial towns (it formed the largest part of the reserve in the Subsidiaries of the Bank of France). Silver was now predominantly located in the countryside, which, being more costly to reach had not participated in the previous arbitrages. After 1865, substitution of gold for silver stalled as rising silver output relieved part of the excess demand for that metal. In 1868, a second survey documented the geograph-

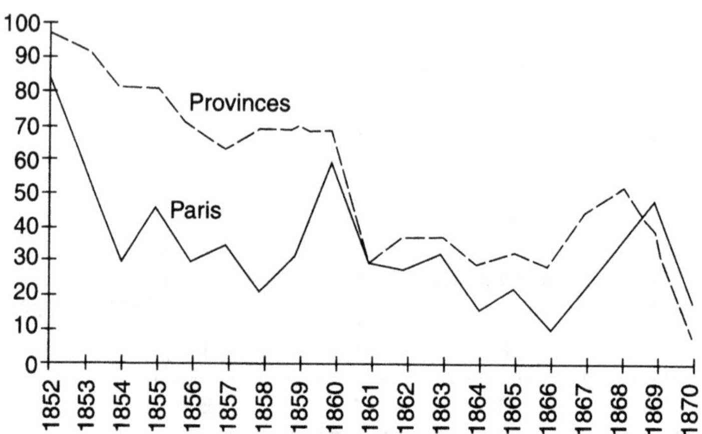

Figure 6.5 Proportion of silver in the reserves of the Bank of France (percentage)
Source: Archives of the Bank of France

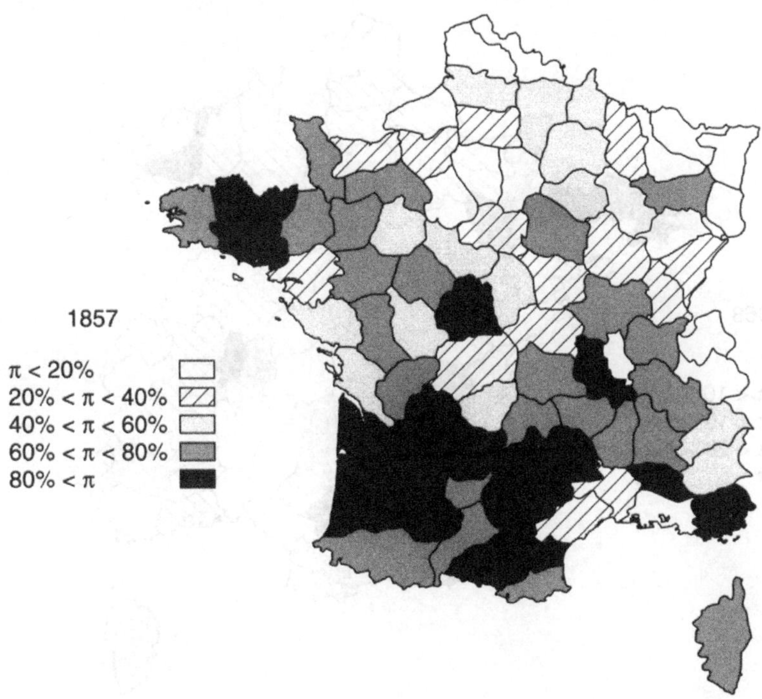

Figure 6.6 Proportion of silver in each department's circulation, 1857

ical composition of France's metallic currency. It displayed a characteristic pattern (Figure 6.7): the portion of the country located above the Saint Malo–Montpellier line was predominantly using gold. This portion coincided with the more industrialized, and more financially developed, part of France. In contrast, the other portion, predominantly devoted to agriculture and financially backward (Brittany, the south-west), was still using large amounts of silver (more than 50 per cent in several departments). Hence, the extent to which industrialization had reduced transaction costs in the various regions, by influencing the expenses involved in bimetallic arbitrages, had drawn a contrasted geography of the French monetary circulation.

Moreover, comparing Figures 6.6 and 6.7 illustrates the considerable progress of the substitution process between 1857 and 1868, as well as the combination of both macroeconomic and geographical effects. The gold–silver structure of the bimetallic circulation had clearly evolved towards a general predominance of gold, as reflected in the general fall in the proportion of silver from Figure 6.6 to Figure 6.7. Yet the geography of bimetallic arbitrages produced an uneven substitution. In regions closely related to national or international bullion markets, gold had almost fully

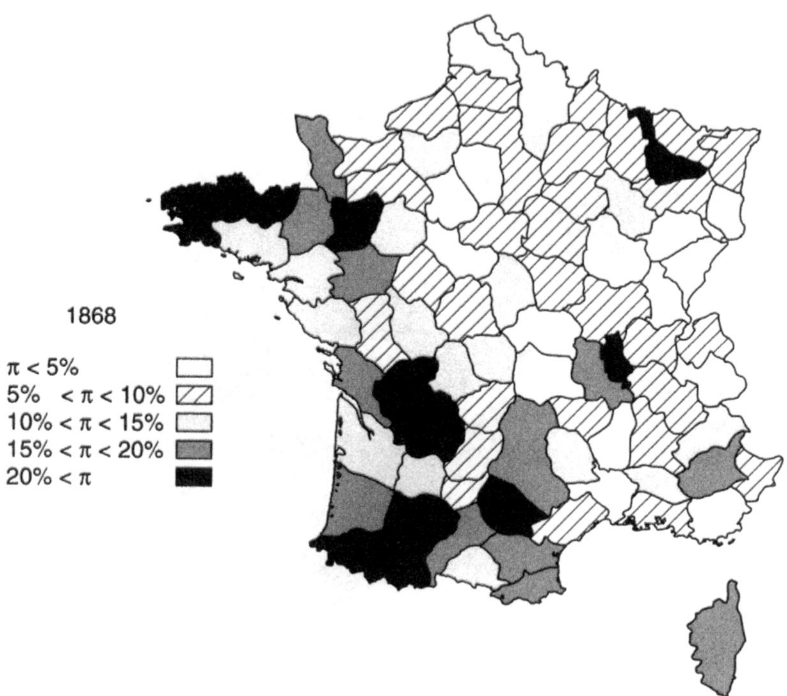

Figure 6.7 Proportion of silver in each department's circulation, 1868

driven silver out of circulation. On the other hand, more distant districts experienced substantially less substitution. From this account the similarities between the two maps are striking.

Estimating gold–silver points

To estimate the costs associated with the arbitrage mechanism, I have relied on a series of contemporary sources, which were found to display a fair level of consistency. In particular, I used Seyd's (1868) bullion brokers' handbook, *Bullion and Foreign Exchanges*, which contains details about the costs associated with operations on gold and silver. In addition, the Rothschild Archives authorized me to investigate their "Matières" files.[27] These files include letters (starting in late 1857) which give a vivid picture of the activities of the Rothschild Bank on bullion markets, and some details about the costs involved in arbitrage activities. These sources were completed by some casual details found in the Archives of the Bank of France, and the Archives de France, Paris. Components of arbitrage cost are shown in Table 6.1.

Table 6.1 Estimating gold–silver points costs for 1000 francs, 1851–70

	Upper Bound				*Lower Bound*		
Period	*1851: 1* *1870: 9*	*1851: 1* *1854: 3*	*1854: 4* *1854: 12*	*1855: 1* *1856: 12*	*1857: 1* *1860: 12*	*1861: 1* *1866: 12*	*1867: 1* *1870: 9*
Transportation	0	0	0	0.5	4	4	1
Abrasion	0.17 × α[a]	0.16 × β[b]	0.16 × β	0.16 × β	0.16 × β	0.16 × β	0.16 × β
Brokerage	2.00	2.25	2.25	2.25	2.25	2.25	2.25
Coinage	7.5	2	2.2	2.2	2.2	2.2	2.2
Interest loss	0.041 × i[c]	0.041 × i	0.041 × i	0.041 × i	0.041 × i	0.055 × i	0.041 × i

Notes: [a] α is the average age for gold coins from Flandreau (1995b)
[b] β is the average age for silver coins from Flandreau (1995b)
[c] i is the interest rate

Transportation

Throughout the entire period, gold could be easily found in Paris. Hence the transportation charge for the upper bound (gold melted, silver coined) can be set equal to zero. For the lower bound however, transportation costs changed over time along with the location of the marginal arbitrageur. The prices we found for consignments within the continent were the following: from Lille to Brussels (a few kilometers by train); less than 0.1 per cent and usually around 0.05 per cent.[28] From Marseilles to Paris (related by train): 0.4 per cent.[29] From Marseilles to Rome: 1 per cent.[30] These figures imply the following transportation costs for the lower bound: until December 1854, silver can be found in Paris, so that we neglect transportation costs. Until December 1856, the towns surrounding Paris are searched for silver, suggesting an expense comparable to the Lille–Brussels figure (0.05 per cent). After that date, we know that towns like Marseilles participated in the arbitrages, so we take 0.4 per cent as an estimate. After 1860, the cost of finding silver probably increased above 0.4 per cent; but since the Marseilles–Rome shipment probably overstates the true amount, we assumed that the expense remains under 0.5 per cent. We took 0.4 per cent as a conservative estimate. Finally, after 1867, we know that silver did flow back in France (it was found in relatively large quantities in Lyons, which obtained it from sales of cloth to Italy), suggesting that the lower bound was certainly reduced to 0.1 per cent.[31]

Abrasion

This expense was one of the main concerns of the arbitrageurs and probably the most substantial cost. In France coins having lost 0.7 per cent of their value through wear and tear were still legal tender. Exporting them, on the other hand, involved a loss. Seyd (1868), for instance, describing a shipment of 5-franc silver coins, assumes as an example that it displays a 0.588 per cent reduction in weight: we found even higher figures in the Rothschild Archives for actual consignments.

In practice, we computed abrasion by evaluating the average age of the silver and the gold currency, and applying to it the yearly rate of abrasion. This rate was estimated from Chevalier (1851) and Malou (1880), who reported figures respectively equal to 0.016 per cent per year for silver and 0.017 per cent per year for gold.[32] Since the average degree of abrasion is variable over time and depends on the average age of coins, the table reports only the mean value.[33]

Brokerage and assays

The brokerage charge or courtage is taken from Seyd (1868: e.g., 389). In Paris, it represents 0.1 per cent of the value of the transaction. Usually, only the seller paid the *courtage*, but the buyer could have had to pay a commission. To be on the safe side, we considered only that the *courtage* was paid by the seller. Since the arbitrage implies both a purchase and a sale, the reported cost provides a conservative bound for the true amount.

Besides, we must take into account the expenses associated with melting and assaying the metal to be sold. The Rothschild Archives mention that for silver this expense was of 0.125 per cent. Seyd, on the other hand, reports that the corresponding expense for gold was about 0.1 per cent.

Coinage fee

The coinage charges for one kilogram 9/10 fine were, respectively, 6 francs for gold and 1.5 francs for silver. In March 1854, the fee for gold was raised to 6.7 franc. The charges reported in Table 6.1 are obtained by dividing these figures by the prices of one kilogram of gold or silver (respectively, 3100 francs and 200 francs).

Interest loss

When bullion was brought to the Mint, the supplier was given a "Mint Certificate" or "Bon de Monnaie" payable after about ten days.[34] Although those certificates were not discounted, it was possible to ask the Mint Director to make the certificate payable to the Bank of France. The Bank then credited the account of the depositor an amount equivalent to the value of the *Bon* from which the waiting period was discounted on the basis of the Bank's rate, which changed over time. In addition, although we can neglect the interest loss associated with transporting bullion when the arbitrage is achieved from a town related to Paris by train, sending from the countryside could take about five days, including "three or four days overland by ox cart,"[35] especially from Brittany and the south-west of

France, where roads were not yet developed. We took a 15-day period when bullion was easily found (i.e., until December 1860 and after 1867) and a 20-day period between 1860 and 1867 (when silver was hard to retrieve), and multiplied this by the Bank rate.

The gold–silver points were computed for the period 1851–70.[36] The quotations on the Paris market were taken from the daily quotations found in the Archives of the Mint of Paris.[37] This allowed us to construct a series of end-of-month gold–silver exchange rates, which is represented in Figure 6.8. The series is compared with the gold–silver points. The conclusion is straightforward: during the period 1851–70, *bimetallism remained in equilibrium*. No violation of the gold–silver points was observed, implying that throughout the 1850s and 1860s the commercial ratio remained "in equilibrium" within the gold–silver points.

The arbitrageur of last resort

In the previous paragraph, we argued that the commercial ratio on the Paris market was found between the gold–silver points, supporting the conclusion that bimetallism remained effective. In view of Figure 6.8, one may even be tempted to argue that bimetallism remained "remarkably effective," because the gold–silver exchange rate tended to be turned away from the edges of the band, towards the center. To clarify this, it is important to recognize that bimetallic arbitrages as we described them earlier can in fact be decomposed into two distinct operations.

The value of one given metal (gold or silver) on the bullion market cannot depreciate below the rate at which the Mint is set to work. This gives to bullion producers a "reservation price," which corresponds to the

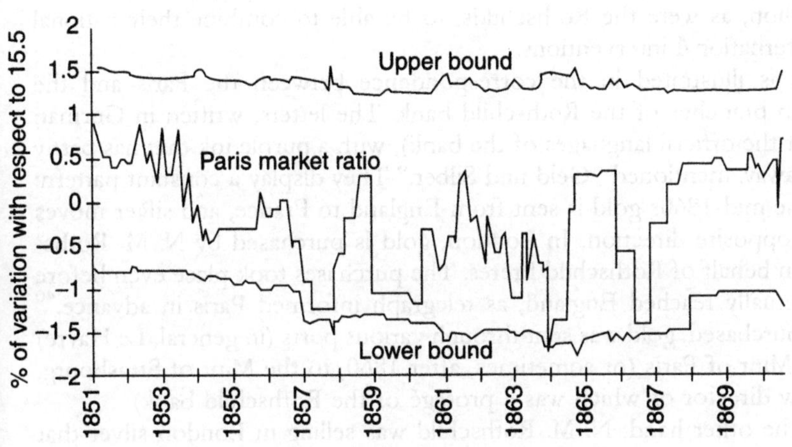

Figure 6.8 The Paris market ratio and the gold–silver points, 1851–70

lowest price at which they will be able to sell their output. Conversely, the value of one given metal cannot rise above the price at which it becomes profitable to melt coins into bullion (as long as there remain coins of that metal in circulation). Thus, the price of each metal cannot diverge from its Mint parity by more than a tiny discount (smaller than the costs associated with coinage) or premium (smaller than the cost of bringing bullion to the market): for instance, if gold bullion depreciates by an amount equal to the coinage charge, holders of gold bars will coin them. By so doing, they switch from bullion to coins, not from silver to gold. This implies that coinage of the depreciating metal or melting of the appreciating one *may occur even before the point where the gold–silver ratio reaches its upper or lower bound.* The existence of metal-specific arbitrages implied that within the gold–silver points a certain amount of "intra-marginal interventions" was taking place.

Obviously, these intra-marginal interventions were likely to contribute to the stabilization of the commercial ratio, for they acted as a check on bullion appreciation or depreciation *even in the absence of bimetallic arbitrages.* In fact, the observation that the gold–silver points were virtually never reached suggests that these intra-marginal interventions were a very important factor in determining the dynamics of the gold–silver exchange rate within its band.

This, in turn, raises the question of the interaction between the Paris market ratio and other market ratios.[38] While Paris was one of the main markets for silver (indeed, France was holding considerable amounts of silver in its circulation), London dominated the gold market.[39] During the 1850s and 1860s, gold from Australia and California arrived primarily in London, from where it was dispatched to its final destinations. This rendered particularly desirable, for bankers actively engaged in operations on bullion, as were the Rothschilds, to be able to combine their national and international interventions.

This is illustrated in the correspondence between the Paris and the London branches of the Rothschild bank. The letters, written in German (one of the official languages of the bank), with a purple ink that has partly faded away, mentioned "Geld und Silber." They display a constant pattern: until the mid-1860s gold is sent from England to France, and silver moves in the opposite direction. In London, gold is purchased by N. M. Rothschild on behalf of Rothschild Frères. The purchases took place even before gold actually reached England, as telegraph informed Paris in advance.[40] Once purchased, gold was sent through various ports (in general, Le Havre) to the Mint of Paris (or sometimes, after 1860, to the Mint of Strasbourg, the new director of which was a protégé of the Rothschild bank).

On the other hand, N. M. Rothschild was selling in London silver that had been collected by the Paris branch. In general, the customers were English Indian banks who needed to send silver to Asia. In France, silver currency was purchased either directly on the Paris market or regionally through various correspondents, and shipped to Southampton, via Le Havre or Brussels and Antwerp, or directly to Asia via Marseilles.[41]

One interesting feature of the "Geld und Silber" letters is that they display virtually no cases of direct gold–silver substitution. Often, gold was purchased by means of bills of exchange, that could have been initially issued to finance good exports from France to England. Similarly, the proceeds of a sale of French silver in London were not necessarily used to purchase gold from England. Instead, these bills could be used to finance imports from England. Here again, we find that a substantial proportion of the arbitrage was carried through metal-specific interventions, not by currency substitution in the bimetallic economy.

This suggests that bimetallic arbitrage be viewed not as the main stabilizing mechanism for the gold–silver exchange rate, but rather as a last line of defense which was rarely (if ever) reached. Being on both a gold and a silver standard, France could supply either metal to the rest of the world, while being paid in the other one, leaving its aggregate demand for money constant: in the pre-gold standard system, France was the *arbitrageur of last resort*, and thus provided for the credibility of the overall regime.[42] Much of the adjustment, however, did not work through direct currency substitution, but rather, through separate interventions, either in gold, or in silver.

CONCLUSION

Finally, our analysis leads to several important conclusions. First, the construction of gold–silver points shows that it is possible to characterize bimetallism between 1850 and 1870 as having been "in equilibrium." Contrary to what some authors have suggested (Oppers 1992; Redish 1992), the variations of the commercial ratio were always smaller than the (rather small) costs associated with arbitraging these very variations. This implies that bimetallism was effective throughout the period under study. Moreover, we found that the commercial ratio was often located quite away from its bounds, suggesting that a substantial part of the stabilisation of the ratio operated through "metal-specific arbitrage" (i.e., sales of the appreciating metal *or* purchases of the depreciating one) rather than through bimetallic arbitrages (i.e., sales of the appreciating metal *and* purchases of the depreciating one). This finding definitely deserves closer scrutiny in future research.

Our second important conclusion relates to the actual functioning of bimetallic regimes. As we demonstrated, the existence of transaction costs produced a spatial differentiation of gold and silver circulation: as excess supply of gold kept arriving on bullion markets during the 1850s and early 1860s, silver was exported primarily from spots that were "closer" to arbitrage networks. This led to a regionalization of specie circulation, gold dominating in some areas, silver dominating in others. This feature sheds an interesting light on the debates on bimetallism: indeed, some authors have relied on contemporary accounts of the gold–silver structure of the circulation to determine whether or not bimetallism was effective (e.g., Oppers 1992). Obviously such an approach is flawed: depending on where the sample is taken, opposite conclusions may be reached.

This in turn suggests that one recast the controversy on bimetallic regimes. Usually, the bulk of the debate focuses on determining whether bimetallism can provide for the "joint circulation" of gold and silver monies in a given economy. We claim that such a wording is misleading because of the spatial dimension of arbitrages. From a regional perspective, it is obvious that bimetallism could not provide for the joint circulation of gold and silver *everywhere and at every date.* On the other hand, from the point of view of *aggregate* circulation, French bimetallism did provide for the joint circulation of gold and silver monies, because between 1850 and 1870, there always remained *at least one region* where both metals circulated, implying that arbitrage could keep operating, thus stabilizing the gold–silver ratio. This ambiguity may explain most of the contradictory statements about bimetallism. As a system to stabilize the relative value of gold and silver through arbitrages, while preserving positive amounts of both metals in circulation, French bimetallism was a success. But the very operation of the system drew rather fascinating geographical contours.

NOTES

1 This chapter is a revised version of a paper written in 1992 while the author was Fulbright Scholar at University of California, Berkeley. The author is grateful to B. Eichengreen, M. Friedman, J. James, L. Officer, R. Michener, C. Marcuzzo, A. Rosselli, C. Wyplosz and seminar participants at Paris, Bonn, Berkeley, Stanford, Rutgers, and the University of Virginia for their comments on earlier drafts. Financial support was provided by the George Lurcy Trust, the Fulbright Scholar program, and the Bank of France, the help of which is gratefully acknowledged. Finally, special thanks are due to the IBER at Berkeley for its hospitality.

2 "[It is the assumption of Jevons] that the bimetallic system is essentially a system of an alternating standard in the sense that it allows only one metal in circulation: sometimes gold, sometimes silver. Now, it is certain that that is erroneous. Our reasoning has established and experience shows that bimetallism can be effective."

3 The following typology corresponds to the situation of the international monetary system *circa* 1868. See Eichengreen and Flandreau (1994).

4 Until the late 1860s, the expression "double standard" (to which corresponded in French the phrase "double étalon") was commonly used. In the late 1860s as debates on the optimal monetary constitution spread, economists started to look for more adequate ways to qualify such a regime. Seyd (1868) proposed "double valuation." At the same period, the word "bimétallisme" was reportedly

coined in France by Henri Cernuschi, one of the leading bimetallists of the next decade. In the 1870s "bimetallism" was widely used in books and pamphlets. In the 1880s, it appeared in official documents.

5 In contrast, after 1873, a number of authors (de Laveleye 1891; Cernuschi 1878), advocated "international bimetallism" by which they meant a coordinated reintroduction of the bimetallic ratio throughout the world.

6 Yeager (1976: 296). A similar view is shared by Friedman (1990a, 1990b) who argued that the United States should have played the same role after 1873 in stabilizing the gold–silver price ratio that France did before 1873.

7 Friedman (1990b: 1174).

8 De Cecco (1974) has documented the episode of the fall of the silver-based rupee, after 1880.

9 See, e.g., Woodford (1990) and Weil (1991).

10 Similar views may be found in De Cecco (1990).

11 De Cecco (1990: 7). Analogous statements may be found in Garber (1986), Rolnick and Weber (1986). As noted by Friedman (1990a, 1990b), most textbooks take the same view.

12 Throughout the chapter we abstract from explicitly modeling bullion production. The rationale for this is that we believe that the discovery of gold and silver is largely fortuitous and not very much related to general production costs (see, e.g., Warren and Pearson 1935: 122). Hence, it can be adequately represented as "rainfalls." It is important to recall, however, that introducing production would not affect the results.

13 In other words, the supply of monetary gold (silver) is the outstanding stock of gold (silver) minus the aggregate demand for nonmonetary gold (silver).

14 Note that if either constraint is binding, the system turns out to be a *de facto* gold or silver standard.

15 The results surveyed in this section were developed in earlier research on the theory of bimetallism (Walras 1881; Fisher 1894; Chen 1972; Niehans 1978; Barro 1979). In the first four works, the indeterminacy result is interpreted as an indeterminacy in the equilibrium gold–silver exchange rate. In contrast, in Barro's framework, the gold–silver exchange rate is determined, but the equilibrium quantities of gold and silver monetary holdings cannot be computed: in effect, Barro's model of bimetallism has no equilibrium. This arises because his definition of the steady state introduces a dichotomy between the monetary and the nonmonetary uses of bullion. He assumes that along the steady state, nonmonetary metal depreciates, but specie does not. Thus, the equilibrium flow of newly produced gold (silver) equals the equilibrium flow of nonmonetary demand (resulting from a depreciation of nonmonetary gold (silver)): Barro's model of bimetallism is analogous to a nonmonetary economy, implying that the gold–silver exchange rate is unique, but leaving the relative quantities of monetary gold and silver in the dark. Adapting Barro's framework with more realistic assumptions (e.g., (a) specie is allowed to depreciate, or (b) the economy is growing) produces the traditional indeterminacy result: the government can define the ratio, thus solving the indeterminacy.

6 If it used more of either metal, the economy would be inefficient, because in terms of welfare it would be strictly dominated by one of the two single-standard regimes.

7 Problems of "improper targeting" of the gold–silver ratio may be easily interpreted in this framework. The classical example is Newton's 1717 "overshooting" of the ratio: Newton, who was Master of the Mint, set too high a silver price for the gold guinea. As a result, Britain's silver coins were quickly

driven from circulation. One way to interpret this is to say that Newton had set the ratio above p_G^{max}. The legal ratio was thus larger than any possible equilibrium exchange rate: in any equilibrium, monetary silver was undervalued. Hence nobody was willing to give silver in payment at the legal rate. As gold alone was given in payment, the economy moved to the gold standard equilibrium associated with point G_0.

18 It can be shown that, consistently with what we have explained earlier, the range of possible resources is an increasing function of the relative propensity of the economy to hold bullion in the shape of coins.

19 Gold–silver points tests are analogous to the usual tests performed in the literature on gold standard efficiency (Morgenstern 1959; Clark 1984; Officer 1986), i.e., we are investigating the possibility of "gold–silver points violations." However, in our case, rejection of the null hypothesis receives two possible interpretations. It may arise because changes in the production of gold and silver have rendered the legal ratio incompatible with the new level of outstanding resources – this relates to an "intrinsic" contradiction of bimetallism. Alternatively, it may result from inefficiencies in the arbitrage mechanism, implying that there remain unexploited opportunities for bimetallic arbitrage – this relates to an "extrinsic" problem, i.e., the market's inability to operate efficiently a system that could theoretically be successful.

20 Quoted in Soetbeer (1889: 25).

21 Alphonse de Rothschild, in *Enquête sur la Question Monétaire*, vol. 1: 99. See Flandreau (1995b).

22 "Bimetallic arbitrages" may be shown to result from two distinct operations. See Flandreau (1995b) and also pp. 167–9.

23 Friedman (1990) calls this a "seignorage charge." However, the expression is not appropriate, because seignorage historically designated the King's tax on coinage, and resulted in a partial debasement of the coin. By contrast, the coinage charge (aimed at covering the coinage expenses) did not affect the intrinsic value of the coins.

24 Note that several other expenses should be considered, although we do not include them in the evaluation. For instance, the arbitrage involves a substantial informational cost (coin holders must learn about the exchange rate in Paris: this may not be so simple in the countryside where information took a couple of days to arrive). In practice, the existence of several fixed costs associated with organizing the arbitrage led to specialization. Large holders of currency, and people well informed of the exchange rate, as bankers, were more likely to arbitrage. In this case, they had to search for coin holders, and purchase the holdings after some bargaining.

25 Flandreau (1995b). The 1857 survey was published under the title: *Documents Relatifs à la Question Monétaire*, (hereafter DRQM) Ministère des Finances, Paris: Imprimerie Impériale, 1858. The Abstract of the 1868 Survey was published by the Ministère des Finances under the same title in 1868.

26 DRQM (1857: 104).

27 Archives Nationales de Paris: 132 AQ 891ff.

28 Archives of the Bank of France. The figure refers to an operation performed in the early 1870s.

29 Rothschild Archives, Letter dated December 1, 1860.

30 *Circa* 1868. Insurance not included. Papiers Rouher, Archives Nationales de France, Paris. As a matter of comparison, we report some figures for shipments made between London and the continent: they may be thought of as benchmarks for the following evaluations. The prices are: from Paris to

London *circa* 1868: 0.3 per cent (Seyd 1868: 385ff.). The price refers to a shipment of 10,000 British Sovereigns. (It includes freight and insurance, but no commission.) From London to Hamburg or Amsterdam: 0.2 per cent (Seyd 1868: 385ff.). The price refers to shipments of silver bars. (It includes the same items as in the Marseilles to Rome figure.) From London to Switzerland: 0.5 per cent and London to Milan: 0.6 per cent (these last figures correspond to operations on gold and silver in 1873). They are reported in the Minutes of the 1874 Conference of the Latin Union.

31 Assuming that (Paris→Lyons) = (Paris→Milan) – (Lyons→Milan), figures are taken from the Rothschild Archives. Neglecting this expense, as in Flandreau (1995b), would not change the conclusion.

32 See Flandreau (1995b).

33 This abstracts from "trébuchage" operations, in which heavier coins were searched to be exported in priority. Hence our computed average abrasion probably overestimates the actual wear and tear of exported coins. On the other hand, "trébuchage" involved costs which we do not include in the estimation. On balance, our estimate should be close to the truth.

34 Hendriks declared before the Royal Commission on International Coinage (1868) that

> M. Dumas, the Director of the French Mint, has been good enough to communicate to me, through M. De Parieu, the full particulars of the rules respecting the exchange of coin for bullion in Paris. It appears that the delay in delivery depends upon the quantity of bullion which the Mint may have to coin. A Ministerial decree of 25th February 1835 had fixed at eight days the maturity of warrants for payments made in Paris. The execution of this measure became impossible after the Californian gold discoveries, because more bullion was then brought to the Mint than could be coined in the eight days delay. A ministerial decree of 18th December 1850 . . . [stated] that the maturity of the coin warrants delivered in payment for gold bullion brought to be changed at the Paris Mint shall be calculated in such a manner as that the director of the coinage shall only have to pay each day the sum of one million francs, following the order in which the bullion shall have been delivered.

According to Hendriks this implied that the maturity could be of "one month and sometimes a more lengthened period of delay." However, it is more reasonable to assume that the 1850 decree corresponded to the need – for the Mint workshops – to adjust to mass production of gold currency (after decades of mass silver coinage). Plessis (1985: 176) reports that in 1856, the Mint of Paris could deliver 3 millions per day (i.e., about 1 billion per year), notwithstanding the occasional help of provincial workshops (e.g., Lyons), as in 1857. Since the annual production always remained below 1 billion, the delay was probably close to the eight-day rule. This is supported by Seyd (1868), who repeatedly assumes that the average delay for coining gold was about ten days, as well as by another broker, Jourdan (Royal Commission: 90), who argues that it was about "a fortnight" (this included transportation from Paris), and by several examples of eight-day (or even less) contracts found in the Rothschild Archives.

35 See Weber (1976: 216ff.).

36 Before 1851 gold was still "scarce" in France, and since we do not know exactly where it was located, we cannot evaluate the upper arbitrage bound (although we may assume, by symmetry with what we know about silver in the latter period, that gold was rather expensive to obtain).

37 *Cours Authentiques des Matières d'Or et d'Argent*, MS folio 310, Archives de la Monnaie de Paris.

38 In what follows, we seek to provide the reader with only a flavor of the interactions between the Paris and the London ratios. For a thorough study of this question, see Flandreau (1996).

39 For instance, while silver was quoted every day in Paris, it is much harder to find continuous monthly series for London.

40 See, e.g., Gille (1967: 278). This is illustrated in the circular issued by the bullion brokers company Pixley, Abell and Langley (which started business in 1852), and reproduced weekly in *The Economist*. For instance, on November 19, 1859:

> Gold – The 24 700 £ gold brought by the Delta and Armenian as mentioned in our last circular was taken for the Continent. The demand for exportation has however, up to the present time, been met by the following arrivals: the Bremen, Europa, Hammonia all from New York bringing together about 150 000 £. The Red Jacket and Swiftsure from Melbourne with about 150 000 £ are not yet in: their arrivals is now hourly looked for and the gold they have will doubtless be sent away.

41 For instance, in a letter dated September 2, 1864, and sent to the Commercial Bank of India (Bombay), the Bank of Hindustan, China and Japan, and the Oriental Bank Corporation (Bombay), the Paris Branch wrote: "Sir, By order of MM. N. M. Rothschild from London, we ship you through Mr Roux de Fraissinet of Marseilles by the steamer leaving this port the 118 cases containing 118 ingots of silver, number 226–383, value F 760 000." The operations reported in the Rothschild Archives were by no means peculiar. Seyd for instance reports that

> Shipments of silver are frequently made from Paris and Marseilles to India and the East for account of English Indian Banks or Merchants. The shipping from the port of Marseilles saves time, and to the exchange with France this method of shipping silver to the East is sometimes more profitable than shipments via Southampton.
>
> (Seyd 1868: 413)

42 As described by a correspondent of *The Economist* (April 23, 1859):

> France by the dispersion of her silver and absorption of gold, must, while the process lasts, effectually check any important rise [in the price of silver]. I will merely add, that the last rise to 5 s 23/4 d and subsequent fall to 5 s 2 d in the price of silver appears to me to confirm this view, as it shows that when the machinery for collecting [silver] from the Continent is put into action, there is still a supply which can be spared, where gold is legal tender.

REFERENCES

Barro, R.J. (1979) Money and the Price Level Under the Gold Standard, *Economic Journal* 89: 13–33.

Bordo, M.D. (1975) John E. Cairnes on the Effects of the Australian Gold Discoveries, 1851–73: An Early Application of the Methodology of Positive Economics, *History of Political Economy* 7 (3): 337–59.

Cairnes, J.E. (1873) *Essays in Political Economy*, London.

Cernuschi, H. (1878) *La Diplomatie monétaire en 1878*, Paris: Guillaumin.

Chen, C. (1972) Bimetallism: Theory and Controversy in Perspective, *History of Political Economy* Spring: 89–112.

Chevalier, M. (1851) *La Monnaie*, Brussels: Méline.
——(1859) *On the Probable Fall in the Value of Gold: The Commercial and Social Consequences which may Ensue, and the Measures which it Invites*, translated by Richard Cobden, New York.
Clark, T.A. (1984) Violations of the Gold-Points, 1890–1908, *Journal of Political Economy* October: 791–823.
Cooper, R.N. (1982) The Gold Standard: Historical Facts and Future Prospects, *Brooking Papers on Economic Activity*.
——(1987) *The International Monetary System – Essays in World Economics*, Cambridge, MA: MIT Press.
De Cecco, M. (1974) *Money and Empire*, Oxford: Blackwell.
——(1990) Editor's introduction, *Collana Storica della Banca d'Italia*, vol. 1, *L'Italia e il Sistema Finanziario Internazionale 1861–1914*, Rome: Laterza.
Del Mar, A. (1902) *A History of the Precious Metals*, New York: Cambridge Encyclopedia Co.
Dermigny, L. (1955) Une carte monétaire de la France à la fin de l'Ancien Régime, *Annales, Economies, Sociétés, Civilisations* October, 4.
Drake, L.S. (1985) Reconstruction of a Bimetallic Price Level, *Explorations in Economic History* 22: 194–219.
Eichengreen, B. (1985) *The Gold Standard in Theory and History* London: Methuen.
Eichengreen, B. and Flandreau, M. (1994) The Geography of the Gold Standard, *CEPR discussion paper*.
Fisher, I. (1894) The Mechanics of Bimetallism, *Economic Journal* September, 527–37.
——(1926) The Purchasing Power of Money, New York: Macmillan.
Flandreau, M. (1995a) Coin Memories: Estimates of the French Metallic Currency, 1840–1878, *Journal of European Economic History* 24 (2): 271–310.
——(1995b) *L'Or du monde: La France et la stabilité du système monétaire international*, Paris: l'Harmattan.
——(1996) Adjusting to the Gold Rush: endogenous bullion points and the French balance of payments, *Explorations in Economic History* 33: 417–39.
Friedman, M. (1990a) Bimetallism revisited, *Journal of Economic Perspectives* 4 (4), Fall: 85–104.
——(1990b) The Crime of 1873, *Journal of Political Economy* 98 (6): 1159–94.
Gallarotti, G.M. (1990) The Scramble for Gold: Monetary Regimes Transformation in the 1870's, Tenth International Economic History Congress, Leuven, Belgium, August 20–24.
Garber, P.M. (1986) Nominal Contracts in a Bimetallic Standard, *American Economic Review* 76 (5): 1012–30.
Giffen, R. (1892) The *Case against Bimetallism*, 2nd edn, London.
Gille, B. (1967) *Histoire de la Maison Rothschild*, vol. II, *1848–1870*, Geneva: Droz.
Grandmont, J.M. (1983) *Money and Value*, Cambridge: Cambridge University Press.
Jevons, W.S. (1884) *Investigations in Currency and Finance*, London: Macmillan.
Kareken J. and Wallace, N. (1981) On the Indeterminacy of Equilibrium Exchange Rates, *Quarterly Journal of Economics* 96: 207–22.
Laughlin, J. (1885) *The History of Bimetallism in the United States*, New York: D. Appleton.
Laveleye, E. de (1891) *La Monnaie et le bimétallisme international*, Paris: Félix Alcan.
McCloskey, D.N. and Zecher, J.R. (1976) How the Gold Standard Worked, 1880–1913, in J. Frenkel and H. Johnson (eds) *The Monetary Approach to the Balance of Payments*, London: Allen and Unwin.
Malou, J. (1880) *Documents Relatifs à la Question Monétaire*, 4 vols, Brussels: Hayez.

Martin, D.A. (1977) The Impact of Mid-Nineteenth Century Gold Depreciation Upon Western Monetary Standards, *Journal of European Economic History* Winter, 641–58.

——(1968) Bimetallism in the United States Before 1850, *Journal of Political Economy* 76: 428–42.

Mertens, J. (1944) *La Naissance et le développement de l'étalon or*, Paris: Presses Universitaires de France.

Morgenstern, O. (1959) *International Fnancial Transactions and Business Cycles*, Princeton, NJ: Princeton University Press.

Niehans, J. (1978) *The Theory of Money*, Baltimore, MD: Johns Hopkins University Press.

Nogaro, B. (1908) *L'Expérience Bimétalliste du 19° Siècle et la Théorie Générale de la Monnaie*, Paris: Sirey.

Officer, L.H. (1986) The Efficiency of the Dollar–Sterling Gold Standard (1890–1908), *Journal of Political Economy* 94 (5): 1038–73.

——(1989) The Remarkable Efficiency of the Dollar Sterling Gold Standard (1890–1906), *Journal of Economic History* XLIX (1): 1–41.

Oppers, S. (1992) Modelling the Bimetallic System: a target zone approach, mimeo, Harvard University.

Plessis, A. (1985) *La Politique de la Banque de France sous le Second Empire*, Genève: Droz.

Redish, A. (1990) The Evolution of the Gold Standard in England, *Journal of Economic History* December: 789–806.

——(1992) The Evolution of the Gold Standard in France, mimeo, University of British Columbia.

Roccas, M. (1987) L'Italia e il sistema monetario internazionale dagli anni '60 agli anni '90 del secolo scorso, Banca d'Italia, *Temi di Discussione del Servizio Studi* 92.

Rolnick, A. and Weber, W. (1986) Gresham's Law or Gresham's Fallacy?, *Journal of Political Economy* 94(1): 185–99.

Salant, S.W. and Henderson, D.W. (1978) Market Anticipations of government Policies and the Price of Gold, *Journal of Political Economy* 86 (4): 627–48.

Sayers, R.S. (1933) The Question of the Standard in the 1850's, *Economic Journal*, Supplement, 2(8): 575–601.

Seyd, E. (1868) *Bullion and Foreign Exchanges, Theoretically and practically considered, Followed by a Defence of the Double Valuation, with Special Reference to the Proposed System of Universal Coinage*, London: Effingham Wilson, Royal Exchange.

Soetbeer, A. (1889) *Matériaux pour faciliter l'Intelligence et l'Examen des Rapports Economiques des Métaux Précieux et de la Question Monétaire*, Paris.

Thuillier, G. (1983) *La Monnaie en France au debut du XIXème Siecle*, Geneva: Droz.

Walras, L. (1881) *Théorie Mathématique du Bimétallisme*, Paris: Guillaumin.

Warren, G.F. and Pearson, F.A. (1935) *Prices*, New York: Wiley, reprinted (1983) *Gold and Prices*, New York: Garland.

Weber, E. (1976) *Peasants into Frenchmen: The Modernization of Rural France, 1870–1914*, Stanford, CA: Stanford University Press.

Weil, Ph. (1991) *Currency Competition and the Transition to Monetary Union: Currency Competition and the Evolution of Multi-currency Regions*, in A. Giovannini and C. Meyer (eds), *European Financial Integration*, Cambridge: Cambridge University Press.

Wolowski, L. (1870) *L'or et l'argent*, Paris: Guillaumin.

Woodford, M. (1990) *Does Increased Competition Between Currencies Lead to Price Level and Exchange Rate Stability*?, NBER, Working Paper n. 3441.

Yeager, L.B. (1976) *International Monetary Relations*, New York: Harper and Row.

7

THE *ANCIEN RÉGIME* AND THE *CLASSICS*

Multimetallism, tabular standards and the classical theory of money[1]

Massimo V. Rostagno

You shall not press down upon the brow of labor this crown of thorns. You shall not crucify mankind upon a cross of gold.[2]

AN OVERVIEW

The internal evolution of the theory of money, from Marshall to Sargent and Wallace, has progressively blurred the boundaries between the theory of money proper and the theory of capital.[3]

This development is most evident in the subfield, reinaugurated in our days by Barro (1979), Whitaker (1984), and Sargent and Wallace (1983), that comes to grips with the mechanics of a system on a commodity-currency footing. Under such an institutional arrangement, given the physical productivity that currency can be thought to retain outside the monetary sector, the theoretical absorption of one discipline into the other becomes almost immediate.

All these models lead to the unequivocal conclusion that "in a stationary economy, production [of gold or silver] is needed solely to make good losses through wear and tear; in a growing economy, also to provide for an increase in the stock of money."[4] All these models espouse a sort of *irrelevance corollary* concerning the role attaching to the unit of account, or rather to the absolute scale of the economy, in a commodity-money setting.[5]

The linear view they convey has gained broad currency within and even outside the discipline. In fact, although the theoretical tradition referred to above does not delve deeply into institutional details and historical caveats, its clear formal treatment of both mono- and bimetallic regimes is perceived to be plausible and compelling. The result of *uniqueness* (one is money and one its price) and the *irrelevance* of the name and the number you attach to those metallic disks which you choose to call money have come to be adopted as an unquestioned premise.

In what follows I question the appropriateness of the institutional vacuum in which the mainstream model studies the emergence of a commodity money, the functions it performs, and the price(s) it fetches. Two major issues are addressed in the following pages: a positive, money theoretic question occupies the second section; the third section tackles the policy side of the matter.

The premise from which the second section departs is a stylized account of the model that the orthodox tradition has used (and still does) to formalize the workings of a monetary system on a (multi)-metallic footing. The main purpose is to assay its robustness by "giving the floor" to first-hand testimonies delivered by a number of seventeenth and eighteenth-century Italian economists debating "on the matter of money." Although sufficiently close to capturing the mechanics of the nineteenth-century (bimetallic) version of the multimetallic regime, assessed against the backdrop of the evidence produced, the mainstream model (complete with Gresham's law and the *irrelevance corollary*) proves to be hardly reliable if applied to the preceding millennium of European monetary history.

The alternative model put forward, laying the groundwork for the more formal treatment expounded in the third section, is centered around the following kingpins.

First, the system in place in continental Europe up till the great Napoleonic reform was more of a *dichotomous* than of a *bimetallic* nature. In fact, Gresham's episodes of misalignment between pure gold and pure silver media are shown to have posed relatively minor problems for the conduct of monetary policy. Carrying the dichotomy to its extremes, my hypothesis holds, rather, that the economy was split in two distinct tiers, populated by low-saving *workers* ("spending retail and living on a daily pay") and by high-saving *merchants* ("treating coins as merchandise"), respectively.

Second, the *tabular*[6] structure of the system (whereby the media of exchange were assigned a price in terms of a unit of account, the *ghost money*) does not seem to have been devised to solve the problem of recurrent misalignments between specie. Tabularity, coupled with a *de facto* asymmetry of the scale of values (used to price the coin) seems to have served the purpose of keeping the two tiers of circulation separated, one provided with a full-bodied medium of transaction, the other with a nonhoardable quasi-coupon (better spent than kept under the mattress). The fine-tuning of the pure metal content of the latter was meant to prevent the leakages between the two. Along these lines of reasoning, as opposed to the consolidated orthodox corollary, the role played by the unit of account in the viability of the whole monetary universe appears to have been all but *irrelevant.*

Third, the tabular-dichotomous monetary system defined two types of money, and assigned to each its own price. In the upper circuit, where wholesale traders systematically used good money, the price of the medium was dictated by the relative value of the metal(s) with respect to the n-1 (n-2) tradables being transacted, nicely along the most orthodox tradition. In the lower tier, where low-saving workers systematically exchanged a *quasi-coupon* (devoid of any store-of-value functions) for, say, a nondurable, money fetched the price determined by the quantity of the units of account made available for circulation, as monetarists would expect.

The third section expands on the policy theme. The model of a dichotomous economy with hoarding *merchants* and non-saving *workers* proves the superiority of a split monetary circuit with quasi- (but not completely) fiat-money in the lower tier coexisting with full-bodied coin in the upper. A bit of comparative statics shows that, provided the seignorage collected on the overvalued money is not "too large," separation of money circuits lends the system one more degree of freedom to counter deflationary shocks.

The *classics* and the *Ancien Régime*

A full standard formalization of systems using more than one metal for producing their means of payments starts with Napoleon. More exotic regimes in force in continental Europe prior to the great Napoleonic reform (which set the world monetary fabric on the solid bases still praised and mourned by some scholars) were never deemed worthy of further money-theoretic analysis. They were simply left in the realm of other disciplines.[7] Yet it is unquestionable that they pose a number of money theoretical questions that are worth dealing with on purely theoretical terms.

A few lines suffice to sketch the coordinates of the orthodox map in the territory of a multi-commodity-money regime. The following points do this. Some (points A1 to A4) will be given the status of Assumptions: they will merely list the main institutional features that the *Classics* almost instinctively ascribe to historical multimetallism. The last two deserve the status of Propositions: Given A1 to A4, an economy populated with utility maximizing representative consumers will behave as in P1 and P2. The complete classical model can thus be set out as follows.

A1 The system was on a bimetallic footing. The mint issued fine-gold and silver coins on demand. Small change was also minted, generally not in pure bullion.

A2 The gold and silver coins were inscribed with their values in terms of a single unit of account (the *pound*, the *ducat*, the *écu* or whatever). Both the full-weight currency and the divisional units were denominated in the same unique scale of absolute values.

A3 Fine-gold and silver coins were given universal legal tender status for all payments. The petty coins, legally limited in quantity and not necessarily good for discharging every kind of obligation, were nevertheless granted full *pro-rata convertibility*.[8]

A4 A uniform (generally small) mintage fee was charged by the *prince* on every type of specie circulating.[9]

P1 Thus, the relative price of coined silver in terms of coined gold was bound to be equal to their ratio if expressed in terms of the monetary, or accounting, unit. This statement sets the necessary and sufficient condition for a bimetallic regime to be both operative and stable *as such*, that is to be preserved from degenerating into a sort of unstable alternating monometallism. In the instances in which this alignment condition was not met (which were not rare, actually), Gresham's law could be expected to do its job:[10]

> The coin made of metal undervalued at the mint will be melted for use as a commodity, and the overvalued metal will be brought in for coining. . . . "Bad" (i.e., overvalued at the mint) money thus will drive "good" (i.e., undervalued at the mint) money out of circulation.
>
> (Laidler 1991: 157)

P2 The price of money in terms of goods was the relative price of its metallic content (expressed in either metal) in terms of the remaining n-2 goods.[11]

In fact, this map portrays the workings of nineteenth-century European bimetallism with a fair degree of exactitude. It is hardly reliable if put to other uses, however.

Einaudi (1982), Patinkin (1965), and White (1984), among the few theorists who ventured beyond the Pillars of Hercules marked by the years 1800–3,[12] unfortunately came back with a fantastic representation. In their thought experiments, they did allow for the existence of institutional settings not subject to constraint A2. In other words, they did realize that a system striking unlabeled (nonpriced) coins, that is specie not linked once-and-for-all (as they leave the Mint) to their statutory value in terms of the accounting unit, quite naturally gives rise to the ghost (or imaginary) money phenomenon. To state the issue in terms somewhat reminiscent of Jevons (1875), they did implicitly recognize that prior to the Napoleonic Wars the system was in essence a tabular one (in which money itself deserved a price to be fixed by law *pro tempore*), in that the act of coinage left the denomination of the physical media of trade (the coins) absolutely indeterminate. Nevertheless, the picture they rendered and the conclusion they sometimes drew are, I think, wide of the mark and more apt to dismiss the issue than to provide the economic explanation that it demands. White's discussion on the historical systems that divorced the medium of payment from the measure in which prices were specified concludes that

> While it is true that a ghost money unit had no exact counterpart among existing coins, each of *these coins bore a fixed value relationship to the unit based on relative bullion content*. . . . The unit of account value of any particular coin in circulation is a question of its weight and fineness, not the variable market exchange rate. . . . The unit of account and the medium of exchange have not become distinct commodities, only distinct quantities of the same commodity.
>
> (White 1984: 705)

This statement, an extended elaboration of Proposition 2, is actually the kingpin of the above conception, complete with the uniqueness and irrelevance axioms. True, the pre-1800 system may well have been messy and malfunctioning, ruled as it was by greedy princes seeking to extract as much precious metal as they could by imposing extravagant seignorage fees on coinage or by clipping coins already in circulation. That is, constraint A3 may in some instances require slight qualifications to make it more binding and adherent to historical conditions. The rest holds on its own, however, and no further qualifications are deemed to be necessary.

THE *ANCIEN RÉGIME*

The *Ancien Régime*, the institutional abstraction that is here contrasted to the standard formalization of a metallic standard, is a purely analytical construct stretching its temporal domain from 1789 back to, say, Charlemagne,[13] and extending its spatial boundaries to comprise the whole of continental Europe. From this enormous mass of historical record, I extract a small sample focusing on mid-eighteenth-century Italy, when (and where) the thousand-year-old system was close to final collapse.

The guide I have selected to conduct the discussion through the mechanisms regulating the Italian (and continental) pre-revolutionary money market is the evidence gleaned from a number of contemporary essays, tracts, *pamphlets*, memoranda, and ordinances "*on the matter of money*" by philosophers, economists, merchants, and high public servants. Some of them took part personally in the great *debate on money* promoted around 1750 by the severe currency disorders that had been afflicting the Italian peninsula since the end of the golden Renaissance.

Some of these writers, such as Montanari, Galiani, and Beccaria, still enjoy considerable international reputation; others, while much admired and broadly quoted in their day, are now almost forgotten.[14] In those days the standard academic dissertations, even on quite technical subjects, combined useful analysis with countless (and tiresome) literary allusions, as well as ancient fables on this and that, so preference is given, where possible, to citations drawn from *ad hoc* memoranda explicitly addressed to the policy maker.

The discussion is structured, admittedly with some exaggeration, in a theorem-like fashion, as a list of assumptions followed by two propositions and a corollary. This serves mainly to replicate the order imposed on the *orthodox view* as traced above. An order which the latter surely deserves.

The assumptions 1 to 4, as well as the two propositions that "close" this model of bimetallism, are replaced here by a specular set of assumptions and propositions. These alternative assumptions and propositions are set forth in detail in the rest of this section.

Multimetallism

Assumption 1a The system was multimetallic. Pure silver and gold pieces were produced along with (overvalued) coins struck in an alloy of silver and copper whose fine-metal (silver) content as a proportion of their total weight varied over a wide continuum, ranging from slightly less than one to zero. Coins containing a positive amount of silver were collectively dubbed black (or small or vellon) currency.[15]

The published evidence supporting the substitution of A1a for A1 is overwhelming.[16] On these grounds, I shall not dwell on the point. The importance of emphasizing multi- rather than (silver–gold) bimetallism, however, is worth one additional remark. The system was more dichotomous (in a sense hopefully made clear below) than bimetallic. What rendered it dichotomous was the coexistence of the black currency, on the one side, and the white and yellow species, on the other, i.e., the joint production and circulation of *hard* and *soft* currency, not simply the *free coinage of silver and gold* at a fixed exchange rate. But let us proceed one step further.

The tabular standard

*Assumption 2a The system was tabular. Coins did not carry a price on the obverse but were decreed from time to time to be current at certain par values in terms of an absolute scale of accounting units (*pounds, ducats, écus, *etc.), also called* imaginary, *or* ghost monies, *for they performed a purely scaling function.*[17] *Devaluations (termed* augmentations, enhancements *or* raisings*), which were not infrequent, meant upgrading the value of foreign coins as well as nationally issued species in terms of the unit of account.*

This has also become common knowledge, though not so much among theorists, and is not worth separate treatment. What really matters is not tabularity *per se* but the use to which this curious complication was put. This should become clear in what follows.

The asymmetric scale

Assumption 3a The scale was asymmetric. The statutory ratios between the coins in terms of the monetary (ghost) unit were fully operative only moving from the top of the table (where the national and foreign full-bodied high-value coins were positioned) down (where the national and foreign black currencies were listed). Climbing up the scale, law was implicitly suspended.

In other words, nobody would have prevented you from exchanging a *zecchino*[18] for as many *black-quattrini*[19] as the lawful ratios prescribed (although, for reasons to become clear below, it would have been foolish of you to do so), but the reverse was certainly forbidden. Legal-tender dispositions limited the discharging power of the small pieces at the bottom of the ladder. Commercial practices were even more drastic on this.

This would be no novelty, as far as legal tender provisions *per se* were concerned. After all, similar laws, limiting the purchasing power of small change were also enforced during the bimetallic era, as Assumption 3 recalls.

However, what sets the pre-Napoleonic system far apart from any later multi-, monometallic, or even fiat-currency arrangements, is the absence of any (banking) institution legally obliged to credit the bearer of small change for any sum, on a *pro-rata* basis, in terms of the monetary unit. In other words, the bottom-up conversion was made possible, in the nineteenth-century type of bimetallic regime, *at no more and no less than the lawful terms*, by requiring the "bank" to draw up the bearer's deposit held with it, and to stand ready to pay out the entire accumulated balance in full-bodied coins or in the National Bank's notes convertible into full-bodied coins. This was not the case before Napoleon.

In short, before Napoleon the tabular scale operated only one-way, in the sense that to climb up the scale, you had to resort to money changers. But this will be the subject of the next Assumption.

In a 1784 technical report on the monetary disorders in the territory of Milan, G.R. Carli calculates that

> In Italy the black currency bears a proportion of imaginary value equal to 36 1/6 [per cent, over its total *pound* price]. If we allow for a 4% coinage cost and a further 3 1/3% due to expenses for the copper contained in it,[20] we are left with an average figure of 30 per cent of non-real value conferred upon the low coins in Italy. As a consequence, if in Milan, in Venice, in Genoa or in any other city one were to barter 100 *filippi*[21] for small currency, he would lose in this barter 30 *filippi*, for in 100 *filippi*'s worth of small currency [in terms of accounting *pounds*] there is no more value than in 70 *filippi* [in pure bullion].
>
> (G.R. Carli 1784: 261)

Later on, he adds:

> There are two values or, to be more precise, two measures for the currency: One for good money and the other for small coins. . . . One for the everyday transactions of the common people, the other for paying taxes, for large-scale and external commerce. Since ancient times the Florentine people have used both white and black money, the latter being by 1/4 less valuable than the former, so that 4 *shillings* payable in white money were equivalent to 5 *shillings* payable in black money. . . . Also in Venice, the silver *ducat* is current [on the free market] at 8 *pounds*, while its official price is £6, 4s, and the current *zecchino* fetches £22, being officially worth only £17.
>
> (G.R. Carli 1784: 275)

Elsewhere, Carli clarifies how the two monetary circuits could be kept separate and thus safeguarded from reciprocal contamination:

> The law confers upon the *zecchino* the value of £14, 10s, but, in the market place, it is current at £17, and in Pavia even at £17, 10s. Now, it is opportune to make clear which *pounds* we are referring to. For in terms of Milanese *pounds*, the statutory price is right, and for £14, 10s one can always get 1 *zecchino* and there will never be anyone who will refuse to pay £14, 10s for it. So there is no abuse so far. Yet, the *zecchino* is current at 17 £ and even at £17, 10s if measured in Genoese *parpajole*, in *bhlozer*, in *marchetti*,[22] in *quattrini.*
>
> (G.R. Carli 1770: 106–7)

The meaning of all this should be clear. If applied to the financial obligations originating from a *written contract*, signed by professional members of the trading community, the lawful scale was absolutely operative. Indeed, the classical irrelevance corollary as to the choice of the unit of account, in which the parties were to label the full-bodied metallic disks they usually exchanged, was perfectly valid. Both established commercial conventions and the legal-tender provisions ensured that no one would dare discharge a debt by handing in black coins at the dummy ratio decreed by law.[23]

Marquis G. Belloni, a wealthy merchant from Bologna, in his 1752 treatise on money dedicated to the Pope, puts it in terms of an implicit gold-clause contractually pending upon the specie to be presented for payment. Note the interchangeable reference to the imaginary money and to a full-weight currency:

> The merchants, who solely evaluate and look after the intrinsic value, absolutely disregarding the numeraire [its price in units of account] and being always in search of the real money, by means of their use of the imaginary money reduce and equate each type of coin to the measure

> dictated by its physical nature, and ask for as many pieces thereof as it suffices to make up the real value they wish to obtain.
>
> (Belloni 1752: 125)

In fact, within written contracts (disposing mainly of wholesale commodities) the use of the unit of account (the imaginary money) was quite naturally another way of stating prices in terms of gold or silver weights *tout court.*

In case of spillovers[24] from one circuit to the other, as mentioned, the money-changers entered into play.

Private seignorage

Assumption 4a Seignorage was not uniform along the scale. The money-changers often acted as partners of the prince, sharing in the seignorage extracted from the overvalued black coins. More often, the two-tier circuit for money was even detrimental to the prince and worked to the exclusive advantage of the money-traders.

The free-market exchange rate between good and bad money was calculated as the ratio of the intrinsic values of the coins bartered: the (free) money market transaction involving spillovers on the side of either party, that is, a deal in which either party was *expected* to pay in a currency not routinely used by the other, was conducted on genuine classical (Modigliani-Miller type) bases, as stated by White in the passage quoted above.

Beccaria (1762: 225) puts it plainly:

> Foreigners, goldsmiths, and money-changers accept solely coins at their intrinsic value, while the common people prefer the coins which are more broadly accepted.

This implies that the money-changers, positioning on the borderline between the two circuits, were operating with a bid-ask spread (expressed in units of account) approximately equal to the rate of overvaluation of the small coins with respect to their par value. Why this had to be so, why, in other words, the *bankers'* ask-price for small coins should have been driven down to the floor represented by the *pound* price of these coins' fine metal content, I try to show later on.[25]

Here it will suffice to give voice to the vehement protests that these lucrative practices aroused within circles of economists and political scientists. The protests were directed both against the arbitrage opportunities for money-changers, who exploited the intermediate position they had come to enjoy and against their taking part in the decision process presiding over the issue of small coins.

In fact, it is possible that at some times and in some places free coinage was even extended, *de facto,* to black currency, to the great advantage of a small circle of businesspeople, who became open partners of the prince in the overvaluation of bullion to be minted as base money.[26] This latter possibility appears to be alluded to in the following piece drawn from Montanari (1680):

> These small coins are necessary for the use of the common people who spend retail and live on a daily pay. But, if the princes of Lombardy had not been too often persuaded by unlearned ministers to issue or to allow the merchants to strike exorbitant amounts of this low currency, and had they limited the issues thereof to the need to replenish what on average had gone lost, they would not have caused the value of the doubloons to rise by 1/3 in the course of the last 30 years; which has dealt a big blow to their own finances.
>
> (Montanari 1680: ch. III)

The explanation of the last clause is found elsewhere in the same work:

> If a tax is paid on corn, this is calculated as so many *shillings* per pound. . . . Now, if this tax yielded as much [in terms of *shillings*] when the *zecchino* stood at 100 *shillings*, as it does now, when the *zecchino* is exchanged for 400 *shillings*, it is perfectly plain that now the revenue in gold is barely 1/4 of what it used to be. To conclude, the prince's receipts have always been counted in small currency. If the gold and silver real monies rose in value, would this not amount to debasing the imaginary money and the lower currencies, and to cutting public revenues?
>
> (Montanari 1683: 323)

Further on, however, Montanari displays the other side of the issue, as perceived by the private sector:

> As the good money increases in value, the merchants do not accordingly adjust the pay of Labour or the price of the poor craftsmen's petty manufactures. The silk weaver who used to be paid 3 *pounds* a yard for his velvet manufacture when the *écu*[27] was worth 9 *pounds*, now has to weave 4 yards for an *écu*, which he used to earn for 3 yards, as the *écu* meanwhile has been raised to 12 *pounds*.
>
> (Montanari 1683: 326)

Gresham's fallacy

Proposition 1a The dichotomous nature of the system and the existence of a free market for coins of all kinds were the necessary and sufficient conditions for a stable multimetallic system (as such): good money and bad money could coexist.

That the second condition (the existence of a free market for coins of all types) obtained is clear from what has been said about the asymmetry of the scale of values and the role played by the money-changers.[28] At any rate, this clearly runs counter to the traditional formalization of a multimetallic system, which rests on the stringency of the official exchange rate provisions, on the one hand, and on Gresham's paradigm, on the other.

As the triggering of Gresham's mechanism depends on strict enforcement of the legal price stipulated in the *Mint's indenture*,[29] the following argument borrowed from Galiani (1750) does not seem to lend it much credit:

> Experience has taught sovereigns that it is better to allow [fine-metal coins] to circulate by weight than by authority of the coins [by tale], and this is why everyone is in the custom of weighing them and using the imprint to assure the price by weight. In other words, it is already treated as merchandise.
>
> (Galiani 1750: 106)

Furthermore, as we shall see in the corollary below, in the lower tier of monetary circulation Gresham's result might even have been reversed. Under certain circumstances, relatively better (less overvalued) money could drive out relatively worse (more overvalued).

To clarify the first condition, the dichotomous nature of the system, some further discussion is required.

The one-price-of-money fallacy

Proposition 2a In a world populated by high-saving merchants *trading in durables and low-saving* workers *consuming nondurables, the monetary system was dichotomous. Each agent was provided with the currency he needed.*

Having in mind Montanari's common people, who "*spend retail and live on a daily pay*," and Galiani's merchants, who "*treat coins as merchandise*," let us consider the following description of the different monies in use, offered by Neri (1751), a widely respected economist and advisor to the Austrian administration in Milan:

> Money is not a pure measure and representation of value, which can be done even with paper, but is or should be a pledge of value as well. . . . This double and combined function it performs is generally sought by mankind. It follows that, referring to the value conferred upon the coins in excess of their metal content, money can perform only the first role, that of representation, just as notes or tokens do. But the function as a pledge is not present if not in the real quantity of metal which money contains. What is not real pledge, is esteemed for nothing in the universal trade of men. . . . Now, good and real money transfer the command on and the property of value, while the petty money, which represents a value in excess of its intrinsic content, renders, to this extent, the bearer's condition akin to that of a pure creditor. The latter

> is never in a position equal to that of the one who *owns* the pledge. Firstly, be he indebted to foreigners, these purely representative tokens he has, this dummy money, melt down like snow and are held for nothing beyond the pure and real value of the metal they are made with. Secondly, it often happens that the government itself refuses such currency for the payment of taxes and customs duties. Also, they are refused in the payments which merchants make among themselves, and particularly in the payment of bills of exchange and for other business of substance. Therefore, this representation of value gives the bearer a credit which will not be paid for by anyone. . . . The realization of this token, its conversion into good money, turns out to be very difficult, for everyone finds it more advantageous to be owner of value, rather than only creditor thereof, and everyone prefers to keep the good money which performs all of the functions of money, serves all needs. It is solely out of pure necessity that one might be induced to divest himself of money in exchange for a pure representation of money.[30]
>
> (Neri 1751: 121, 186)

The tabular-dichotomous monetary system was a clever technology. It did not serve the purpose imagined (with enthusiastic admiration) by Einaudi (1982), i.e., solving the problem of gold–silver misalignments, just by daily adjustment of the ghost money prices of the different species to bring them back into line with their relative value in the market place. As we have seen, this was a minor problem, after all.

Rather, it was a system that deliberately provided everyone with the kind of money that each needed. *Merchants*, trading in durables, need a durable as a temporary store of their purchasing power. For them the price of the money they happen to hold is the yield on the capital they have parted with in the process of portfolio diversification, and to which they will sooner or later return.

On the opposite side, *workers* with a very low propensity to save, mainly interested in the routine conversion of their daily pay into quickly perishable goods, need no more than a pure *record-keeping device* that gives evidence (as Neri would say) of a *claim*. Within the short circuit in which this record is to circulate, however, the chances of this *claim* being ever collected on (converted into good money for hoarding or other purposes) are actually very low.[31] As a consequence, workers are provided with a quasi-coupon, nonhoardable currency, what Hicks (1989: 45) would call a *quasi-money*.

The black currency had at least three essential features.

First, it was nonhoardable, better spent than kept under the mattress. The recurrent general rescalings of the whole spectrum of coins dissuaded the bearer from keeping them out of circulation.[32] Montanari (1680: 356–7) describes a *hot-potato* episode prompted by fear of future devaluation: "In

Venice, at the time of the *augmentation* of the other coins, the merchants hid the *bezzo* and the *soldo*[33] in order to get rid of overvalued coins being afraid that they will be suddenly devalued by the authorities." The currency was always at risk of being taxed (devalued), the more so the more overvalued it was in terms of the good species.[34] Galiani (1750) explains:

> A country which has base coins finds it necessary to use them; they cannot be hidden away, melted down, or sent abroad in their entirety, as gold and silver may be. For since they are more necessary to trade, as payment for small purchases, no man would ever destroy copper coins in order to make a small profit and allow all industry and the rapid pace of employment to vanish. . . . It is no less evident that something which all consider so bad can circulate quite as much as if it were thought of as good, as long as the common deception endures and as long as everyone can live in hope that his neighbour will not refuse it.
>
> (Galiani 1750: 101)

Second, it was not fiat money. In a regime of free coinage, some bullion content was the guarantee that money would not be turned into a free good. The bullion content was set to bear a certain relationship to the tradability of the petty commodities being exchanged in the lower circuit of the economy, in order to shelter the latter from international arbitrage. The higher the degree of international tradability of those goods, the lower the rate of overvaluation of the petty coin, the larger the bullion equivalent of a *pound* paid in bad money. This will be more extensively treated in the third section. The monetary role of fine bullion within this sector was essentially downgraded to that of an entry barrier device against international arbitrage.

Third, it was an anti-deflationary device. A conjectural treatment of this issue is given in the third section.

A corollary

Corollary 1a In the lower currency circuit, Gresham's law was not only non-operative, but sometimes actually reversed.

The reason for good money displacing bad money in the lower tier of the economy is simple. Being provided with nationally issued overvalued coins, always subject to the risk of devaluation and thus serving merely as an instrument for quick transactions, the *workers* were in search of a full-bodied money that could also serve as a store of value. This could be achieved by importing divisional coins from the countries where the low currency contained comparatively more bullion per unit of the numeraire value.

For example, a foreign black coin officially worth a *shilling* was purchased for something less than a *shilling* (at the intrinsic value) by international money arbitrageurs and spent in the countries, whose 1-*shilling* coin contained comparatively less silver. Both parties gained from the deal, of course: the money trader pocketed the arbitrage profit, the *worker* received more bullion per *shilling*.

Carli (1766) confirms this account:

> Many complain about this introduction [of foreign black coins], but nobody knows the boundaries of what is good and what is evil. Indeed, one finds that all these foreign coins, given the price at which they are introduced, are better than ours: that is, they have more intrinsic value than our *quattrini*.
>
> (Carli 1766: 40)

Further on, he sets out some calculations:

> 50 *marchetti* [the foreign coin], worth 3 [domestic] *quattrini* [i.e., 12 shillings] each are equal in value to 150 *quattrini*. In 50 *marchetti* there are *denari* 3. 2. 11 1/2 of fine silver, and *denari* 65.15.12 1/2 of copper.[35] If we price silver at 8 *pounds* and 8 *shillings* the *mark*,[36] and copper at 17 *shillings* the *mark*, we conclude that the true value of the 50 *marchetti* is equal to 1. 7. 6 5/12 *pounds*. But 150 *quattrini* have a true value of 17 *shillings*. Thus, 50 *marchetti* carry a higher value than 150 *quattrini* by as much as 38 1/7 per cent.
>
> (Carli 1766: 42–4)

The result applies, as well, to *bhlozers* (from Switzerland), *parpajole* (from Genoa), *pounds* of Parma, and so on. The statement made at the outset of this subsection is then brought out.

A SIMPLIFIED MODEL

This section presents a highly simplified model,[37] which portrays a fully dichotomous economy consisting of two sectors, the one exchanging a nondurable good and the other trading in a "luxury" durable. The two sectors are first supposed to *use the same medium*, a full-weight silver coin denominated in the home unit of account, the *pound* (£), at the face value assumed fixed at 1. In a second version, the two separate circuits are provided with media made of different metals, but still priced in the same numeraire.

A single money

Sector d (durables) is populated by *merchants* who have to balance their need to consume a luxury good (d), which they produce, with their inclination to accumulate a stock of silver in the form of ornaments and pieces of jewelry. Their choice between consumption as a flow (of d) and a stock (of silver in the form of *jewelry*) is depicted by equation (1), which renders the desired stock of silver (T^*) held in non-monetary form by *merchants* as a (positive) function of the price of good d (P_d, in terms of silver-money), a (negative) function of the expected rate of increase in the price of d (π), and a (positive unit-elastic) function of the flow of real income (y_d) accruing to the merchants:[38]

(1) $T^* = f(P_d, \pi)y_d$, $f_1 > 0$, $f_2 < 0$,

As P_d rises, the opportunity cost of freezing silver for one's sumptuary consumption (in the form of T) diminishes. On the other hand, if P_d is expected to rise in the future (π suddenly becoming positive), it pays to revise one's hoarding target (T^*) to diversify from one durable (nonminted silver frozen in one's vaults) to the other (d).

The flow demand for silver to be added to the stocks held for non-monetary (ornamental) purposes is expressed as a function of the difference between the target T^* and current holdings (S_n). On the other hand, since silver hoarded in nonmonetary form is assumed to deteriorate geometrically, at the rate δ, the *net* demand for silver in nonmonetary forms (s^d_n), presented in equation (2), also takes account of the additions to existing stocks needed to mantain the desired stock constant in physical terms:

(2) $s^d_n = \alpha(f(P_d, \pi)y_d - S_n) + \delta f(P_d, \pi)y_d$

Equation (1) and equation (2) together define the net additions to the silver hoards (ΔS_n) as follows:

(3) $\Delta S_n = s^d_n - \delta S_n = (\alpha + \delta)\ (f(P_d, \pi)y_d - S_n)$

Agents operating in *Sector n*, that is consuming one unit of a nondurable good n each, are all employed in the industry mining and minting silver (henceforth, *the mint*), to which they inelastically supply their labor, the unique factor of production. Given the (inverse) of the technology function $n(Q)$ linking silver output Q to employment n (with $n' > 0$), by the optimality condition applying to *the mint* and the no-saving hypothesis affecting the spending behavior of the workers, we can define a supply function of silver:

(4) $s^p = s^p(P_n | k)$, $\quad s^{p\prime}(.|k) < 0$,

where P_n is the *pound*-price of the perishable good and k is a constant capturing the physical constraints placed on the mining (and minting) activity.[39]

Since capital is accumulated solely in the form of uncoined silver (recall equation (1)), and borrowing for consumption is ruled out, the amount of silver demanded for monetary purposes is determined by the need of both *merchants* and *workers* to buy their goods (y_d and y_n, respectively) on the market.[40] The equilibrium condition in the money market thus requires

(5) $S_m = P_d y_d + P_n y_n$

where S_m is the stock of silver money in circulation, expressed in £. The economy adds to this stock residually, once the *merchants'* hoarding propensity is taken into account; the injections of silver coin into the system (ΔS_m) are as follows:

(6) $\Delta S_m = s^p - s_n^d = s^p(P_n) - \alpha(f(P_d, \pi)y_d - S_n) - \delta f(P_d, \pi)y_d$

It is clear that the dichothomous nature of the system rests upon the twin assumptions that the merchants do not like (and thus, within certain bounds to be made more explicit below, value at zero) the *workers'* consumption good (n), and that the workers do not save (having, for example, an infinite discount factor applying to any future consumption streams).

The steady state

In the long run, when no additions to existing stocks are being made ($\Delta S_n = \Delta S_m = 0$), the system settles on an equilibrium defined, for given values of y_d, y_n and π (the latter being equal to zero in the long run) by the values of P_n, P_d, S_n and S_m implicitly defined by the following four conditions:

(7) $s^p(P_n{}^*) = P_n{}^* y_n$

(8) $s^p(P_n{}^*) = \delta f(P_d{}^*) y_d$

(9) $S_n{}^* = f(P_d{}^*) y_d$

(10) $S_m{}^* = P_d{}^* y_d + P_n{}^* y_n$

Equation (7) consolidates the no-profit condition in the mining sector, the no-saving constraint on workers, and the clearing of the n market; equation (8) conveys the result that, under stationary conditions, silver production is exactly sufficient to replenish the continuously decaying target stock held for non-monetary uses. Figure 7.1 depicts the situation in the $P_d - S_m$, and the $S_m - S_n$ spaces. In the left-hand portion, equation (10) is treated as an implicit function of S_m in terms of P_d. In the right-hand section, the two stationarity conditions (loci $\Delta S_n = 0$ and $\Delta S_m = 0$, respectively) intersect to nail down the equilibrium vector of the stocks of silver held in monetary and non-monetary forms.[41]

In what sense do conditions (7)–(10) have a truly classical flavour? Even a cursory inspection yields several particularly noteworthy insights.

First, "*The value of money is determined, temporarily by demand and supply, permanently and on average by the cost of production*" (Mill 1871: 507). As a consequence, the causal sequence linking money and (durables) prices runs, between one stationary point and the next, from the latter to the former and not vice versa. In few words, the system (which regulates mainly large-scale trade) is price-making and quantity-taking.[42]

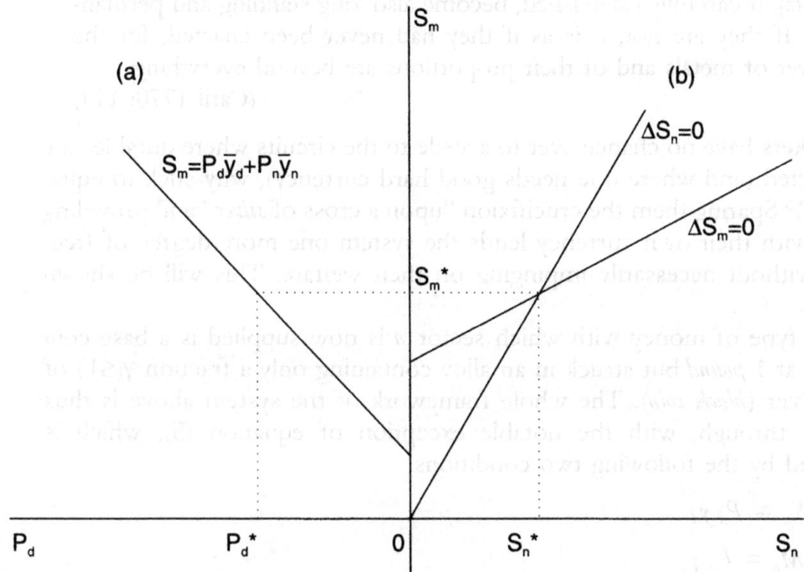

Figure 7.1 The steady state

Second, equation (10), in particular, has a Fisherian tone to it. In the short run, the interaction between (durables) prices and money is one between a pure flow of money expenditure (S_m) and a pure *flow* of goods offered for sale. In other words, the money that we shall consider is only what is in *active circulation*, excluding any hoards accumulated in the form of coin.[43]

Third, as for sector *n*, the need for the currency used in the lower tier of the economy is totally extraneous to the terms of the choice (accumulation of S_n versus consumption of *d*) that regulates the demand for money within sector *d*. The connection of the purchasing power in sector *n* to the physical production of the precious metal is dictated by the no-profit constraint on the extractive and minting industry. The money that goes to feed this sector (worth, in equilibrium, $P_n{}^*y_n$) is, for all practical purposes, *a short-circuit currency*.

Of course this strays a good way from an authentic account of the classical wisdom on the subject, at least as far as the classics in the Anglo-Saxon tradition are concerned.

Separation

The double value of money is not a great evil. It does constitute a nuisance, though, if the limits of it are not firmly traced by law. [These

> limits], if carefully established, become also long standing and permanent. If they are not, it is as if they had never been enacted, for the power of metals and of their proportions are beyond everything.
>
> (Carli 1770: 114)

If workers have no chance ever to accede to the circuits where durables are transacted (and where one needs good hard currency), why stick to equation (5)? Sparing them the crucifixion "upon a cross of *silver*" and providing them with their own currency lends the system one more degree of freedom without necessarily impinging on their welfare. This will be shown below.

The type of money with which sector *n* is now supplied is a base coin valued at 1 *pound* but struck in an alloy containing only a fraction $\gamma(\leq 1)$ of fine silver (*black coin*). The whole framework of the system above is thus carried through, with the notable exception of equation (5), which is replaced by the following two conditions:

(5a) $S_m = P_d y_d$

(5b) $M_n = P_n y_n$

where M_n is the amount of value in accounting units (*pounds*) made available to the workers (in the form of clipped coins) for their petty expenses (the purchase of *n*). Defining M_n^* as the supply of base currency that, given equation (5b), keeps the price of non-durables fixed at P_n^*, we have:

(11) $Q^s = s^P(\gamma M_n^*/y_n) > Q^* = s^P(P_n^*)$

In other words, for $\gamma<1$, the quantity of silver produced under *separation* (splitting of monetary circuits), Q^s, is larger than the output under conditions (7)–(10), Q^*. Moreover, from equations (7) and (11) it follows that

(7a) $s^P(\gamma M_n^*/y_n) - \gamma M_n^* = \Sigma^s > 0$

Thus, provided the "right" quantity M_n^* of the numeraire is supplied to the lower tier of the economy (i.e., the quantity that stabilizes P_n at its pre-separation level P_n^*), the saving of bullion made by *the mint* thanks to being authorised to pay in a cheaper coin (in terms of fine metal) shows up, in the new version of equation (7), as a positive rent term, the seignorage Σ^s. We assume that the rent (expressed in ounces of fine metal) is cashed-in by the merchants and is added to their hoards of nonmonetized silver (S_n).[44]

The steady state

Conditional to the stability of the pound price for good *n*,

(12) $P_n^* = M_n^*/y_n$

the new system portraying stationarity under separation of the currencies is as follows:

(7a) $s^p(\gamma M_n^*/y_n) = \gamma M_n^* + \Sigma^s$

(8a) $s^p(\gamma M_n^*/y_n) = \delta\, f(P_d^s)\, y_d$

(9a) $S_n^s = f(P_d^s)\, y_d$

(10a) $S_m^s = P_d^s\, y_d + \gamma M_n^*$

where P_d^s, Σ^s, S_n^s, and S_m^s (the last three of which are in real terms) are defined for a given vector of exogenous ($P_n^*(M_n^*)$, y_n, y_d, $\pi = 0$), and choice variables (γ).

To be sure, the pure metal content per unit of value, γ, cannot be entirely treated as a choice variable. As Carli puts it in a proposal for a general monetary reform:

> It is Nations' most fatal blunder that some may think that this base money be *always* kept out of the universal trade. This trade has its regulator in the exchange rate and the latter finds its own in the fine metal content of the shillings and of the pounds issued by each Nation.
> (Carli 1784: 276, emphasis added)

As noted earlier, the *financier* (the money dealer), placed on the border line between the two systems, was in a position to buy the black coinage at its intrinsic value ($\gamma \leq 1$) and sell it at the par price stipulated by law (in our case, 1).[45] This implied the opportunity for theoretically unbounded profits. Actually, for a given M_n, the lower γ, the cheaper the price of good *n* expressed in fine silver, the more handsome the gain from arbitraging among different monetary jurisdictions. In other words, once the initial amount of *pounds* granted to *sector n* in the form of black coins (M_n) is set, as we have assumed, at the level that guarantees a stable price in the lower tier of the economy (P_n^*), there is nothing in the economy, but γ itself, that prevents the international arbitrageurs from flooding the home country with γ-coins, thus swelling M_n, putting upward pressures on P_n, and upsetting and undoing the new equilibrium under separation.

As a matter of history, free-coinage provisions or international-arbitrage possibilities (or both combined) opened up dangerous leakages between the *home* and the *international* circulations. This possibility rendered the lower basin of the home circulation particularly vulnerable to *endogenous changes* in M_n. However, since good *n* is, by assumption, perishable, there are built-in (physical) impediments to the full-fledged working of the kind of disruptive mechanisms outlined above. In other words, there can be defined a whole continuum of values that γ may take on (between a ceiling of 1 and a floor γ_{min}) at which the arbitrage is not profitable and thus non-operative, given the transaction and transportation costs lying on the international mobility of goods.

It is precisely for values of γ comprised within our stability range ($\gamma_{min} \leq \gamma \leq 1$), that the notion of a managed money available for deployment in the cause of macroeconomic stability gains plausibility. Let us now return to this case.

From inspection of equation (8a), recalling equation (11), we immediately conclude that $P_d^s > P_d^*$. Also, from equation (9a), $S_n^s > S_n^*$.

Shocks

It is thus clear that the transition from a system that "pools" the two basins of circulation and provides them with the same full-weight medium of exchange to one which targets each circuit with its own currency (the full-weight coin being devoted to wholesale trade, and the quasi-fiat money to retail expenses, possibly of perishables) carries an implicit *inflationary* bias with it. But, more interestingly, once the monetary standard based on separation has been established, the same built-in inflationary bias can be turned into a powerful tool of macroeconomic management deployed against the insurgence of *deflationary* episodes. A bit of comparative statics will demonstrate this.

Let us examine what happens when the system so described is hit by potentially deflationary shocks. To begin with, we concentrate on the transmission mechanism set into motion by such shocks within the unified system, the one that offers to both markets the same full-weight coin. Later on (pp. 199–200), account will be given of the kind of propagation mechanism being unleashed under split circulation.

Drop without parachute

Less and less cheaply worked sources of the precious metal may here be rendered through an increase in k (see equation 4). This, other things being equal, exerts a downward pressure on s^p, the flow of silver production, which in turn, by way of the monopsonic position ruling in the labor market, acts on P_n. Equation (5) suggests that, for given y_n, a fall in the price of n will shift the curve represented in the left-hand side of Figure 7.1 downward (see Figure 7.2). On the other side of the graph, locus $\Delta S_m = 0$ will also slip downward, as for given desired additions to S_n less and less silver is made available for monetary use.[46] Of course, the sensitivity of the desired stocks of silver held in nonmonetary forms to its opportunity cost does play a role. The less responsive T^* is to P_d (the steeper $\Delta S_m = 0$ in our space) the larger is the adjustment P_d is called upon to make in order to bring the money market back to equilibrium, the more harshly will the deflationary bias implicit in the commodity money regime be felt by the traders.

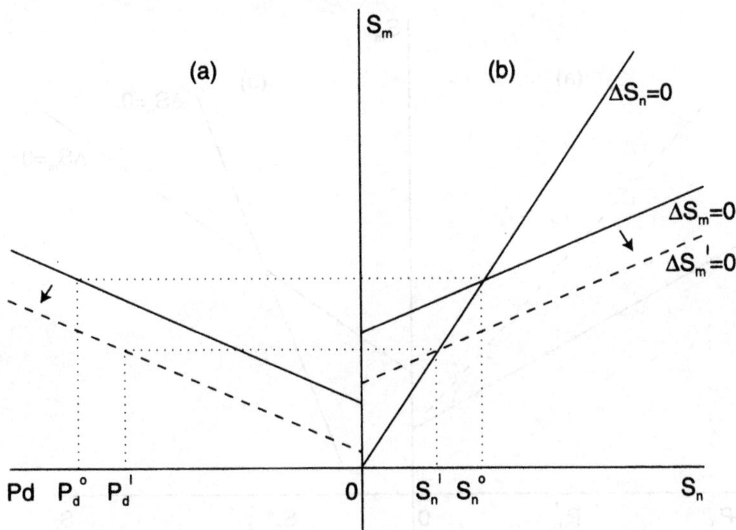

Figure 7.2 The unified system: effects of technological progress

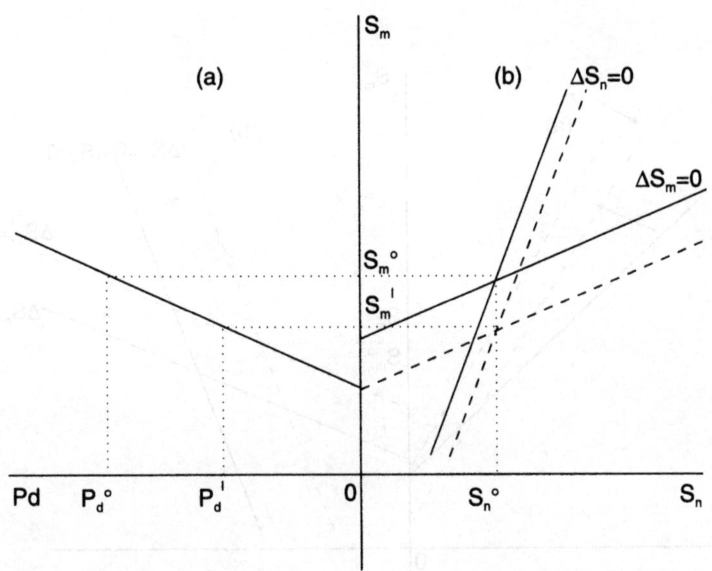

Figure 7.3 The unified system: effects of an increased propensity to hoard

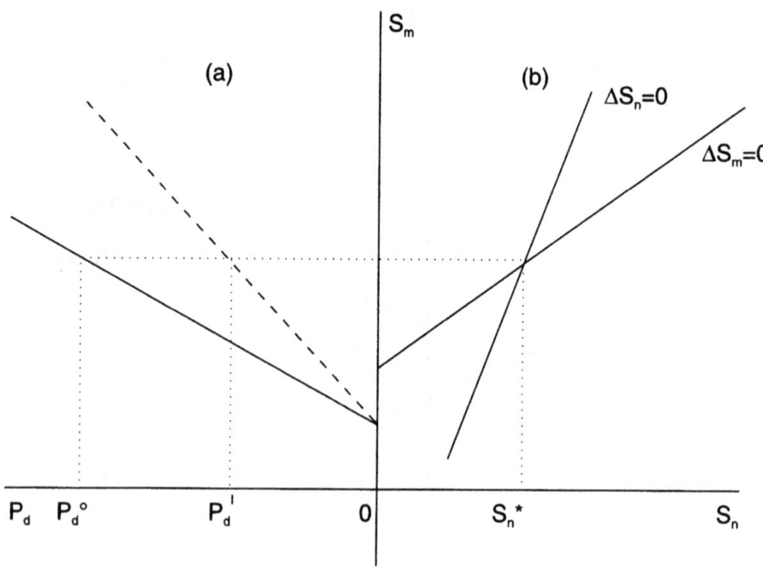

Figure 7.4 The unified system: effects of output growth

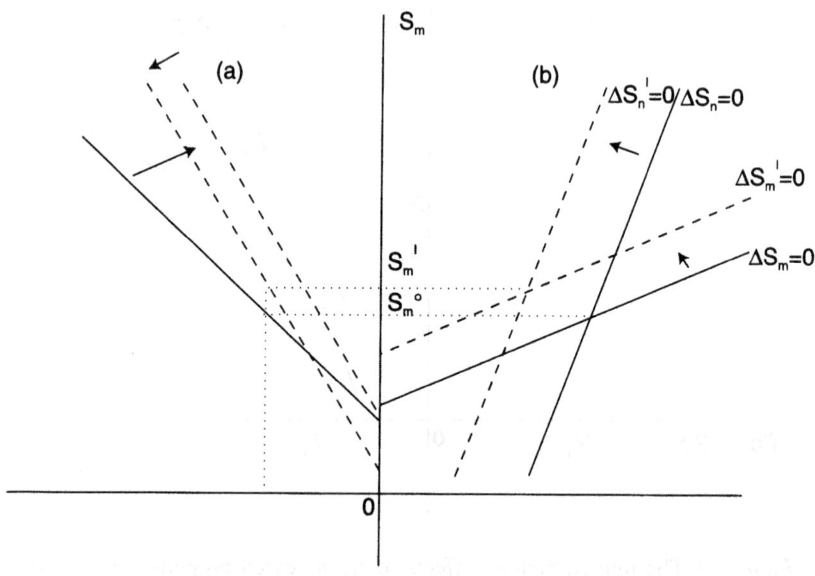

Figure 7.5 The split system: effects of output growth

Figure 7.2 depicts the situation of a unit elastic f(P_d), which causes the new equilibrium value for P_d to be unambiguously lower than its starting point.

An increase in y_d, which is tantamount to accelerated productivity growth for *d* beyond the rate at which silver is being injected into the economy, rotates the curve of graph (*a*) clockwise. Again, in the case of a unit-elastic function for target metal hoards, both the curves of graph (*b*) remain as they are and the burden of the adjustment is now entirely borne by P_d (see Figure 7.4).[47]

A sudden shift in the merchants' propensity to hoard, or accumulate silver in the form of S_n, captured here by π turning negative, while leaving everything unchanged in section (*a*) of Figure 7.3, will displace both curves in section (*b*) either through clockwise rotation or through lower intercepts.[48] Again, deflationary waves that the system is unable to withstand will rather be propagated up to the point where the new equilibrium, with an unambiguously lower P_d, is established.

It is true that we cannot *see* how the agents' (traders') utilities will be affected by a free-falling P_d, in all of the above instances. Within the stylized framework of the present model it is hard to connect the general degree of prosperity and an index of the profit opportunities to the kind of purely *nominal recession* we are here able to define. What is clear, at any rate, is that the writers of the *Ancien Régime* generally described price deflation as putting a severe strain upon the whole economy. We are consequently justified in considering P_d deflation to be detrimental.

Drop with parachute

The second version of the model allows some scope for countercyclical intervention. Provided the shocks to the system are not too intense, so that γ can be maintained well within what we have defined the feasible range ($\gamma_{min} \leq \gamma < 1$), γ itself together with M_n affords the monetary authority some leverage on the general price level.

Assume an equilibrium in which $\gamma = 1$(and $\Sigma=0$), where a *de facto* non-discriminating monetary arrangement is enforced. In the case of an expansion in y_d, as depicted in Figure 7.5 with reference to a unit-elastic $f(P_d)$, the curve in section (*a*) turns rightwards around its stable intercept.[49] Pressures are starting to be exerted on P_d to do its job, which is accommodating a now augmented flow-demand for money in the sector trading durables.

Given the number of small coins to be kept in circulation, M_n is a given. Now, while M_n will take care of P_n, the availability of silver needed to transact y_d can be increased, at a close to stable price level, by *fine-tuning* γ, which amounts simply to decreasing the fine silver content of the small coins below 100 per cent (γ below 1), while freezing their tabular price at par (1 *pound*). As far as our scheme is concerned, what this does, of course, is to shift the curve in graph (*a*), while causing an equal vertical translation of both the stationarity loci on (*b*). It is in this way easy to conceive of a new $\gamma(\geq\gamma_{min})$ that eventually stabilizes P_d.

What is most remarkable is that while the introduction of a γ-money, to be devoted to supplying the short circuit in the home market for non-durables, frees resources to sustain the trading sector, it will not disturb *workers* either. As long as their saving rate is zero, their only concern is the equation of exchange in the terms stated by equation (5b), which we have not modified.

CONCLUSIONS

It is fair to recall that, conscious of the miracles of a managed-money standard for stabilization purposes (as opposed to the rigidities and the potential instability of the nineteenth-century both mono- and bimetallic standards), taking part in the great debate on money of the 1870s and 1880s, Léon Walras himself was to advocate:

> A gold monometallism coupled with a silver billon [precisely what we called *vellon*, base coinage] . . . which is alternatively issued and retired in such a way as to keep the multiple standard from fluctuating.[50]

The somehow surprising evidence produced by the preceding three sections has shown that what Walras presented as a clever finding of a highly sophisticated scientist, was actually the consolidated device on which a thousand years of European monetary history had rested.

What was the price of money in the historical systems using metallic means of payments? Was it the transformation coefficient (in terms of *the* consumable output) attached by the production technology to the circulating commodity outside the monetary circuit? Or was it, rather, more in keeping with the monetarist tradition, simply the inverse of the price level? F. Galiani, having in mind equations (7a) and (8a), would have answered arguing that the price of money was equal to its metal content, equal to γ:

> If the metal used but not consumed is much greater in quantity than the quantity coined, then the destruction which is done to the uncoined metal is incomparably greater, by comparison, than that done by the destruction of money. From which anyone who still doubted it should be convinced, with new and stronger arguments, that gold and silver are valued more as metals than for their use as money.
>
> (Galiani 1750: 43)

On the opposite side, C.A. Broggia, a Neapolitan merchant with scientific ambitions, would have contended, with particular regard to equation (12):

> Accustumed to their money, the people do not generally pay attention, which is understandable as far as their home currency is concerned, to

> the shrinking of the latter's metal content. They more often pay attention solely to money in its serving as money proper. . . . They rather devote all their efforts to finding out whether the stuff for sale in the market place is more or less scarce and valued, in order to update, according to such measure, the price of money itself.
>
> (Broggia 1743: 326)

Loose though his argument might sound, the meaning is that the price of money was actually the inverse of P_n, not γ.

They both grasped a bit of the truth, which, in turn, was a blend of the (Neo)Classics' and the Monetarists' paradigms. A tabular-dichotomous monetary system operating on a multimetallic footing, such as the one in effect prior to the great Napoleonic reform, defined two types of money and assigned to each its own price. In the upper circuit, where wholesale traders systematically used good money, the price of the medium was dictated by the *relative value* of the metal(s) with respect to the n-1 (n-2) durables being transacted, nicely along the most orthodox (Neo)Classical tradition. In the lower tier, where low-saving agents systematically exchanged a *quasi-coupon* (devoid of any store-of-value functions) for non-durables, money fetched the price determined by the quantity of the units of account made available for circulation, as Friedman would expect. Which is another way to say that its price was, within that circuit, the inverse of the price level.

Gresham did not haunt either the former or the latter type of money market: not the former, as the professional traders operating there knew how to undo fantastic provisions and silly prohibitions; and not the latter, where, in some instances, good (or better) money even displaced the bad (or worse) money.

The economy was less rigid than its bimetallic offspring inaugurated by Napoleon, although certainly more prone to both public mismanagement and private greed. It was not entirely built as an *inverted pyramid*, and consequently did not so desperately rely on the quantity of precious metals that it happened to attract (as its nineteenth-century post-Napoleonic version), for it was equipped with an ingenious bullion-saving device which potentially preserved it from the deflationary consequences of the recurrent episodes of drains of species and the attendant financial panics which afflicted the century of Bagehot ("the foreign drain empties the Bank till, and that emptiness, and the resulting rise in the rate of discount, tend to frighten the market").[51] Black money and the absence of *pro-rata* convertibility (the asymmetry of the scale of values along which all media of exchange were quoted in terms of the unit of account) freed precious resources that otherwise would have been frozen in barren petty exchanges.

NOTES

1 The author wishes to thank the editors of this volume for helpful comments on an earlier draft of this chapter, and Rosario La Rocca for excellent editing assistance. Any mistake remains in his own responsibility. Moreover, what follows expresses the author's views, not necessarily those of the Bank of Italy.

2 William Jennings Bryan, candidate in the 1896 US presidential election, running on a free-silver-coinage ticket. He lost. This famous passage is cited, among others, by Fisher (1932: 4).

3 Of course, the dominance of the capital theory over what used to be the purely monetary domain is reinforced by the fact that in a general-equilibrium framework the stock-of-value role of money (which it shares with physical capital) is more readily accommodated than its function as a pure *device* for everyday transactions. On the conception of money as a record-keeping device, see the wonderful piece by Ostroy and Starr (1990) and their pair of *Robinson Crusoes.* McCallum (1983: 10) argues that: "The [neo-classical] model is designed so that nothing in it distinguishes a priori the demand for assets that one may wish to identify as monies from the demands for other assets. . . . Either all assets serve as media of exchange, or none of them do". In this sense, money is equivalent to other forms of capital.

4 The passage, from Milton Friedman, is quoted in Laidler (1991: ch. 6).

5

> Setting up a government mint to stamp coins costlessly, even assigning the government mint a monopoly, has in itself no effect in our models because private agents can costlessly assay and melt down coins. Private agents can easily be imagined to render innocuous government decisions to stamp differing amounts of gold, silver, and other metals as "one dollar".
>
> (Sargent and Wallace 1983: 178)

6 I have somewhat subverted Jevons' conception of *tabularity.* Whereas the author of *Money and the Mechanism of Exchange* (1875) advanced a proposal to index money, here the same term is meant to represent a system in which *money itself* (in the sense of the physical record used in transaction) *is priced.*

7 Most recently, see the assertion that "It is convenient to begin a modern history of the international monetary systems after the Napoleonic Wars" (Mundell, p. 13 in this volume). Of course, we have superb *economic historical* accounts of how the system worked here and there or from an international perspective. To name only a few, Zerbi (1955), Cipolla (1952, 1956, 1958, 1987), Felloni (1969), Vilar (1971), Grierson (1977), Boyer-Xambeau, Deleplace, and Gillard (1986), Spufford (1988).

8 Einaudi (1982: 501), the most classic among the classics on this matter, puts it in these terms:

> These coins [small change under nineteenth-century style bimetallic provisions] have currency only as images of the gold coin, into which, however, if accumulated in sufficient amount, they are legally convertible.

9 The argument for this seignorage being small in an international framework can be conducted along the following lines taken from White (1984: 704):

> Each mint strives to mantain a reputation for uniformly high quality, lest it lose customers to its rivals by imposing higher authentication costs. In a competitive equilibrium, the mintage fee would be just sufficient to earn each minter the normal rate of return on investment. Self-interest will lead all mints in an economy to denominate coins in terms of a unit of standard weight and fineness. A mint doing otherwise would inconvenience its customers.

10 Rolnick and Weber (1986), in a rather challenging piece further referred to (p. 204, n. 28), give two versions of the law, the weaker being the one allowing for a fixed and fully compulsory exchange rate between silver and gold coins.

11 In the sense *à la* Sargent and Wallace:

> Evidently, the quantity theory result is not robust in models like ours. . . . That being so, either our model is defective or one should not be concerned if one's model of commodity money does not give results resembling those of the quantity theory. . . . It is not clear to us that these discoveries [of precious metals] have been [historically] accompanied by anything other than the outcomes that would proceed from ordinary price theory, according to which a large discovery of *x* is likely to be accompanied by a large price decrease in *x*, whether *x* is gold, oil, cotton, or Picassos.
>
> (Sargent and Wallace 1983: 172)

12 In 1800 Napoleon founded the Bank of France and instituted the French franc as the national currency on a sound bimetallic footing. The following "Law of the Year Eleven" (1803) finally launched bimetallism in Europe with a relative mint price of silver to gold at 15.5 to 1. For an account of the difficult transition between the silver *livre tournois* of Louis XVI, to the paper *assignat* denominated in *livres* of the National Assembly, to the Termidorian *mandat*, and then to Napoleon's silver-gold franc, see Sargent and Velde (1990).

13 This choice of the time span is consistent with that proposed by Einaudi (1982) in his classical piece on the theory of the imaginary money.

14 The contributors to the mid-eighteenth-century great debate on money were later collected and published jointly in Milan by Baron P. Custodi from 1803 to 1816. The Custodi edition is the one I draw on for the quotations that follow.

15 This latter label, current in Italy and France, was taken from a Spanish coin circulating during the great Castilian inflation that bore a design representing a lamb (*vellon*).

16 Again, see the economic history literature, particularly Cipolla (1956) and Boyer-Xambeau, Deleplace, and Gillard (1986).

17 The *pound* (the *lira*, the *livre*, or the *pound sterling*) was the monetary unit in the small republics and principalities of central and northern Italy, in France, in England, and in the Netherlands. It was subdivided into 20 *shillings* (*soldi*, *souls*), each divided in 12 *pence* (*denari* or *deniers*). The *ducat*, with its *carlini* and *grani* submultiples, was the accounting unit in Naples, the *écu* (divided in 100 *baiocchi*) in Rome. Every government published a price-*table*, in which both the national and the foreign species were assigned a value for use within the state. G. R. Carli, a famous economist and advisor to the Austrian administration in Milan, reports (Carli 1770) that around 1750 Venice declared its own golden *zecchino* current within its territory at 22 Venetian *pounds*, the Spanish golden *dobloon* at 37 Venetian *pounds* and 10 *shillings*, its own silver *ducat* at 8 Venetian *pounds*, and so on. At the same time, Genoa declared the Venetian *zecchino* legal tender at 13 Genoese *pounds*, 6 Genoese *shillings* and so on.

18 The gold *zecchino*, first coined by Venice in the mid-thirteenth century, was the highest value specie issued in Italy. Its par value was fixed, in Milan, at 14 *pounds* 10 shillings. (i.e., £14.5), but in the market, if purchased with black currency, it fetched up to £17.

19 The *quattrino*, a coin struck in a debased alloy of silver and copper, owed its name to its value, in terms of the scale, fixed at 4 *shillings*.

20 Carli seems to be too generous on this point. Beccaria (1762: 208), for instance, does not share Carli's view that the value of the copper should be taken into account for the *right* pricing of the black coin:

> As far as the alloy is concerned, it is so base and of such a low value that it can be overlooked. . . . Thus, a coin struck in an alloy should be considered as falling short of so much weight as the portion of the copper in it.

21 The *filippo* was a Milanese heavy good silver coin, valued at 7.5 Milanese *pounds*.

22 These were foreign black coins used as *vellon*-currency in the state of Milan. For example, the Genoese *parpajole* were valued 2.5s.

23 Indeed, the established commercial practices were so deeply rooted in contrast to the law that, for example, the state of Milan felt obliged to issue some *grida* (ordinances) to assure the small coin at least *some* measure of acceptability. See, for example, the ordinances of November 1585 and April 1598 cited by Cipolla (1952) requiring tax officials to accept up to 10 *pounds*' payment in black coins.

24 That is, climbing (upward or downward) past the line separating full-bodied and overvalued coins.

25 Note the many characteristics these money-dealers share with the financial operators imagined by Hicks:

> We should be thinking of a fully monetized economy, which includes a sector of merchants, who use bills as a means of payment between each other, while the rest of the economy uses cash. . . . We need to incorporate a reason why bills, in practice, nearly always stand at a discount in terms of cash, the rate of interest on them being positive. A sufficient reason within our model might perhaps be found in the consideration that they are only acceptable *within* the mercantile sector, while cash is acceptable within that sector and outside. So whether the mercantile sector is large or small, cash must always have a wider acceptability. But it is probably more fundamental that cash is a standard of value as well as a means of payment, so it is fully money. It is the standard in terms of which contracts are expressed and enforced at law: bills being only a means of payment, are no more than quasi-money. The discount is the expression, by the market, of this inferiority.
>
> (Hicks 1989: 49)

Replace "bills" with "black coins," "cash" with "full-bodied media," invert the roles of the mercantile sector and the circuit using cash, and you have precisely our case.

26 In 1592, the Pope's Chancellor, Cardinal Caetani, issued an edict reading as follows:

> We ban from the State of the Church all the monies called *bajocchella*, ordering that this coin never be tendered in payment again in the future, nor minted under any excuse whatever in the mints of our State.
>
> (De Gennaro 1970: 35)

Such a prohibition is suggestive of a situation in which the public entity was not the only one involved in the decision to issue the small currency.

27 The *écu* is here a heavy silver coin.

28 This result bears out the conclusion reached by Rolnick and Weber (1986), starting from evidence they draw from seventeenth-century England and nineteenth-century America. Theirs, in particular, is the contention that Gresham's Law was actually a fallacy.

29 See, again, Rolnick and Weber (1986).

30 P. Neri (1706–76) was professor of economics in Florence before being called by Maria Theresa to cover the presidency of the census office in Milan.

31 The worker spends money for perishables, produced by other workers.

32 Rescalings, called *raisings* or *augmentations* (of good specie with respect to the

unit of account), involved a devaluation of the black coins in terms of the numeraire in which prices were quoted.

33 These were black coins carrying a comparatively larger bullion content in proportion to their face value.

34 The idea of an anti-deflationary *taxed* money was re-invented, on the eve of the great depression, by Fisher (1933) and was made popular under the label of *stamp-scrip*. This was a time-currency which got taxed every Wednesday: the one who happened to bear it on that day had to validate it by paying a weekly tax accounting for 5 per cent of its value. This, of course, was intended to speed up circulation and to discourage hoarding.

35 The *denaro* is here a measure of weight.

36 The *mark* was a measure of weight.

37 The system of equations presented in the text draws extensively on the one-sector model of Barro (1979), which in many respects epitomizes *the* representative way of formalizing systems on a commodity money standard.

38 As Beccaria (1762: 226) puts it: "Silver and golden objects are like a treasure to which one can resort in the extremes, without increasing our circulating stock; in this way we can shelter our merchandise from foreign competition." To understand my ruling out of the possibility of the merchants piling up hoards denominated in coined silver as well, the following passage by Giffen (1892) is illuminating: "The demand for precious metals as reserves, . . . is thus, in fact, a demand for them as a merchandise; and in all respect accordingly the precious metals are merchandise only" (quoted in Laidler 1991: 142).

39 Note that, since each worker consumes one perishable good n per period and does not save, the wage rate in real (silver) terms is simply P_n, the *pound*-price of n. Hence, through the optimality condition $n'(Q) = 1/P_n$, we implicitly define the supply function of silver in equation (4).

40 The assumption of absence of speculative (and precautionary) motives supporting the demand for coined silver, together with the ruling out of borrowing for consumption purposes, amount to imposing a cash-in-advance constraint upon the general equilibrium framework formalizing the monetary exchange in our dichotomized economy. This is precisely what equation (5) does.

41 The two curves in the (*b*) portion of Figure 7.1 have the following shape:

$$S_n = f((S_m/y_d - P_n y_n/y_d), \pi) y_d \text{ for } \Delta S_n = 0$$

$$S_n = (\alpha + \delta) / \alpha \, f((S_m/y_d - P_n y_n/y_d), \pi) y_d - (1/\alpha) \, s^P(P_n), \text{ for } \Delta S_m = 0$$

Clearly, for $\delta > 0$, locus $\Delta S_m = 0$ is steeper than $\Delta S_n = 0$.

42 Pure monetary standards can be ranged along a whole spectrum stretching from a purely endogenous to a purely exogenous money arrangement. See Leijonhufvud (1981, 1990).

43 Laidler (1991: 75) argues: "For Fisher money's means of exchange role was of the essence, and money not so functioning had by that very fact ceased to be money."

44 This assumption amounts to consolidating the entity that manages the extraction of silver and runs the mint into the mercantile sector. On the plausibility of such assumption, see, for example, Montanari (1683).

45 Zerbi (1955), in an illuminating study on the balance sheets of certain banks and money-changers operating in Milan during the sixteenth century, concludes:

> The ancient banker usually retained the possibility to apply an internal exchange rate on the legal value of the *national* current coins; that is, he could credit the clients' accounts with what we would now call a buy-price, in the same way they did when trading in foreign currencies whose intrinsic value was different from their price at par.
>
> (Zerbi 1955: 25, emphasis added)

46 On this side, therefore, the system seems to be endowed with a sort of built-in parachute to counter the deflationary impact of jumps in the marginal cost of silver production. This countervailing effect is due to the decreased silver production being automatically reflected (one-to-one) in a decrease in the portion of money used as medium of exchange for *n*.

47 The case in which the elasticity of $f(P_d)$ is less than one strengthens the result, while the opposite case weakens it, but without inverting the sign of the change in P_d.

48 Depending, of course, on whether the functional form of $f(P_d)$ is or is not separable in π.

49 I omit the treatment of the other two cases, which would just replicate the present result.

50 The passage, borrowed from Walras' contribution prepared for the *Final Report* delivered by the "Royal Commission Appointed to Enquire into Recent Changes in the Relative Values of the Precious Metals" in 1889, is quoted by Laidler (1991: 172).

51 The piece, from Bagehot's most celebrated *Lombard Street* (1873), is quoted in Laidler (1991: 21).

REFERENCES

Barro, R. (1979) Money and the Price Level Under the Gold Standard, *Economic Journal* 89: 13–33.

Beccaria, C. (1762) *Del disordine e de' rimedi delle monete*, Milan: P. Custodi (1803), reprinted in Rome: Edizioni Bizzarri (1966).

Belloni, G. (1752) *Trattato del commercio*, Milan: P. Custodi (1803), reprinted in Rome: Edizioni Bizzarri (1966).

Boyer-Xambeau, M.T., Deleplace, G., and Gillard, L. (1986) *Monnaie privée et pouvoir des princes*, Paris: Editions du CNRS, Presse de la Fondation Nationale des Sciences Politiques.

Broggia, C.A. (1743) *Trattato delle Monete*, Milan: P. Custodi (1803), reprinted in Rome: Edizioni Bizzarri (1966).

Carli, G.R. (1751) *Dell'origine e del commercio della Moneta*, Milan: P. Custodi (1803), reprinted in Rome: Edizioni Bizzarri (1966).

Carli, G.R. (1766) *Osservazioni preventive al piano intorno alle monete di Milano*, Milan: P. Custodi (1803), reprinted in Rome: Edizioni Bizzarri (1966).

Carli, G.R. (1770) *Nuove Osservazioni su la riforma delle monete*, Milan: P. Custodi (1803), reprinted in Rome: Edizioni Bizzarri (1966).

Carli, G.R. (1784) *Dissertazione VI sulle monete*, Milan: P. Custodi (1803), reprinted in Rome: Edizioni Bizzarri (1966).

Cipolla, C.M. (1952) *Mouvements monétaires dans l'Etat de Milan (1580–1700)*, Paris: Librairie Armand Colin.

Cipolla, C.M. (1956) *Money, Prices and Civilization in the Mediterranean World: Fifth to Seventh Centuries*, Princeton, NJ: Princeton University Press.

Cipolla, C.M. (1958) *Le avventure della lira*, Milan: Edizioni Comunità.

Cipolla, C.M. (1987) *Money in Sixteenth Century Florence*, Berkeley: University of California Press.

De Gennaro, G. (1970) *L'esperienza monetaria di Roma in età moderna (secc. XVI–XVIII)*, Naples: Edizioni Scientifiche Italiane.

Einaudi, L. (1982) Teoria della moneta immaginaria nel tempo da Carlomagno alla Rivoluzione Francese, *Bancaria* 5: 494–510.

Felloni, G. (1969) *Il mercato monetario in Piemonte nel secolo XVIII*, Torino: Cassa di Risparmio di Torino.

Fisher, I. (1932) *In Search of a Stable Currency*, Chicago: University of Chicago Press.

Fisher, I. (1933) *Stamp*, Chicago: University of Chicago Press.

Galiani, F. (1750) *On Money*, Chicago: University of Chicago Press (1977).

Grierson, P. (1977) *The Origins of Money*, London: Athlone Press of the University of London.

Hicks, J. (1989) *A Market Theory of Money*, Oxford: Oxford University Press.

Jevons, W.S. (1875) *Money and the Mechanism of Exchange*, London: Kegan Paul.

Laidler, D. (1991) *The Golden Age of the Quantity Theory*, Princeton, NJ: Princeton University Press.

Leijonhufvud, A. (1981) *Information and Coordination*, Oxford: Oxford University Press.

Leijonhufvud, A. (1990) The Monetary Economics of John Hicks, *Greek Economic Review* 12: 133–51.

McCallum, A. (1983) The Role of Overlapping Generations Models in Monetary Economics, *Carnegie-Rochester Conference Series on Public Policy*, 18: 9–44.

Marshall, A. (1871–1975) Money, in J. Whitaker (ed.) *The Early Economic Writings of A. Marshall*, 2 vols, London: Macmillan (1975).

Mill, J.S. (1871) *The Principles of Political Economy with Some of their Applications to Social Philosophy*, reprinted in 2 vols by J.M. Robson (ed.), Toronto: University of Toronto Press (1965).

Montanari, G. (1680) *Breve trattato del valore delle monete in tutti gli stati*, Milan: P. Custodi (1803), reprinted in Rome: Edizioni Bizzarri (1966).

Montanari, G. (1683) *Della Moneta*, Milan: P. Custodi (1803), reprinted in Rome: Edizioni Bizzarri (1966).

Montanari, G. (1683) La zecca in consulta di stato, reprinted in A. Graziani (ed.) *Economisti del Cinque e Seicento*, Bari: Laterza (1913).

Neri, P. (1751) *Osservazioni sopra il prezzo legale delle monete*, Milan: P. Custodi (1803), reprinted in Rome: Edizioni Bizzarri (1966).

Ostroy, J. and Starr, R. (1990) The Transactions Role of Money, in B.M. Friedman and F.H. Hahn (eds) *Handbook of Monetary Economics*, vol. 1, ch. 1: 4–61, Amsterdam: Elsevier Science Publishers.

Patinkin, D. (1965) *Money, Interest and Prices*, New York: Harper and Row.

Rolnick, A. and Weber, W. (1986) Gresham's Law or Gresham's Fallacy?, *Journal of Political Economy* 94 (1): 185–99.

Sargent, T. and Velde, F. (1990) An Economic Theory of the French Revolution, mimeo.

Sargent, T. and Wallace, N. (1983) A Model of Commodity Money, *Journal of Monetary Economics* 17: 163–87.

Spufford, P. (1988) *Money and its Use in Medieval Europe*, Cambridge: Cambridge University Press.

Vilar, P. (1971) *A History of Gold and Money*, London and New York: Verso.

Whitaker, J. (1984) An Essay on the Pure Theory of Commodity Money, *Oxford Economic Papers* 31: 339–57.

White, L. (1984) Competitive Payments Systems and the Unit of Account, *American Economic Review* 74 (4): 699–712.

Zerbi, T. (1955) *Moneta effettiva e moneta di conto nelle fonti contabili di storia economica*, Milan: Marzorati.

Part III

EXCHANGE-RATE BEHAVIOR UNDER THE GOLD STANDARD

8

INTEGRATION IN THE AMERICAN FOREIGN-EXCHANGE MARKET, 1791–1931[1]

Lawrence H. Officer

This chapter explores the methodology of exchange-market integration, meaning the extent of perfection of the foreign-exchange market, with empirical application to the American (dollar–sterling) historical experience. The focus is on measurement rather than determination. The two traditional approaches, centering on exchange-rate variation and the gold-point spread, respectively, are reviewed. Then a new and formal model, which integrates the approaches and overcomes their limitations, is developed. Empirical findings of earlier authors are summarized, followed by results based on superior data.

EXCHANGE-RATE VARIATION APPROACH TO EXCHANGE-MARKET INTEGRATION

Davis and Hughes (1960: 58, 62–3) compute the range of their dollar–sterling quarterly exchange-rate series (expressed as the per cent premium over parity) by decade from the 1830s to the 1890s. From 18 per cent of parity in the 1830s the range falls precipitously (excluding the 1860s) to 1 per cent in the 1880s and 1890s. Davis and Hughes compute a second measure of variation, what they call the variance.[2] The finding is the same: a steady decrease in exchange-rate variability, interrupted only by the upheaval of the Civil War. From "fairly stable" in the 1850s, the exchange rate is "permanently stabilized" by the mid-1870s, so that the stability of exchange rates associated with the international gold standard emerged.

Exchange-market integration, then, is measured inversely by the variability of the exchange rate. In Officer (1996) I develop a long-run quarterly exchange-rate series admirably suited for this analysis, because not only is it expressed as the percentage deviation from true mint parity (whereby divergent monetary standards in the two countries are made comparable via the gold/silver market price) but also it is corrected for paper standards (whence it has the interpretation of the percentage deviation from mint parity throughout). Neither property holds for the Davis-Hughes series.[3] Also, the long-run series, denoted as *R*, runs from 1791 to 1931, covering all periods of an Anglo-American specie standard plus floating-exchange-rate episodes with a free gold market that intervened between such periods.[4] In contrast, Davis and Hughes develop their series only for the 1835–95 time period.

Figure 8.1 plots the long-run exchange-rate series. The Davis-Hughes result of reduced variability appears true for their time period and with their exception of the Civil War years. Prior to 1820 exchange-rate variation is high indeed. Also, the stability of the exchange rate in the years just prior to World War I appears greater than that in 1925–31.

For a fuller data picture to extend the analysis, decadal periods may be used from 1791 to 1910, followed by 1911–14 (terminated by World War I), 1919–25 (floating pound, though adjusted), and 1925–31 (interwar gold standard). Then five alternative measures of variation are utilized, and their values by period presented in Table 8.1.

The mean of algebraic values (column two) measures the extent to which deviations from parity compensate for one another. The measure suggests that there were six broad periods of ever-increasing exchange-market integration: 1791 to 1810, 1811 to 1830, 1831 to 1850, 1851 to 1870, 1871 to 1890, and 1891–1914, with 1919–31 most comparable to 1871–90. One must be cautious in interpreting this statistic, because in permitting positive and negative deviations from parity to offset each other, the measure understates variation. Consider the maximum divergence from

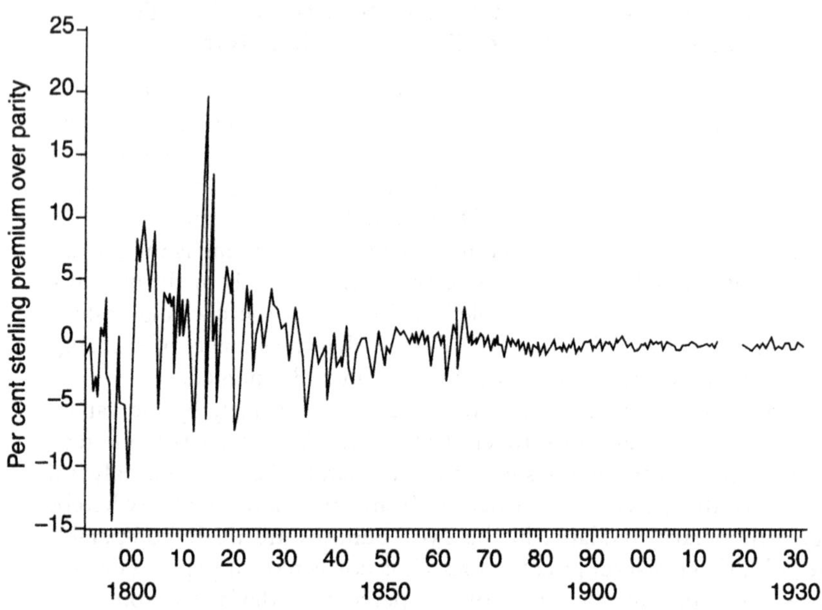

Figure 8.1 Exchange rate (quarterly), 1791–1931

Table 8.1 Exchange-rate statistics, by period, 1791–1931 (per cent sterling premium over parity)[a]

Period	*Mean*		*Standard deviation*		*Maximum observation*
	Algebraic values	*Absolute values*	*About mean*	*About zero*	
1791–1800	−2.70	4.55	5.06	5.75	−14.58
1801–10	3.46	4.17	3.48	4.93	9.52
1811–20	0.97	4.57	6.19	6.27	19.90
1821–30	1.23	2.01	2.06	2.40	−5.55
1831–40	−0.72	1.47	1.87	2.01	−6.10
1841–50	−0.73	1.11	1.26	1.46	−3.60
1851–60	0.42	0.65	0.68	0.80	−2.24
1861–70	0.32	0.87	1.20	1.25	−3.13
1871–80	−0.16	0.37	0.44	0.47	−1.09
1881–90	−0.19	0.33	0.36	0.41	−0.90
1891–1900	0.02	0.25	0.30	0.51	−0.61
1901–10	−0.03	0.14	0.19	0.19	−0.49
1911–14[b]	−0.04	0.12	0.15	0.15	−0.28
1919–25[c]	−0.12	0.24	0.27	0.29	−0.60
1925–31[d]	−0.14	0.22	0.20	0.25	−0.43

Notes: [a] A negative sign denotes a sterling discount
[b] First and second quarter, respectively
[c] Fourth and second quarter, respectively
[d] Third and second quarter, respectively

parity (column six), deemed more meaningful than the range. By this criterion there is a tremendous increase in integration in the 1820s, as well as confirmation of the general trend to enhanced integration thereafter to World War I. From 1881 to 1931 (always allowing for gaps) exchange-market integration is continuously strong, with every quarterly observation below 1 per cent premium or discount, suggesting a smooth working of the gold standard.

Superior statistics are the mean of absolute values and the standard deviation about the mean deviation from parity (the customarily defined standard deviation), shown in columns three and four. The first measure has the advantage that the norm deviation from parity is zero rather than the mean deviation; the second that deviations are squared, thus penalizing observations heavily for being further away from parity. Combining both properties is the standard deviation about zero (essentially the root mean square of the observations), shown in column five.

All three statistics (and the maximum observation) show surprisingly large variability in 1791–1820, with the deviation from parity reaching levels unimaginable under the gold standard in its prime. Also present is the trend of reduced exchange-rate variation, that is, enhanced market integration, all the way to 1914, as well as the profound jump in integration in the 1820s. The measures also exhibit maximum, and truly amazing, tightness of the exchange rate around parity, in 1901–14. The progressive improvement in integration is interrupted in 1811–20 and 1861–70, probably explained by the impact of the War of 1812 and the Civil War.

Associating exchange-market integration with the variability of the exchange rate over time, in particular over decadal or related periods, provides great insight into the rate of development of the foreign-exchange market. The conceptual defects are the heuristic nature of the approach and the lack of a framework to separate and explain the roles of internal and external elements in determining the level of integration. In particular, there is need of a model incorporating specie points and their role in constraining exchange-rate movements.

GOLD-POINT SPREAD APPROACH TO EXCHANGE-MARKET INTEGRATION

In the first section an approach to exchange-market integration – and associated measures – involving only the exchange rate was examined. A radically different focus ignores the exchange rate and considers nothing but gold points. Market integration, logically termed "external integration," is represented by the specie-point spread. The gold-export and gold-import points are defined, respectively, as the cost of specie export (CX) and the negative of the cost of specie import ($-CM$), expressed in percentage terms (per cent of parity). Then the gold-point spread (more generally, specie-point spread), also in percentage terms, is the difference of the gold points: $CX - (-CM) = CX + CM$, the sum of the specie-shipment costs. The narrower the spread, the greater the integration. The spread measures the extent of external integration in the sense of the amount yet to be achieved.

Three authors adopt this technique and put it in practice by collecting data on the movement of specie points over time. Johnson (1905: 90, n. 1) comments that during the last quarter of the nineteenth century the gold-export point fell from three to two cents per pound. Cole (1929: 405–6, 419–20, n. 3) states that the gold-export point fell from over 4 per cent in 1760 to $1\frac{1}{4}$ to $2\frac{1}{4}$ per cent in the 1830s. Taking the dates 1886, 1905, and 1929, he mentions the diminution in the gold-point spread over time. Myers (1931: 74–5, 342–3) observes the specie-export point for 1811, 1829, 1848, 1882, 1906, and 1908; the specie-import point for 1883, 1906, and 1908. Both gold points move closer to parity as time goes on, and she remarks in 1931 that "the drawing together of the gold points is still going on."

In sum, the three authors agree on a narrowing of dollar–sterling specie points in the nineteenth century and beyond. Without displaying data,

Einzig (1970: 172–3) discusses the "very gradually . . . narrowing of the spread between specie points" from 1815 over the nineteenth century. He also asserts that "not until the concluding decades of the 19th century and the early years of the 20th century" did the spread narrow to figures comparable to those of the interwar period.

There are four deficiencies with how these authors apply the gold-point-spread approach to external integration. First, to the extent they use explicit data (which Einzig fails to do) and that the sources of the data are identified (not done by Johnson), the authors (Cole and Myers) rely on contemporary estimates of specie points. These estimates are inconsistent and of varying quality. Second, the dates of comparison are haphazard rather than systematic, in part because of the scattered nature of the known contemporary specie-point estimates. Third, the gold export and import points are examined separately rather than their spread computed and considered as such.

Fourth, no distinction is made between the gold-point arbitrage (GPA) and gold-effected transfer of funds (GTF) spread. Both gold-point arbitrage (GPA) and gold-effected transfer of funds (GTF) involve purchasing specie in one country and transporting it across the ocean to be sold in the other country. Under GPA the indirect foreign-exchange transaction via the medium of gold is combined with a direct foreign-exchange transaction in the opposite direction, resulting in a profit. Under GTF the indirect foreign-exchange transaction via gold substitutes for a direct foreign-exchange transaction in the same direction. The gold and foreign-exchange transactions are complements under GPA, substitutes under GTF. The objective under GPA is to make a sure profit, that under GTF is to transfer funds from one country to the other cheaper than via a direct foreign-exchange transaction.[5] Practically, the cost of specie export and import – and therefore the gold points and gold-point spread – is lower under GTF than GPA.[6]

All four problems are overcome here. First, in Officer (1996) the gold points are derived by generating a time series of each cost component of GPA or GTF using all existing information over 1791–1931, so the gold-point estimates are consistent and of the highest possible quality. Second, the subperiods of 1791–1931 are carefully construed, and comprehensive except for the omission of 1801–20 and 1919–25.[7] Third, the gold-point spread is computed and considered as such, the individual gold points deemed forgettable once they are used for the calculation. Fourth, the spread is separately constructed for GPA and GTF. Results are shown in Table 8.2.

Hypotheses emanate from conjoining the conclusions of the authors exploring external integration with the findings of the exchange-rate variation approach to market integration (see first section).

Table 8.2 Gold-point spread (per cent), period averages, 1791–1931

Period	*Gold-point spread*[a]	
	Gold-point arbitrage	*Transfer of funds*
1791–1800	14.2585	8.6881
1821–30	7.9146	4.6480
1831–40	7.2231	3.3068
1841–50	5.0436	2.6999
1851–60	3.1937	1.3097
1861–70	2.9792	1.2817
1871–80	2.2071	0.7080
1881–90	1.3725	0.5392
1891–1900	1.2824	0.8889
1901–10	1.0993	0.7332
1911–14[b]	1.0940	0.7878
1925[c]–31[b]	1.0752	0.8973

Notes: [a] Gold export point–gold import point
[b] Second quarter
[c] Third quarter

Hypothesis 1: There is enhanced integration over time

This is true without qualification for the GPA gold-point spread. The spread falls continuously from 1791–1800 to 1925–31. The hypothesis holds for the GTF spread through 1881–90. If the change from the 1790s to World War I, that is, 1791–1800 to 1911–14, is considered, the reduction in the GPA (GTF) spread is 13.16 (7.90) percentage points, or 92 (91) per cent.

Hypothesis 2: The progressive improvement in integration is interrupted in the 1811–20 and 1861–70 decades

Specie-point data were not developed for 1811–20. The gold-point spread shows no such interruption for 1861–70, whether under GPA or GTF.

Hypothesis 3: The 1820s decade involved a tremendous increase in integration

Consider the change in external integration among the following three periods: 1790–1800, 1821–30, and 1911–14. From the 1790s to 1820s, the (GPA, GTF) spread fell by (6.34, 4.04) percentage points, and from the 1820s to 1911–14 by (6.82, 3.86) percentage points. Therefore by the 1820s about half (48, 51 per cent under GPA, GTF) the total improvement in integration to World War I – as measured by the decline in the gold-point spread – had been achieved.

The specie-point spread under (GPA, GTF) narrowed from (14.26, 8.69) per cent in the 1790s to (7.91, 4.65) per cent in the 1820s – a decline of (6.34, 4.04) percentage points, as stated above. Much of this giant improvement in external integration could be related to war, present in the 1790s and absent in the 1820s. Therefore there is some rationale for delineating the trend in external integration from the 1820s, rather than the 1790s, to 1911–14 (see hypothesis 1). In a relative sense, the improvement in integration remains impressive, with the GPA (GTF) gold-point spread falling by 86 (83) per cent.

Hypothesis 4: From 1881 to 1931 (allowing for gaps) integration is at a high level

For the GPA spread, the hypothesis holds, in the sense that, for all periods of that time span, the spread is substantially narrower than in all prior periods. However, the hypothesis is qualified by the continuing decline in the spread to 1925–31. For the GTF spread, the higher level of integration had been reached one decade earlier. From 1871–80 to 1925–31 the gold-point spread is noticeably less than in the prior periods.

Hypothesis 5: Not until 1881–1910 did the spread narrow to a value comparable to that of 1925–31

This hypothesis is contradicted by the evidence. For GPA, only after the nineteenth century, in 1901–14, was a gold-point spread of the same order of narrowness as that in 1925–31 reached. For GTF, the narrowness of the spread of 1925–31 was surpassed earlier, in 1871–80.

Hypothesis 6: Integration just prior to World War I exceeds that in 1925–31

True for the GTF, not true for the GPA spread. In the next section the external-integration approach, which involves representing exchange-market integration by the gold-point spread, is assessed and reinterpreted in the context of a complete model of integration of the foreign-exchange market.

A MODEL OF INTERNAL AND EXTERNAL INTEGRATION

The one existing approach to exchange-market integration uses exchange-rate data without reference to gold points, the other employs gold-point data without reference to the exchange rate. Thus each uses its data in a compartmentalized fashion.

One problem with the research of previous authors is the use of inappropriate exchange-rate or gold-point data – a defect corrected in the first and second sections through the employment of the data generated in Officer (1996). Other limitations, however, are methodological in nature and were retained in the earlier sections.

First, it is not stated why the gold-point spread itself rather than some transformation is the appropriate measure of external integration. Second, internal integration – the logical complement to external integration – is not even considered conceptually, let alone measured. Third, and consequently, there is the failure to assess quantitatively the relative importance of external and internal forces in fostering integration. Fourth, mint parity is adopted as the exchange-rate norm about which deviations from integration occur, whereas in historical fact dollar–sterling gold points were asymmetric: the gold-point spread midpoint diverged from parity.[8] The spread midpoint (SM), expressed as the percentage deviation from parity, is half the sum of the algebraic gold points:

$$SM = (CX + (-CM))\ /2 = (CX - CM)/2.$$

Fifth, the gold-point spread alone provides only a potential envelope for the exchange rate. An alternative interpretation is that the location of the exchange rate itself is viewed as irrelevant. On the other hand, examining exchange-rate variation outside the context of gold points biases measured integration by neglecting the influence of the gold-point spread on the exchange rate.

The basic problem, therefore, is that the exchange-rate-variation approach ignores the gold points, while the gold-point-spread ("external integration") analysis pays no attention to the exchange rate. Exchange-market integration must be examined by means of a model that incorporates both exchange rate and gold points, and that distinguishes between internal and external integration. The following formal model combines the exchange-rate-variation and gold-point-spread approaches, but not in an additive way.

Recalling that the gold-export and gold-import points are expressed as per cent of parity (CX and $-CM$), consider external integration (EI) anew. However, let this integration be measured by half the gold-point spread (rather than the full spread, as in the previous section). Equivalently, external integration is the average of the absolute values of the gold points. Symbolically,

$$EI = (CX + |-CM|)\ /2 = (CX + CM)\ /2.$$

EI, expressed as a per cent of parity, measures the extent of external integration, the amount of integration yet to be achieved. As EI decreases, external integration increases.

The gold points can be redefined as deviations from the spread midpoint (but still expressed as percentage points of parity). Denoting the redefined gold-export and import points as CX^* and $-CM^*$, respectively,

$$CX^* = CX - SM = CX - (CX - CM)\ /2 = (CX + CM)\ /2 = EI$$
$$= -\ (-CM - SM) = -\ (-CM^*) = CM^*.$$

Therefore EI can be interpreted as the gold-export point (the negative of the gold-import point) with respect to the spread midpoint rather than with respect to parity.

In a similar vein the long-run exchange-rate (R) series is re-expressed as R^*, the deviation from the spread midpoint (though still expressed as percentage points of parity):

$$R^* = R - SM = R - (CX - CM)\ /2.$$

Of course, the spread midpoint (or gold points) used in the computation is specific to the period to which the exchange-rate values belong.

Internal integration is concerned with the amount of exchange-rate variation not in and of itself but rather given the gold-point spread or, equivalently, the level of external integration. Should exchange-rate variation decrease for a given level of external integration, internal integration increases. However, a higher level of external integration (a narrower gold-point spread) reduces the internal integration associated with a given amount of exchange-rate variation.

For a given period, consider exchange-rate variation as measured by mean $|R^*|$, the mean of the absolute values of R^*. For a given gold-point spread, or, equivalently, a given value of EI, internal integration varies negatively with mean$|R^*|$. For a given value of mean $|R^*|$, internal integration varies positively with EI.

What is the norm value of mean $|R^*|$, that which involves full internal integration? Perfect internal integration is achieved by $R^* =$ mean $|R^*| = 0$. The exchange rate is always at the midpoint of the gold-point spread. This is a "maximalist" criterion, extreme in its ideal. As an alternative, consider that external integration (EI) is the gold (export or negative import) point; a "minimalist" criterion of internal integration would involve the exchange rate simply respecting the gold point as a limit. While a particular value of R^* might exceed EI, on average it should not do so. Therefore a "minimalist" criterion of internal integration is mean $|R^*| \leq EI$. "Full" or "expected" internal integration is logically a compromise between the "maximalist" and "minimalist" standards; the criterion is mean $|R^*|$ midway between zero and EI, that is, mean $|R^*| = EI/2$.

So the expectation of internal integration is that the exchange rate on average be midway between the spread midpoint and a gold point. This standard for internal integration can be obtained in another way. Suppose that the exchange rate takes on all values within the spread with equal probability and any value outside the spread with zero probability. Formally, the probability density of $|R^*|$, f $(|R^*|)$, has zero value beyond *EI* and is distributed uniformly (rectangularly) between 0 and *EI*. Therefore the function is described as: (1) f $(|R^*|) = 0$ for $|R^*| > EI$, (2) f $(|R^*|) =$ constant $= 1/EI$, for $|R^*| \leq EI$. (The constant is $1/EI$ because the sum of the probabilities of all values must be unity.) With equal probability of all values of $|R^*|$ between 0 and *EI*, the mean (or expected) value of $|R^*|$, which is mean $|R^*|$, is $EI/2$.

How can conditions (1) and (2) be realized? Defining a gold-point "violation" as $|R^*| > EI$, either the absence of such violations ($|R^*| \leq EI$ for all R^*) or "perfect" GPA (instantaneous removal of a violation) yields (1). Within the gold-point spread, there is no reason for the "natural" distribution of the exchange rate to be other than uniform. In fact, a "law of large numbers" might guarantee that over a sufficiently long time period the exchange rate takes on all values within the spread with equal probability. Assuming that the behavior of exchange-market participants (speculators and arbitrageurs) is "neutral" in the sense that it does not disturb the distribution, (2) results. There is an admitted lack of realism in some of these specifications (in particular, perfect GPA and neutral behavior of economic agents within the spread), but the issue is generation of a standard for internal integration rather than a set of realistic conditions under which integration operates.

With full (or expected) internal integration represented by mean $|R^*| = EI/2$, the level of internal integration (*II*) is the shortfall from full internal integration: $II =$ mean $|R^*| - EI/2$. So, consistent with the interpretation of external integration (*EI*), *II* measures the extent of internal integration, the amount of integration yet to be achieved.

Maximum external integration is at $EI = 0$; so $EI \geq 0$, and realistically (because there are positive costs of GPA and GTF) $EI > 0$. Maximum (perfect) internal integration is at $II = -EI/2$, corresponding to mean $|R^*| = 0$, again unrealistic (on three counts, with *R* not only constant, not only locked at the spread midpoint of the current period, but also jumping instantaneously to the new spread midpoint in the next period). However, it is certainly possible for $II < 0$ (corresponding to mean $|R^*| < EI/2$). A negative value of *II* simply means that there is overfull internal integration (*II* is less than its expected value).

The model of exchange-market integration is used to re-examine the integration of the foreign-exchange market from 1791 to 1931. Values for the mean absolute value of the exchange rate (mean $|R^*|$), external integration (*EI*), and internal integration (*II*), for both GPA and GTF gold points, are shown by period in Table 8.3. The external-integration (*EI*) values are simply half those of the gold-point spread shown in Table 8.2. Therefore the analysis of external integration in the second section stands.

What remains to be done is a corresponding investigation of internal integration. Exchange-rate variation in the form of the mean absolute value

Table 8.3 Internal and external integration, period averages, 1791–1931 (percentage points of parity)

Period	Exchange rate[a] mean of absolute values		External integration gold export point[a]		Internal integration[b]	
	GPA	GTF	GPA	GTF	GPA	GTF
1791–1800	4.1854	4.5699	7.1292	4.3440	0.6208	2.3979
1821–30	2.1443	1.8886	3.9573	2.3240	0.1656	0.7266
1831–40	1.4438	1.4115	3.6115	1.6534	−0.3619	0.5848
1841–50	1.0414	1.0289	2.5218	1.3500	−0.2195	0.3539
1851–60	0.8634	0.6106	1.5968	0.6548	0.0650	0.2832
1861–70	0.8703	0.8195	1.4896	0.6409	0.1255	0.4991
1871–80	0.3791	0.4456	1.1036	0.3540	−0.1727	0.2686
1881–90	0.3207	0.3628	0.6863	0.2696	−0.0224	0.2280
1891–1900	0.2470	0.2426	0.6412	0.4445	−0.0736	0.0204
1901–10	0.1466	0.1518	0.5496	0.3666	−0.1282	−0.0315
1911–14[c]	0.1167	0.1325	0.5470	0.3939	−0.1568	−0.0645
1925[d]–31[c]	0.2764	0.2757	0.5376	0.4487	0.0076	0.0514

Notes: [a] Expressed as deviation from midpoint of gold-point spread
[b] Exchange rate minus half gold export point
[c] Second quarter
[d] Third quarter
GPA = gold-point arbitrage
GTF = transfer of funds

of the exchange rate, as a representation of exchange-market integration, was examined in the first section and shown by period in Table 8.1. How does that concept differ from internal integration (*II*)? The measure in the first section is mean $|R|$; the one here is mean $|R^*| - EI/2$, denoted as *II*. Therefore the current measure, *II*, differs from the former in two respects: (1) divergence from the spread midpoint rather than from parity, that is, the computation of mean $|R^*|$ rather than mean $|R|$, (2) subtraction of an adjustment factor representing external integration ($EI/2$). Internal integration is exchange-rate variation adjusted for (1) the deviation of the spread midpoint from parity, and (2) external integration.

Hypotheses concerning exchange-market integration were examined for mean $|R|$ and *EI*, in the first and second sections respectively. It is natural to investigate the applicability of these same hypotheses to (mean $|R^*| - EI/2) = II$. The hypotheses are taken from their convenient assembly in the second section.

Hypothesis 1: There is enhanced internal integration over time

This hypothesis is true period-by-period from 1791–1800 to 1911–14, except for a temporary reverse movement lasting three periods (1841–70) for GPA and one period (1861–70) for GTF. The figures for GTF, because steadier than those for GPA, appear to be a better measure of internal integration.

Considering the change from the 1790s to World War I, the reduction in adjusted exchange-rate variation (improvement in internal integration, ΔII) is 0.7776 (2.4624) percentage points, or 125 (103) per cent. The excess over 100 per cent reflects overfull internal integration. Amazingly, this happens as early as 1831–40 for GPA.

Hypothesis 2: The progressive improvement in integration is interrupted in the 1811–20 and 1861–70 decades

This holds for 1861–70, but data on *EI* and therefore *II* are not available for 1811–20.

Hypothesis 3: The 1820s decade involved a tremendous increase in integration

Indeed, a profound jump in internal integration occurs in the 1820s. From the 1790s to 1820s, *II* declined by 0.4552 (1.6713) percentage points for GPA (GTF), and from the 1820s to 1911–14 by 0.3224 (0.7911) percentage points. So by the 1820s about 60 per cent or more (59, 68 per cent under GPA, GTF) of the total improvement in internal integration to World War I had occurred – an even stronger performance than external integration.

Hypothesis 4: From 1881 to 1931 (allowing for gaps) integration is at a high level

The hypothesis holds excellently for GPA, with overfull integration from 1881 (in fact, 1871) to 1914 and full integration in 1925–31. For GTF, the hypothesis applies with a decade's delay. From the 1880s to 1890s, integration improves by 0.21 percentage points. From 1891 onward, *II* does not exceed 0.05 per cent. Certainly, by 1891–1914 exchange-market integration is unambiguously strong in both external and internal respects.

Hypothesis 5: Not until 1881–1910 does integration reach a value comparable to that of 1925–31

An amended hypothesis is true for GTF; the starting decade is the 1890s rather than 1880s. However, the hypothesis is decidedly rejected by GPA. In the 1830s and 1840s internal integration is not only higher than in 1925–31 but also at maximum strength (*II* at minimum algebraic value).

Hypothesis 6: Integration just prior to World War I exceeds that in 1925–31

This statement is true for both GPA and GTF.

IMPORTANCE OF INTERNAL VERSUS EXTERNAL INTEGRATION

In explaining the dampening of exchange-rate variation over the nineteenth century, Davis and Hughes (1960: 58–9) contrast "factors external to the American economy," that is, "reduced ocean-transport cost coupled with the increased speed and reliability of transport and communications and the development of adequate ocean insurance," with "fundamental changes within the U.S. economy," such as reduced frequency of bank specie suspensions and improved communication and transportation facilities in the US financial market.

Davis and Hughes describe the external factors as "important," but they are said to be "powerfully reinforced" by the internal developments. In fact, from 1791–1800 to 1911–14, $\Delta EI/\Delta II = 8.46$ (1.60) under GPA (GTF). The external factors in the form of EI had about $8\frac{1}{2}$ ($1\frac{1}{2}$) times the impact of the internal forces, represented by II. Narrowing of the specie points dominated developments internal to the American foreign-exchange market in enhancing integration, a result that contradicts Davis and Hughes and those who cite their view with implicit approval.[9]

It must be acknowledged that external versus internal integration is not the same as external versus internal factors. Some external factors impinge causally on internal integration. Examples are international transportation and communication and the alliance of British firms (House of Baring, Liverpool branch of House of Brown) with American foreign-exchange dealers. Correspondingly, internal factors play a role in determining external integration. For example, government policy sets the prices at which specie is transacted by arbitrageurs and transferors. In sum, there are relationships between internal and external integration beyond the identity that relates internal integration, external integration, and exchange-rate variation: $II =$ mean $|R^*| - EI/2$.

Nevertheless, the analysis is continued. As mentioned in the second section, there is some rationale for delineating the trend in exchange-market integration from the 1820s (rather than 1790s) to World War I. Now $\Delta EI/\Delta II = 10.58$ (2.44) under GPA (GTF). The improvement in external relative to internal integration, a multiple of about $10\frac{1}{2}$ ($2\frac{1}{2}$), is even greater than with the 1790s starting period.

Internal integration is an important concept and its enhancement over time was fundamental to the development of the American foreign-exchange market. However, the improvement in external integration, meaning narrowing of the gold-point spread, was the much more important element in the process of perfecting the market.

DETERMINANTS OF EXTERNAL AND INTERNAL INTEGRATION

A full analysis of the determinants of internal and external integration in the American foreign-exchange market would be too involved for this chapter. However, the proximate elements that serve as determinants, some of which are mentioned in the previous section, are outlined in this concluding section. The elements underlying the phenomenal improvement in external integration over time are (for GPA and GTF) declines in the freight, insurance, and handling rates in shipping specie; reductions in transactions costs; improvement in oceanic transportation in speed, regularity and reliability, associated with substantial reductions in interest loss; and (for GPA) decrease in normal profit and risk premium.

Turning to internal integration, this concept has three dimensions: integration across space (geographic integration, in reference to the divergence of the exchange rate in the various American port cities), across time (temporal integration, pertaining to the variability of the exchange rate), and with respect to the midpoint of the gold-point spread (placement integration, referring to the location of the exchange rate).

Geographic integration is ignored in the model of exchange-market integration developed in the third section. Yet the dispersion of the early American foreign-exchange market in the various port cities involved a geographic variation in the exchange rate the reduction and elimination of which was an inherent part of the integration process. The omission of geographic integration is a limitation of the model, albeit the traditional approaches share this deficiency.

Temporal integration, incorporated in the model of internal integration via the term mean $|R^*|$ = mean $|R - SM|$ for a given value of *SM* (spread midpoint), has two components: recurring exchange-rate variation (for example, seasonal or cyclical variation) and non-recurring exchange-rate movements (due to exogenous shocks or random events). Improved temporal integration involves damping or eliminating seasonal and other recurring variation, and moderating the non-recurring movements, thus reducing mean $|R^*|$ even for a given spread midpoint (*SM*).

Placement integration is concerned with the location rather than the variation of the exchange rate. The closer the exchange rate is to the midpoint of the gold-point spread, the stronger is internal integration. This dimension of integration is included in the model via the parameter *SM* in mean $|R^*|$ = mean $|R - SM|$.

Forces determining the amount of internal integration fall into two categories. First, there are elements that constitute background to the foreign-exchange market. The level of transportation and communication, both international and domestic, clearly relates positively to the extent of internal integration. The state of expectations of participants in the foreign-exchange market is another background element, affecting their desire to hold one or the other currency. Expectations regarding the future value of the exchange rate are the proximate object, but ultimately the expectations are with reference to external events, such as suspension of specie payments. Therefore underlying the expectations is the state of nature, in this example, the stability of the banking system.

Note that the level of transportation and communication either remains the same or improves over time; so decade-by-decade this force can only enhance, never diminish, internal integration. Expectations regarding exchange-rate change and external events are another matter; they can be favorable or unfavorable for internal integration. As for stability of the American banking system, it generally increased over time, although certainly there were fits and starts.

The second category is the foreign-exchange market itself, which has two components. One is the role of brokers and dealers. Brokers bring ultimate buyer and seller together. Because brokers do not take uncovered positions in foreign exchange, there is a limit to the improvement they can achieve in temporal integration, and also in geographic integration where it is conjoined with temporal integration. Dealers may act as brokers, but in addition they perform three other functions. Dealers (1) buy and sell exchange on their own account, (2) act as wholesalers in that they buy and sell exchange to institutions (brokers) that deal directly with ultimate buyers and sellers of exchange, and (3) transact exchange with other dealers.

Dealers enhance integration by virtue of their special roles. In transacting with other dealers and retail institutions (brokers), they facilitate the operations of these market participants. In transacting on their own account, dealers take uncovered foreign-exchange positions across space, across time, and with respect to midpoint of the gold-point spread. They also undertake GPA and GTF operations. In so doing, they improve the three dimensions of internal integration.

How so? If the exchange rate differs in two locations at the same time (or, realistically, for the same time period), brokers alone improve geographic integration by spatial arbitrage. If the exchange rate differs in the same location at two points in time (or in two time periods), dealers improve temporal integration by arbitrage over time (if the situation systematically recurs) or exchange-rate speculation (if otherwise). If the exchange rate differs in two locations, each for a different point in time or time period, dealers engage in joint geographic and temporal arbitrage (or speculation), thereby improving both geographic and temporal integration. It is the dealers' undertaking of uncovered positions in foreign exchange that reduces exchange-rate variation over time, thereby enhancing temporal integration (and geographic integration where intertwined with temporal integration).

What about operations that foster placement integration? Two situations should be distinguished. First, the exchange rate is located outside the gold-point spread (beyond a gold point, wherefore a "gold-point violation"). Symbolically, $|R^*| > EI$. GTF and GPA are the operations of relevance. The first prevents the exchange rate from going even further beyond the gold point, that is, from moving even further away from the spread midpoint (*SM*); the second returns the exchange rate to within the spread, thus bringing it closer to *SM*.[10]

Second, the exchange rate is within the spread ($|R^*| \leq EI$), either naturally or by virtue of GPA. In this situation GTF and GPA are inapplicable; for they are cost-effective or profitable, respectively, only when the exchange rate is outside the spread. Rather, a special form of exchange-rate speculation is in order. Such speculation, which operates only within the spread, acts to turn the exchange rate away from the gold points and, ideally, to place the exchange rate right at the spread midpoint ($|R| = SM$, or $|R^*| = 0$).

Assuming that dealers have a uniform subjective probability distribution of the future exchange rate within the spread and a zero probability of the exchange rate outside the spread (implying, among other things, absolute confidence in the maintenance of the gold standard), the probability density function $f(|R^*|)$ is exactly as in the third section: $f(|R^*|) = 0$ for $|R^*| > EI$, $1/EI$ for $|R^*| \leq EI$. Then dealers engaged in numerous transactions will (1) buy pounds in the range $-EI \leq R^* < 0$, for the probability that the pound will appreciate exceeds 50 per cent, and (2) sell pounds in the range $0 < R^* \leq EI$, for the probability that the pound will depreciate exceeds 50 per cent. This type of exchange-rate speculation, under ideal assumptions, would always return the exchange rate to the midpoint of the gold-point spread ($R = SM$ or $R^* = 0$).[11] Thus placement integration is achieved. Absent ideal assumptions, this speculation improves placement integration but does not make it complete.

The second component of the foreign-exchange market is the market structure. Is the market purely competitive, controlled by a monopolist, strongly influenced by a price leader, or subject to intense competition among oligopolists? A market with strong competition – whether purely competitive or oligopolistic – enhances internal integration by driving down profit margins in arbitrage and speculation activities. However, one dominant market participant, in the form of a giant exchange dealer, can have a much more beneficial effect on integration. Such a dealer would possess financial strength and economies of scale, both of which would foster the arbitrage and speculation operations required for improved internal integration.

Indeed, it is arguable that the principal force that fostered internal integration in the nineteenth century was the growth and operations of two giant American foreign-exchange dealers. One was a chartered bank, the Second Bank of the United States under the presidency of Nicholas Biddle; the other a private banker, the House of Brown.[12] If not monopolists, they certainly were effective price leaders – the Second Bank in 1826–36, the House of Brown in the fifteen years before the hegemony of the Second Bank and in the period from the demise of Biddle's successor bank in 1841 to the resumption of specie payments in 1879. The steady (GTF) or almost steady (GPA) improvement in internal integration observed over 1821–80 (see Table 8.3) owes much to the managerial and technological innovation emanating from the market power of these two institutions. In contrast, the high level of integration in 1901–14 – compared to the surrounding decades before and after – was associated with intense price competition among specialized dealers in an oligopolistic foreign-exchange market, with both private banks and incorporated institutions involved.

In conclusion, the model of exchange-market integration not only provides measurement of the extent of market perfection in both internal and external aspect but also enables plausible explanation of changing and improved integration over time.

NOTES

1 This chapter is based on material in Officer (1996).
2 The values are much too low for this measure to be the variance as ordinarily defined.
3 In fact, Davis and Hughes (1960) recompute their variance for those quarters excluding periods of paper standards.
4 The only discontinuity in the series is the period from the third quarter of 1914 to the third quarter of 1919, during which time the London gold market was nonoperational.
5 For details, see Officer (1996). Rare is the author who distinguishes GPA from GTF. Einzig (1931: 18) writes:

> The terms exchange transaction [GTF] and arbitrage transaction [GPA] are usually used indiscriminately, though there is a considerable difference between them. The object of the exchange transaction is to substitute the shipment of gold for the transfer of funds through the intermediary of the Foreign Exchange Market. The object of the pure arbitrage transaction is the shipment of gold, without any intention of transferring funds, to take advantage of the discrepancy between exchanges and their gold points.

6 The main reasons why GPA cost exceeded GTF cost are the following. (1) Exchange-rate cost is positive for GPA, negative for GTF. (2) In 1791–1914, when the bill of exchange was the dominant exchange-market instrument, there was a GPA interest cost for the duration of a round-trip Atlantic voyage but a zero GTF interest cost. (3) Normal profit and risk premium are a component of GPA but not GTF cost. For details, see Officer (1996).
7 The 1801–10 and 1811–20 decades are excluded for two reasons. First, they embody periods of American trade embargoes against Britain (intermittently

from 1807), as the United States was caught in the middle of Anglo-French wars, and the American-British War of 1812–15. Anglo-American specie flows under these circumstances were subject to great difficulty not reflected in arbitrage/transfer costs. Second, data on such costs are virtually nonexistent for these decades, as they are for 1919–25 (until Britain returned to the gold standard).

8 For details, see Officer (1996).

9 Perkins (1975: 155–6) and Officer (1983: 607). The latter author has since changed his view.

10 For explanation, see Officer (1996).

11 Among the ideal assumptions are zero transactions cost, zero interest-rate differential between the two countries, no taxation in the countries, and risk neutrality on the part of the speculators. For details on this speculation and its effect, see Officer (1996).

12 For discussions of the role of the Second Bank and House of Brown, see Perkins (1975) and Officer (1996).

REFERENCES

Cole, A.H. (1929) Evolution of the Foreign-Exchange Market of the United States, *Journal of Economic and Business History* 1: 384–421.

Davis, L.E. and Hughes, J.R.T. (1960) A Dollar–Sterling Exchange, 1803–1895, *Economic History Review* 13: 52 – 78.

Einzig, P. (1931) *International Gold Movements*, 2nd edn, London: Macmillan.

——(1970) *The History of Foreign Exchange*, 2nd edn, London: Macmillan.

Johnson, J.F. (1905) *Money and Currency*, rev. edn, Boston, MA: Ginn.

Myers, M.G. (1931) *The New York Money Market*, vol. 1, *Origins and Development*, New York: Columbia University Press.

Officer, L.H. (1983) Dollar–Sterling Mint Parity and Exchange Rates, 1791–1834, *Journal of Economic History* 43: 579–616.

——(1996) *Between the Dollar–Sterling Gold Points: Exchange Rates, Parity, and Market Behavior*, Cambridge: Cambridge University Press.

Perkins, E.J. (1975) *Financing Anglo-American Trade*, Cambridge, MA: Harvard University Press.

9

ITALY, THE FISCAL-DOMINANCE MODEL, AND THE GOLD-STANDARD AGE[1]

Giuseppe Tattara and Mario Volpe

Large government deficits experienced in recent years in various countries, mainly developing economies, and evidence of a positive relation between government deficits and the growth of money and prices are at the heart of the debate on fiscal policy.[2] The situation is rather similar to that experienced by many European countries just at the beginning of their industrialization process. Many countries lacked a single central bank and had a plurality of small banks of issue, the government was frequently pressed by new tasks and by the need to face large infrastructure expenditures, and it lacked an efficient fiscal administration to raise the required taxes.

The connection between the budget deficit and inflation can be articulated as follows (Buchanan and Wagner 1977). At first, a very direct link arises when the central bank is not independent of the government, so that at least part of the deficit is financed, through government pressure, by printing additional money. In the same vein, when finance is raised through debt creation, the government competes with private borrowers for scarce loanable funds; this will drive up interest rates and crowd out private spending on both consumer and capital goods.[3] Although government and central banks are completely independent, the high interest rates due to the large government borrowing are an incentive to the central bank to purchase at least part of the newly issued government debt through open-market operations. This reduces pressure on interest rates but at the same time leads to a more rapid growth of the money supply and prices; the result is money growth and inflation, and the outcome is not very different from financing the budget deficit through the printing of money.[4]

Barro (1987) used long-term British data, spanning from the first years of the eighteenth century to World War I to assess the effects of temporary changes in government purchases on interest rates, the quantity of money, the price level, and the budget deficit. He found that temporary spending increased interest rates, but raised prices and the quantity of money only when the gold standard was suspended, i.e., during two wars, in 1797 and in 1914. In peacetime the ratio of public debt to GNP tended constantly to fall.

Barro's results are grounded on two main points. First, the gold-standard fixed-exchange regime pegged domestic prices to the international level and enforced a strict control over the money supply.[5] A flexible-exchange regime would have provided room for much greater flexibility: different monetary-expansion rates and different price levels are brought to compatibility with external equilibrium via exchange-rate variations. Second, in an open economy with high capital mobility – as under the gold standard (Fishlow 1985) – a temporary increase in government purchases shows up in borrowing from abroad rather than high interest rates at home and there is no incentive for the central bank to change its portfolio composition and inflate circulation (Ahmed 1987).

Fratianni and Spinelli claim that Italian historical development provides a good illustration of the fiscal-dominance model, as in the long period Italian monetary policy proved endogenous to fiscal policy and such endogeneity explains the process generating Italian inflation (Fratianni and Spinelli 1982; Spinelli and Fratianni 1991; Favero and Spinelli 1992).

The mechanism hypothesized by the authors is based essentially on evidence from two historical periods: the years from the reunification of the kingdom to World War I and the more recent period from the early 1970s up to the mid-1980s. During both periods the state deficit proved significant, and for the larger part of both periods the lira exchange rate was not formally tied either to gold or to other currencies.

Italy, from the unity of the kingdom in 1861 to 1913, provides an interesting case because it was a small, open economy and the lira had no fixed link to gold. The Italian government ran a deficit for two-thirds of the period, although the main deficits were clustered in 1861–70 and 1886–91. Open recourse to the printing press was the way used to finance the first deficit; government debt financed the second.

The government shifted readily off commodity standard toward paper standard during the Austrian war in 1866 and the domestic credit crisis of the 1890s. In this it paralleled movements out of gold in other countries – Austria-Hungary, Greece, the United States, etc. – during wartime or other emergencies (Eichengreen and Flandreau 1996; Bordo and Rokoff 1995; Bordo and Schwartz 1996). Unlike many other European countries, Italy did not come back to gold once the bad years had passed away. It stayed on gold for a very limited period, from 1861 to 1866, and for a short time in 1883, but it maintained a remarkably stable exchange rate and price level so that it is commonly said to have "shadowed" gold for the 52 years under scrutiny, notwithstanding government deficits (Bordo and Rokoff 1995; Bordo and Schwartz 1996). The exchange never departed measurably from the gold-standard currencies and relative prices kept rather stable: the lira depreciation was limited and the exchange fluctuated for more than four-fifths of the whole period within a hypothetical ± 5 per cent band with respect to the average quotation.

This puzzle is specifically addressed in this chapter. Only under the gold-standard myth is there postulated a strict relationship among the exchange, metal reserves, and circulation – working mainly through the price level and the following balance-of-payments adjustment. In reality, the gold standard worked mainly through capital movements in an integrated financial market. An excess demand for or supply of money in one country leads to a once-and-for-all re-allocation of money and assets and to a one-shot transfer of gold as world portfolio equilibrium is re-established. The differential between domestic and foreign interest rates does not move, except for a change in the risk perception of international investors. This balance-of-payments adjustment is largely independent of relative price levels and commodity flows (Dick and Floyd 1992).

A stable exchange rate system was compatible with an expansion of the role of the state in building infrastructure and adding to global demand in the early phases of development in the Atlantic economies – as well as in Italy – where new unemployed resources were brought to work and money issued on account of the Treasury did not put too much pressure on relative prices. Eventually the excess supply of money was disposed of through assets purchases from abroad. There were minor reflections on interest rate differential and on the exchange, as budget deficits were huge but limited in time and foreign investors' long-term confidence was never shaken.

This vision provides a very different framework from the explanation of the Italian inflation in more recent years – when capital flows were restrained and the exchange was explicitly allowed to depreciate – and fails to support the Fratianni and Spinelli long-run vision of the relationship between budget deficit and inflation. At the same time, it enlightens some neglected points on how the gold standard functioned in the European periphery.

The chapter is organized in four main sections. First, the link between the money supply and the state budget deficit in the Italian historical context is described. Second, the process of monetization of government deficit is related both to the fixity of the exchange and the situation of free capital mobility typical of the 1860–1913 period. These two elements are, as is well known, the gold standard's two fundamental principles. Third, the empirical evidence supporting the view of Italy "shadowing" gold is discussed. The effect of government financing on the money supply is tested. Finally, the fundamental difference of the process of financing government deficit in the gold-standard age and in the more contemporary period is outlined.

BUDGET DEFICITS AND MONETARY CIRCULATION: HISTORICAL EVIDENCE

The Italian budget deficit

With the reunification of the kingdom, Italy adhered to the bimetallic regime of French origin and the lira rate of exchange was fixed with respect to both gold and silver at an established ratio. The largest part of domestic circulation was metallic (Tattara 1997).

Immediately after unification, Italian public finance had to face new problems. Public administration was to be completely reorganized: the debts of the various component states were undertaken by the new state (the capital value of the old debts amounted to 50 per cent of the country's national product); the country was in need of the most basic public services and a permanent revolt – *brigantaggio* – inflamed the south for more than five years.[6] Public expenditure over national income varied between 15 and 20 per cent, a relatively high level in comparison with other European countries with larger wealth (Brosio and Marchese 1986: 51, Table 3.1).

Expenditure growth went very high just after reunification; as expected, interest on the debt stock made up a large part of it. From 1867, under the conservative government, expenditures declined, although the political program of "state restraint" of the right was based more on raising taxes (tax on wheat milling) than on contracting expenditures.

The left-wing government of Agostino Depretis (1879–87) was characterized by a climate much more favorable to industry and developed in a decade of relatively high economic growth. Expenditure composition changed. Military expenses declined and government intervention in the economy, mainly to build railway infrastructure, increased. Depretis was succeeded by Francesco Crispi, whose government was characterized by a new surge in military expenditures (in 1888–90 due to the military convention with Germany and later on to the African campaign).[7]

During the Italian take-off in the first years of the twentieth century, government expenditure rose less than proportionate to national product, and government surplus added to private savings and relieved global demand in a period of rapid export growth. Military expenditures were still at the root of the new expansion after 1905; railway expenditures had two peaks in 1905 and 1908 corresponding to the indemnity paid to the railway companies.

Taxes deviated from expenditures basically in two periods: the early 1860s and the 1880s and the 1890s (1883–97). The budget deficit consequently reached high levels in 1866–70 and in 1888–90 (see Figure 9.1). An immediate increase in taxation just after the reunification of the country was politically unfeasible, and the same fiscal system was inadequate to the new tasks posed by the country's reunification. In the early 1860s only 50 per cent of state expenditures were covered by fiscal revenues, and the budget deficit rose in the early years of the decade to about 7 per cent of the national income; it was financed by public-estate sales and by an increase in public debt.[8] State debt started at about 45 per cent of GDP to reach 80 per cent in 1865 and almost 100 per cent five years later (debt data from Spinelli and Fratianni 1991: 66–77).

After an initial slow start, taxes jumped in 1870 to almost 11 per cent of national product and maintained roughly the same level until 1887, when they reached a level of 15 per cent. Direct and indirect taxes shares remained approximately constant through time (with a quota of about 50 per cent each). Among indirect taxes, the left-wing government abolished the tax on wheat milling and substituted it in 1878 with a new, higher, tariff (Federico 1996).

In 1872 the current budget was almost brought under control and the deficit remained very limited from 1874 to 1885. From 1897 it turned into a surplus, and remained positive to 1904 (Figure 9.1).

Other European countries ran deficits during the nineteenth century, mainly connected with episodes of war finance or railways and public-work construction, not very dissimilar from the Italian ones. In a comparative perspective, the ratio of Italian debt to GNP looks rather high and the way it was financed appears important in understanding Italian inflation, or better the lack of it. In Europe, Italian debt stock per head can be valued third, after the French and the Portuguese (*Fenn's Compendium* 1889).

Deficit finance

The Italian budget deficit in the early 1860s was largely financed through debt. Most of the Italian debt was represented by irredeemable consols, the Rendita Italiana: a part of these was subscribed on the internal market, with the active participation of the main banks of issue – particularly the Banca Nazionale – that operated a sequence of rather profitable "open market" operations (Di Nardi 1953: 76–7). A large part – more than half – was placed abroad, mainly in Paris through the Rothschild's intermediation (Luzzatto 1968: 44). The Paris market at that time was a big source of foreign funds, financing mainly the government expenditures of European nations (Fishlow 1985: 392–400). The effective rate of interest paid on Italian debt during the 1860s varied from 7 to 13.5 per cent, and the Rendita was placed easily on the international market. In the Paris stock market the Rendita had a yield premium in relation to the French and the English state funds, because of the larger risk attributed by foreign investors to a new debtor state with uncertain repute, as was the case of the new Kingdom of Italy.

In a decade the Rendita stock piled up to around 5 billion lire face value, corresponding to 3.3 billion market value: half of this stock was probably

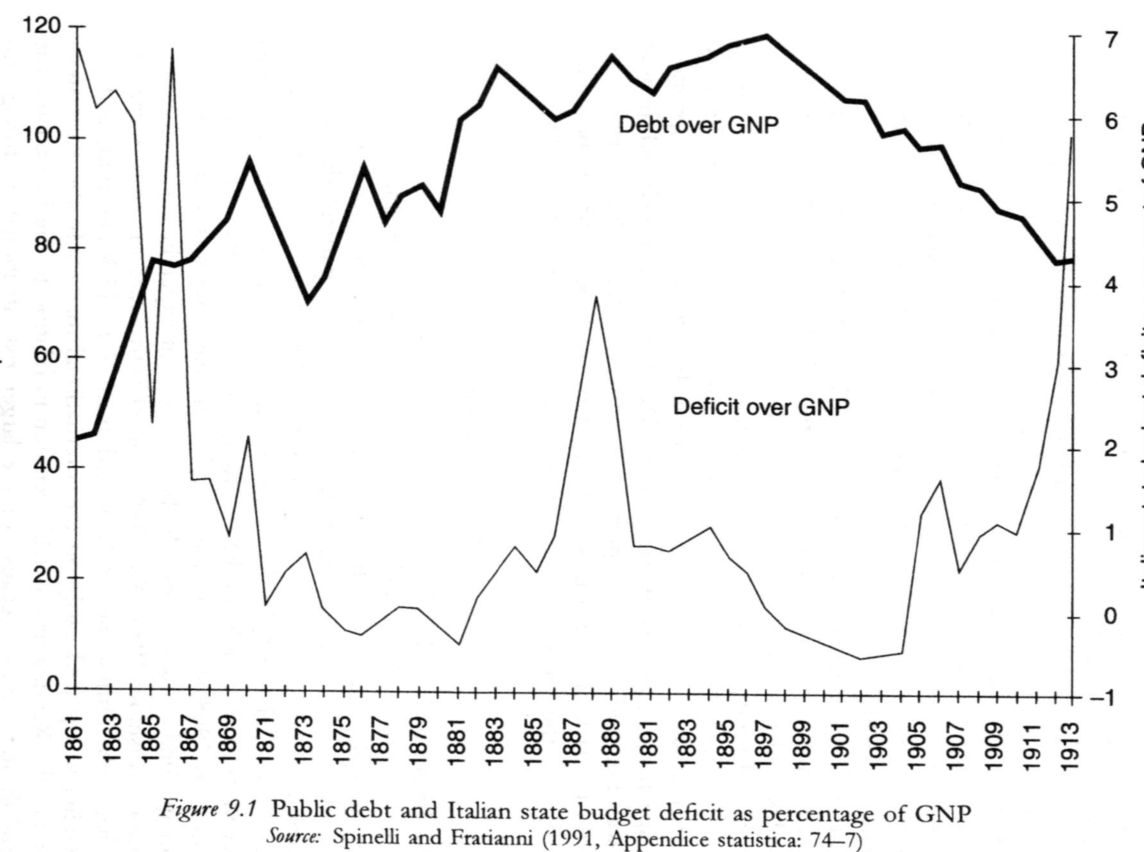

Figure 9.1 Public debt and Italian state budget deficit as percentage of GNP
Source: Spinelli and Fratianni (1991, Appendice statistica: 74–7)

kept abroad (Gille 1968: 211). On average during the nineteenth century, no less than one-third of the entire stock was kept abroad.

At the beginning of 1866, with the incipient war against Austria-Hungary, the budget situation deteriorated rapidly and the price of the Rendita halved, making external finance extremely expensive. In December 1865 Rendita prices in Paris went as low as 36.[9] In Spring 1866 a law was passed giving the government full powers in financial matters; the following day the government issued a decree arranging a large loan from the Banca Nazionale to the Treasury at a very low rate of interest and, at the same time, declared the *corso forzoso* (forced currency, namely suspension of convertibility of bank notes) for the notes of the same bank and introduced legal tender for some debt certificates issued by southern banks. Inconvertibility marked the clear pre-eminence of the Banca Nazionale on the Italian financial market.[10] Its notes could be used to settle any obligation once negotiated in commodity money and gave a big impulse to the diffusion of the paper currency among the population (see Figure 9.2).

After 1869, Finance Minister Sella[11] signed four agreements with the Banca Nazionale allowing it to finance the Treasury and widen the circulation.[12] As a result, circulation "by the Treasury" increased continuously until 1873 (Figure 9.3), although metallic reserves had been drastically curtailed.[13] The budget deficit had been reduced to low levels, but in the

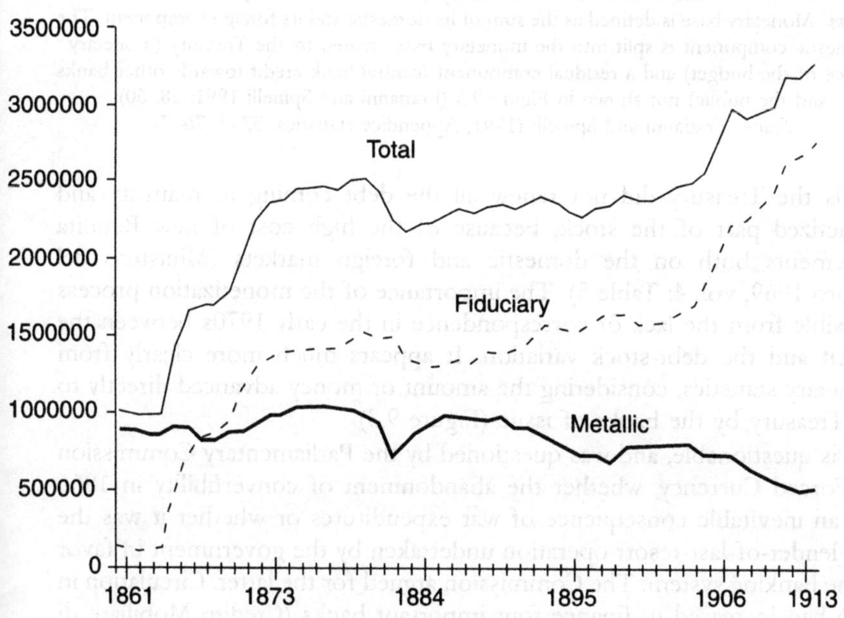

Figure 9.2 Metallic and paper circulation (thousands of lire)
Source: De Mattia (1967, vol 1: Tables 5, 13)

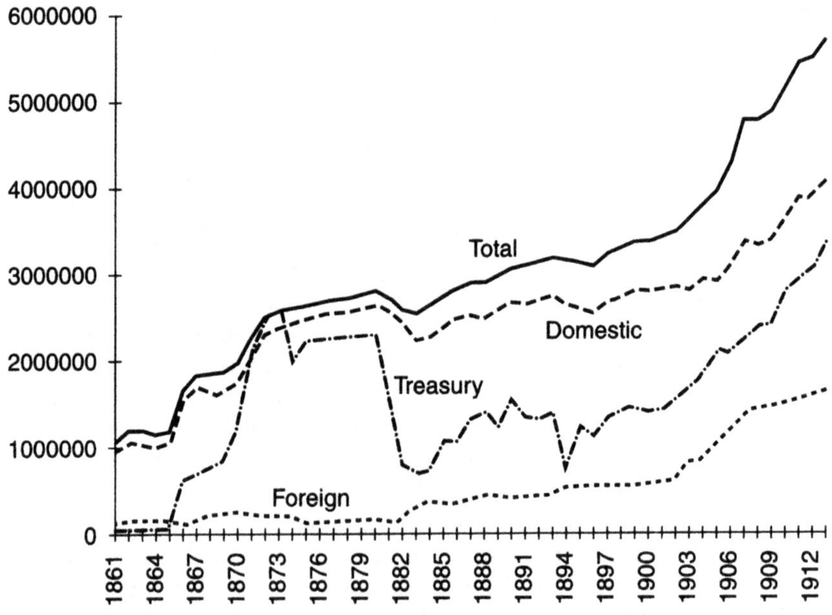

Figure 9.3 Circulation (M1): total, domestic, foreign. Circulation issued on behalf of the Treasury (thousands of lire)

Method: Monetary base is defined as the sum of its domestic and its foreign component. The domestic component is split into the monetary base created by the Treasury (monetary finance of the budget) and a residual component (central bank credit towards other banks and the public) not shown in Figure 9.3 (Fratianni and Spinelli 1991: 58, 60)

Source: Fratianni and Spinelli (1991, Appendice statistica: 52–3, 76–7)

1870s the Treasury did not renew all the debt coming to maturity and monetized part of the stock, because of the high cost of new Rendita placements both on the domestic and foreign markets (Ministero del Tesoro 1969, vol. 4: Table 5). The importance of the monetization process is visible from the lack of correspondence in the early 1970s between the deficit and the debt-stock variation. It appears much more clearly from monetary statistics, considering the amount of money advanced directly to the Treasury by the banks of issue (Figure 9.3).

It is questionable, and was questioned by the Parliamentary Commission on Forced Currency, whether the abandonment of convertibility in 1866 was an inevitable consequence of war expenditures or whether it was the first lender-of-last-resort operation undertaken by the government in favor of the banking system. The Commission argued for the latter. Circulation in 1866 had increased to finance four important banks (Credito Mobiliare di Torino e Firenze, Banco di Sconto e Sete di Torino, Cassa Generale di Genova and Cassa di Sconto di Genova) the activities of which were locked up, and were not able to face the run of depositors (Di Nardi 1953: 122ff). The Banca Nazionale – to which these banks were tied – devoted to them the largest part of its operations (discount and advance operations) and the credit market experimented an unprecedented stringency. This raised strong demand for new monetary issues and the abandonment of convertibility. Instead, the members of the Commission had viewed rather tranquilly the Treasury financial situation in 1866.

Although the origin of *corso forzoso* is debatable, the Treasury was very quick to thread its way through it and get cheap finance out of monetary issues, disconnected as they were from any metal backing.

In principle, freedom for the banks of issue was never without limits: the law enforced a proportional backing and a ratio of one-third between gold and silver reserves,[14] and in 1868 a maximum amount of issues of the Banca Nazionale at approximately the amount then in circulation was established. But the law allowed the loans to the Treasury to be accounted as a reserve component (Di Nardi 1953: 143) and the rigid control of money supply lasted only few months, after which the limit to the new issues was raised and the Banca Nazionale was authorized to print additional currency. Abusive circulation by the minor banks – the number of which virtually quadrupled over the decade – was tolerated and control over the plurality of banks of issue was rather wanting. No wonder that circulation increased even when the current budget was once again balanced. We can estimate that from 1866 to 1881 circulation (M1, namely circulation of paper and metal) increased by 67 per cent and total money creation (M3, defined as M1 plus postal and bank deposits) by 113 per cent (De Mattia 1990, vol. 2, part 3: 1324–31, Tables 3, 4.1).

As Minister Sella said to the Deputy Chamber in 1872:

> I know that paper currency is no more than paper . . . but circulation did not grow too much and the exchange against gold did not depreciate too much from 1865 onwards. But this system was an evil incomparably less serious than the one we would have faced if we had gone on issuing public debt certificates. In such a case, in a couple of years, the Rendita quotations would have reached a quotation below that reached at the end of 1869. [Rendita price in Paris at that date was around 55, i.e., interest was 9 per cent.]
>
> (Tivaroni 1908, vol. 1: 76)

During the second period, the government deficit was financed exclusively through debt creation. Debt stock grew rather rapidly, reaching 120 per cent of GNP in 1897 (see Figure 9.1).

The domestic situation was now profoundly different. The government had announced the return to convertibility in 1881 and had backed it with the issue of a large loan in Britain in 1883: gold entered the Treasury coffers (about 640 million lire) and built a metallic base over which to increase circulation. Private short-term capital flowed from foreign to Italian banks roughly in the same amount (500 million lire), anticipating an appreciation of the lira. Convertibility was declared in 1883. In fact, convertibility was never effective and throughout the 47 years from 1866 to 1913 the lira remained inconvertible.

Money (M3) and prices increased rapidly in 1884 and in 1885.

The situation deteriorated in one year, the exchange tended to exceed the lower gold point and gold and short-term capital started to flow out of the country as rapidly as they had entered. Banks restrained reserve reduction in several ways. They openly refused to convert paper money into gold, converting only to silver – for which nobody was willing to ask. Opening hours and days of operations were contracted, bank employees were asked to queue outside in an attempt to discourage the public from withdrawing their deposits (Di Nardi 1953: 348).

As gold continued to flow out of the country two options remained. First, reduce credit to the economy and make it more expensive, as the gold standard rules would have recommended. Second, purchase gold on the market, provide the required backing, and do not contract credit.

The second option was, of course, not profitable, because banks would have paid for gold with depreciated lire and converted them back at par on demand. It might have turned out to be profitable if banks had been allowed to print additional money from their reserves while convertibility requests were in practice denied. Many banks were as locked up as their customers and, with the tacit consent of the government, they pursued the second option, at first timidly, and later more openly.[15]

Banks had a limit to circulation expansion not exceeding three times the minimum of the two ratios: reserves to circulation and nominal capital to circulation. Additional issues should have full gold coverage. Fiduciary money substituted metal on the domestic market, reserves overall increased, and circulation (M3) did even more but banks overissued with respect to the nominal capital limit without the necessary backing. The attitude of the government was very tolerant, and in 1891 the existing situation of excess money creation was openly recognized and the legal ratio of circulation to the banks' nominal capital was increased to four to one.[16]

As Minister Luzzatti said to the Deputy Chamber in 1890:

> If banks were to comply with all private claims, all claims from abroad, the exchange would not exceed the gold point, but they would be compelled to reduce monetary circulation and reduce discount operations; but this they would not be able to do without limits because of their capital locking up due to the present economic and financial crisis.
>
> De Cecco (1990b: 715, doc. 140)

Government deficit, the printing press and inflation

When inconvertibility was declared in 1866, money supply grew six-fold but did not degenerate under high inflation. Making payments in paper lire legal generated a sudden rise in money demand and enlarged the monetized part of the economy. Diffusion of paper over metallic money had a sharp increase, as Figure 9.2 shows.

A new market, that for paper currency, was created that did not exist; and an increase in money supply was made possible, granting new profitability to the active operations of the Banca Nazionale. Loans to the government were remunerated at 1.5 per cent, rather low in respect to the 7–10 per cent banks could get from the Rendita. But banks were allowed to count advances to the Treasury as reserves and could lend out of them and made remarkable profits. This advantage, granted to the Banca Nazionale by the 1866 law, was extended in 1874 to all the banks of issue, and during the period 1874–84 about 50 per cent of banks-of-issue reserves were paper money. The Banca Nazionale, Banco di Napoli and Banca Nazionale della Toscana had the largest quotas (De Mattia 1967, vol. 1, part 2: Table 23).

Possibly, the banking system – pressed to finance current deficits and to monetize the debt stock by the Treasury – created more money than domestic residents wanted to hold and the latter reestablished their portfolio equilibrium by exporting gold to buy assets in the world market, mainly Rendita Italiana in Paris. From 1864 to 1876 the estimated share of the Italian Rendita kept in Paris declined rather continuously (see Figure 9.4).[17] Capital outflows reduced domestic money and brought it in line with demand. Fiscal incentives made profitable the repurchase of the Italian Rendita and at the same time the *affidavit* (see p. 241) made investing in Rendita abroad less lucrative. As substitution among different assets was not perfect we could expect some reflection on domestic interest and prices.

Various sources, reported by Luzzatto (1968: 69), estimate the outflow of metal from 1866 to 1873 at about 600 million lire, more than half of the stock of metal estimated to be used as money. According to Romanelli, much of the Italian debt previously abroad was repatriated, also as a consequence of sales from the French as a consequence of the war with Prussia (De Cecco 1990b: 633, doc. 123).

In the 1880s state finance was raised through debt creation and the government competed with private borrowers on the domestic capital market. The fiscal-dominance literature predicts a consequent increase of private spending on both consumer and capital goods. Banks of issue have an incentive to rearrange their portfolio and purchase part of the newly issued government debt through open market operations. This reduces pressure on interest rates but at the same time leads to a more rapid growth of the money supply and prices.

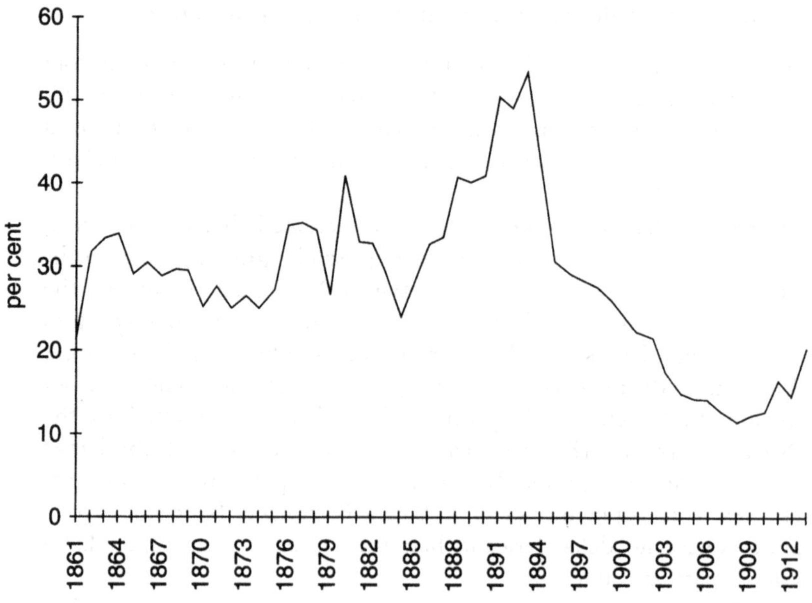

Figure 9.4 Estimated share of Italian Rendita held in France (percentage of total interest payments paid in Paris)
Source: Zamagni (1988)

However, when the country is part of the international capital market, the situation can evolve along an entirely different path. The government pressure on the financial market in the late 1880s did show up in borrowing from abroad, while domestic rates of interest remained rather stable. Credit to the government from all banks of issue declined in the same period from 26 per cent to 9–10 per cent of total asset value (computed from De Mattia 1967, vol. 1, part 1: Table 2)[18] while short-term credit that had been granted from foreign banks to the Italian banks of issue just after convertibility, in the form of commercial-paper discounts, had been recalled. There was more a change in portfolio composition than an injection of fresh finance from abroad. Banks substituted private for state financing and the state raised funds abroad that had previously flown into the banks.

The banks of issue did not inflate circulation because of the budget deficit. Then money supply appeared completely endogenous and independent of the budget deficit, and no relation with the level of prices could be expected after a limited burst in 1884.

The domestic long-run rate of interest grew later on, in 1891–2 and 1896, when the state deficit had already reduced, because of the domestic banking crisis. The Rendita yield increased because the risk of default had augmented, state solvency was jeopardized, and the quantity of debt certificates abroad experienced a sudden drop.[19]

ASSET MARKETS, CAPITAL MOBILITY AND MONETARY EQUILIBRIUM

Italy and the international financial market

As we have already mentioned, a large part of the Italian public debt was issued in foreign markets – mainly in Paris – and was represented by a consolidated bond, the Rendita Italiana. Capital was transferable and flowed in large amounts between the Italian market and foreign markets for a large part of the period, and by far the largest part of the Italian portfolio investment abroad went on the Rendita.

The stock of the Italian public debt held abroad was very big in relation to other items affecting the exchange; it was approximately ten times the average annual current-account balance and double import value. In such a situation, even a small shift in asset preferences could lead to a capital transfer that was very large in relation to what could be effected through the current account, and expectations on the exchange were much more dependent on the mood of the international financial markets than on arbitrage on the commodity markets. Rendita purchases and sales in and out of Italy were the real factors moving the lira exchange (De Cecco 1990a: 269).[20]

Capital invested in the Rendita was subject to some changes in tax regime during this period. Rendita yields were subject to a specific 8 per cent tax in 1868, subsequently increased to 13.2 per cent in 1871 and to 20 per cent in 1895 (De Cecco 1990b, docs 64 and 123).

Interest paid on the Rendita varied according to where it was paid. Interest in foreign markets was paid in gold at a fixed rate of exchange while in Italy it was paid in paper lire. For a long time Rendita owners could transfer their consols abroad, without actually selling the original certificate for a new one, and have interest paid in gold.

Investments in the Rendita in Paris and domestic financial investments were very close substitutes, as facilities in such transactions were rather well organized and free transferability of capitals across national borders was never denied.

The possibility for Italian citizens to receive interest in gold abroad was removed with the introduction of the *affidavit* in 1874, abolished in 1881, reestablished in 1894 and removed again 10 years later (De Cecco 1990b, doc. 123; editor's note: 37). *Affidavit* was a sworn declaration that the bond presented to the foreign bank did not belong to an Italian citizen, and was requested when collecting interest abroad.

The *affidavit* never prevented capital from flowing out of the country.

Figure 9.4 might suggest a possible correlation between the reintroduction of the *affidavit* in 1894 and the sharp decline in the estimated Rendita quota abroad and attribute to the *affidavit* an efficacy that it never had. But other important factors had intervened: by the end of 1894, expectations on the exchange started to turn towards appreciation and people were now transferring back capital previously held abroad.

The price approach suggests that the internationalization of a market is complete when its prices are brought into international equilibrium. Many authors use the interest-parity relationship as a measure of price equilibrium; when deviations from covered-interest parity are small, markets are assumed to be integrated under the price approach (Cosh *et al.* 1992: 24–5).

Since it is especially in the nature of financial-asset prices to adjust swiftly to important developments, it appears appropriate to examine those prices, rather than inter-country capital flows. Integration in capital markets does not require a large volume of cross-border transactions. The necessary price adjustments in interdependent financial markets often take place without any transaction occurring. Financial-asset prices can change to incorporate new information, changes in legal or institutional arrangements and the like, before any new transaction takes place, or can eliminate the profit of arbitrage before any arbitrageurs have traded (Zevin 1992: 43–4).

With a well-integrated capital market, *ex post* differences in yield represent differences in the perceived risk of default among various classes of assets. In equilibrium the yield premium on Italian bonds was a measure of the perceived possibility of default on the Italian debt; an increase in the premium means that equilibrium had changed and risk had increased (Fenoaltea 1988: 624ff; Dick and Floyd 1992: ch. 3).

Italy's international financial position can be discussed taking into account three different kind of assets: (1) Rendita priced on the domestic market, (2) Rendita priced abroad, that was exactly the same certificate as before but negotiated in foreign currency abroad (in Paris, Berlin and London) – buying Rendita abroad was a safeguard against lira devaluation and (3) British consols acting as safe-reference bond against both devaluation and default.[21]

The Rendita yield premium is defined as the difference between the Paris Rendita interest and the Rome Rendita interest and measures a currency risk premium. It varied from zero to about 1 per cent.

The consols yield premium is defined as the difference between the Rome Rendita and the British interest and measures both a currency risk and a default risk premium. It was positive and varied between 0.5 per cent and 6 per cent throughout the period.

Whenever the Italian domestic situation was perceived as very risky, to be on the Rendita in Paris did not provide any reasonable hedge against the risk of default. The fear was state bankruptcy, not the lira losing value on the foreign-exchange market. People able to move funds in the international market abandoned Italian bonds in favor of foreign government bonds, the Paris Rendita prices decreased, and the consols yield premium increased (in the 1890s).

In this situation the *affidavit* never prevented arbitrage, although it made it more expensive: arbitrage could take place only through purchases and sales of consols in the international capital market, not just moving them around and collecting interest in different currencies.

The endogeneity of monetary policy

Monetary policy in a small country, with interest rates determined in world capital market and integration of assets markets, is endogenous. This is a well-known result, due to the seminal works of Mundell (1968), McKinnon and Oates (1966), and Fleming (1962).

The model is strictly short term: there is no consideration of price adjustment or of the implications of balance of payments disequilibrium regarding the ability of the monetary authority to finance these flows (Dornbusch 1980: 175). The model introduces two assets: money and bonds. Bonds are an aggregate of all interest earning assets.

We consider the implication of asset-market integration for the small-country case and assume that individuals are free to buy and sell a wide variety of domestic and foreign bonds in an international market. If holders of securities are indifferent between domestic and foreign bonds, their yields must be equalized, taking account of risk divergence and exchange uncertainty. We assume that portfolio adjustments are instantaneous. These two assumptions imply that yields are continuously equalized and that asset holders are in portfolio equilibrium.

Consider *monetary equilibrium*. Let us start from a bookkeeping identity representing the active and passive side of a bank-of-issue assets and liabilities account.

(1) $R_t + D_t = C_t$

where D_t is the domestic source of monetary base, R_t reserves or the foreign component of the monetary base, and C_t circulation (monetary base) within the public.

We assume that at each point of time (t) money demand is represented by the familiar relation

(2) $M_{td} = P_t L(Y_t, i_t)$

where M_{td} is the demand for money balances, Y_t real income, P_t the price level, and i_t the rate of interest in the domestic market. We now look at (1) as an equilibrium relationship. Monetary equilibrium requires that money demand (M_{td}) equals supply (M_{ts}) and that both these are "desired" levels, given income, interest rates, and all other independent variables. Money (monetary-base) supply is equal to foreign assets (reserves) R_t plus the domestic component D_t.

Let us take domestic monetary base (D_t) and income (Y_t) as given at each moment of time. The equilibrium stock of reserves R_t is a function of the rate of interest.

(3) $R_t = P_t L(Y_t, i_t) - D_t$

We prefer not to model the real side of the economy, mainly on the grounds of the rather questionable estimates available for Italian national income. The ISTAT (Italian Institute for National Statistics) figure is basically a trend with a white noise added; we rather refer to Maddison's constant-value figures (Maddison 1991) after transformation at current prices. For the time being let us assume Y_t as exogenous.

The capital market integration assumption constrains the domestic interest rate in relation to interest rates in the international market. It results in the uncovered interest-parity condition:

(4) $i_t = i_t^* + \rho_t + (S_t^e - S_t)/S_t$

where i_t^* is the foreign interest rate, ρ_t the risk premium on domestic assets, S_t the current rate of exchange, S_t^e the expected one.

Given ρ_o, S_o, S_o^e, a given level of the world rate of interest, i_o^*, establishes the domestic rate of interest. Given Y_o, P_o, D_o, (3) determines the reserve level (R_o) at which we have asset-market equilibrium and the magnitude of the endogenous supply of money. In other words equations (3) and (4) solve for the two variables R_t, i_t (or P_t), given Y_t, P_t, D_t, (or i_t), i_t^*, ρ_t and $(S_t^e - S_t)/S_t$.

Money being created on account of the Treasury or the banking system does not affect the result. Total money supply is endogenous, because of the endogeneity of its foreign component, due to the effect of world capital market equilibrium on the domestic interest rate in equation (4). What we observe empirically is substantially the money–demand relationship.

If the banking system, through its domestic loan and discount policies, creates less money than domestic residents want to hold, domestic residents re-establish portfolio equilibrium by selling non-monetary assets on the world market. As the foreign currency acquired is converted into domestic currency at the banks, the domestic banking system is forced to create additional domestic money balances to meet the demand for them and to acquire international reserves in the process. The banking system has no control over the money supply. The latter always equals whatever domestic residents want to hold (Dick *et al.* 1996: 2, 9).

If the nominal exchange rate is stable and if we believe purchasing power parity to hold, given the level of prices abroad, the domestic price level will depend on the foreign money stock and foreign prices but will not depend on the domestic stock of money (Dick *et al.* 1996: 9). These assumptions are hard to verify even in the long run, and some limited effect on prices can be expected.

The model does not require *perfect substitutability* of domestic and foreign assets in portfolios accounts: domestic and foreign securities bear different interest rates and a different degree of risk. The previous equation (4) takes all that into account and expresses an equilibrium condition in the international capital market; the interest rate differential can change only when wealth owners perceive that the relative risk of the two countries has changed. Capital does not flow between countries in response to interest rate differentials.

Let us now assume that *portfolio adjustments are not instantaneous.* The mechanism through which monetary expansion occurs, following a budget deficit is as follows. An increase in public debt is financed through selling bonds to the banks of issue. Banks sell their international reserves and add domestic assets to their portfolios with a consequent expansion of domestic money – money that is not wanted. Private asset holders – at home and abroad – reduce their net domestic asset holdings and increase their reserve assets, for example buying Rendita in Paris for the same amount. If domestic and foreign assets are not perfect substitutes, an increase in interest-rate differentials can occur, as banks will have to give the public an inducement to alter its portfolio mix. *Variations in the spread between domestic and foreign rates of interest* can allow some degree of flexibility for monetary policy and explain some possible differences in relative price trends and in exchange expectations.

The fundamental argument of the portfolio theory is that the basic capital-mobility model holds without essential modifications when capital is not perfectly mobile internationally (Dick *et al.* 1996: 12–13).

In Italy the government lacked control over the stock of money through its note issue. The quantity of government notes held depended on the public's and the banking system's demand for them – any excess would be converted into Rendita abroad. Fiscal and legislative measures introduced to discriminate between the domestic and foreign capital markets had some temporary effects, but did not alter the results.

THE EMPIRICAL EVIDENCE

We now turn to our empirical tests. First, the claim that the Italian lira, although inconvertible during almost all the period, "shadowed gold" is discussed. Second, stationarity of money (M1) is tested and the proposition that monetary expansion was compatible with exchange and relative prices stability is examined. Then the reserve-flow equation suggested by portfolio theory is estimated and shown to be consistent with empirical evidence. Substitutability between domestic and foreign assets is considered. The final section concludes summarizing time series and estimation results.

The shadow of gold

As we said, the lira exchange rate with gold standard countries showed a remarkably stable pattern around the mean within a rather narrow band. Stationarity of a time series means that its mean, variance, and autocovariances are independent of time. Informal examination of data in Figure 9.5 suggests that the lira exchange rate is a typical stationary series, or a I(0) series.[22]

The meaning of the phrase "gold shadowing" is nonetheless more complex. It implies some assumptions about the mechanism under which exchange stationarity has been achieved.

A rather general starting point is to look at domestic prices relative to competitors' prices. A country is said to "shadow the gold standard" if relative prices are stationary over time for the whole period, independently of any change in the exchange regime. Relatively stable prices and a stable real exchange allow for different "mechanisms" at work, which can be investigated in various historical situations.

Figure 9.5 plots the lira nominal exchange rate and Italian wholesale prices relative to foreign prices. In building the indexes we consider two foreign countries – the United Kingdom and France (weighted) – as their

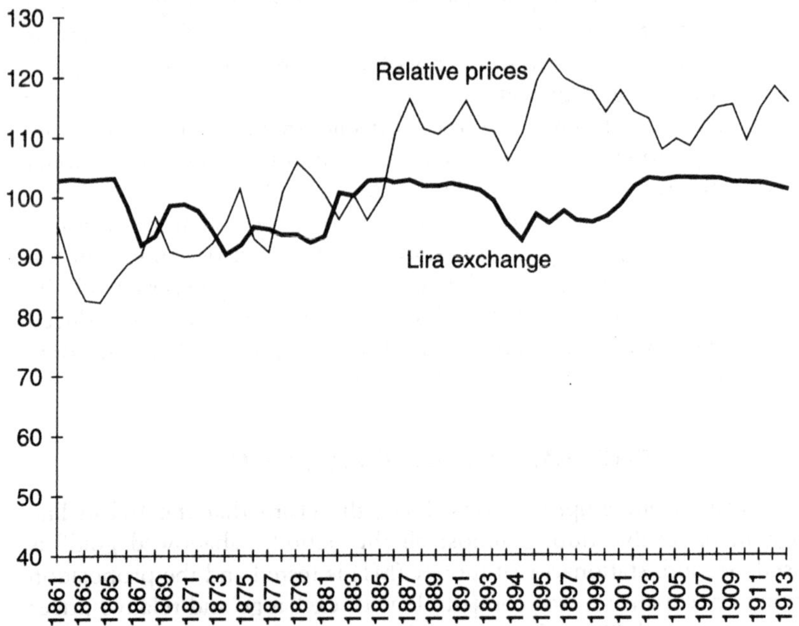

Figure 9.5 Italian prices and lira exchange relative to UK and France (index numbers, 1882=100)

Source: Ciocca and Ulizzi (1990: Tables 2,4)

rates of exchange were stable against gold and our claim is to test Italian prices relative to the prices of the gold-standard countries: other countries used to compute the lira effective exchange rate by Ciocca and Ulizzi (USA, Germany, and Austria) were discarded, as their currencies fluctuated against gold for part of the period.

Tests for unit roots for the two series were performed using DF, ADF, and the Za test suggested by Phillips and Perron (Perron 1994). The null hypothesis is that the exchange rate has a unit root, against the alternative that it has not. Test values do not lead to the rejection of the null, and both exchange rate and prices series are possible stationary series, I(0).[23]

As the series include the years of the lira inconvertibility, the formal return to bimetallism, and the 1890s international financial crisis, it seems sensible to evaluate the unit root hypothesis in a setting that allows for the possibility of structural breaks. We used a recursive technique that allows for structural breaks at any point in time: a model that permits an exogenous change in the level of the series (a "crash" or additive outlier model), a model that permits an exogenous change in the rate of growth (a trend model) and a mixed model were tested (Holden and Perman 1994; Perron 1994). Our results are then reinforced: the assumption of a unit root is not rejected, and the "trend stationary" hypothesis is the most appropriate (Holden and Perman 1994).

Money creation and money demand

Investigating the relationship through which price and exchange stability have been achieved is, of course, much more troublesome. The classical gold-standard myth assumes a direct connection between metallic reserves and money, and money and prices, through the price-specie-flow mechanism.

The introduction of capital movements into models of the gold standard has drawn attention to the role of central banks in managing the monetary mechanism. Nurske (1944) and Bloomfield (1959) studied the 1920s and 1930s and demonstrated that the domestic and foreign assets of central banks moved together – as required by the "rules of the game" – on only a minority of occasions. Nurske's analysis was replicated by Bloomfield for the pre-1914 period, and he found no greater propensity to obey these rules. These results raised the question of how the gold standard worked so successfully if central banks systematically sterilized reserve flows.

Goodhart (1972), studying the behavior of the Bank of England, found little evidence that the Bank played by the "rules of the game." The same was claimed with respect to Germany (Gall *et al.* 1995). Pippenger (1984) suggested a way to reconcile the paradox, claiming that there was considerable sterilization in the short run but that in the long run central banks had to reduce monetary liabilities in response to a decline in gold reserves. It comes as no surprise to know that Italian banks of issue, not formally linked to gold, did sterilize the two big declines in metallic reserves experienced in the early 1870s and in 1885–6, with complacency from the Treasury. They did not play by the "rules of the game" in the 1890s either, when they increased paper issues to face the domestic emergency and did not check overall credit expansion.

In Italy the quantity of money in circulation, M1, appears to have drifted upward over time, and it does not look to be stationary at all. Our battery of integration tests partially confirm the result (except for the non-trended case) and points to the rejection of the null hypotheses. The additive outlier model, the trend model, and the mixed model do not change our conclusions.[24] Testing the first difference of M1 rejects the null hypothesis of a unit root. These tests are broadly consistent with the hypothesis that the M1 time series is I(1).

The trending nature of M1 and the stationary trend in relative prices and the exchange suggest much more cautious conclusions about the process generating domestic inflation. A six-fold increase in money supply accompanied by rather stable relative prices was already explained by a parallel increase in demand reflecting the ample monetization of the economy that followed the inconvertibility law of 1866. Portfolio adjustment supplies a compatible explanation, as capital outflow possibly took care of the excess money supply with only a limited effect on relative prices. A similar shift in portfolio composition was also at the heart of the 1887 expansion in public debt.

From (3) and (4) we get the reduced form equation for estimation in current prices:

(5) $R_t = a_o Y_t + a_1(i_t^* + (\Delta S_t / S_t) + a_2 D_t + u_t$

Expected variations in the exchange are approximated by actual spot-rate variations.

The following variables are used in estimation:

R_t is defined as foreign metallic reserves, from De Mattia (1967, vol. 2: Table 5).

Y_t is the value added of Italian manufactures, from Maddison (1991), reflated with the wholesale price index from Ciocca and Ulizzi (1990).

S_t is the lira rate of exchange with gold-standard countries. It is defined as lire per unit of foreign exchange, the British–French average. Basic series are from Ciocca and Ulizzi (1990).

i_t^* is the long-run rate of interest in the United Kingdom – the leading financial center – from Spinelli and Fratianni (1991). We also computed the interest rate on Rendita Italiana in Paris, and called them $RendP_t$ and $RendR_t$. $Rend_t$ is the difference between them.

D_t is the currency in circulation, from De Mattia (1967, vol. 2: Table 13), which is C_t circulation, net of the foreign component, R_t.

$Deficit_t$ is the budget deficit over GNP, from Spinelli and Fratianni (1991).

The following signs of the coefficients are expected: $a_o > 0$, a_1, $a_2 < 0$. We do not expect the state deficit to enter significantly into (5), both because money creation by the Treasury did not reflect the current deficit and because any shift in the source of monetary expansion does not affect the result.

The strategy followed for estimation is reported only very briefly and the more technical points are given in the appendices.

Money, income, reserves, foreign interest rate net of exchange variation, and risk variables are I(1) variables.[25] All I(1) variables have been tested for broken-trend stationarity and all series entering our reduced-form equation are represented by stochastic nonstationary processes. Differentiated series have been tested to be I(0) – the null hypothesis. Results are reported in the appendix.

As our variables cointegrate and trace, and maximum-eigenvalue tests indicate a unique cointegrating vector, a linear combination between them, exists that is stationary. The cointegrating vector, normalized in R_t, estimated through the Johansen FIML procedure, is reported in Table 9.1 (equation 1).

OLS estimation of the cointegrating vectors are a super-consistent estimate. Test statistics with appropriate asymptotic distributions can be computed using the Phillips-Hansen modifications – Fully modified OLS estimators. Various equations estimates were run following this procedure and are reported in Table 9.1 as equations (2), (3), (4), (5), (6).

We can distinguish between a long-run relationship between metallic reserves and the other explanatory variables, that is, the manner in which the two sets of variables drift upward together, and the short-run dynamics, that is, the relationship between deviations of the variables from their long-run trend.

In the long-run function, the highly significant and positive coefficient of income points to the strong transaction motive for holding money. The

Table 9.1 Equation 5: long-run foreign reserves function, 1862–1913

Eq.		*Constant*	*Y*	*D*	*RendP*	*i**	*ΔS*	*i*+ΔS/S*	*Deficit*
1	coeff.		0.008	−0.05		−246.50	−100.55		
2	coeff.	452.79	0.001	−0.12	−87.74		−14.80		
	t-value	*1.81*	*6.99*	*−1.90*	*−4.36*		*−1.41*		
3	coeff.	677.41	0.001	−0.18	−22.77	−282.17			
	t-value	*4.11*	*15.43*	*−4.85*	*−1.60*	*−4.83*			
4	coeff.	740.71	0.001	−0.22	−23.21	−260.86			−7.44
	t-value	*4.64*	*15.98*	*−4.47*	*−1.68*	*−4.22*			*−1.14*
5	coeff.	678.14	0.001	−0.17	−22.77			−282.16	
	t-value	*4.13*	*14.43*	*−4.85*	*−1.59*			*−4.83*	
6	coeff.	741.38	0.001	−0.23	−23.21			−260.86	−7.44
	t-value	*4.64*	*15.98*	*−4.47*	*−1.68*			*−4.22*	*−1.11*

Note: t statistic based on Phillips-Hansen FM estimator is N(0,1) (see Phillips 1990)

conditions of the international capital market are seen in variations in the exchange variable and by the level of the interest rate in the leading financial market at that time – the United Kingdom – and by the interest rate on the Rendita in Paris net of the risk element, measured by the exchange variations. Long-run interest rates (in London and on the Rendita in Paris) and interest net of the variation in the exchange appear with the expected sign.

The negative coefficient of the domestic-circulation variable verifies the portfolio assumption: an increase in circulation by the banks of issue that is "not wanted" flows abroad through a decrease in metallic reserves. If people want more money than is created by the banks of issue, they obtain it by selling assets on the foreign markets.

The budget deficit is never significant. Reserve movements are indifferent to the reason why an excess demand or supply of money is created, and money created by the Treasury reflects monetization of the debt stock and not solely the current budget deficit.

The positive sign of the income coefficient allows us to say something on the question of whether the data support our portfolio model against the traditional price-specie-flow adjustment mechanism.

Under the price-specie-flow mechanism, the income term in (5) might be assumed to represent the real side of the economy, so that reserves reflect the adjustment in the commodity market. Capital flows are induced by the deficit or surplus on current account: an autonomous increase in domestic activity will have a consequent increase in import demand, and a deficit in the commodity account will result. This would generate a long-run decline in reserves and show up in a negative income coefficient.

Additionally, the stationarity behavior of relative prices seems at odds with the price-specie-flow mechanism, as one would expect higher money circulation to be reflected in a reserve decline through an explicit relative-prices movement.

Residuals of the cointegration relationships pertaining to our model have been computed and are symmetrically distributed around zero with constant variance. They represent the stationary series obtained as a linear combination of the cointegrated series, i.e., a long-run equilibrium position to which a possible short-run model adjusts. We represent the short-run dynamics through an error correction model (ECM).

Let us recall equation (3). A rather general ECM formulation of the dynamics is

$$(6)\quad \Delta R_t = \alpha_o \Delta Y_t + \alpha_1 \Delta(i_t^* + \Delta S_t/S_t) + \alpha_2 \Delta D_t + \alpha_3\,[R - (i^* + \Delta S/S) + D]_{t-1} + u_t$$

The difference in the foreign-reserves function is modeled and estimated as a function of the differences in the explanatory variables, of lagged values of both these variables, of the lagged value of the long-run residuals and possibly of lagged values of the same reserves.[26]

Economic theory does not give us many hints about short-run dynamics. The procedure we followed starts from a model with a rather general form, and moves along more reduced models. The final parsimonious function is listed in Table 9.2, together with a set of diagnostic statistics.

The plot of actual versus fitted variables, according to the ECM equation, for the whole period, can be seen in Figure 9.6.

A measure of the leverage of the data – which is not reported here – assures us that no particular data points have a disproportionately large influence on the coefficient estimates of the model (Otto 1994).[27]

The process of money creation and the reserve policy of the banks, during this period, has been influenced by various institutional arrangements and the total variance is only partially explained by our "long-run level variables." Banks tend to adapt their reserve policy to the circulation according to a proper "reaction" function. Short-run behavior explains a large part of the phenomena, and describes the short-run adaptation. As

Table 9.2 ECM of the reserve function based on long-run equation 3 (Table 9.1), 1864–1913

Variable	*Coefficient value*	*t-value*
const	108.26	2.49
R(−1)	0.41	3.32
R(−2)	−0.40	−3.30
ΔY(−1)	−0.0001	−1.94
ΔY(−2)	−0.0001	−1.87
Δi*(−1)	−37.79	−2.16
ΔRend	35.79	4.12
ΔRend(−2)	−31.92	−4.39
ΔRend(−3)	−23.10	−3.09
ΔΔS	32.25	3.59
ΔΔS(−1)	44.75	4.14
ΔΔS(−2)	19.11	2.53
ΔRendP(−2)	63.41	4.12
ΔD	−0.23	−4.48
ΔD(−1)	0.25	3.02
ΔD(−2)	−0.34	−3.92
ΔD1(−1)	−0.99	−2.44
ΔD1(−2)	0.24	5.63
Res(−1)	−0.13	−2.26

Notes: i is the long-run interest rate in Italy (on the Rendita)
D1 is defined as M3–R. M3 is from De Mattia (1967, vol. 2: Table 13)
Res(−1) are lagged residuals from long-run equation (3)

Statistics

R^2	0.788
adj. R^2	0.650
D.W.	2.00
F stat.	5.68
Log. lkh.	−225. 21

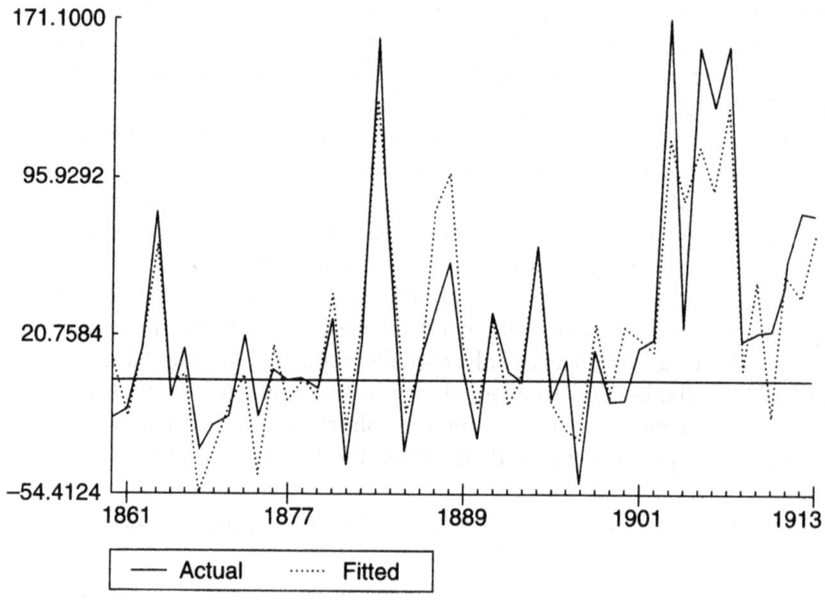

Figure 9.6 Yearly variations of metallic reserves: actual and fitted values
Source: see text

expected from the plurality of forces at work and their, sometimes, contradictory behavior, the movement toward the long run level is rather slow.

CONCLUSIONS

The fiscal-dominance model has reinterpreted Italian monetary experience during the "gold-standard" age as supporting the general view of a positive relation between government deficits and the growth of money and prices. Can this model fit Italian history in a period unanimously regarded as a period of stability of the exchange rate and integration among the international markets?

The lira maintained its metallic anchor during only 5 years out of the 52 years from the declaration of the unification of the country to World War I. When it was necessary, recourse to limited flexibility of the exchange was preferred to strict adherence to the gold-standard rules that would have required more severe limits to circulation. Several elements conjured up to a rather loose regulation of the money supply. The plurality of banks of issue made controls difficult to implement. The huge stock of public debt made the government attentive to the cost of financing, so that an atmosphere of solidarity developed between banks and the government to keep stable or to depress the rate of interest and not use it to protect metallic reserves and control credit.[28] The fiscal structure was rather fragile: banks of issue were much involved in business financing, with a large part of their assets locked up in industrial and commercial activities, and a monetary restraint could develop into a liquidity crisis for the whole financial system. They were, in fact, the most important commercial banks of the time, at least until the late 1890s.

Lack of control of the money supply and the recurrent monetization of the state deficit did not develop into depreciation and inflation. The lira exchange rate never departed significantly from stability with the gold-standard countries, so that the lira is correctly said to have "shadowed" gold along all the period.

The very rapid growth in the money supply in 1866–8 was accompanied by an increase of the monetized part of the economy, so that demand increased with supply; the unwanted money was sold abroad in exchange for foreign bonds, mainly purchasing Italian Rendita in Paris. This is why there was no price explosion when the money supply grew six-fold in a few years in the early 1870s.

In 1885 financing of the state deficit was done through debt ultimately provided by the international markets through purchase of Rendita Italiana abroad and capital imports. Foreign capital did not create excessive money supply and, within the banks' balance sheets, substituted for short-term capital that had entered the country in 1881–3 and had left at the rising of the first political and economic uncertainty. It did not show up in domestic interest-rate movements.

In the following years, during the 1890s domestic crisis, capital left the country and only gradually returned to Italy, once the external situation was brought to surplus by the huge capital inflows due to emigrant remittances around the turn of the century.

The money supply in a small country such as Italy, open to international financial markets, is endogenous. Variations in its Treasury component do not show up either in a variation in money supply or in relative price differentials.

Our study suggests one plausible interpretation for the role of capital mobility and endogenous money in the context of the gold-standard international monetary arrangement. It was the international mobility of capital rather than adherence to any automatic proportion between metal and paper that made the gold-standard system work smoothly (Dick and Floyd 1992: 170–4). Any foreign account imbalance was wiped out not in the commodity market through relative prices variations but mainly in the capital market through asset movements. The presence of some element of imperfection in international financial markets, such as the *affidavit* on the Rendita certificates abroad, does not alter this general view of the equilibrium process.

The empirical evidence we have provided is conditioned by the institutions and the history of the time. Government deficits never exploded and their duration was limited in time, although their amount was of a large magnitude, in comparison with other European countries of the time. Liberal attitudes favoring limitations on the scope of government activity (on this general point, see Yeager 1984) were a deep part of Italian policy-makers' training and education, both from the right and from the left. As soon as possible, policy-makers made strong efforts to cut public expenditure and return to balance. A very different attitude from that prevailing among Italian politicians in the more recent period!

APPENDIX 9.1: ORDER OF INTEGRATION OF TIME SERIES

Unit root tests: variables in levels

Constant

Variable	*DF*	*ADF(1)*	*L*	*ADF(L)*	*Za*	*L*	*Za(L)*
Y	1.91	2.55	3	2.80	4.08	3	4.71
R	1.91	1.18	2	1.18	2.52	2	2.37
Prices[a]	−2.34	−2.43	4	−1.78	−4.02	4	−2.82
i	−1.39	−1.92	4	−3.03*	−1.66	4	−2.45
i*	−0.40	−1.01	6	−1.54	−0.93	6	−3.14
RendP	−1.20	−1.26	2	−0.86	−1.42	2	−1.90
RendR	−1.10	−1.14	2	−0.99	−1.01	2	−1.56
Rend	−1.90	−2.07	9	−2.26	−10.07	9	−11.48
S	−1.71	−1.96	9	−2.77**	−8.97	9	−10.60**
D[b]	−1.33	−2.00	3	−4.02*	−5.57	3	−6.49
D1[c]	4.34	2.77	3	1.18	1.87	3	1.76
Deficit	−0.24	−1.15	3	−1.70	15.41	3	−12.54
Res	−6.60*	−5.71*	10	−3.84*	−46.64*	10	−39.11*

Notes: [a] Italian relative prices, from Ciocca and Ulizzi (1990)
[b] D = M3 − R
[c] D1 = M1 − R
* *values are accepted at the 5 per cent significance level.*
** *values are accepted at the 1 per cent significance level.*

Constant and trend

Variable	*DF*	*ADF(1)*	*L*	*ADF(L)*	*Za*	*L*	*Za(L)*
Y	0.09	0.83	3	1.53	1.34	3	2.49
R	−0.67	−0.98	3	−0.67	−0.18	3	−0.97
Prices	−2.82	−3.19**	3	−1.81	−15.95	3	−17.22**
i	−2.25	−1.92	4	−3.01	−5.59	4	−9.36
i*	0.96	0.12	6	−0.57	2.54	6	1.21
RendP	−1.94	−1.72	2	2.66	−9.04	2	−11.02
RendR	−2.03	−1.97	2	−2.48	−7.27	2	−9.82
Rend	−2.19	−2.43	10	−4.38	−12.16	10	−10.03
S	−2.24	−2.56	9	−4.42*	−10.60	9	−9.97
D	−1.86	−2.69	3	−4.20	−4.73	3	−5.34
D1	1.13	0.31	3	−0.17	2.16	3	1.10
Deficit	−0.56	−1.47	3	−1.09	−13.88	3	−10.05
Res	−6.67*	−5.80*	2	−4.42*	−46.17*	2	−41.92*

Notes: DF = Dickey, Fuller (tau) test
ADF = augmented Dickey-Fuller test
L = optimal lag according to the AIC2 (Akaike Information Criterion)
Za = Phillips-Perron variation of the Dickey-Fuller (z) test
L = number of lags, equal to the order of the autocorrelation-robust long-run variance estimate
* *values are accepted at the 5 per cent significance level.*
** *values are accepted at the 1 per cent significance level.*

Unit root tests: first difference of variables

Constant

Variable	*DF*	*ADF(1)*	*L*	*ADF(L)*	*Za*	*L*	*Za(L)*
ΔY	−6.45*	−3.58*	2	−3.37*	−52.78*	2	−55.80*
ΔR	−4.58*	−3.15*	2	−3.00*	−34.51*	2	−35.73*
ΔPrices	−5.93*	−6.19*	4	−4.72*	−46.49*	4	−33.55*
Δi	−11.41*	−10.77*	2	−3.40*	−36.34*	2	−35.57*
Δi*	−3.52*	−2.64*	5	−1.34	−29.59*	5	−32.65*
ΔRendP	−8.50*	−6.65*	2	−3.37*	−40.09*	2	−38.29*
ΔRendR	−8.65*	−7.29*	2	−3.34*	−37.02*	2	−36.04*
ΔRend	−6.07*	−4.83*	9	−2.41	−45.31*	9	−35.62*
ΔS	−6.02*	−4.41*	9	−2.47	−41.73*	9	−32.85*
ΔD	−5.05*	−4.52*	2	−3.67*	−28.77	2	−29.52*
ΔD1	−3.92*	−2.66	3	−2.01	−26.36*	3	−25.83*
ΔDeficit	−3.44*	−3.67*	3	−2.73	−72.75*	3	−73.46*

* *values are accepted at the 5 per cent significance level.*
** *values are accepted at the 1 per cent significance level.*

Constant and trend

Variable	*DF*	*ADF(1)*	*L*	*ADF(L)*	*Za*	*L*	*Za(L)*
ΔY	−7.63*	−4.64*	2	−4.28*	−59.34*	2	−60.79*
ΔR	−5.07*	−3.58*	2	−3.69*	−39.74*	2	−40.81*
ΔPrices	−5.91*	−6.23*	4	−4.93*	−45.87*	4	−32.42*
Δi	−11.47*	−10.86*	2	−3.37*	−35.82	2	−35.02*
Δi*	−4.33*	−3.48*	5	−1.73	−32.56*	5	−34.18*
ΔRendP	−8.36*	−6.56*	2	−3.32	−39.83*	2	−37.98*
ΔRendR	−8.44*	−7.06*	2	−3.27	−36.65*	2	−35.67*
ΔRend	−5.98*	−4.74*	9	−2.28	−45.13*	9	−34.51*
ΔS	−5.93*	−4.32*	9	−2.34	−41.57*	9	−31.69*
ΔD	−4.94*	−4.36*	2	−4.20*	−30.64*	2	−31.20*
ΔD1	−5.20*	−3.79*	2	−3.35*	−29.93*	2	−30.80*
ΔDeficit	−3.62*	−4.02	3	−3.37*	−75.69*	3	−72.27*

Notes: DF = Dickey, Fuller (tau) test
ADF = augmented Dickey-Fuller test
L = optimal lag according to the AIC2 (Akaike Information Criterion)
Za = Phillips-Perron variation of the Dickey-Fuller (z) test
L = number of lags, equal to the order of the autocorrelation-robust long-run variance estimate
* *values are accepted at the 5 per cent significance level.*
** *values are accepted at the 1 per cent significance level.*

Tests are based on the following alternative models for any variable y:

	H_0	H_1
$\Delta y_t = a_0 + a_2 y_{t-1} + \sum_{j=1}^{q} \gamma_j \Delta y_{t-j} + u_t$	$a_2 = 1$	$a_2 < 1$
$\Delta y_t = a_0 + a_1 t + a_2 y_{t-1} + \sum_{j=1}^{q} \gamma_j \Delta y_{t-j} + u_t$	$a_2 = 1$	$a_2 < 1$

The search for a trend break and test for a unit root with a trend break were performed using a sequential procedure. Tests are available from the authors.

An AR model with drift and trend has been defined as

$$\Delta y_t = a_0 + a_1 d_t^b + a_2 t + a_3 t d_t^b + e y_{t-1} + \sum_{j=1}^{q} \gamma_j \Delta y_{t-j} + u_t$$

where d are the lag differences to eliminate the residual autocorrrelation.

$d^b_t = 0,\ t < 6,\ t \geqslant 40$

$d^b_t = 0$, if $b < t,\ 7 \leq t, b < 40$

$d^b_t = 1$ otherwise.

The AR model with drift and trend has been estimated. H_0 is that the process has a unit root. Informative summary statistics from these sequences are the minimum ADF; if looking at the minimum we do not reject it, we can be quite confident about the stochastic non-stationarity of the series.

APPENDIX 9.2: COINTEGRATION AMONG MODEL VARIABLES (VAR 2)

Johansen maximum likelihood procedure, trended case, with trend in data generation process

Cointegration LR test based on maximal eigenvalue of the stocastic matrix.

Fifty observations from 1864 to 1913. Maximum lag in VAR=2.
List of variables included in the cointegrating vector: R, i*, Y, D, S
List of eigenvalues in descending order: 0.66349 0.37015 0.26972 0.25375 0.053659

Null	*Alternative*	*Statistic*	*95% critical value*	*90% critical value*
r = 0	r = 1	54.46	33.46	30.90
r ≤ 1	r = 2	23.11	27.07	24.73
r ≤ 2	r = 3	15.72	20.97	18.60

Johansen maximum likelihood procedure, trended case, with trend in data generation process

Cointegration LR test based on trace of the stochastic matrix.

Fifty observations from 1864 to 1913. Maximum lag in VAR=2.
List of variables included in the cointegrating vector: R, i*, Y, D, S
List of eigenvalues in descending order: 0.66349 0.37015 0.26972 0.25375 0.053659

Null	*Alternative*	*Statistic*	*95% critical value*	*90% critical value*
r = 0	r = 1	110.68	68.53	64.84
r ≤ 1	r = 2	56.22	47.21	43.95
r ≤ 2	r = 3	33.11	29.68	26.78

NOTES

1 We thank Stefano Fachin, Marc Flandreau, Diego Lubian, Cristina Marcuzzo, Lawrence Officer, Annalisa Rosselli and the participants to the Perugia workshop for very helpful discussions. We are grateful to the Consiglio Nazionale delle Ricerche (1994) and to the Ministero per l'Università e la Ricerca Scientifica (1993, 1994) for supporting our research.

2 For evidence that the association between deficit and money growth is common and is present particularly when the central bank is politically and economically not independent. See Alesina (1988).

3 Barro defines conditions under which government borrowing does not crowd out private spending but erodes private savings: when a larger deficit today is accompanied by lower current tax revenue. See Barro (1974).

4 Part of the relationship between variations in money and the budget deficit can prove a little spurious. Barro (1978) presents a model in which a positive relationship between government deficit and money growth is observed even if the government does not monetize its debt. The government is assumed to be concerned with the real rather than the nominal value of its debt; consequently it allows its nominal debt to grow by 1 per cent (as compared with what it otherwise would have been) for each anticipated 1 per cent increase in the price level. This leads to a positive association between the rate of inflation and the nominal government deficit, and if the rise in prices and in money are positively related, then one would observe a positive association between money growth and nominal government deficit.

5 The fixed exchange constraint might not have been binding in the case of England, the currency of which enjoyed an international-reserve status sufficient to explain both the Bank of England's leadership role in monetary management and the powerful effects of variations of bank rate on gold flows (Eichengreen 1987). But it was certainly binding for a small economy at the periphery of the system, as in the case of Italy.

6 According to Carocci (1975: 366) the repression of *brigantaggio* occupied more than half of the Italian army and cost more than the Italian Risorgimento.

7 Crispi was in power from 1887 to 1891 and from 1893 to 1896.

8 Official national-accounts data are from Istituto Centrale di Statistica (1957). Unification took place on March 17, 1861 and immediately afterwards Finance Minister Bastogi asked Parliament to issue the Rendita – a consolidated Treasury bond – in the internal and foreign markets. On financial problems in the 1860s, see Izzo (1962).

9 The yearly rate of interest on Italian consols reached almost 10 per cent in 1867. In a single day the rate went as high as 14 per cent.

10 The two other banks of issue could enjoy the advantages of inconvertibility only in a rather indirect way because they were obliged to convert their paper money on demand into the paper money of the Banca Nazionale. They were also much less important and had a much more limited territorial diffusion.

The Parliamentary Commission, established in 1868, to investigate the forced currency, defined it as a "hateful device" supported by the Banca Nazionale to bring to a practical solution the problem of the single bank of issue. See Sannucci (1990: 187).

11 Sella was Finance Minister in 1862, 1864–5, and 1869–73.

12 Di Nardi (1953: 138–45). The increase in circulation was mainly due to the financial needs of the state and this operation was not included in the reserve requirement. On some occasions the Banca Nazionale was allowed to count

Treasury money orders among metallic reserves, and during the same period other banks overissued in limited amounts. See Di Nardi (1953: 150–60).

13 Reserves decreased because of a flight of metal and a high commodity deficit in the Italian external accounts. They declined from 35 per cent of paper circulation in the late 1860s to around 20 per cent in the 1870s. See De Mattia (1990, vol. 2, part 3: Tables 3 and 49.2).

14 The regime was that of the old Piedmont state, as usual, see Martello and Montanari (1874: 10–11). Before that, different banks of issue operating in different states had different statutory rules; some had a proportional backing, others had to keep a ratio between the stock of currency issued and the bank's capital stock.

15 This was the case of the Banca Nazionale, which was authorized by the government to increase issues by 50 million, without any backing at all, to refinance the Banca Tiberina. See Di Nardi (1953: 332).

16 Monetary issues were not completely out of control, and the ratio between reserves and circulation was kept to around 3 to 1.

17 The amount of the Rendita in Paris is inferred from interest paid abroad, as Paris was by far the most important market for the Rendita. At first only coupons could be transferred, just to collect interest, and there was no connection between interest paid abroad and capital movements; but from 1872 the government required that coupons be accompanied by the debt certificate. See De Cecco (1992, doc. 123).

18 Credit to the Treasury was granted by domestic as well as foreign institutions. The most important were Società ordinarie di credito, Banche Popolari, Casse di Risparmio, etc., but these were not banks of issue and could not monetize government debt.

19 The debt burden as a percentage of GNP was at a maximum from 1892 to 1897 (see Figure 9.1), mainly due to the GNP decline. In the late 1890s the interest quota of public debt paid abroad declined from 50 to 25 per cent of the total (Zamagni 1988: Table A.6.1).

20 The causal link from capital imports to the current-account balance was put forward by Williamson (1964) in his pioneering study on American growth. Williamson speculated that cycles in capital imports were caused by cycles in domestic construction, through an upward pressure on the level of the interest rate. Fenoaltea (1988) believes that what was valid for the countries of the Atlantic economy also held true for Italy.

21 On the importance of the British market, as a point of reference, see Fenoaltea (1988: 629).

22 For a more precise statement, see Dickey *et al.* (1994).

23 Our sample is 52 annual observations, which can be considered not a large number. But, as discussed in Perron (1994) the power of the unit-root tests depends much more on the span of the data than on the number of observations *per se.* Our data span over a significant – relatively homogeneous – period in world monetary history.

We have tested stationarity of the level variables about a non zero mean, stationarity about a deterministic time trend, and stationarity about a time trend and a drift.

Tests performed on the difference of the variables lead to the rejection of the null hypothesis of a unit root.

24 Only when a very specific outlier is used – an exogenous shift in M1 level for the period 1866–8 – is the null hypothesis rejected and the series apparently stationary. Removing the big increase in money supply after the late 1860s

devaluation, through "appropriate dummies", leaves us with an "almost stationary" series, but this, of course, misrepresents the "real" story. Statistically, a too-constrained model implies a substantial loss of power and even tests that are inconsistent. See Perron (1994: 121).

25 Currency risk can be measured as the yield difference between the average Paris and Rome Rendita prices. General risk is measured by the interest yield between Italy and the UK, as already noticed.

Exchange expectations are assumed to equal actual spot variations and are also stationary, as the exchange itself is stationary. The difference between foreign interest and the yield difference and/or exchange expectations is I(1), as the difference between I(1) and I(0) series.

26 Differenced variables are I(0). Obviously, one needs to be careful about nonstationarity of the lagged dependent variable. Particularly, inference on the stationary variables coefficients can be conducted according to standard distributions, while inference on lagged reserve coefficients relates to a non standard unknown distribution, approximated by Dickey and Fuller.

27 The ECM model provides better fit for the period 1861–1904, avoiding the 1907 financial crisis. In the most recent period reserves were composed both of metal and of foreign bonds, and an explicit policy for the stability of the exchange had been undertaken by the Bank of Italy. Both elements influenced particularly the short run dynamic of the model, leaving the long-run formulation unchanged.

28 There was also a very practical formal reason to prevent it. For most of the period banks had to ask the Finance Minister's consent each time they wanted to vary the rate of discount. See Di Nardi (1953: 187–8 and 281–4).

REFERENCES

Ahmed, S. (1987) Government Spending, the Balance of Trade and the Terms of Trade in British History, *Journal of Monetary Economics* 20: 195–200.

Alesina, A. (1988) Alternative Monetary Regimes: A Review Essay, *Journal of Monetary Economics* 21: 175–83.

Barro, R.J. (1974) Are Government Bonds Net Wealth?, *Journal of Political Economy* 82: 1095–117.

Barro, R.J. (1978) Comment from an Unreconstructed Ricardian, *Journal of Monetary Economics* 4: 569–81.

Barro, R.J. (1987) Government Spending, Interest Rates, Prices and Budget Deficits in the United Kingdom, 1701–1918, *Journal of Monetary Economics* 20: 221–47.

Bloomfield, A.I. (1959) *Monetary Policy under the International Gold Standard, 1880–1914*, New York: Federal Reserve Bank of New York.

Bordo, M. and Rokoff, H. (1995) The Gold Standard as a "Good Housekeeping Seal of Approval," paper presented at the Economic History Association Annual Meetings, September 8–10, Chicago.

Bordo, M. and Schwartz, A. (1996) The Specie Standard as a Contingency Rule: Some Evidence for Core and Peripheral Countries, 1880–1990, in J. Braga de Macedo, B. Eichengreen and J. Reis (eds) *Currency Convertibility: The Gold Standard and Beyond*, London and New York: Routledge.

Brosio, G., and Marchese, C. (1986) *Il potere di spendere*, Bologna: Il Mulino.

Buchanan, J.M. and Wagner, R.E. (1977) Democracy in Deficit: The Political Legacy of Lord Keynes, New York: Academic Press.

Carocci, G. (1975) *Storia d'Italia dall'unità ad oggi*, Milan: Feltrinelli.

Ciocca, P. and Ulizzi, A. (1990) I tassi di cambio nominali e "reali" dell'Italia dall'unità nazionale al sistema monetario europeo (1861–1979), in *Ricerche per la storia della Banca d'Italia*, vol. 1, Rome and Bari: Laterza.

Cosh, A.D., Hughes, A. and Singh, A. (1992) Openess, Financial Innovation, Changing Patterns of Ownership, and the Structure of Financial Markets, in T. Banuri and J.B. Schor (eds) *Financial Openess and National Autonomy: Opportunities and Constraints*, Oxford: Clarendon Press.

De Cecco, M. (1990a) The Italian National Debt Conversion of 1906, in R. Dornbusch and M. Draghi (eds) *Public Debt Management: Theory and History*, Cambridge: Cambridge University Press.

De Cecco, M. (ed.) (1990b) *L'Italia e il sistema finanziario internazionale, 1861–1914*, Introduzione, Rome and Bari: Laterza.

De Mattia, R. (ed.) (1967) *I bilanci degli istituti di emissione italiani dal 1845 al 1936, altre serie storiche di interesse monetario e fonti*, vol. 1, Parts 1, 2, Rome: Banca d'Italia.

De Mattia, R. (ed.) (1990) *Storia delle operazioni degli istituti di emissione italiani dal 1845 al 1936 attraverso i dati dei loro bilanci*, vol. 2, Parts 1, 2, 3, Rome: Banca d' Italia.

Dick, J.O. and Floyd, J.E. (1992) *Canada and the Gold Standard: 1871–1913*, Cambridge: Cambridge University Press.

Dick, J.O., Floyd, J.E. and Pope, D. (1996) Adjustment Under the Gold Standard Policies: Canada and Australia Compared, in T. Bayoumi, B. Eichengreen and M. Taylor (eds) *Modern Perspectives on the Gold Standard*, New York: Cambridge University Press.

Dickey, D.A., Jansen, D. and Thornton, D.L. (1994) A Primer on Cointegration with an Application to Money and Income, in B.B. Rao (ed.) *Cointegration: Expository Essay for the Applied Economist*, New York: St. Martin's Press.

Di Nardi, G. (1953) *Le banche di emissione in italia nel secolo XIX*, Torino: UTET.

Dornbush, R. (1980) *Open Economy Macroeconomics*, New York: Basic Books.

Eichengreen, B. (1987) Conducting the International Orchestra: Bank of England Leadership Under the Classical Gold Standard, *Journal of International Money and Finance* 6.1: 5–29.

Eichengreen, B. (1992) The Gold Standard since Alec Ford, in S.N. Broadberry and N.F.R. Crafts (eds) *Britain in the International Economy*, Cambridge: Cambridge University Press.

Eichengreen, B. and Flandreau, M. (1996) The Geography of the Gold Standard, in J. Braga de Macedo, B. Eichengreen and J. Reis (eds) *Currency Convertibility: The Gold Standard and Beyond*, London and New York: Routledge.

Favero, C. and Spinelli, F. (1992) *Deficits, Money Growth and Inflation in Italy: 1865–1990*, London: Queen Mary and Westfield College.

Federico, G. (1996) L'Italia era un paese protezionista?, mimeo.

Fenn's Compendium of the English and Foreign Funds, Debts and Revenues of All Nations (1889), London: Effingham Wilson, Royal Exchange.

Fenoaltea, S. (1988) International Resource Flows and Construction Movements in the Atlantic Economy: the Kuznets Cycle in Italy, 1861–1913, *Journal of Economic History* XLVIII, 3 (9): 605–36.

Fishlow, A. (1985) Lessons from the Past: Capital Markets during the Nineteenth Century and the Interwar Period, *International Organization* 39: 383–439.

Fleming, J.M. (1962) Domestic Financial Policies Under Fixed and Under Flexible Exchange Rates, *IMF Staff Papers* 9: 369–80.

Fratianni, M. and Spinelli, F. (1982) The Growth of government in Italy: Evidence from 1861 to 1979, *Public Choice* 39 (9): 221–43.

Fratianni, M. and Spinelli, F. (1984) Italy in the Gold Standard Period, 1861–1914, in M.D. Bordo and A.J. Schwartz (eds) *A Retrospective on the Classical Gold Standard, 1821–1931*, Chicago and London: University of Chicago Press.

Gall, L., Feldman, G.D., James, H., Holtfrerich, C-L. and Buschen, H.E. (1995) *The Deutsche Bank 1870–1955*, London: Weidenfeld and Nicolson.

Gille, B. (1968) *Les Investissements français en Italie, 1815–1914*, Torino: Archivio storico dell'unificazione italiana.

Goodhart, C.A.F. (1972) *The Business of Banking, 1891–1914*, London: Weidenfeld and Nicolson.

Holden, D. and Perman R. (1994) Unit Root and Cointegration for the Economist, in B.B. Rao (ed.) *Cointegration: Expository Essay for the Applied Economist*, New York: St. Martin's Press.

Istituto centrale di statistica (1957) *Indagine statistica sullo sviluppo del reddito nazionale dell'Italia dal 1861 al 1956*, Annali di statistica, series 8, vol. 9, Rome.

Izzo, L. (1962) *La finanza pubblica nel primo decennio dell'unità italiana*, Milan: Giuffrè.

Joines, D.H. (1985) Deficits and money growth in the United States 1872–1993, *Journal of Monetary Economics* 16: 329–51.

Luzzatto, G. (1968) *L'economia italiana dal 1861 al 1894*, Torino: Einaudi.

McKinnon, R. and Oates, W. (1966) *The Implications of International Economic Integration for Monetary, Fiscal and Exchange Rate Policy*, Princeton Studies in International Finance, 39, Princeton, NJ: Princeton University Press.

Maddison, A. (1991) Una revisione della stima della crescita economica italiana, 1861–1989, *Moneta e Credito* 174: 143–61.

Martello, T. and Montanari, A. (1874) *Stato attuale del credito in Italia e notizie sulle istituzioni di credito straniere*, Padova: F.lli Salmin editori.

Ministero del Tesoro, Ragioneria generale dello stato (1969) *Il bilancio dello stato italiano dal 1862 al 1967*, vols 3, 4, Rome: Istituto Poligrafico dello Stato.

Mundell, R.A. (1968) *International Economics*, New York: Macmillan.

Nurske, R. (1944) *International Currency Experience*, Geneva: League of Nations.

Perron, P. (1994) Trend, Unit Root and Structural Change in Macroeconomic Time Series, in B.B. Rao (ed.) *Cointegration: Expository Essays for the Applied Economist*, New York: St. Martin's Press.

Pippenger, J. (1984) Bank of England Operations, 1893–1913, in M. Bordo and A. Schwartz (eds) *A Retrospective on the Classical Gold Standard*, Chicago: University of Chicago Press.

Phillips, P.C.B. (1990) Statistical Inference in Instrumental Variables Regression with I(1) Processes, *Review of Economic Studies* 57: 99–125.

Otto, G. (1994) Diagnostic Testing: An Application to the demand for M1, in B.B Rao (ed.) *Cointegration: Expository Essays for the Applied Economist*, New York: St. Martin's Press.

Sannucci, V. (1990) Molteplicità delle banche di emissione: ragioni economiche ed effetti sull'efficacia del controllo monetario (1860–1890), in *Ricerche per la storia della Banca d'Italia*, vol. 1, Rome and Bari: Laterza.

Spinelli, F. and Fratianni, M. (1991) *Storia monetaria d'Italia*, Milan: Mondadori.

Tattara, G. (1997) Was Italy Ever on Gold?, in P. Martin Acena and J. Reis (eds) *Monetary Standards in the Periphery*, London: Macmillan.

Tivaroni, J. (1908) *Storia del debito pubblico del Regno d'Italia*, vols 1, 2, Pavia: Successori Marelli.

Williamson, J.G. (1964) *American Growth and the Balance of Payments, 1820–1913: A Study of the Long Swings*, Chapel Hill, NC: University of North Carolina Press.

Yeager, L.B. (1984) The Image of the Gold Standard, in M.D. Bordo and A.J. Schwartz (eds) *A Retrospective on the Classical Gold Standard, 1821–1931*, Chicago and London: University of Chicago Press.

Zamagni, V. (1988) Il debito pubblico in Italia 1861–1945, mimeo.
Zevin, R. (1992) Are World Financial Markets More Open? If So, Why and With What Effects?, in T. Banuri and J.B. Schor (eds) *Financial Openess and National Autonomy: Opportunities and Constraints*, Oxford: Clarendon Press.

10

TERMS-OF-TRADE VARIABILITY AND ADHERENCE TO THE GOLD STANDARD

The cases of Portugal and Spain[1]

Agustín Llona Rodríguez

INTRODUCTION

For the entire period that it was in effect, adherence to the gold standard in Southern and Eastern Europe as well as Latin America was paradoxical. While the standard was definitively established in Germany, the Netherlands, and Scandinavia in the early 1870s and long before in France and the United Kingdom, Austria-Hungary, Greece, Italy, Portugal and Spain in Europe, and Argentina and Chile in Latin America went in and out of it. Although chronic fiscal imprudence caused the suspension of convertibility in Argentina, Greece and Italy, this does not appear to be the case of Chile, Portugal and Spain. Ruling out chronic fiscal imbalances, it is difficult to explain long spells of inconvertibility in a world under the gold standard. This chapter studies the two sources of difficulties faced by peripheral countries, taking the Iberian ones as examples, that made their adherence to the gold standard trying. The first source is variability of the terms of trade and the second, the degree of flexibility of the price of nontraded goods. One of the results from the dependent economy model is that the higher the variability of the terms of trade and the more rigid domestic prices, the harder it is to remain within a fixed exchange rate regime.

Including this Introduction, the chapter has seven sections. The second gives a brief historical background of Portugal and Spain. The third section discusses the adjustment mechanism for a dependent economy under the gold standard as well as under inconvertibility. The fourth section measures the variability of the terms of trade. The fifth describes the Portuguese path towards inconvertibility, and the sixth, the Spanish gyrations in terms of currency regimes. The seventh section summarizes the conclusions.

HISTORICAL BACKGROUND

Portugal and Spain inaugurated the nineteenth century with the overhauling of their political systems. The Napoleonic invasion disseminated the French Revolution ideals of political and economic liberalism. And the War of Independence proved that the royals were of no use when it came to defend the country: the Portuguese royal family fled to Brazil and the more abject Spanish royals brought their truly Freudian family feuds to the Emperor, who easily took their throne for his brother Jose. The War of Independence was fought by the commoners and, finally, won by the British.

The socio-political consequence of these disruptions was the surge of political forces supporting political democratization and economic liberalism. The political aim of these groups was to establish constitutional monarchies in which the power of the crown would be checked by a relatively democratically elected parliament. Their economic proposals included the liberalization of domestic markets and a substantial trade liberalization. This two-pronged agenda generated strong opposition: political democratization eroded the power of traditional groups, particularly the church, and economic liberalization meant the elimination of perks and privileges given to these groups during the mercantilist era.

In Portugal fighting lasted until 1851, with the definite establishment of a constitutional monarchy and the rise to power of the Regeneração party. In Spain political instability lasted for longer than in Portugal. Ferdinand VII's absolutist ambitions clashed with the liberal political environment arising from six years of war and self government. Political turmoil plagued the reign of Isabella II until the queen was finally deposed by the "Glorious Revolution" of 1868. During the next six years, Spain had a provisional government for two, a new king for another two, and the First Republic, lasting one and a half years. This long period of instability ended with the Bourbon Restoration of 1875 (Tortella 1994: 24–8).

Under these circumstances, economic policy-making followed a classical "stop and go"; it was not possible to pursue a consistent liberalization of the economy. However, some structural reforms took place; the most important of them was a substantial reduction of the church political and economic clout and the gradual control of the state by a liberal bourgeoisie. Once a "new law and new order" were established – in 1851 in Portugal and 1875 in Spain – policy-makers were able to follow a moderate but consistent plan for the modernization of these economies as well as the adoption of relatively orthodox fiscal and monetary policies. Not surprisingly the Iberian countries were underachievers during the nineteenth century. Politically and economically, they turned into small underdeveloped nations. Their exports were concentrated in a few commodities, particularly common wine, in which they were relatively small and thus were price-takers. Lack of domestic savings made investment dependent on foreign capital, which concentrated in railroads. Investment in traded sectors required a high profitability, due to the variability of their international price.

THE WORKING OF THE GOLD STANDARD: A VIEW FROM THE PERIPHERY

First, this section gives a stylized representation of the economies of the periphery; second, it deals with practical issues arising from the adoption of a fixed exchange rate regime.

The dependent economy

The dependent economy model is a good representation of the economies of peripheral countries during the nineteenth century. This model, developed by Salter (1959) and expanded by Dornbusch (1980) and Llona (1989) among others, assumes a small economy producing and consuming two kinds of goods: traded, Q_T, and nontraded, Q_N. The price of traded goods is set internationally, while that of nontraded goods is set domestically. In term of relative size, nontraded sectors were not small: a gross estimate for Spain gives a figure of 38 per cent of gross domestic product (GDP), not including the effect of tariff protection.

On the supply side, production functions for both goods are linear homogeneous, and the supply of capital and labor services is fixed in the short run. Therefore, the economy shows rising opportunity cost for increasing the production of one type of commodity. General-equilibrium supply functions depend on relative prices and the economy's capital–labor ratio. Assuming that the economy is on its steady-state-path equilibrium, we can disregard the relationship between the capital–labor ratio and commodity production. Under these conditions, an increase in the relative price of traded goods shifts resources into this sector and vice versa. On the demand side, relative expenditure depends on relative prices, the scale variable being wealth or permanent income. In this case, an increase in the relative price of traded goods will shift expenditure towards nontraded commodities.

Commodity arbitrage ensures that the domestic price of traded goods, P_T, equals their international price, $P_T{}^*$, times the exchange rate, E. The price of nontraded goods, P_N, is set domestically in response to supply and demand conditions. Assuming no changes in preferences and technology, there would be only one real exchange rate consistent with general equilibrium, p, defined as

$$(1) \quad p = (E\ P^*_T)\ /P_N$$

Figure 10.1 is a textbook representation of this economy's general equilibrium. The production possibility frontier represents the supply side and social preferences the demand side; equilibrium is reached at point A where the quantity demanded and supplied of both commodities are equal and their relative price is p.

Imagine that the economy experiences a negative external shock, e.g., a deterioration of the terms of trade. Since this economy takes the price of traded goods from abroad, the real exchange rate appreciates, decreasing to p′. The production mix shifts to B in Figure 10.1, increasing the quantity supplied of nontraded and decreasing that of traded goods. The desired consumption bundle is now represented by C. Given that B and C are on the same price line, income and expenditure are equal, but there is an excess demand for traded goods, equal to $p'*(QT_C - QT_B)$ and an excess supply of nontraded goods, equal to $(QN_B - QN_C)$. Given the new relative prices, the market for nontraded goods would reach equilibrium only if expenditure rises so as to reach D, where there would be a substantial disequilibrium in the traded sector. Alternatively, the market for traded goods would clear if expenditure decreases so as to reduce demand to a point like E. If the economy moves toward D, it must borrow from abroad and/or consume its accumulated reserves. On the other hand, traversing towards E implies a recession, which might be politically unpalatable.

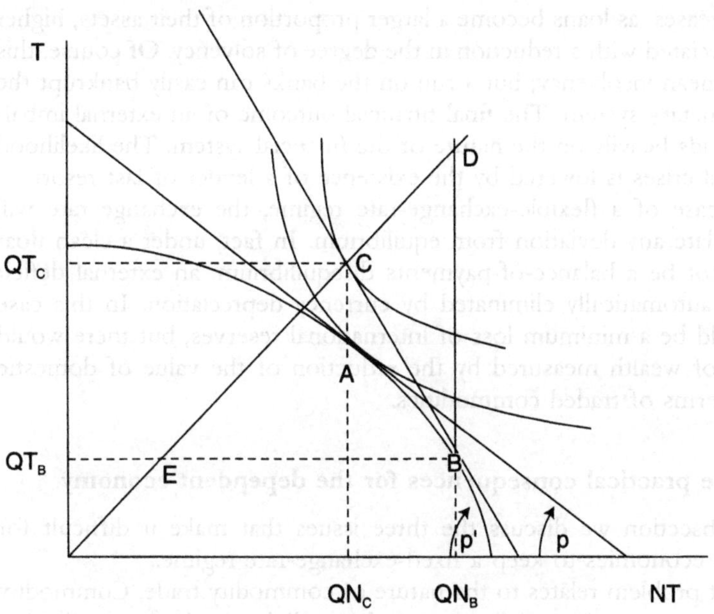

Figure 10.1 Dependent economy model

The adjustment mechanism has to eliminate both imbalances. In order to reduce consumption and increase production of traded goods, their relative price needs to rise. In order to reach equilibrium in both markets, the real exchange rate has to depreciate to reach its pre-shock level. However, the price of traded goods is given by the world markets, thus the road to the original real exchange rate requires a decline in the price of nontraded goods and/or nominal exchange rate depreciation.

This adjustment mechanism differs from that postulated by the classical economists in two important ways. First, having more than one sector allows the economy to depart from its fundamentals for relatively long periods of time. Second, the final relative adjustment comes via a mixture of currency depreciation and price deflation in the nontraded sector.

The above description does not explore the transmission mechanism through which the relative-price adjustment takes place. An external imbalance sets in motion a series of processes in the financial markets that induce prices to move in the right direction (Tobin and Braga de Macedo 1982). Under a fixed-exchange-rate regime, which is the one described by the classical economists, there is a direct link between the external balance and the monetary base. If there are no delaying interventions, the stock of high-powered money varies directly with any external imbalance. Therefore, shocks originating in commodity markets disturb portfolio equilibrium; in particular, financial institutions will see their cash reserves going down and deposit destruction on the part of their customers. Risk in banks' balance sheets increases, as loans become a larger proportion of their assets; higher risk is associated with a reduction in the degree of solvency. Of course, this does not mean insolvency; but a run on the banks can easily bankrupt the whole monetary system. The final financial outcome of an external imbalance depends heavily on the nature of the financial system. The likelihood of financial crises is lowered by the existence of a lender of last resort.

In the case of a flexible-exchange-rate regime, the exchange rate will accommodate any deviation from equilibrium. In fact, under a clean float there cannot be a balance-of-payments disequilibrium: an external deficit would be automatically eliminated by currency depreciation. In this case there would be a minimum loss of international reserves, but there would be a loss of wealth measured by the reduction of the value of domestic assets in terms of traded commodities.

Some practical consequences for the dependent economy

In this subsection we discuss the three issues that make it difficult for dependent economies to keep a fixed-exchange-rate regime.

The first problem relates to the nature of commodity trade. Commodity trade is the result of specialization, and we all know that specialization improves social welfare. However, from the point of view of short and medium-run macroeconomic stability, it could be a source of difficulties. The structure of commodity trade depends on comparative advantage, which in turn is a function of relative factor endowment. Factor endowment of peripheral countries tends to be relatively abundant in natural resources and unskilled labor, while that of central economies is relatively abundant in human and physical capital. Therefore, peripheral countries' comparative advantage lies in natural resources and unskilled-labor-intensive goods, while that of central countries lies in increasingly sophisticated manufactures and traded services.

Therefore it does not come as a surprise that peripheral countries' exports are concentrated on relatively unprocessed agricultural and mining products while their imports are manufactures, intermediate and capital goods, and services. Besides, peripheral countries lack of capital investment and Dutch disease contribute to concentrating exports in a relatively small bundle of goods. An intuitive application of the central limit theorem, plus the dictum that the world market generates prices that follow a random walk, predicts that export prices for peripheral countries are more volatile that their import prices: they import a wide variety of commodities whose prices follow the general price level of the central countries.

Highly volatile terms of trade and export prices constitute an obstacle for maintaining convertibility because they make the external balance unstable. In order to keep the economy in equilibrium, prices of nontraded goods have to behave with the same degree of variability as those of traded goods. In the event they do not, the external imbalance will be transmitted into the real economy, with dire consequences.

The second problem comes from the functioning of the international capital markets. Robert Triffin pointed out long ago that the global adjustment mechanism of the gold standard is not symmetrical. A balance-of-payments deficit in one of the central countries would raise that country's domestic interest rate; but this rate was not purely domestic: it was one of the world-reference interest rates, e.g., the London discount rate. A hike in one of the central key rates siphons gold from peripheral countries; thus a balance-of-payments problem in a central country could become a nightmare for a peripheral economy. The Baring crisis of 1890 and the German banking crisis of 1906–7 are good examples of this problem.

The third problem lies in the dependent economy's institutional arrangements for its financial system. These arrangements should be designed to preserve the system's overall solvency, but at the same time allowing for market corrections within the banking system. In this respect the existence of a central bank and efficient clearing mechanisms are of the utmost importance.

VOLATILITY OF TERMS OF TRADE

This section compares the fluctuations and volatility of the Portuguese and Spanish terms of trade with those of France, Germany and the United Kingdom. Maravall and Bentolila (1986) distinguish between variability and volatility; the first refers to the range of fluctuation of a series and the second to the predictability of a series. Here countries are compared in terms of both concepts.

A simple way of measuring and comparing the fluctuation range of a random series is to compute its coefficient of variation. The larger the coefficient, the larger the deviations from the sample mean, i.e., the larger the fluctuation range. Table 10.1 shows these coefficients for overlapping ten-year periods for the countries indicated above. Simple inspection shows that the fluctuation range for Portugal and Spain is larger than that for France, Germany, and the United Kingdom.

Table 10.2 shows the results of conducting an F-test for inequality of variances, specifically, for testing the hypothesis that terms-of-trade variability was larger in Portugal and Spain than in the central countries considered here.

Excess variability does not help a country to remain within the rules of the gold standard, but volatility is even worse: excess volatility implies relative unpredictability of terms-of-trade level and variation. Maravall and Bentolila (1986) proposed the construction of a variable that represents volatility at each particular period. In the case of time series that follow a random walk, such as the terms of trade, this variable is defined as

Table 10.1 Coefficient of variation of terms of trade, 1845–1913

Period	*France*	*Germany*	*UK*	*Portugal*	*Spain*
1845–55	0.059	na	na	na	0.061
1850–60	0.059	na	na	na	0.086
1855–65	0.055	na	na	na	0.102
1860–70	0.047	na	na	na	0.077
1865–75	0.061	na	na	0.056	0.092
1870–80	0.021	na	0.058	0.065	0.149
1875–85	0.029	na	0.040	0.057	0.052
1880–90	0.028	0.034	0.035	0.041	0.079
1885–95	0.053	0.010	0.029	0.042	0.074
1890–1900	0.039	0.016	0.031	0.155	0.084
1895–1905	0.039	0.045	0.031	0.169	0.109
1900–13	0.042	0.072	0.035	0.046	0.072

Note: na = not available

Sources: The original export and import price indices come from the following sources: *France*: Bourguignon and Levy-Leboyer (1990: Table A VI); *Germany*: Hoffmann (1985: 515, 603); *United Kingdom*: Feinstein (1976, Table 64); *Portugal*: Lains (1986: 413–14); *Spain*: Prados de la Escosura (1991: 255–9).

Table 10.2 One-tail F-test for inequality of variances, 1820–1913

Period	*F-statistics*	*Rejection* 1%	*Values* 5%
1820–1913	Sp/Fr = 2.33	1.39	1.59
1865–1913	Po/Fr = 6.85	1.60	1.94
	Sp/Fr = 5.85		
1870–1913	UK/Fr = 0.64	1.65	2.03
	Po/Fr = 7.15		
	Sp/Fr = 5.73		
	Po/UK = 11.1		
	Sp/UK = 8.93		
1880–1913	Ge/Fr = 2.63	1.77	2.18
	UK/Fr = 0.77		
	Po/Fr = 7.15		
	Sp/Fr = 5.73		
	UK/Ge = 0.29		
	Po/Ge = 4.10		
	Sp/Ge = 2.62		
	Po/UK = 11.1		
	Sp/UK = 8.93		

Notes: Ho: $\sigma^2_1 = \sigma^2_2$
Ha: $\sigma^2_1 > \sigma^2_2$
F-statistic $= s^2_1/s^2_2$
s^2_1 and s^2_2 are estimates of σ^2_1 and σ^2_2

(2) $V = 100\sigma\ (\Delta\log \text{(terms of trade)})$

Figures 10.2 to 10.6 show this index for the five countries considered here. Again, simple visual inspection indicates that terms-of-trade volatility in peripheral countries vastly surpasses that of central economies.

PORTUGUESE PATH TO INCONVERTIBILITY

Portugal officially adopted the gold standard in 1854. The authorities defined the gold content of the milreis as 1.626 mg. of fine gold, thereby fixing an exchange rate of 4.5 milreis per pound sterling. The standard was to work within a system of competitive banks of issue with full note backing; however, only notes issued by Banco de Portugal had national circulation, those issued by the remaining banks were accepted only in the northern provinces. In 1887 Banco de Portugal was granted a monopoly of note issue. With the exception of a few months during the crisis of 1876, Portugal was under the gold standard until 1891 (Reis 1990; Sousa 1991). That year, a balance-of-payments crisis turned into a severe financial crisis, forcing the authorities to abandon convertibility. The country did not attempt to restore convertibility in later years.

Given the relatively large variability and volatility of its terms of trade, Portuguese adherence to the gold standard from 1854 to 1891 seems

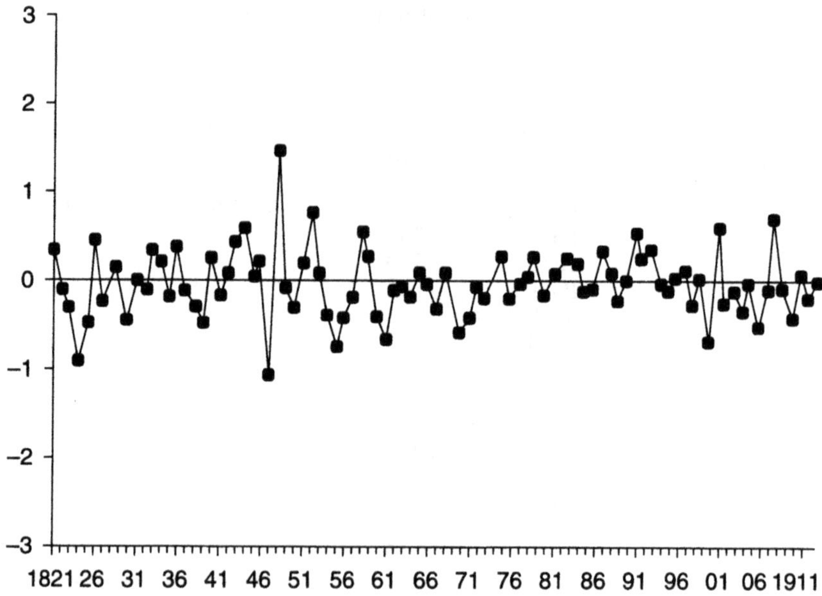

Figure 10.2 Volatility of terms of trade in France

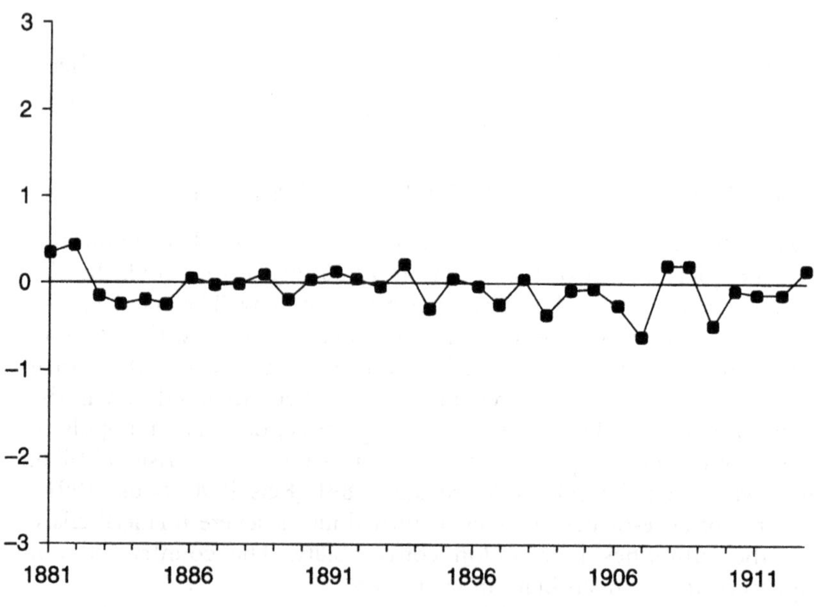

Figure 10.3 Volatility of terms of trade in Germany

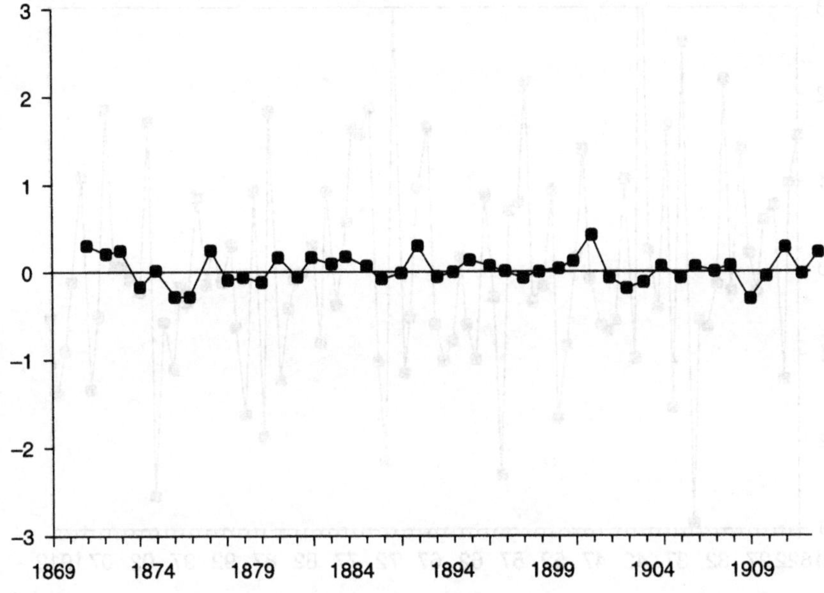

Figure 10.4 Volatility of terms of trade in the United Kingdom

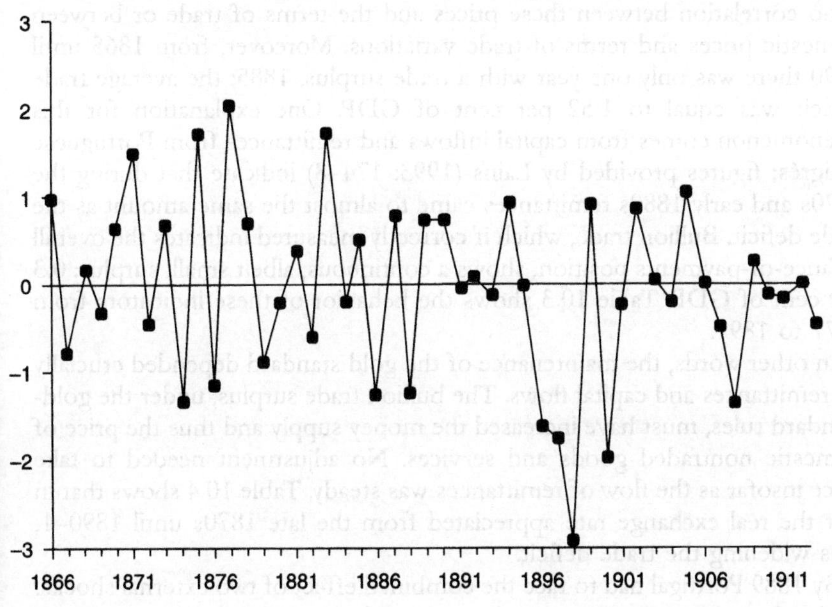

Figure 10.5 Volatility of terms of trade in Portugal

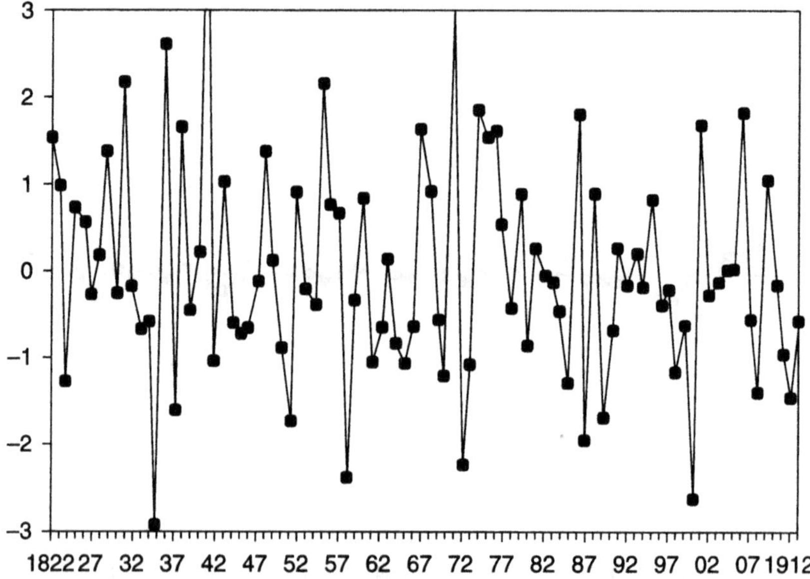

Figure 10.6 Volatility of terms of trade in Spain

paradoxical, unless domestic prices were extremely flexible. However, there is no correlation between these prices and the terms of trade or between domestic prices and terms-of-trade variations. Moreover, from 1865 until 1890 there was only one year with a trade surplus, 1885; the average trade deficit was equal to 1.52 per cent of GDP. One explanation for this phenomenon comes from capital inflows and remittances from Portuguese émigrés; figures provided by Lains (1993: 174–8) indicate that during the 1870s and early 1880s remittances came to almost the same amount as the trade deficit. Bullion trade, which if correctly measured indicates the overall balance-of-payments position, shows a continuous, albeit small, surplus: 0.3 per cent of GDP. Table 10.3 shows the behavior of these indicators from 1877 to 1891.

In other words, the maintenance of the gold standard depended crucially on remittances and capital flows. The bullion trade surplus, under the gold-standard rules, must have increased the money supply and thus the price of domestic nontraded goods and services. No adjustment needed to take place insofar as the flow of remittances was steady. Table 10.4 shows that in fact the real exchange rate appreciated from the late 1870s until 1890–1, thus widening the trade deficit.

By 1889 Portugal had to face the combined effect of two external shocks. In the first place, there was a substantial reduction in the volume of wine exports – about 50 per cent – due to the recovery of the French

Table 10.3 Portugal: external imbalance and fiscal deficit, 1877–91 (thousands of reis, nominal figures)

Year	*Trade balance* (1)	*Bullion trade* (2)	*Remittances* (3)	*Fiscal deficit* (4)	*GDP* (5)
1877	−567.30	−730.80	3365	−9272.00	506000.00
1878	−5735.00	1701.50	2557	−7640.00	502500.00
1879	−12971.50	−1383.70		−7550.50	497500.00
1880	−4176.60	2561.60		−8047.00	505000.00
1881	−7217.60	2882.10		−7638.00	521500.00
1882	−9565.20	850.30		−6634.50	532000.00
1883	−4567.60	3503.10		−5663.50	539000.00
1884	−7538.40	2492.40		−6803.50	556000.00
1885	1096.20	3331.20		−8854.50	580500.00
1886	−598.30	9419.80		−8209.00	604500.00
1887	−2981.80	5025.60		−6915.50	629000.00
1888	−1782.60	6063.80	4355	−9336.00	657000.00
1889	−9659.00	8474.40	3237	−12860.50	676000.00
1890	−14522.20	3994.20	1915	−12402.50	680000.00
1891	−5945.70	−21534.70	824	−13079.00	685000.00

Sources: (1) and (2) Lains (1993: 333–42); (3) Lains (1993: 178); (4) Mata (1993: 175); (5) Mata (1993: 40)

vineyards that had been affected by phylloxera during the early 1880s. In the second place, political problems in Brazil added to the abolition of slavery in that country caused a sharp reduction of remittances, as indicated in Table 10.3. The gold drain provoked a run on the banks, forcing the authorities to abandon convertibility (Reis 1990). Consequently, the nominal exchange rate depreciated by 23 per cent. Table 10.4 shows that the real exchange rate for exports depreciated by 20 per cent and that for imports 18 per cent.

Table 10.5 indicates how the change in relative prices turned the trade deficit into a surplus for most of the 1890s. During that decade Portugal faced a severe worsening of its terms of trade that did not generate an external imbalance, because the nominal exchange rate depreciated, thus maintaining the real exchange rate. At the same time, relatively tight fiscal and monetary policies contributed to macroeconomic stability, in particular price stability.

SPAIN UNDER A QUASI-FIXED, QUASI-FLOATING REGIME

Spain never officially adopted the gold standard. In the years before 1868 the country was under a bimetallic standard; but the Mint overvalued silver, thus the country was under a *de facto* silver standard. The closest Spanish

Table 10.4 Portugal: real exchange rate indices, 1875–1913 (base: 1913)

Year	*Real exchange rate (1)*	*Real exchange for exports (2)*	*Real exchange for imports (3)*
1875	130.05	159.45	111.11
1876	128.29	142.96	107.11
1877	121.45	151.85	100.63
1878	106.57	139.50	88.72
1879	106.44	140.54	94.53
1880	116.60	144.86	98.83
1881	117.95	151.32	100.99
1882	112.98	140.54	97.65
1883	110.62	142.19	89.00
1884	109.03	146.77	93.22
1885	108.17	149.73	92.20
1886	101.78	133.98	89.29
1887	100.75	137.28	87.31
1888	105.82	133.03	91.36
1889	104.7	135.81	89.31
1890	94.21	130.53	82.24
1891	99.90	140.81	89.02
1892	112.68	167.57	105.37
1893	104.06	163.96	103.86
1894	96.64	168.54	100.95
1895	98.09	171.81	103.04
1896	101.35	160.15	106.20
1897	107.48	156.20	115.65
1898	113.74	158.67	140.43
1899	104.05	140.23	117.63
1900	119.04	144.60	136.94
1901	115.53	146.15	140.65
1902	103.23	134.12	122.48
1903	93.11	118.51	107.92
1904	97.34	121.74	112.37
1905	96.00	115.04	99.58
1906	100.39	112.25	97.17
1907	100.55	108.55	96.89
1908	98.74	113.98	110.71
1909	101.33	115.90	110.64
1910	118.93	129.60	124.60
1911	93.79	97.73	94.92
1912	97.92	95.93	93.17
1913	100.00	100.00	100.00

Notes: (1) Real exchange rate = (Nominal exchange rate * Sauerbeck price index)/Domestic price index; (2) Real exchange rate for exports = (Nominal exchange rate * Export price index)/Domestic price index; (3) Real exchange rate for imports = (Nominal exchange rate * Import price index)/Domestic price index

Sources: Nominal exchange rate: Mata (1993: 40); exports and imports price indices: Lains (1986: 423–4); domestic price index: Justino (1990); Sauerbeck price index: Mitchell (1988: 474)

Table 10.5 Portugal: external balance, fiscal deficit and prices, 1892–1913 (thousands of reis)

Year	*Trade balance* (1)	*Fiscal deficit* (2)	*GDP* (3)	*Domestic price index* (4)
1892	18964.50	−10294.50	695500.00	78.55
1893	6608.30	−2470.00	705500.00	83.05
1894	8160.80	−428.50	725000.00	85.72
1895	8226.90	432.50	757500.00	81.75
1896	15062.40	−2580.50	779500.00	80.00
1897	18842.80	−7310.50	785500.00	86.10
1898	27647.80	−5389.50	793000.00	90.83
1899	11284.10	−5418.00	808500.00	91.21
1900	6554.80	−3194.50	819000.00	90.37
1901	4286.90	−976.00	817000.00	87.78
1902	176.20	−2730.50	822000.00	86.87
1903	−4936.40	−2201.50	840500.00	93.88
1904	−11899.40	−678.50	856500.00	88.39
1905	−19503.80	30.00	865500.00	81.60
1906	−12581.80	−689.00	878500.00	79.77
1907	−14160.80	−2298.00	902000.00	83.89
1908	−17374.10	−2971.50	925000.00	87.24
1909	−9252.50	−1514.00	939000.00	85.95
1910	699.10	796.00	935000.00	87.78
1911	−10522.80	−320.50	923500.00	94.65
1912	−8786.50	365.50	932000.00	98.00
1913	−13847.70	5383.00	924500.00	100.00

Sources: same as Table 10.3.

authorities got with respect to the gold standard was to join informally the Latin Monetary Union in 1868. However, they did not sign the Union's treaty; therefore they did not participate in the Union decision-making process. In 1868 the peseta was introduced as the national monetary unit; its silver and gold content were equal to those of the French franc. Spain did not move into the gold standard when the rest of the Latin Monetary Union adopted it. The authorities decided to remain in silver and finally, in 1883, any convertibility was abandoned. The Spanish banking system was similar to that of Portugal: since 1844 it was one of competitive banks of issue. In 1874, however, Banco de España was granted the monopoly of note issue.

Spain experienced the largest variability and volatility of terms of trade of all the countries considered in the fourth section. The dependent-economy model predicts a bumpy ride for such an economy under a fixed- exchange-rate regime. Perhaps this is the clue for understanding Spanish authorities' ambivalence about a firm and clear adherence to the gold standard.

Judging from figures in Table 10.6, the Spanish economy did not have a

Table 10.6 Spain: external imbalance, fiscal deficit and gross domestic product, 1850–1914 (millions of current pesetas)

Year	*Trade balance*	*Fiscal deficit*	*GDP*	
	(1)	*(2)*	*Nominal (3)*	*Real (4)*
1850	−9.80	−4.00	4688.00	5053.05
1851	−24.30	−27.00	4796.00	5127.43
1852	−48.50	−10.00	4407.00	5174.29
1853	−4.10	−11.00	5363.00	5352.82
1854	−83.60	−27.00	5419.00	5378.10
1855	65.50	−52.00	5826.00	5531.54
1856	−8.30	−66.00	6218.00	5590.89
1857	−39.90	−54.00	6314.00	5816.40
1858	−176.20	−42.00	6061.00	6026.63
1859	−69.80	−6.00	6219.00	6102.97
1860	−102.10	−65.00	6504.00	6312.00
1861	−149.50	−131.00	6598.00	6438.86
1862	−217.70	−130.00	6726.00	6563.78
1863	−269.30	−121.00	6954.00	6674.82
1864	−247.80	−186.00	7165.00	6706.03
1865	−211.00	−139.00	7195.00	6758.16
1866	−130.00	−101.00	6852.00	6564.94
1867	21.20	−118.00	7307.00	6209.18
1868	−57.90	−149.00	7005.00	6224.04
1869	−48.70	−270.00	5934.00	6037.30
1870	−57.70	−331.00	6722.00	6475.77
1871	−16.20	−238.00	6939.00	7087.21
1872	−105.90	−219.00	8088.00	8197.09
1873	170.90	−227.00	7980.00	7773.11
1874	−20.30	−10.00	7788.00	7656.99
1875	62.70	−111.00	7614.00	7672.35
1876	−76.90	−6.00	8165.00	8291.10
1877	73.40	−13.00	8158.00	8252.13
1878	53.20	−30.00	7987.00	7867.34
1879	22.00	−78.00	8300.00	8252.93
1880	112.90	−58.00	8258.00	8704.83
1881	184.70	−1.00	8854.00	8956.16
1882	60.50	−31.00	9683.00	9328.31
1883	0.00	−45.00	10037.00	9758.71
1884	20.40	−28.00	9384.00	9697.41
1885	70.60	−82.00	9376.00	9670.15
1886	97.50	−15.00	9149.00	9362.60
1887	70.50	−73.00	8695.00	9277.02
1888	141.10	−122.00	8647.00	9397.36
1889	23.80	−67.00	8044.00	9340.27
1890	31.50	−50.00	8152.00	9261.23
1891	220.40	−54.00	8432.00	9517.67
1892	354.60	−19.00	8674.00	10206.99
1893	291.20	75.00	8866.00	9901.31
1894	149.40	6.00	8556.00	9956.76

Table 10.6 Continued

Year	*Trade balance*	*Fiscal deficit*	*GDP*	
	(1)	*(2)*	*Nominal (3)*	*Real (4)*
1895	207.70	−26.00	8569.00	9927.96
1896	437.70	40.00	8149.00	9023.95
1897	447.30	−54.00	8957.00	9694.20
1898	488.10	8.00	10146.00	10464.31
1899	63.50	134.00	9762.00	10522.16
1900	133.20	52.00	10386.00	10817.89
1901	15.30	38.00	11067.00	11527.21
1902	52.80	71.00	10772.00	11219.94
1903	16.00	23.00	11528.00	11270.87
1904	73.60	54.00	11560.00	11095.91
1905	73.30	72.00	11555.00	11131.74
1906	296.70	103.00	11631.00	11742.62
1907	297.60	65.00	12668.00	11920.16
1908	151.00	56.00	11929.00	12255.18
1909	178.10	−51.00	11962.00	12337.28
1910	163.10	−6.00	11410.00	11860.99
1911	176.70	6.00	670.00	13223.06
1912	160.10	−62.00	12640.00	13011.04
1913	−28.30	−71.00	13077.00	13077.00
1914	−213.30	−166.00	12822.00	12725.23

Sources: (1) Prados de la Escosura (1991: 250–4); (2) Estadísticas Históricas de España (p. 443); (3) and (4) Prados de la Escosura (1993: 89–90).

bumpy ride until the great depression of the second half of the 1860s. The table indicates that real GDP fell by eleven per cent from 1865 to 1869. Tortella (1982: 243–92) identifies as the main culprit of this crisis the bankruptcy of the railroad companies, which in turn provoked a major financial crisis. Stock-market quotations fell by almost 50 per cent in 1865. Under these circumstances one would have expected strong speculation against the domestic currency; however, the Spanish silver currency held ground and easily retained its full value. The explanation of such an odd behavior lies in an improvement of the terms of trade, which boosted the value of exports, and a reduction of imports due to the income fall; these two effects turned the trade balance into surplus after years of heavy deficits.

The adoption of the peseta in 1868 did not change matters greatly. As the economy began to gain strength in 1870, imports rose faster than exports, turning the trade balance into a deficit again. Table 10.7 shows the terms of trade following a random walk and the real exchange rate for exports and imports moving up and down accordingly. The peseta remained within the silver points of the Latin Monetary Union and domestic prices did not follow the terms-of-trade movements. Fluctuations of the real exchange

Table 10.7 Spain: real exchange rate and domestic price indices, 1850–1913 (base: 1913)

Year	*Real exports exchange rate (1)*	*Real imports exchange rate (2)*	*Terms of trade (3)*	*GDP deflator (4)*	*Consumption deflator (5)*
1850	103.18	74.70	138.23	92.78	95.83
1851	91.15	74.16	123.01	93.54	95.83
1852	105.08	80.37	130.85	85.17	97.22
1853	92.45	71.53	129.34	100.19	98.61
1854	93.68	74.18	126.38	100.76	108.33
1855	98.22	67.13	146.42	105.32	104.17
1856	102.43	66.36	154.46	111.22	109.72
1857	108.31	66.94	161.92	108.56	109.72
1858	99.24	72.13	137.69	100.57	94.44
1859	95.16	70.55	134.98	101.90	100.00
1860	95.05	66.45	143.16	103.04	104.17
1861	97.71	73.33	133.35	102.47	104.17
1862	96.00	75.11	127.90	102.47	106.94
1863	103.49	80.04	129.40	104.18	106.94
1864	105.03	85.87	122.40	106.84	108.33
1865	92.79	81.51	113.92	106.46	97.22
1866	96.99	88.79	109.32	104.37	97.22
1867	88.40	72.24	122.46	117.68	102.78
1868	94.18	72.16	130.61	112.55	100.00
1869	103.03	81.94	125.83	98.29	87.50
1870	86.90	74.98	115.98	103.80	91.67
1871	109.32	76.77	142.52	97.91	94.44
1872	112.95	92.01	122.85	98.67	94.44
1873	108.59	95.06	114.32	102.66	94.44
1874	113.03	86.98	130.04	101.71	100.00
1875	114.92	79.59	144.49	99.24	95.83
1876	113.05	70.26	161.03	98.48	102.78
1877	113.60	67.95	167.30	98.86	100.00
1878	102.50	63.07	162.65	101.52	97.22
1879	98.92	57.22	173.00	100.57	100.00
1880	104.75	64.13	163.46	94.87	97.22
1881	98.26	58.81	167.20	98.86	97.22
1882	96.08	57.66	166.74	103.80	94.44
1883	95.99	57.84	166.08	102.85	97.22
1884	96.34	59.63	161.68	96.77	93.06
1885	87.73	59.24	148.20	96.96	93.06
1886	99.25	59.22	167.73	97.72	90.28
1887	85.25	58.00	147.09	93.73	87.50
1888	94.79	60.60	156.53	92.02	87.50
1889	98.07	70.43	139.33	86.12	87.50
1890	104.41	78.40	133.28	88.02	91.67
1891	102.76	75.57	136.08	88.59	91.67
1892	108.99	80.87	134.86	84.98	87.50
1893	101.05	73.59	137.42	89.54	91.67
1894	102.73	75.67	135.85	85.93	87.50

Table 10.7 Continued

Year	*Real exports exchange rate (1)*	*Real imports exchange rate (2)*	*Terms of trade (3)*	*GDP deflator (4)*	*Consumption deflator (5)*
1895	99.61	69.14	144.19	86.31	90.28
1896	98.15	69.87	140.59	90.30	94.44
1897	106.49	76.79	138.78	92.40	95.83
1898	123.68	96.37	128.44	96.96	90.28
1899	105.51	85.44	123.59	92.78	91.67
1900	114.44	110.66	103.49	96.01	95.83
1901	121.42	104.53	116.25	96.01	93.06
1902	100.78	88.28	114.24	96.01	93.06
1903	101.54	89.37	113.70	102.28	95.83
1904	102.02	89.69	113.83	104.18	100.00
1905	97.58	85.54	114.16	103.80	98.61
1906	104.17	80.53	129.46	99.05	97.22
1907	100.44	80.55	124.79	106.27	100.00
1908	98.03	86.32	113.64	97.34	95.83
1909	95.01	77.57	122.58	96.96	94.44
1910	97.93	80.63	121.54	96.20	98.61
1911	101.51	88.89	114.28	95.82	98.61
1912	99.41	95.92	103.71	97.15	98.61
1913	100.00	100.00	100.00	100.00	100.00

Notes: (1) Real exchange rate for exports = (Nominal exchange rate * Export price index)/ GDP deflator; (2) Real exchange rate for imports = (Nominal exchange rate * Import price index)/GDP deflator.
Sources: Export and import price indices: Prados de la Escosura (1991: 255–9); GDP deflator: Prados de la Escosura (1993: 87–8); Consumption deflator: Prados de la Escosura, work in progress

rate are not cost free: they increase the risk of domestic investment, thus raising the cost of capital and reducing investment levels. On top of these, the fiscal situation deteriorated enormously from 1868 to 1874; the fiscal deficits observed during those years are the highest for the whole period, measured in absolute terms and as percentage of GDP. Tortella (1982) claims that this fiscal situation forced the authorities to grant the monopoly of note issue to Banco de España: issuing money and granting credit to the state was to be the role of the bank. Although the reasoning is correct, financing the government should have produced an explosion in the money supply and an inflationary outburst with dire consequences for the peseta. Moreover, there should have been a run against the peseta. Again the peseta weathered the storm without difficulties, and until 1874–5 it was traded at par with the French franc. This time the explanation might come from the difficulties faced by the French franc as a result of the temporary abandonment of convertibility due to the Franco-Prussian War.

The depreciation of silver that began in 1874 had a minor impact on the peseta: the nominal exchange rate depreciated by 2.5 per cent. However, as Table 10.7 indicates, the real exchange rate for exports and that for imports appreciated steadily until 1883. The terms of trade turned increasingly favorable, due to a larger fall in the price of imports than those of exports. The situation did not evolve into a balance-of-payments crisis, due to phylloxera: as in Portugal, Spain expanded its wine exports enormously. Prados de la Escosura (1991: 199–201) states that common wine explains 60 per cent of the increase in total exports during the 1880s. Table 10.6 indicates that the trade balance turned into surpluses, reaching a maximum in 1881. The trade surplus and a tightening up of the fiscal accounts certainly helped the peseta not to devalue with silver.

The decision to abandon convertibility in 1883 is complex. Figures in Table 10.6 indicate a healthy real side of the economy: real GDP had been growing since 1878 and the trade account shows a consistent surplus. The problem lies on the capital account of the balance of payments. Banco de España had been accumulating gold reserves since 1874; by 1878 they were 53 million pesetas and in 1881 they reached 125 million pesetas. However, the French crisis of 1882 sucked gold worth 75 million pesetas from Banco de España. Fearing a run on the bank, the authorities declared inconvertibility (Martín-Aceña 1995). This is an example of the Triffin mechanism, described on p. 269.

During the next five years the Spanish economy came to a halt. As shown in Table 10.6, real GDP stagnated. Exports remained stagnant, while imports fell from their peak of 1883; consequently, the trade balance shows an increasing surplus. Table 10.7 shows that the real exchange rate for both exports and imports also remained at the level of 1883. From 1883 to 1886 Banco de España had recovered gold reserves worth 60 million pesetas. One explanation for the stagnation is the combination of tight fiscal and monetary policy followed during those years.

Banco de España changed its monetary policy in 1888. After five years of an almost constant money supply, it rose by 8.5 per cent from 1887 to 1889. Domestic prices did not respond; but as shown in Table 10.8, this time the peseta began to depreciate, slowly first and then accelerating, as a consequence of the Baring crisis of 1890.

Nominal depreciation was accompanied by real depreciation, as shown in Table 10.7, which certainly helped exports while restraining imports. A looser monetary policy, the worsening of the terms of trade, and the Spanish–American War contributed to the further depreciation of the peseta.

Once the war was over, the tendency of the real exchange rate is reversed: there is currency appreciation. Martín-Aceña (1995) states that this development may be explained by capital repatriation from Cuba and the Philippines; but it is also true that there was a sizable trade surplus. The same author explains that at the turn of the century fiscal policy became

Table 10.8 Depreciation of the peseta, 1888–1913

Year	*Pesetas per British Pound*
1888	25.6
1889	26.0
1890	26.3
1891	26.9
1892	29.0
1893	30.0
1894	30.1
1895	29.0
1896	30.4
1897	32.6
1898	39.2
1899	31.4
1900	32.8
1901	34.8
1902	31.1
1903	34.0
1904	34.7
1905	32.9
1906	28.4
1907	28.1
1908	28.4
1909	27.1
1910	27.1
1911	27.1
1912	27.0
1913	27.1

Source: Martín-Aceña (1995: 479)

even tighter and so did monetary policy, thus stabilizing domestic prices (see Table 10.7) and also allowing for nominal appreciation.

CONCLUSIONS

The aim of this chapter is to find empirical evidence for two sources of difficulties that make it hazardous trying to stay within the rules of the gold standard or any fixed exchange rate regime. One important difficulty lies in the variability of the terms of trade. The evidence described in the fourth section clearly indicates that this was a severe problem for Portugal and Spain. Their terms of trade varied in a substantially larger range than those of the central countries. In addition to this, the fifth and sixth sections indicate that the real exchange rate in both countries did not behave as needed to maintain internal and external balance under a fixed-exchange-rate regime. In the case of Portugal, the final blow was the Baring crisis, that made capital unavailable in the context of an overvalued real exchange rate. The case of Spain is more complex than that of its neighbor, because the country was under no clear standard. However, in 1883, after mild overvaluation of the real exchange rate and fears of a run on the reserves of the Banco de España, the authorities declared inconvertibility. In both countries, inconvertibility led to a more stable real exchange rate; and during the 1890s their export growth was important, although both faced a deterioration of the terms of trade.

It is interesting to note that Triffin's hypothesis regarding the global adjustment of specie flows under the gold standard is supported by the experience of these two countries. The 1882 French crisis provoked a major drain in reserves of the Banco de España, and the Baring crisis had dire effects for Portugal and it also contributed to a depreciation of the peseta.

STATISTICAL APPENDIX

Table 10.9 Central economies: export price indices, 1820–1913 (base: 1913=100)

Year	*France*	*Germany*	*UK*
1820	162.50	NA	NA
1821	160.58	NA	NA
1822	155.77	NA	NA
1823	150.00	NA	NA
1824	141.35	NA	NA
1825	148.08	NA	NA
1826	140.38	NA	NA
1827	127.88	NA	NA
1828	125.00	NA	NA
1829	125.00	NA	NA
1830	118.27	NA	NA
1831	112.50	NA	NA
1832	113.46	NA	NA
1833	118.27	NA	NA
1834	124.04	NA	NA
1835	125.96	NA	NA
1836	135.58	NA	NA
1837	125.00	NA	NA
1838	123.08	NA	NA
1839	119.23	NA	NA
1840	119.23	NA	NA
1841	118.27	NA	NA
1842	114.42	NA	NA
1843	117.31	NA	NA
1844	125.96	NA	NA
1845	127.88	NA	NA
1846	130.77	NA	NA
1847	111.54	NA	NA
1848	113.46	NA	NA

Table 10.9 Continued

Year	*France*	*Germany*	*UK*
1849	122.12	NA	NA
1850	128.85	NA	NA
1851	127.88	NA	NA
1852	139.42	NA	NA
1853	153.85	NA	NA
1854	152.88	NA	NA
1855	147.12	NA	NA
1856	157.69	NA	NA
1857	153.85	NA	NA
1858	144.23	NA	NA
1859	150.96	NA	NA
1860	148.08	NA	NA
1861	140.38	NA	NA
1862	141.35	NA	NA
1863	142.31	NA	NA
1864	141.35	NA	NA
1865	136.54	NA	NA
1866	129.81	NA	NA
1867	123.08	NA	NA
1868	119.23	NA	NA
1869	117.31	NA	NA
1870	115.38	NA	122.00
1871	116.35	NA	122.00
1872	118.27	NA	135.00
1873	114.42	NA	140.00
1874	108.65	NA	132.00
1875	106.73	NA	124.00
1876	105.77	NA	114.00
1877	103.85	NA	110.00
1878	98.08	NA	106.00
1879	99.04	NA	99.00
1880	101.92	128.90	103.00
1881	100.96	130.40	99.00
1882	100.00	133.60	101.00
1883	98.08	129.20	97.00
1884	93.27	119.60	94.00
1885	90.38	109.30	90.00
1886	88.46	105.10	86.00
1887	87.50	105.70	86.00
1888	88.46	107.50	86.00
1889	91.35	110.70	87.00
1890	91.35	110.50	91.00
1891	90.38	105.90	90.00
1892	87.50	99.50	86.00
1893	88.46	98.90	86.00
1894	81.73	92.30	82.00
1895	79.81	91.90	79.00
1896	78.85	94.00	79.00
1897	79.81	93.70	78.00

Table 10.9 Continued

Year	*France*	*Germany*	*UK*
1898	80.77	94.00	79.00
1899	86.54	98.90	82.00
1900	87.50	102.20	95.00
1901	85.58	97.20	90.00
1902	85.58	94.70	86.00
1903	86.54	95.00	86.00
1904	85.58	96.40	87.00
1905	87.50	97.60	87.00
1906	91.35	97.00	92.00
1907	92.31	102.30	96.00
1908	91.35	96.40	93.00
1909	93.27	95.00	89.00
1910	97.12	95.60	93.00
1911	99.04	96.20	95.00
1912	99.04	98.90	96.00
1913	100.00	100.00	100.00

Sources: France: Bourguignon and Levy-Leboyer (1990: Table A VI); Germany: Hoffmann (1985: 603–15); United Kingdom: Feinstein (1976: Table 64).

Table 10.10 Central economies: import price indices, 1820–1913 (base: 1913=100)

Year	*France*	*Germany*	*UK*
1820	122.43	NA	NA
1821	116.82	NA	NA
1822	114.95	NA	NA
1823	114.02	NA	NA
1824	117.76	NA	NA
1825	129.91	NA	NA
1826	117.76	NA	NA
1827	110.28	NA	NA
1828	106.54	NA	NA
1829	105.61	NA	NA
1830	104.67	NA	NA
1831	100.00	NA	NA
1832	101.87	NA	NA
1833	102.80	NA	NA
1834	105.61	NA	NA
1835	109.35	NA	NA
1836	113.08	NA	NA
1837	105.61	NA	NA
1838	107.48	NA	NA
1839	109.35	NA	NA
1840	106.54	NA	NA
1841	107.48	NA	NA
1842	102.80	NA	NA
1843	100.93	NA	NA
1844	101.87	NA	NA
1845	102.80	NA	NA
1846	102.80	NA	NA
1847	98.13	NA	NA
1848	85.98	NA	NA
1849	93.46	NA	NA
1850	101.87	NA	NA
1851	99.07	NA	NA
1852	100.00	NA	NA
1853	109.35	NA	NA
1854	113.08	NA	NA
1855	117.76	NA	NA
1856	131.78	NA	NA
1857	130.84	NA	NA
1858	115.89	NA	NA
1859	117.76	NA	NA
1860	120.56	NA	NA
1861	122.43	NA	NA
1862	125.23	NA	NA
1863	127.10	NA	NA
1864	128.97	NA	NA
1865	123.36	NA	NA
1866	117.76	NA	NA
1867	114.95	NA	NA
1868	110.28	NA	NA

Table 10.10 Continued

Year	*France*	*Germany*	*UK*
1869	108.41	NA	NA
1870	113.08	NA	134.00
1871	118.69	NA	127.00
1872	122.43	120.50	136.00
1873	120.56	122.60	136.00
1874	114.02	120.90	133.00
1875	109.35	117.40	126.00
1876	110.28	116.50	123.00
1877	108.41	110.60	126.00
1878	101.87	104.60	117.00
1879	100.00	103.20	112.00
1880	104.67	102.70	118.00
1881	102.80	100.20	116.00
1882	100.93	97.80	115.00
1883	96.26	96.20	112.00
1884	89.72	91.70	106.00
1885	87.85	85.60	100.00
1886	86.92	84.60	93.00
1887	83.18	84.60	92.00
1888	83.18	86.30	94.00
1889	87.85	89.10	96.00
1890	87.85	87.90	95.00
1891	82.24	86.20	95.00
1892	77.57	80.70	91.00
1893	75.70	79.00	89.00
1894	70.09	73.50	84.00
1895	69.16	73.60	81.00
1896	68.22	73.60	82.00
1897	68.22	75.80	81.00
1898	71.03	75.90	82.00
1899	75.70	80.20	84.00
1900	82.24	85.00	90.00
1901	75.70	80.40	87.00
1902	77.57	81.60	86.00
1903	79.44	82.60	88.00
1904	81.31	84.70	88.00
1905	83.18	88.30	89.00
1906	91.59	93.80	93.00
1907	93.46	96.80	97.00
1908	85.98	89.30	93.00
1909	88.79	92.70	95.00
1910	96.26	94.00	101.00
1911	97.20	96.10	98.00
1912	99.07	100.40	100.00
1913	100.00	100.00	100.00

Sources: France: Bourguignon and Levy-Leboyer (1990: Table A VI); Germany: Hoffmann (1985: 603–15); United Kingdom: Feinstein (1976: Table 64)

Table 10.11 Portugal: exports and imports price indices, exchange rate and domestic price index, 1850–1913 (indices base: 1913=100)

Year	*Exports price index*	*Imports price index*	*Exchange rate (milreis/pound)*	*Domestic price index*
1850	NA	NA	NA	47.89
1851	NA	NA	NA	48.89
1852	NA	NA	NA	47.21
1853	NA	NA	NA	55.14
1854	NA	NA	NA	68.26
1855	NA	NA	4.50	71.69
1856	NA	NA	4.50	83.89
1857	NA	NA	4.50	82.75
1858	NA	NA	4.50	71.38
1859	NA	NA	4.50	74.66
1860	NA	NA	4.50	74.05
1861	NA	NA	4.50	74.97
1862	NA	NA	4.50	77.41
1863	NA	NA	4.50	76.42
1864	NA	NA	4.50	77.03
1865	139.44	112.87	4.50	73.21
1866	147.91	112.87	4.50	76.11
1867	140.41	112.49	4.50	78.55
1868	141.80	112.47	4.50	76.72
1869	129.90	105.32	4.50	72.53
1870	134.19	104.85	4.54	70.70
1871	143.52	102.57	4.50	69.10
1872	140.19	103.32	4.54	71.00
1873	141.91	100.44	4.50	71.08
1874	124.87	96.29	4.50	73.67
1875	138.48	96.50	4.47	74.89
1876	124.54	93.31	4.52	75.96
1877	138.26	91.63	4.52	79.39
1878	133.98	85.21	4.52	83.74
1879	128.94	86.72	4.53	80.23
1880	128.62	87.75	4.48	76.80
1881	128.30	85.62	4.56	74.59
1882	122.94	85.42	4.56	76.95
1883	124.01	77.62	4.56	76.72
1884	120.36	76.45	4.56	72.15
1885	117.26	72.20	4.57	69.10
1886	106.86	71.21	4.51	69.40
1887	109.00	69.33	4.51	69.10
1888	103.54	71.10	4.51	67.72
1889	109.86	72.25	4.51	70.39
1890	117.36	73.95	4.53	78.63
1891	119.40	75.48	4.83	79.09
1892	118.97	74.81	5.73	78.55
1893	126.05	79.84	5.60	83.05
1894	129.26	77.43	5.79	85.72
1895	127.76	76.62	5.70	81.76
1896	113.40	75.20	5.85	80.00

Table 10.11 Continued

Year	*Exports price index*	*Imports price index*	*Exchange rate (milreis/pound)*	*Domestic price index*
1897	106.00	78.49	6.57	86.10
1898	105.04	92.96	7.11	90.83
1899	107.82	90.44	6.159	1.21
1900	107.18	101.50	6.32	90.37
1901	104.18	100.26	6.38	87.78
1902	105.47	96.31	5.728	6.87
1903	103.32	94.08	5.58	93.88
1904	103.00	95.07	5.41	88.39
1905	101.50	87.86	4.79	81.60
1906	101.29	87.68	4.58	79.77
1907	101.61	90.69	4.64	83.89
1908	99.14	96.30	5.20	87.25
1909	99.57	95.05	5.188	5.95
1910	100.00	96.14	5.89	87.78
1911	98.07	95.25	4.89	94.65
1912	97.96	95.15	4.97	98.00
1913	100.00	100.00	5.23	101.00

Sources: Exports and imports price indices: Lains (1986: 381–419); exchange rate: Lains (1993); domestic price index: Justino (1990)

Table 10.12 Spain: exports and imports price indices and exchange rate, 1821–1913
indices base: 1913=100

Year	*Exports price index*	*Imports price index*	*Exchange rate (peseta/pound)*
1821	132.74	148.56	24.85
1822	135.98	136.96	24.65
1823	141.87	133.50	24.62
1824	127.29	130.66	24.79
1825	129.96	126.86	24.62
1826	126.82	118.73	25.53
1827	109.49	104.32	26.42
1828	106.50	100.01	25.26
1829	110.98	95.02	24.57
1830	106.80	93.02	25.09
1831	108.60	81.75	24.41
1832	110.86	84.40	25.09
1833	109.56	87.12	25.60
1834	116.14	96.01	25.70
1835	117.56	118.07	26.03
1836	131.14	110.39	25.61
1837	122.37	114.90	23.94
1838	117.07	98.25	24.85
1839	121.75	105.27	25.42
1840	113.29	96.26	24.33
1841	121.07	80.09	24.83
1842	116.80	82.89	24.53
1843	120.21	79.45	24.53
1844	118.01	81.25	24.49
1845	116.44	83.94	24.64
1846	112.67	84.72	24.90
1847	115.85	87.62	25.29
1848	109.02	75.07	26.97
1849	108.06	73.68	24.71
1850	106.63	77.14	24.32
1851	96.00	78.04	24.06
1852	100.27	76.63	24.18
1853	104.60	80.87	23.99
1854	106.46	84.24	24.02
1855	116.48	79.55	24.06
1856	127.26	82.39	24.25
1857	130.70	80.72	24.37
1858	109.46	79.50	24.70
1859	108.24	80.19	24.27
1860	111.72	78.04	23.75
1861	110.71	83.02	24.50
1862	109.89	85.92	24.25
1863	120.45	93.08	24.25
1864	122.83	100.35	24.75
1865	109.23	95.88	24.50
1866	111.93	102.39	24.50
1867	115.59	94.39	24.38

Table 10.12 Continued

Year	*Exports price index*	*Imports price index*	*Exchange rate (peseta/pound)*
1868	116.02	88.83	24.75
1869	112.48	89.39	24.39
1870	100.39	86.56	24.34
1871	120.97	84.88	23.97
1872	123.38	100.43	24.47
1873	123.07	107.65	24.54
1874	126.70	97.43	24.58
1875	123.83	85.70	24.95
1876	120.69	74.95	24.99
1877	120.44	71.99	25.26
1878	112.00	68.86	25.17
1879	106.57	61.60	25.29
1880	108.03	66.09	24.92
1881	104.97	62.78	25.07
1882	105.33	63.17	25.65
1883	104.55	62.95	25.58
1884	99.16	61.33	25.47
1885	89.63	60.48	25.71
1886	102.23	60.95	25.70
1887	85.05	57.82	25.45
1888	92.23	58.92	25.62
1889	88.03	63.18	25.99
1890	94.63	71.00	26.31
1891	91.61	67.32	26.92
1892	86.46	64.11	29.02
1893	81.82	59.54	29.96
1894	79.42	58.46	30.11
1895	80.34	55.72	28.99
1896	79.01	56.20	30.39
1897	81.74	58.90	32.61
1898	82.79	64.46	39.24
1899	84.40	68.29	31.42
1900	91.41	88.33	32.56
1901	90.80	78.11	34.78
1902	84.17	73.68	31.14
1903	82.77	72.80	33.99
1904	83.07	72.98	34.66
1905	83.38	73.04	32.91
1906	98.39	76.00	28.41
1907	102.94	82.49	28.09
1908	91.05	80.12	28.39
1909	91.92	74.99	27.15
1910	94.17	77.48	27.10
1911	96.73	84.64	27.24
1912	97.00	93.53	26.97
1913	100.00	100.00	27.09

Sources: Exports and imports prices: Prados de la Escosura (1991: 255–9)

Table 10.13 Spain: domestic price indices, 1850–1913 (base: 1913=100)

Year	*GDP deflator*	*Private consumption deflator*
1850	92.78	95.83
1851	93.54	95.83
1852	85.17	97.22
1853	100.19	98.61
1854	100.76	108.33
1855	105.32	104.17
1856	111.22	109.72
1857	108.56	109.72
1858	100.57	94.44
1859	101.90	100.00
1860	103.04	104.17
1861	102.47	104.17
1862	102.47	106.94
1863	104.18	106.94
1864	106.84	108.33
1865	106.46	97.22
1866	104.37	97.22
1867	117.68	102.78
1868	112.55	100.00
1869	98.29	87.50
1870	103.80	91.67
1871	97.91	94.44
1872	98.67	94.44
1873	102.66	94.44
1874	101.71	100.00
1875	99.24	95.83
1876	98.48	102.78
1877	98.86	100.00
1878	101.52	97.22
1879	100.57	100.00
1880	94.87	97.22
1881	98.86	97.22
1882	103.80	94.44
1883	102.85	97.22
1884	96.77	93.06
1885	96.96	93.06
1886	97.72	90.28
1887	93.73	87.50
1888	92.02	87.50
1889	86.12	87.50
1890	88.02	91.67
1891	88.59	91.67
1892	84.98	87.50
1893	89.54	91.67
1894	85.93	87.50
1895	86.31	90.28
1896	90.30	94.44
1897	92.40	95.83

Table 10.13 Continued

Year	*GDP deflator*	*Private consumption deflator*
1898	96.96	90.28
1899	92.78	91.67
1900	96.01	95.83
1901	96.01	93.06
1902	96.01	93.06
1903	102.28	95.83
1904	104.18	100.00
1905	103.80	98.61
1906	99.05	97.22
1907	106.27	100.00
1908	97.34	95.83
1909	96.96	94.44
1910	96.20	98.61
1911	95.82	98.61
1912	97.15	98.61
1913	100.00	100.00

Sources: GDP deflator: Prados de la Escosura (1993: 87–8); private consumption deflator: Prados de la Escosura (1993).

NOTE

1 This chapter has benefited from helpful comments and suggestions from Barry Eichengreen, Erika Fellinger, Lawrence Officer, Leandro Prados de la Escosura, Jaime Reis, Antonio Tena, Mario Tomba, Pedro Videla, participants at the II Congress of the European Association of Historical Economics, and workshops at the American University and Universidad Carlos III de Madrid. Any remaining errors and misinterpretations are the sole responsibility of the author. This research has been partially funded by the Spanish Ministry of Education, DGICYT, grant PB 94-0373.

REFERENCES

Bourguignon, F. and Levy-Leboyer, M. (1990) *The French Economy in the Nineteenth Century*, Cambridge: Cambridge University Press.

Dornbusch, R. (1980) *Open Economy Macroeconomics*, New York: Basic Books.

Feinstein, C.H. (1976) *Statistical Tables of National Income, Expenditure and Output of the United Kingdom, 1855–1965*, Cambridge: Cambridge University Press.

Hoffmann, W. (1985) *Das Wachstum der deutschen Wirtschaft seit der Mitte der 18. Jahrhunderts*, Berlin: Springer Verlag.

Justino, D. (1990) *Preços e Salarios em Portugal 1850–1912*, mimeo, Lisbon: Universidade Nova de Lisboa, Faculdade de Ciências Sociais e Humanas.

Lains, P. (1986) Exportações portuguesas, 1850–1913: a tese da dependência revisitada, *Análise Social* XXII (91): 381–419.

——(1993) Foreign Trade and Economic Growth in the European Periphery: Portugal, 1851–1913, unpublished Ph.D dissertation, Florence: European University Institute.

Llona Rodriguez, A. (1989) Chilean Monetary Policy: 1860–1925, unpublished Ph.D dissertation, Boston, MA: Boston University.

Maravall, A. and Bentolila, S. (1986) Una Medida de Volatilidad en Series Temporales con una Aplicación al Control Monetario en España, *Investigaciones Económicas* X (1): 185–99.

Martín-Aceña, P. (1995) Spain during the Classical Gold Standard Years, 1880–1914, in P. Martín-Aceña and J. Simpson (eds) *The Economic Development of Spain since 1870*, London: Edward Elgar.

Mata, E. (1993) *As Finanças Públicas Portuguesas da Regeneração à Primera Guerra Mundial*, Lisbon: Banco de Portugal.

Mitchell, B.R. (1988) *British Historical Statistics*, Cambridge: Cambridge University Press.

——(1992) *International Historical Statistics: Europe 1750–1988*, London: Macmillan-Stockton Press.

Prados de la Escosura, L. (1993) *Spain's Gross Domestic Product, 1850–1990: A New Series*, Madrid: Ministerio de Economía y Hacienda, Secretaria de Estado de Hacienda, Dirección General de Planificación: Documento de Trabajo D-93002.

——(1991) *De Imperio a Nación, Crecimiento y Atraso Económico de España (1780–1930)*, Madrid: Alianza Editorial.

Reis, J. (1990) *A Evolução da Oferta Monetária Portuguesa 1854–1912*, Lisbon: Banco de Portugal.

Salter, W. (1959) Internal and External Balance: The Role of Price and Expenditures Effects, *Economic Record* 36: 51–66.

Sousa, R. (1991) Money Supply in Portugal, 1834–1891, *Estudos de Economia* XII (1): 33–42.

Tobin, J. and Braga de Macedo, J. (1982) The Short-run Macroeconomics of Floating Exchange Rates: An Exposition, in J. Tobin (ed.) *Essays in Economics, Theory and Policy*, Cambridge, MA: MIT Press.

Tortella, G. (1994) *El desarrollo de la España contemporánea, Historia económica de los siglos XIX y XX*, Madrid: Alianza Editorial.

——(1982) *Los Origenes del Capitalismo en España*, 2nd edn, Madrid: Editorial Tecnos.

INDEX

For Product Safety Concerns and Information please contact our EU representative GPSR@taylorandfrancis.com Taylor & Francis Verlag GmbH, Kaufingerstraße 24, 80331 München, Germany

For Product Safety Concerns and Information please contact our EU representative GPSR@taylorandfrancis.com Taylor & Francis Verlag GmbH, Kaufingerstraße 24, 80331 München, Germany